UNDE[illegible] SECURITIES LAW

Marc I. Steinberg

Radford Professor of Law
Southern Methodist University

LEGAL TEXT SERIES

Matthew Bender

Times Mirror
Books

Printed in United States of America
Library of Congress Catalogue Number: 89-062199
ISBN#: 0-256-14728-0

1993 Reprint

MATTHEW BENDER & CO., INC.
EDITORIAL OFFICES
11 PENN PLAZA, NEW YORK, NY 10001–2006 (212) 967-7707
2101 WEBSTER STREET, OAKLAND, CA 94612–3027 (510) 446-7100

LEGAL EDUCATION PUBLICATIONS

Acknowledgements

I wish to thank a number of individuals for their help regarding this project. In particular, my thanks to Professors Alan Bromberg, Dennis Honabach, and Mark Sargent for their comments. I thank Ralph Ferrara, Robin Goldman, Sam Gruenbaum, Will Kaulbach, Joe Kempler and Richard Starr, all of whom were my coauthors for certain publications, portions of which appear herein. My thanks also to Callaghan & Co., publishers of my treatise on *Securities Practice: Federal and State Enforcement* (1985) (updated annually) (coauthored with Ralph Ferrara), and to Law Journal Seminars-Press, publisher of my treatise on *Securities Regulation: Liabilities and Remedies* (1989), for granting their permission for me to use excerpts from the respective treatises. I also thank several law reviews in which I authored articles for granting their permission to use certain portions thereof herein, including the *Cornell Law Review* (67 Cornell L. Rev. 557 (1982), 66 Cornell L. Rev. 27 (1980)) and Fred B. Rothman & Co., the *Emory Law Journal* (30 Emory L.J. 169 (1981)), the *Journal of Corporation Law* (11 J. Corp. L. 1 (1985)), the *Loyola of Los Angeles Law Review* (13 Loyola Univ. (L.A.) L. Rev. 247 (1980) (coauthored with Samuel Gruenbaum), the *University of Maryland Law Review* (46 Md. L. Rev. 923 (1987)) (coauthored with Robin Goldman), the *University of Pennsylvania Law Review* (129 U. Pa. L. Rev. 263 (1980)) (coauthored with Ralph Ferrara) and Fred B. Rothman & Co., and the *Vanderbilt Law Review* (40 Vand. L. Rev. 489 (1987)) (coauthored with Will Kaulbach).

From the University of Maryland Law School, I thank Bob Krusen and Haywood Miller for their research assistance, Anne Rollins for her comments, and LuAnn Marshall, Gwen Davis, and Eileen Gretes for their expert secretarial help. This book was written while I was a member of two faculties, the faculties of the University of Maryland Law School and the Southern Methodist University School of Law. I thank both institutions and their respective deans, Mike Kelly at Maryland and Paul Rogers at SMU, for their support of this project.

I wish to dedicate this book to my friends at the University of Maryland School of Law. I've been fortunate to teach during the past six years at this superb institution with wonderful colleagues and students. As I enthusiastically join the SMU law faculty on a more permanent basis, I will miss my friends at the Maryland Law School.

TABLE OF CONTENTS

CHAPTER 1

INTRODUCTION

CHAPTER 2

DEFINITION OF A "SECURITY"

Page

CHAPTER 3

ISSUER EXEMPTIONS FROM REGISTRATION

CHAPTER 4

THE REGISTRATION PROCESS

CHAPTER 5

RESALES AND REORGANIZATIONS

CHAPTER 6

DUE DILIGENCE AND SECURITIES ACT LIABILITY

CHAPTER 7

SECTION 10(b) AND RELATED ISSUES

Page

CHAPTER 8

ALTERNATIVE REMEDIES

CHAPTER 9

SELECTED DISCLOSURE ISSUES

CHAPTER 10

CORPORATE CONTROL ACQUISITIONS AND CONTESTS

Page

CHAPTER 11

SEC ENFORCEMENT

CHAPTER 1

INTRODUCTION

§ 1.01 Purpose of Text

The purpose of this reference text is to provide a general understanding of the key issues that a student will face in the basic securities regulation course. As a consequence, the text's scope principally focuses on the Securities Act of 1933 (hereinafter called the "Securities Act" or "1933 Act") and the Securities Exchange Act of 1934 (hereinafter called the "Exchange Act" or "1934 Act"). State securities statutes (also known as "blue sky" laws) are covered to a lesser extent.

For students wishing a broader subject matter treatment or more intense coverage of a particular issue (such as tender offers or SEC enforcement), the sources cited in § 1.03 should be consulted.

Securities regulation is a difficult course. At the same time, it is intellectually challenging and generates provocative policy issues. It thus has the potential of being one of the more interesting yet demanding courses in the law school curriculum. This text hopefully will stimulate student interest and help make the course's subject matter more understandable.

§ 1.02 Overview

Enacted in the aftermath of "The Great Crash," the Securities Act of 1933 and the Securities Exchange Act of 1934 have become the principal governors of federal securities law regulation. Basically, the 1933 Act deals with the initial offer and sale of securities while the 1934 Act primarily concerns trading and regulation in the secondary markets. Both Acts also prohibit manipulative and deceptive practices. Undoubtedly, the central focus of the securities laws is that of disclosure, thereby providing shareholders and the marketplace with sufficient information to make relevant decisions and to be apprised of significant developments. Congress thus sought to promote investor protection and the maintenance of fair and orderly markets. Generally, Congress, in enacting these Acts, declined to adopt a merit approach. Rather, irrespective of the value or fairness of a transaction or other corporate action, the investor may decide for him or herself after receiving disclosure of pertinent information.

It bears mentioning that the Exchange Act addresses a number of other matters, including oversight of brokers, dealers, and the stock exchanges, as well as proxy and tender offer regulation. In addition, the Exchange Act, as amended by the 1975 Amendments, directs the Securities and Exchange Commission to facilitate the establishment of a national market system.

In addition to the 1933 and 1934 Acts (and amendments thereto), Congress has enacted other securities legislation: the Public Utility Holding Company Act of 1935, the Trust Indenture Act of 1939, the Investment Company Act of 1940, the Investment Advisers Act of 1940, and the Securities Investor Protection Act of 1970. Also, the individual states have passed their own securities statutes, called "Blue Sky" laws.[1] A number of these statutes, depending on the particular state, provide for significant investor protection and substantive regulation.

The Securities and Exchange Commission (hereinafter called the "SEC" or the "Commission") is the agency which administers and enforces the federal securities laws. Not surprisingly, the Commission during the years has had both its ardent supporters and outspoken critics.[2] Nonetheless, as described in the *New York Times* on the fiftieth anniversary of the stock market crash of 1929, "the agency created in 1934 to enforce [the securities] laws, the Securities and Exchange Commission, is still widely regarded as the nation's finest independent regulatory agency."[3]

Turning to state securities regulation, the first such statute was enacted in Kansas over seventy years ago. Today, all the states have enacted some form of "blue sky" law designed to apply to securities activities within their individual borders. In general, these statutes seek to regulate such activities by one or more of the following routes:

> (1) to prohibit fraud in the offer and sale of securities; (2) to require and regulate licensing of investment advisors, broker-dealers, and their agents; (3) to require the registration of securities, and (4) to determine that the securities meet certain standards which are often referred to as "merit" or "fair, just, and equitable" standards.[4]

---

[1] This term came into being due to the original purpose of the "blue sky" laws which was to prevent "speculative schemes which have no more basis than so many feet of blue sky." *Hall v. Geiger-Jones Co.*, 242 U.S. 539, 550 (1917).

[2] See R. Karmel, *Regulation by Prosecution — The Securities and Exchange Commission Versus Corporate America* (1982); H. Kripke, *The SEC and Corporate Disclosure: Regulation in Search of a Purpose* (1979); J. Seligman, *The Transformation of Wall Street — A History of the Securities and Exchange Commission and Modern Corporate Finance* (1982); M. Steinberg, *Corporate Internal Affairs — A Corporate and Securities Law Perspective* (1983).

[3] Miller, *S.E.C.: Watchdog 1929 Lacked*, New York Times, Oct. 31, 1979, at D 1.

[4] Walker & Hadaway, *Merit Standards Revisited*, 7 J. Corp. L. 651, 653 (1982). See generally L. Loss, *Commentary on the Uniform Securities Act* (1976).

§ 1.03 Selected References

There are a number of useful books and treatises on securities regulation. These works include:

Bloomenthal, Harold S., *Going Public and the Public Corporation* (1988).

Bloomenthal, Harold S., *Securities and Federal Corporate Law* (1980).

Borden, Arthur M., *Going Private* (1982).

Bromberg, Alan & Lowenfels, Louis, *Securities Fraud and Commodities Fraud* (1988).

Clark, Robert Charles, *Corporate Law* (1986).

Contemporary Issues in Securities Regulation (M. Steinberg ed. 1988).

Ferrara, Ralph, Brown, Meredith & Hall, John, *Takeovers: Attack & Survival* (1987).

Fleischer, Arthur, *Tender Offers: Defense, Responses and Planning* (1983).

Frankel, Tamar, *The Regulation of Money Managers* (1980).

Hazen, Thomas Lee, *The Law of Securities Regulation* (1984).

Hicks, J.W., *Limited Offering Exemptions: Regulation D* (1987).

Jacobs, Arnold, *Litigation and Practice Under Rule 10b-5* (2d ed. 1983).

Karmel, Roberta S., *Regulation by Prosecution — The Securities and Exchange Commission Versus Corporate America* (1982).

Kripke, Homer, *The SEC and Corporate Disclosure: Regulation in Search of a Purpose* (1979).

Legislative History-Securities Law Committee, Federal Bar Association, *Federal Securities Laws: Legislative History 1933-1982* (1983).

Lipton, Martin & Steinberger, Erica, *Takeovers and Freezeouts* (1984).

Long, Joseph C., *Blue Sky Law* (1986).

Loss, Louis, *Fundamentals of Securities Regulation* (2d ed. 1988).

Loss, Louis, *Securities Regulation* (2d ed. 1961, Supp. 1969).

Phillips, Susan M. & Zecher, J. Richard, *The SEC and the Public Interest* (1981).

Securities Law Techniques (A.A. Sommer ed. 1985).

Securities Underwriting: A Practitioner's Guide (K. Bialkin & W. Grant eds. 1985).

Seligman, Joel, *The SEC and the Future of Finance* (1985).

Seligman, Joel, *The Transformation of Wall Street — A History of the Securities and Exchange Commission and Modern Corporate Finance* (1982).

Shapiro, Susan, *Wayward Capitalists* (1984).

Soderquist, Larry, *Understanding the Securities Laws* (1987).

Steinberg, Marc I., *Corporate Internal Affairs: A Corporate and Securities Law Perspective* (1983).

Steinberg, Marc I., *Securities Regulation: Liabilities and Remedies* (1989).

Steinberg, Marc I. & Ferrara, Ralph C., *Securities Practice: Federal and State Enforcement* (1985).

Tender Offers: Developments and Commentaries (M. Steinberg ed. 1985).

Wolfson, Nicholas, *The Modern Corporation: Free Markets vs. Regulation* (1984).

APPENDIX TO CHAPTER 1

THE WORK OF THE SEC

(Published by the SEC) (1982)

The Securities and Exchange Commission (SEC) was created on July 2, 1934 by an act of Congress entitled the Securities Exchange Act of 1934. It is an independent, bipartisan, quasi-judicial agency of the United States Government.

The Commission is composed of five members not more than three of whom may be members of the same political party. They are appointed by the President, with the advice and consent of the Senate, for five-year terms, the terms being staggered so that one expires on June 5th of each year. The Chairman is designated by the President.

The Commission's staff is composed of lawyers, accountants, security analysts and examiners, engineers and other professionals, together with administrative and clerical employees. The staff is divided into Divisions and Offices (including nine Regional Offices), each under charge of officials appointed by the Chairman.

The laws administered by the Commission relate in general to the field of securities and finance, and seek to provide protection for investors and the public in their securities transactions. They include (in addition to the Securities Exchange Act of 1934) the Securities Act of 1933 (administered by the Federal Trade Commission until September 1934), the Public Utility Holding Company Act of 1935, the Trust Indenture Act of 1939, the Investment Company Act of 1940, and the Investment Advisers Act of 1940. The Commission also serves as advisor to Federal courts in corporate reorganization proceedings under Chapter 11 of the Bankruptcy Reform Act of 1978. . . .

. . . .

It should be understood that the securities laws were designed to facilitate informed investment analyses and prudent and discriminating investment decisions by the investing public. It is the investor, not the Commission, who must make the ultimate judgment of the worth of securities offered for sale. The Commission is powerless to pass upon the merits of securities; and assuming proper disclosure of the financial and other information essential to informed investment analysis, the Commission cannot bar the sale of securities which such analysis may show to be of questionable value.

. . . .

SECURITIES ACT OF 1933

This "truth in securities" law has two basic objectives: (a) to provide investors with material financial and other information concerning securities offered for public sale; and (b) to prohibit misrepresentation, deceit and other fraudulent acts and practices in the sale of securities generally (whether or not required to be registered).

Registration of Securities

The first objective applies to securities offered for public sale by an issuing company or any person in a control relationship to such company. Before the public offering of such securities, a registration statement must be filed with the Commission by the issuer, setting forth the required information. When the statement has become effective, the securities may be sold. The purpose of registration is to provide disclosure of financial and other information on the basis of which investors may appraise the merits of the securities. To that end, investors must be furnished with a prospectus (selling circular) containing the salient data set forth in the registration statement to enable them to evaluate the securities and make informed and discriminating investment decisions.

Exemptions From Registration

The registration requirement applies to securities of both domestic and foreign private issuers, as well as to securities of foreign governments or their instrumentalities. There are, however, certain exemptions from the registration requirement. Among these are: (1) private offerings to a limited number of persons or institutions who have access to the kind of information registration would disclose and who do not propose to redistribute the securities, (2) offerings restricted to the residents of the State in which the issuing company is organized and doing business, (3) securities of municipal, State, Federal and other governmental instrumentalities, of charitable institutions, of banks, and of carriers subject to the Interstate Commerce Act, (4) offerings not in excess of certain specified amounts made in compliance with regulations of the Commission discussed below, and (5) offerings of "small business investment companies" made in accordance with rules and regulations of the Commission. The anti-fraud provisions referred to above, however, apply to all sales of securities involving interstate commerce or the mails, whether or not the securities are exempt from registration.

Purpose of Registration

Registration of securities does not insure investors against loss in their purchase, nor does the Commission have the power to disapprove securities for lack of merit — and it is unlawful to represent otherwise in the sale of securities. The only standard which must be met in the registration of securities is an adequate and accurate disclosure of the material facts concerning the company and the securities it proposes to sell. The fairness of the terms of securities (whether price, promoters' or underwriters' profits, or otherwise), the issuing company's prospects for successful operation, and other facts affecting the merits of securities have no bearing on the question whether securities may be registered [under the Securities Act].

The purpose of registration is to provide disclosure of these and other important facts so investors may make a realistic appraisal of the merits of the securities and thus exercise an informed judgment in determining whether to purchase them. Assuming proper disclosure, the Commission cannot deny registration or otherwise bar the securities from public sale whether or not the price or other terms of the securities are fair or the issuing company offers reasonable prospects of success. These are factors which the investor must assess for himself in the light of the disclosures provided; and if the facts have been fully and correctly stated, the investor assumes whatever risks may be involved in the purchase of the securities.

Nor does registration guarantee the accuracy of the facts represented in the registration statement and prospectus. The law does, however, prohibit false and misleading statements. . . . In addition, if an investor suffers loss in the purchase of a registered security, the law provides him with important recovery rights if he can prove that there was incomplete or inaccurate disclosure of material facts in the registration statement or prospectus. These rights must be asserted in an appropriate Federal or State court (not before the Commission, which has no power to award damages); and if such misstatements are proved, the issuing company, its responsible directors and officers, the underwriters, controlling interests, the sellers of the securities, and others (or one or more of such persons) would be liable to the purchaser of the securities for losses sustained.

The Registration Process

To facilitate the registration of securities by different types of issuing companies, the Commission has prepared special registration forms which vary in their disclosure requirements to provide disclosure of the essential facts pertinent in a given type of offering while at the same time minimizing the burden and expense of compliance with the law. In general, the registration forms call for disclosure of information such as (1) a description of the registrant's properties and business, (2) a description of the significant provisions of the security to be offered for sale and its relationship to the registrant's other capital securities, (3) information about the management of the registrant, and (4) financial statements certified by independent public accountants.

The registration statement and prospectus become public immediately on filing with the Commission; but it is unlawful to sell the securities until the effective date. After the filing of the registration statement, the securities may be offered orally or by certain summaries of the information in the registration statement as permitted by rules of the Commission. . . .

Small Issue Exemption

Among the special exemptions from the registration requirement is one adopted by Congress as an aid primarily to small business. The law provides that offerings of securities not exceeding $5 million in amount may be exempted from registration, subject to such conditions as the Commission prescribes for the protection of investors. Pursuant to this authority, the Commission's Regulation A permits certain domestic and Canadian companies to make exempt offerings not exceeding $1,500,000 in amount . . . . The Commission's Regulation D permits certain companies to make exempt offerings not exceeding [$1 million] with only minimal federal restrictions, while more extensive disclosure requirements and other conditions apply for offerings exceeding that amount but less than $5 million . . . .

Interpretations and Rulemaking

As a part of its activities under this Act, the Division of Corporation Finance also renders administrative interpretations of the law and regulations thereunder to members of the public, prospective registrants and others, to help them decide legal questions about the application of the law and the regulations to particular situations and to aid them in complying with the law . . . . Other Divisions render similar advice and assistance.

. . . .

SECURITIES EXCHANGE ACT OF 1934

By this Act, Congress extended the "disclosure" doctrine of investor protection to securities listed and registered for public trading on our national securities exchanges; and the enactment in August 1964 of the Securities Acts Amendments of 1964 applied the disclosure and reporting provisions to equity securities of hundreds of companies traded over-the-counter. . . .

Corporate Reporting

Companies which seek to have their securities listed and registered for public trading on [a national securities] exchange must file a registration application with the exchange and the Commission. A similar registration form must be filed by companies whose equity securities are traded over-the-counter if they meet the size test [of assets exceeding $5 million and at least 500 shareholders]. The Commission's rules prescribe the nature and content of these registration statements, including certified financial statements. . . . Following the registration of their securities, such companies must file annual and other periodic reports to keep current the information contained in the original filing. . . .

The law prescribes penalties for filing false statements and reports with the Commission, as well as provision for recovery by investors who suffer losses in the purchase or sale of . . . securities in reliance thereon.

Proxy Solicitations

Another provision of [the Exchange Act] governs the solicitation of proxies (votes) from holders of . . . securities (both listed and over-the-counter), whether for the election of directors or for approval of other corporate action. In any such solicitation, whether by the management or minority groups, disclosure must be made of all material facts concerning the matters on which such holders are asked to vote. . . . Where a contest for control of the management of a corporation is involved, the rules require disclosure of the names and interests of all "participants" in the proxy contest. Holders of such securities thus are enabled to vote intelligently on corporate actions requiring their approval. . . .

Tender Offer Solicitations

In 1968, Congress amended the Exchange Act to extend its reporting and disclosure provisions to situations where control of a company is sought through a tender offer or other planned stock acquisition of over 10 percent of a company's equity securities. The amount was reduced to 5 percent by an amendment in 1970. These amendments and Commission rules thereunder require disclosure of pertinent information, by the person [acquiring] over 5 percent of the company's securities by direct purchase or by tender offer, as well as by any persons soliciting shareholders to accept or reject a tender offer. Thus, as with the proxy rules, public investors who hold stock in the subject corporation may now make informed decisions on take-over bids.

Insider Trading

The protection provided the investing public through disclosure of financial and related information concerning the securities of registered companies is supplemented by provisions of the law designed to curb misuse of corporate information not available to the general public. . . .

Margin Trading

The [1934 Act] also contains provisions governing margin trading in securities. It authorizes the Board of Governors of the Federal Reserve System to set limitations on the amount of credit which may be extended for the purpose of purchasing or carrying securities. The objective is to restrict the excessive use of the nation's credit in the securities markets. While the credit restrictions are set by the Board, investigation and enforcement is the responsibility of the Commission.

Market Surveillance

The Securities Exchange Act also provides a system for regulating securities trading practices in both the exchange and the over-the-counter markets. In general, transactions in securities which are effected otherwise than on national securities exchanges are said to take place "over the counter." Designed to protect the interests of investors and the public, these provisions seek to curb misrepresentations and deceit, market manipulation and other fraudulent acts and practices and to establish and maintain just and equitable principles of trade conducive to the maintenance of open, fair and orderly markets.

While these provisions of the law establish the general regulatory pattern, the Commission is responsible for promulgating rules and regulations for their implementation. . . .

Registration of Exchanges and Others

In addition, the [1934 Act] as amended requires registration with the Commission of (1) "national securities exchanges" (those having a substantial securities trading volume); (2) brokers and dealers who conduct securities business in interstate commerce; (3) transfer agents; (4) clearing agencies; (5) municipal brokers and dealers; and (6) securities information processors.

To obtain registration, exchanges must show that they are so organized as to be able to comply with the provisions of the statute and the rules and regulations of the Commission and that their rules contain provisions which are just and adequate to insure fair dealing and to protect investors.

. . . .

Broker-Dealer Registration

Applications for registration as broker-dealers and amendments thereto are examined by the Office of Reports and Information Services with the assistance of the Division of Market Regulation. The registration of brokers and dealers engaged in an interstate over-the-counter securities business also is an important phase of the regulatory plan of the Act. They must conform their business practices to the standards prescribed in the law and the Commission's regulations for the protection of investors (as well as to the fair trade practice rules of their association); in addition, . . . they may violate these regulations only at the risk of possible loss of registration with the Commission and the right to continue to conduct an interstate securities business, or of suspension or expulsion from the association and loss of the benefits of such membership.

Investigation and Enforcement

It is the duty of the Commission under the laws it administers to investigate complaints or other indications of possible law violations in securities transactions, most of which arise under the Securities Act of 1933 and the Securities Exchange Act of 1934. Investigation and enforcement work is conducted both by the Commission's Regional Offices and the Division of Enforcement.

. . . .

Assuming that the facts show possible fraud or other law violation, the laws provide several courses of action or remedies which the Commission may pursue:

a. Civil injunction. The Commission may apply to an appropriate United States District Court for an order enjoining those acts or practices alleged to violate the law or Commission rules.

b. Criminal prosecution. If fraud or other willful law violation is indicated, the Commission may refer the facts to the Department of Justice with a recommendation for criminal prosecution of the offending persons. That Department, through its local United States Attorneys (who frequently are assisted by Commission attorneys), may present the evidence to a Federal grand jury and seek an indictment.

c. Administrative remedy. The Commission may, after hearing, issue orders suspending or expelling members from exchanges or the over-the-counter dealers' association [the National Association of Securities Dealers (NASD)]; denying, suspending or revoking the registrations of broker-dealers; or censuring individuals for misconduct or barring them (temporarily or permanently) from employment with a registered firm.

. . . .

PUBLIC UTILITY HOLDING COMPANY ACT OF 1935

. . . .

This statute was enacted by Congress to correct the many abuses which Congressional inquiries had disclosed in the financing and operation of electric and gas public-utility holding-company systems.

. . . .

Interstate holding companies which are engaged through their subsidiaries in the electric utility business or in the retail distribution of natural or manufactured gas are subject to regulation under the statute. The Act requires that they register with the Commission and file initial and periodic reports containing detailed data about the organization, financial structure and operations of each such holding company and of its subsidiaries. Once the holding companies are registered, they and their subsidiaries become subject to regulation by the Commission in accordance with statutory standards designed for the protection of investors, consumers, and the public interest. If, however, a holding company or a subsidiary thereof meets certain specifications, it may be exempted from part or all the duties and obligations otherwise imposed on it by statute.

. . . .

TRUST INDENTURE ACT OF 1939

This Act applies in general to bonds, debentures, notes and similar debt securities offered for public sale which are issued pursuant to trust indentures under which more than $1 million of securities may be outstanding at any one time. Even though such securities may be registered under the Securities Act, they may not be offered for sale to the public unless the trust indenture conforms to specified statutory standards of this Act designed to safeguard the rights and interests of the purchasers.

The Act was passed after studies by the Commission had revealed the frequency with which trust indentures failed to provide minimum protections for security holders and absolved so-called trustees from minimum obligations in the discharge of their trusts. It requires that the indenture trustee be free of conflicting interests which might interfere with the faithful exercise of its duties [on] behalf of the purchasers of the securities. It requires also that the trustee be a corporation with minimum combined capital and surplus; imposes high standards of conduct and responsibility on the trustee; precludes preferential collection of certain claims owing to the trustee by the issuer in the event of default; provides for the issuer's supplying evidence to the trustee of compliance with indenture terms and conditions such as those relating to the release or substitution of mortgaged property, issuance of new securities or satisfaction of the indenture; and provides for reports and notices by the trustee to security holders. Other provisions of the Act prohibit impairment of the security holders' right to sue individually for principal and interest except under certain circumstances, and require the maintenance of a list of security holders which may be used by them to communicate with each other regarding their rights as security holders.

. . . .

INVESTMENT COMPANY ACT OF 1940

This legislation, together with the Investment Advisers Act of 1940, discussed below, resulted from a study of the activities of investment companies and investment advisers conducted by the Commission pursuant to direction of Congress contained in the Holding Company Act. The results of this study were reported to Congress in a series of reports filed in 1938, 1939 and 1940, the legislation being supported both by the Commission and the investment company industry.

Under this Act, the activities of companies engaged primarily in the business of investing, reinvesting and trading in securities and whose own securities are offered and sold to and held by the investing public, are subject to certain statutory prohibitions and to Commission regulation in accordance with prescribed standards deemed necessary to protect the interests of investors and the public.

. . . .

In addition to a requirement that such companies register with the Commission, the law requires disclosure of their financial condition and investment policies to afford investors full and complete information about their activities; prohibits such companies from changing the nature of their business or their investment policies without the approval of the stockholders; bars persons guilty of security frauds from serving as officers and directors; prevents underwriters, investment bankers or brokers from constituting more than a minority of the directors of such companies; requires management contracts (and material changes therein) to be submitted to security holders for their approval; prohibits transactions between such companies and their directors, officers, or affiliated companies or persons, except on approval by the Commission as being fair and involving no overreaching; forbids the issuance of senior securities by such companies except under specified conditions and upon specified terms; and prohibits pyramiding of such companies and cross-ownership of their securities.

. . . .

The securities of investment companies are also required to be registered under the Securities Act; and the companies must file periodic reports and are subject to the Commission's proxy and "insider" trading rules.

The Division of Investment Management is the staff unit concerned with administration of this law and with the processing of investment company registration statements under the Securities Act as well as their proxy statements and periodic reports.

INVESTMENT ADVISERS ACT OF 1940

This law establishes a pattern of regulation of investment advisers which is similar in many respects to Securities Exchange Act provisions governing the conduct of brokers and dealers. It requires, with certain exceptions, that persons or firms who engage for compensation in the business of advising others about their securities transactions shall register with the Commission and conform their activities to statutory standards designed to protect the interests of investors.

The registration of investment advisers may be denied, suspended or revoked by the Commission if, after notice and hearing, it finds that a statutory disqualification exists and that such action is in the public interest. Disqualifications include a conviction for certain financial crimes or securities violations, the existence of injunctions based on such activities, a conviction for violation of the Mail Fraud Statute, the willful filing of false reports with the Commission, and willful violations of this Act, the Securities Act or the Securities Exchange Act. In addition to the administrative sanction of denial, suspension or revocation, the Commission may obtain injunctions restraining violations of this law and may recommend prosecution by the Department of Justice for fraudulent misconduct or willful violation of the law or rules of the Commission thereunder.

The law contains anti-fraud provisions, and it empowers the Commission to adopt rules defining fraudulent, deceptive or manipulative acts and practices. . . . It also requires that investment advisers disclose the nature of their interest in transactions executed for their clients; and, in effect, it prevents the assignment of investment advisory contracts without the client's consent. The law also imposes on investment advisers subject to the registration requirement the duty to maintain books and records in accordance with such rules as may be prescribed by the Commission, and it authorizes the Commission to conduct inspections of such books and records.

. . . .

Moreover, under the Bankruptcy Reform Act, the SEC serves as adviser in certain bankruptcy matters.

CHAPTER **2**

DEFINITION OF A "SECURITY"

§ 2.01 Overview

Failure on counsel's part to recognize that a "security" is present can be disastrous. As will be seen in the following chapters, absent an exemption, no offer or sale of a security generally can take place unless a registration statement is in effect. Because the requirements for meeting any particular exemption may be complex, failure on counsel's part to perceive that his or her client's "deal" involves a security often means that the securities are being sold in violation of the securities laws. Under such circumstances, the Securities and Exchange Commission (SEC), state securities commissioner(s), and private parties may bring suit. Even criminal liability, depending on the circumstances, may be imposed. Hence, many deals have been scuttled, parties held liable, and lawyers sued for failure on counsel's part to recognize that a "security" was present.

The definition of "security" in the Securities Act of 1933 and the Securities Exchange Act of 1934[1] ("the Acts") covers a broad range of transactions. Although the term includes familiar instruments such as stock, notes, bonds, and "in general, any instrument commonly known as a 'security,'" the statutory definition also encompasses a wide variety of irregular devices. In part because of the remedial purposes underlying the federal securities laws, the term "investment contract" has emerged as a catch-all for transactions that do not fit neatly into the conventional categories.

The Supreme Court has construed the definition of "security" on several occasions.[2] In the first such case, *SEC v. C.M. Joiner Leasing Corp.*,[3] the Court recognized that although the statutory definition makes specific reference to a number of "standardized" investment devices, "the reach of the Act does not stop with the obvious and commonplace."[4] Therefore, as the Court suggested, other "[n]ovel, uncommon, or irregular devices" may

---

[1] Securities Act of 1933 § 2(1), 15 U.S.C. § 77b(1); Securities Exchange Act of 1934 § 3(a)(10), 15 U.S.C. § 78c(a)(10).

[2] See *Gould v. Ruefenacht*, 471 U.S. 701 (1985); *Landreth Timber Co. v. Landreth*, 471 U.S. 681 (1985); *Marine Bank v. Weaver*, 455 U.S. 551 (1982); *International Bhd. of Teamsters v. Daniel*, 439 U.S. 551 (1979); *United Hous. Found., Inc. v. Forman*, 421 U.S. 837 (1975); *Tcherepnin v. Knight*, 389 U.S. 332 (1967); *SEC v. United Benefit Life Ins. Co.*, 387 U.S. 202 (1967); *SEC v. Variable Annuity Life Ins. Co. of Am.*, 359 U.S. 65 (1959); *SEC v. W.J. Howey Co.*, 328 U.S. 293 (1946); *SEC v. C.M. Joiner Leasing Corp.*, 320 U.S. 344 (1943).

[3] 320 U.S. 344 (1943) (holding that the sale of assignments of oil leasehold subdivisions constituted a sale of securities).

[4] *Id.* at 351.

fall within one of the definition's more descriptive categories, such as "investment contract," if the facts so warrant.[5]

In *SEC v. W.J. Howey Co.,*[6] the Court subsequently explained that the term "investment contract" had been employed in previously enacted state "blue sky" laws and had come to signify "a contract or scheme for 'the placing of capital or laying out of money in a way intended to secure income or profit from its employment.'"[7] The transaction in *Howey* involved the offering of small parcels of land in a citrus grove in Florida, coupled with a service contract for cultivating and marketing the produce. The prospective purchasers were informed that the venture was not economically feasible without arranging for a service contract. In holding that the instrument offered was an "investment contract" and, hence, a security, the *Howey* Court emphasized that "investment contract" embodies a "flexible rather than a static principle" and that the term had been broadly construed as a means of protecting the investing public. "Form was disregarded for substance and emphasis was placed upon economic reality."[8] Reasoning that Congress was aware of prior judicial interpretation of "investment contract" when it employed the term in defining "security" and noting that a broad construction was consistent with the federal securities laws' remedial intent, the *Howey* Court devised a standard to comport with this background.[9]

Under what has become known as the "*Howey* test," an investment contract is a transaction or scheme that involves "an investment of money in a common enterprise with profits to come solely from the efforts of others."[10] In *Tcherepnin v. Knight,*[11] the Court reiterated that "remedial legislation should be construed broadly to effectuate its purposes" and that "[e]ven a casual reading of [section] 3(a)(10) of the 1934 Act reveals that Congress did not intend to adopt a narrow or restrictive concept of security in defining that term."[12] Therefore, in its early post-*Howey* decisions construing the Acts, the Court adopted a flexible, expansive interpretation of

---

[5] *Id.* The Court looked to such factors as "what character the instrument is given in commerce by the terms of the offer, the plan of distribution and the economic inducements held out to the prospect." *Id.* at 352-53.

[6] 328 U.S. 293 (1946) (holding that the sale of units in a citrus grove development together with service contracts for cultivating and marketing the produce constituted a sale of securities).

[7] *Id.* at 298 (quoting *State v. Gopher Tire & Rubber Co.*, 146 Minn. 52, 56, 177 N.W. 937, 938 (1920)).

[8] 328 U.S. at 298.

[9] *Id.* at 299 (defining the term "investment contract" to encompass "a flexible rather than a static principle, one that is capable of adaptation to meet the countless and variable schemes devised by those who seek the use of the money of others on the promise of profits").

[10] *Id.* at 301.

[11] 389 U.S. 332 (1967).

[12] *Id.* at 336-38 (also stating that "form should be disregarded for substance and the emphasis should be on economic reality").

the three-part *Howey* test. The lower courts, expanding on the *Howey* test, followed suit.[13] By the mid-1970s, however, the Supreme Court retreated from this remedial approach.

The decision that signaled the Court's retreat was *United Housing Foundation, Inc. v. Forman*.[14] In *Forman* the Court held that shares of stock in a cooperative housing project purchased by individuals who were residents of the apartment complex were not securities. The Court assessed the economic realities of the transaction: the shares purchased did not confer the attendant rights that ordinarily accompany stock, were not transferable to a non-tenant, could not be pledged or encumbered, carried no voting rights, and had to be offered back to the cooperative housing corporation at their initial selling price. In determining whether the shares of stock constituted securities, the Court rejected a literal approach and refused to require that the transaction, evidenced by the sale of "stock," be considered a security transaction merely because the statutory definition of a security contains the words "any stock." Instead, the Court stressed that "*economic reality*," not form, should control: "Because securities transactions are economic in character Congress intended the application of these statutes to turn on the economic realities underlying a transaction, and not on the name appended thereto."[15]

After finding that the shares of stock in *Forman* lacked the attributes of ordinary stock, the Court also declined to view the instruments as investment contracts. The Court reasoned that the securities laws are inapplicable when the purchaser is "motivated by a desire to use or consume the item purchased," rather than by the anticipation of receiving a return on his or her investment.[16]

Similarly, in *International Brotherhood of Teamsters v. Daniel*,[17] the Supreme Court applied the "economic reality" concept to constrict, rather than to broaden, the definition of "investment contract." Specifically, the Court held that a noncontributory, compulsory pension plan is not an investment contract and, hence, not a security. In a noncontributory, compulsory pension plan, the employer contributes the necessary payments, not the employee who ultimately benefits from the plan. The Court applied the three-pronged *Howey* test for an investment contract. Concentrating on the economic reality of the plan, the Court observed that "an employee is

---

[13] See, *e.g.*, *SEC v. Koscot Interplanetary, Inc.*, 497 F.2d 473 (5th Cir. 1974) (holding that a franchise-like "pyramid" promotion scheme involved securities even though the investors exerted some effort, provided that the promoters efforts were the undeniably significant ones); *SEC v. Glenn W. Turner Enters., Inc.*, 474 F.2d 476, 482 (9th Cir.) (looking to "whether the efforts made by those other than the investor are the undeniably significant ones, those essential managerial efforts which affect the failure or success of the enterprise").

[14] 421 U.S. 837 (1975).

[15] *Id.* at 849.

[16] *Id.* at 852-53.

[17] 439 U.S. 551 (1979).

selling his labor primarily to obtain a livelihood, not making an investment" and, therefore, concluded that the *Howey* test's "investment of money" element was not satisfied.[18] Moreover, the employer's contributions to the fund were not the equivalent of an "investment" by the employee because no fixed relationship existed between the employer's contributions and the employee's potential benefits. The Court also found that the pension fund's maintenance did not depend on profits yielded by the efforts of others. To the contrary, the vast majority of the income generated derived from the employer's contributions and thus was independent from the efforts of the fund's managers. In addition, actual receipt of benefits from the fund depended on whether employees met certain individual eligibility requirements, not on the financial success of the fund itself.[19]

The *Daniel* Court further supported its holding by concluding that the enactment of ERISA, which expressly regulates pension plans,[20] eliminated the need for coverage under the securities laws:

> The existence of this comprehensive legislation governing the use and terms of employee pension plans severely undercuts all arguments for extending the Securities Acts to noncontributory, compulsory pension plans. Congress believed that it was fulfilling a regulatory void when it enacted ERISA, a belief which the SEC actively encouraged. Not only is the extension of the Securities Act . . . not supported by the language and history of those Acts, but in light of ERISA it serves no general purpose. . . . Whatever benefits employees might derive from the effect of the Securities Acts are now provided in more definite form through ERISA.[21]

Thus, in both *Forman* and *Daniel* the Supreme Court employed the language, if not quite the spirit, of the *Howey* "economic reality" test to exclude transactions that otherwise might fall within the definition of "investment contract." This trend was further evidenced by the Court's decision in *Marine Bank v. Weaver*.[22] At the outset of its analysis, the *Weaver* Court paraphrased the prefatory language to Section 3(a)(10) of the Exchange Act, stating that the terms included in the Act's definitional section are not to be considered securities if "the context otherwise requires." The Court then asserted that "Congress, in enacting the securities laws, did not intend to provide a broad federal remedy for all fraud."[23] It concluded that neither

---

[18] *Id.* at 560-61.

[19] *Id.* at 561-62.

[20] See Employee Retirement Income Security Act of 1974 (ERISA), 29 U.S.C. §§ 1001-1461.

[21] 439 U.S. at 569-70 (citations omitted). See also *Securities Act Release* Nos. 6188 (1980), 6281 (1981) (stating that voluntary contributory pension plans may be securities). But see *Conrad v. Colgate-Palmolive Co.*, 686 F.2d 1230 (7th Cir. 1982) (contributory voluntary pension plans are not securities).

[22] 455 U.S. 551 (1982).

[23] *Id.* at 556.

a conventional certificate of deposit nor an agreement given as consideration for pledging the certificate of deposit to guarantee a bank loan was a security under the federal securities laws.

In addressing the certificate of deposit issue, the *Weaver* Court elevated the presence of other comprehensive regulation, a factor of inferential importance in *Daniel*, to paramount significance in *Weaver*. The Court commenced its analysis by distinguishing the withdrawable capital shares in *Tcherepnin v. Knight* on the ground that the *Tcherepnin* purchasers received dividends based on the savings and loan associations' profits, rather than at a fixed rate of interest, and also received voting rights. The *Weaver* Court observed that the withdrawable capital shares "were much more like ordinary shares of stock and 'the ordinary concept of a security,' . . . than a certificate of deposit."[24] Then, looking to the context of the transaction, the Court turned to the differences it perceived between a certificate of deposit and other long-term debt obligations. The Court focused not on the particular attributes of these instruments, but rather on the existence of comprehensive federal regulation governing the banking industry. Moreover, unlike the holder of a long-term debt obligation who assumes the risk of the borrower's insolvency, the purchaser of a certificate of deposit is almost assured of repayment due to the availability of depositor insurance. Accordingly, the Court concluded that "[i]t is unnecessary to subject issuers of bank certificates of deposit to liability under the antifraud provisions of the federal securities laws since the holders of bank certificates of deposit are abundantly protected under the federal banking laws."[25]

Likewise, the Court observed that the profit-sharing agreement present in *Weaver* was not the type of transaction that "comes to mind when the term 'security' is used" and concluded that the agreement differed in several respects from other unusual arrangements found to involve securities. Specifically, the Court noted that the agreement was a private transaction, negotiated one-on-one, with no prospectus distributed to potential investors; that the agreement was unique (as evidenced by the provisions allowing the Weavers to use the barn and pasture), lacked "equivalent value" to other investors, and was not designed to be traded publicly; and that the Weavers' "veto" power over future loans gave them a measure of control over the business. Therefore, although the Court did not apply the *Howey* test expressly, it held that the agreement was not a security despite the profit-sharing provision.[26]

Indeed, the *Weaver* Court may have impliedly modified the *Howey* test. Although far from clear, an instrument may not be deemed an investment contract, irrespective of the *Howey* three-part test being met, if (1) the transaction involves a novel or unique instrument, (2) that is not capable of mass distribution or public trading, (3) when no prospectus has been

---

[24] *Id.* at 557.
[25] *Id.* at 558-59.
[26] *Id.* at 559-60.

distributed, *and* (4) the transaction is negotiated privately and involves few individuals.

On the other hand, in *Landreth Timber Co. v. Landreth*[27] and *Gould v. Ruefenacht*,[28] the Supreme Court departed somewhat from the economic reality concept in rejecting the restrictive approach embodied by the sale of business doctrine. That doctrine stood for the proposition that the incidental transfer of stock to manifest the sale of a closely-held business is not a security.[29] In refusing to adopt the doctrine, the Supreme Court indicated that scrutiny of a transaction's economic substance is necessary only when the instruments involved are "unusual . . . not easily characterized as 'securities.' "[30] Hence, the Court distinguished *Forman* by reasoning that the stock involved in the cases at bar bore all the characteristics traditionally associated with common stock, which the Court described as follows:

> (i) the right to receive dividends contingent upon an apportionment of profits; (ii) negotiability; (iii) the ability to be pledged or hypothecated; (iv) the conferring of voting rights in proportion to the number of shares owned; and (v) the capacity to appreciate in value.[31]

Looking to the "plain meaning" of the statutory definition of a "security," the Court held that traditional stock necessarily falls within the Acts' coverage.[32]

§ 2.02 Key Issues in Defining the Scope of a "Security"

[A] General and Limited Partnerships

The judicial analysis of whether partnership interests fall within the definition of a security has proceeded along the lines of whether a partnership interest is an "investment contract."

[1] Limited Partnerships

Since state law governing the operation of limited partnerships generally prohibits limited partners from performing management functions, courts have usually held that these interests meet the *Howey* requirement that profits are to be derived from the efforts of others. Analysis has focused upon both the terms of the partnership agreement and on the actual extent of managerial participation by the limited partners.[33]

---

[27] 471 U.S. 681 (1985).

[28] 471 U.S. 701 (1985).

[29] See, *e.g., Christy v. Cambron*, 710 F.2d 669 (10th Cir. 1983); *King v. Winkler*, 673 F.2d 342 (11th Cir. 1982); *Canfield v. Rapp & Son, Inc.*, 654 F.2d 459 (7th Cir. 1981).

[30] *Landreth*, 471 U.S. at 690.

[31] *Id.* at 686. See *Gould*, 471 U.S. at 704-06.

[32] *Landreth*, 471 U.S. at 687; *Gould*, 471 U.S. at 704.

[33] See, *e.g., Mayer v. Oil Field Systems Corp.*, 721 F.2d 59 (2d Cir. 1983).

It should be noted, however, that a court still must make an independent examination of whether the limited partnership interest meets the *Howey* investment contract test. Whether or not a partnership interest is a "limited" partnership for state law purposes is significant but not determinative. This is illustrated by *Gordon v. Terry.*[34] In that case a limited partnership was formed for the purposes of buying and selling undeveloped land. The limited partners had explicit voting power on whether or not specific pieces of land should be sold and at what time. The Eleventh Circuit (ruling on a summary judgment motion) held that these interests were not securities and could not pass the *Howey* test.

[a] "Solely from the Efforts of Others"

One of the issues often present in determining whether limited partnership interests and similar investments are securities under the *Howey* test is how strictly the term "*solely* from the efforts of others" should be construed. A number of federal appellate court decisions have discussed the issue, with the Fifth Circuit case of *SEC v. Koscot Interplanetary, Inc.*[35] being the most well known. That case involved a franchise-like marketing system rather than a limited partnership but its holding has had broad application. The *Koscot* court adopted a test first explicated by the Ninth Circuit in *SEC v. Glenn W. Turner Enterprises, Inc.*[36] In *Turner* the court announced that the critical inquiry is "whether the efforts made by those other than the investor are the undeniably significant ones, those essential managerial efforts which affect the failure or success of the enterprise."[37] This *Koscot/Turner* test rejects a literal interpretation of "solely" and has been applied in several cases involving limited partnerships. For example, in *Goodman v. Epstein,*[38] the Seventh Circuit stated that "solely from the efforts of others" should not be read as a strict or literal limitation on the definition of an investment contract. The court went on to hold that evidence that a limited partner arranged financing for the venture before its inception did not overcome the fact that by state law he could not manage it.[39]

[b] "Expectation of Profits"

Courts in certain circumstances have also been presented with the issue of whether the "expectation of profits" aspect of the *Howey* test has been met. Generally, a number of courts hold that an investor's desire for favorable tax consequences does not prevent the instrument from being a security so long as there is also an expectation of profit in real terms.[40] On the other hand, as alluded to earlier, the securities laws generally will not be applicable where

---

[34] 684 F.2d 736 (11th Cir. 1982).

[35] 497 F.2d 473 (5th Cir. 1974).

[36] 474 F.2d 476 (9th Cir. 1973).

[37] *Id.* at 482.

[38] 582 F.2d 388 (7th Cir. 1978).

[39] *Id.* at 408 n.59.

[40] See, *e.g., Goodman v. Epstein,* 582 F.2d 388 (7th Cir. 1978).

the purchaser is principally motivated by a desire to use or consume the particular item acquired (*e.g.*, the *Forman* transaction involving tenant purchases of shares of stock in a cooperative housing project).

[c] The "Common Enterprise" Requirement

Under the *Howey* test, the "common enterprise" standard must be satisfied. This issue may well surface in determining whether certain partnership interests are securities. Generally, all courts hold that horizontal commonality (which looks to the relationship between an individual investor and the pool of other investors) meets this element of the *Howey* test.[41] Courts widely disagree, however, on whether vertical commonality is sufficient.[42] Vertical commonality generally requires only that the investor(s) and promoter (or third party) be involved in some common venture. Based on *Weaver*, due to the Supreme Court's holding that the one-on-one agreement in that case was not a security, some lower courts have asserted that the vertical commonality approach no longer survives.[43] This view, although plausible, is premature. Indeed, a number of other courts have ruled otherwise, refusing to read *Weaver* in an unduly restrictive manner.[44] This latter interpretation of *Weaver's* implications finds strong support in the Court's post-*Weaver* denial of the petition for a *writ of certiorari* in *Mordaunt v. Incomco.*[45] In *Mordaunt,* Justice White, dissenting from the denial of the petition, surveyed the divergent views among the lower courts concerning the requisite commonality and opined that "[i]n light of the clear and significant split in the Circuits, I would grant *certiorari.*"[46]

[2] General Partnerships

Since general partnerships do not possess the same restrictions on participation in management as limited partnership interests, they usually fail to satisfy the *Howey* "solely from the efforts of others" standard. Several courts have applied *Howey* in a fairly literal manner and have held that general partnership interests are not securities.[47]

The Fifth Circuit, with its decision in *Williamson v. Tucker,*[48] may have "rescued" general partnership interests from being declared outside the scope

---

[41] See, *e.g., Salcer v. Merrill Lynch, Pierce, Fenner & Smith, Inc.*, 682 F.2d 459 (3d Cir. 1982); *Hirk v. Agri-Research Council, Inc.*, 561 F.2d 96 (7th Cir. 1977).

[42] For decisions holding that vertical commonality is sufficient, see, *e.g., McGill v. American Land & Exploration Co.*, [1985-1986 Transfer Binder] Fed. Sec. L. Rep. (CCH) ¶ 92,368 (10th Cir. 1985); *Meyer v. Thomas & McKinnon Auchincloss Kohlmeyer, Inc.*, 686 F.2d 818 (9th Cir. 1982).

[43] See, *e.g., First Nat'l Bank v. Thoele*, [1982 Transfer Binder] Fed. Sec. L. Rep. (CCH) ¶ 98,854 (W.D. Okla. 1982).

[44] See, *e.g., McGill v. American Land & Exploration Co.*, [1985-1986 Transfer Binder] Fed. Sec. L. Rep. (CCH) ¶ 92,368 (10th Cir. 1985).

[45] 469 U.S. 1115 (1985).

[46] *Id.* at 1117 (White, J., dissenting).

[47] See, *e.g., Sandusky Land Ltd. v. Uniplan Group, Inc.*, 400 F. Supp. 440 (N.D. Ohio 1975).

[48] 645 F.2d 404 (5th Cir. 1981).

of the securities laws as a matter of law. The case involved a series of joint ventures each of which owned an undivided interest in certain real estate. The joint venturers seemingly retained substantial control over the prospect through the joint venture agreements that they signed. The court stated that, in spite of the partnership form which the investment took, if the investor was in fact unable to exercise meaningful management powers because of his or her dependence on the promoter or a third party, then the general partnership interest could be designated a security under federal law. The court went on to delineate three sets of circumstances where this could happen: First, an interest could be a security if the agreement between the parties leaves so little power in the hands of the investor that power is distributed as it would be in a limited partnership. Second, a security also could be present if the investor is so inexperienced and unknowledgeable in business affairs as to be incapable of intelligently exercising his or her partnership powers. Finally, the *Williamson* court stated that a security could be present if the investor is so dependent on some unique "entrepreneurial or managerial" ability of the promoter or manager that he or she cannot replace the manager or otherwise exercise meaningful partnership powers.[49]

[B] Property Interests Combined with Service Contracts

The factual setting presented to the Supreme Court in *SEC v. W.J. Howey Co.* has been repeated numerous times in a variety of contexts. Courts repeatedly have looked beyond a strict statutory construction and have examined the economic reality of the transaction to determine whether a property interest combined with some form of service contract constitutes a security. The *Howey* analysis applied by the courts in these cases can usually be broken down into three issues: First, are the investors dependent on other investors and/or the promoter for a return on their investment ("common enterprise")? Second, is the interest bought in order to obtain a financial return or for other reasons ("expectation of profits") and third, do the investors participate in the venture to such a degree that they are not dependent "solely on the efforts of others" for their profits?[50]

An example of the applicability of the securities laws in this context may arise when there is the offer and sale of condominium units, or other units in a real estate development, coupled with an arrangement for the promoter to perform rental services for the purchaser. Such agreements, as asserted by the SEC, may be held to involve the offer and sale of an investment contract or a participation in a profit sharing arrangement within the meaning of the securities acts.[51]

---

[49] *Id.* at 417-25.

[50] See, *e.g., Westchester Corp. v. Peat Marwick Mitchell & Co.*, 626 F.2d 1212 (5th Cir. 1980); *Continental Marketing Corp. v. SEC*, 387 F.2d 466 (10th Cir. 1967).

[51] See *Securities Act Release* No. 5347 (1973).

[C] The Risk Capital Test

The risk capital test is an important alternative to the *Howey* test for ascertaining the existence of an investment contract. Although not generally adopted by the federal courts, the test has been embraced by a number of states by statute or case law. Importantly, application of the risk capital test may lead to a finding of a "security" under the applicable state law where the *Howey* test would hold that no security interest is present.

The risk capital test was recognized by the California Supreme Court in *Silver Hills Country Club v. Sobieski*[52] in an opinion written by Justice Traynor. There, the California Commissioner of Corporations successfully argued that the offer and sale of memberships in a country club to be operated for profit, the proceeds from such memberships to be used for club improvements and which entitled the members and their immediate families to use club facilities, constituted a security. Even though the benefits to be received were not pecuniary, the court, recognizing that the promoters were soliciting risk capital for the purpose of developing a profitable business, held that the membership interests were securities.

The risk capital test has been adopted by a number of state courts and legislatures.[53] Significantly, generally under the risk capital test, (1) there is no horizontal common enterprise requirement, (2) (similar to the *Howey* line of cases) non-pecuniary benefits are sufficient, and (3) the *Howey* "solely" from the efforts of others standard is relaxed.

[D] Debt Securities

A substantial portion of the case law that has developed in attempting to determine what is a security for the purposes of the securities acts has dealt with debt instruments. One threshold problem that has arisen is that the definitions pertaining to debt securities in Section 2(1) of the Securities Act and Section 3(a)(10) of the Exchange Act are not precisely the same. Further, the Securities Act definition, although exempting notes of less than nine months maturity from the registration requirement, specifically includes "evidence(s) of indebtedness". The Exchange Act definition of security (§ 3(a)(10)), on the other hand, specifically excludes notes of less than nine months maturity. Almost all of the lower federal courts that have discussed the issue, however, construe the two Acts as having the same definition. The courts base this approach on *Tcherepnin v. Knight*[54] which contains language that the Exchange Act definition was intended to be substantially the same as that in the Securities Act.

---

[52] 55 Cal. 2d 811, 361 P.2d 906, 13 Cal. Rptr. 186 (1961).

[53] See, *e.g., State, Commissioner of Securities v. Hawaii Market Center, Inc.*, 52 Haw. 642, 485 P.2d 105 (1971); Ga. Code Ann. § 97-102(a)(16); Okla. Stat. tit. 71, § 2(20)(P); Coffey, *The Economic Realities of a "Security": Is There a More Meaningful Formula?*, 18 Case W. Res. L. Rev. 367 (1967).

[54] 389 U.S. 332 (1967).

[1] Notes

The lower federal courts have essentially employed three different modes of analysis in determining whether a note is a security: the "risk capital" test, the "plain language" test, and the "commercial/investment" test. These tests are applied irrespective of whether the note falls within the literal language of Section 2(1) of the Securities Act or Section 3(a)(10) of the Exchange Act. The tests differ in the degree of deference that they give to the statutory language in determining whether the "context otherwise requires" that a note not be declared a security.

[a] The "Plain Language" Test

The Second Circuit gives the most deference to the statute, placing the burden of proof upon the party seeking to avoid the plain language of the statute. Hence, where the note literally is within the scope of the statute, the burden is upon the party seeking to avoid application of the securities laws to show that the context otherwise requires. Conversely, where the note literally falls outside of the statute's reach, the burden is upon the party seeking application of the securities laws to prove that the context otherwise requires. The Second Circuit applied the "plain language" test in *Exchange National Bank of Chicago v. Touche Ross*[55] where the unsecured subordinated notes of a brokerage firm, having a maturity of greater than nine months, were held to be securities. In so holding, however, the Second Circuit stated that the context may require that notes delivered in certain transactions not be deemed securities. The court enumerated the following types of situations where a note would not be deemed a security:

> The note delivered in consumer financing, the note secured by a mortgage on a home, the short-term note secured by a lien on a small business, or some of its assets, the note evidencing a "character" loan to a bank customer, short-term notes secured by an assignment of accounts receivable, or a note which simply formalizes an open account debt incurred in the ordinary course of business (particularly if, as in the case of the customer of a broker, it is collateralized.)[56]

[b] The "Commercial/Investment" Test

Several courts have adopted the commercial/investment test where the focus is on the underlying character of the transaction. Applying the "unless the context otherwise requires" language of Sections 2(1) and 3(a)(10) as well as the economic reality concept, courts adhering to this view hold that a note is not a security where it arises from a commercial transaction even when its terms are literally within the Acts' coverage. In making this determination, the courts have focused on such factors as the use of the funds (to fund current expenses rather than long-term projects), whether the note is

---

[55] 544 F.2d 1126 (2d Cir. 1976).

[56] *Id.* at 1138. See *Chemical Bank v. Arthur Andersen & Co.*, 725 F.2d 930 (2d Cir. 1984) (perhaps departing somewhat from *Exchange National Bank*).

collateralized (and, hence, less "risky"), the number of purchasers (limited to few or marketed to many), the level of sophistication of the purchasers (is the purchaser a bank or an uninitiated investor), and whether the note has a short maturity.[57]

[c] The "Risk Capital" Test

The Ninth Circuit in *Great Western Bank & Trust v. Kotz*[58] adopted the "risk capital" test in the note context. The court's analysis focused on the following factors: the length of the note ("the most important factor [because] the longer one's funds are to be used by another, the greater the risk of loss"), the collateralization ("[t]he unsecured lender is generally more dependent upon the managerial skills of the borrower than is a secured party"), the size of the debt compared to the size of the borrower's business ("the larger the relative amount, the greater the stake, and therefore the risk, of the lender"), and the use of the proceeds (whether used as "an essential ingredient of enterprise formation [rather than] to maintain current financial position"). The Ninth Circuit has applied the risk capital test in subsequent cases.[59]

[2] Certificates of Deposit

Although literally notes, certificates of deposit issued by banks were generally found by courts to present special issues. Several courts, focusing on the fact that a depositor received a fixed rate of return, found that the *Howey* "profits" element was not present. These courts also concluded that the existence of the federal bank regulatory system made including these instruments under the securities laws unnecessary on policy grounds. The definitive case in this area now is *Marine Bank v. Weaver*[60] where the Supreme Court did not apply the *Howey* test to the CD but rather focused on the existence of pervasive federal regulation over banking. Accordingly, the Court held that a certificate of deposit purchased from a federally regulated bank is not a security.

Two post-*Weaver* decisions serve as examples to help highlight the policy questions involved. In *Wolf v. Banco Nacional De Mexico*,[61] the Ninth

---

[57] See, *e.g.*, *Smith International, Inc. v. Texas Commerce Bank, National Association*, [1987-1988 Transfer Binder] Fed. Sec. L. Rep. (CCH) ¶ 93,770 (5th Cir. 1988) (promissory notes offered by a corporation to its trade creditors were commercial in nature, and, hence, not securities); *Bauerer v. Planning Group, Inc.*, 669 F.2d 770 (D.C. Cir. 1981) ("security" includes short term promissory note given in exchange for funds advanced in anticipation of securing a limited partnership interest); *American Fletcher Mortgage Co. v. United States Steel Credit Corp.*, 635 F.2d 124 (7th Cir. 1980) (agreement to participate in a three year collateralized commercial loan held not a security).

[58] 532 F.2d 1252 (9th Cir. 1976).

[59] See, *e.g.*, *AMFAC Mortgage Corp. v. Arizona Mall of Tempe, Inc.*, 583 F.2d 426 (9th Cir. 1978). See generally Sonnenschein, *Federal Securities Law Coverage of Note Transactions: Antifraud Provisions*, 35 Bus. Law. 1567 (1980).

[60] 455 U.S. 551 (1982).

[61] 721 F.2d 660 (9th Cir. 1984). See *West v. Multibanco Comermex*, 807 F.2d 820 (9th Cir. 1987).

Circuit was faced with the issue of whether certificates of deposit (CDs) in Mexican pesos in a Mexican bank were securities under United States law. The district court, relying on *Weaver's* emphasis on the protection given to depositors by the U.S. banking laws, held that, since the Mexican CDs were outside the U.S. banking regulatory system, *Weaver* did not compel a finding that these instruments were not securities. Reversing, the Ninth Circuit, applying *Weaver*, held that the Mexican CDs were not securities in that the issuing bank was sufficiently regulated under Mexican law and repayment in full was virtually guaranteed due to the presence of depositor insurance. The second case arose out of the failure of Penn Square Bank, *Brockton Savings Bank v. Peat, Marwick, Mitchell & Co.*[62] In holding that a certificate of deposit issued by Penn Square and purchased by the plaintiff through a money market broker was not a security, the court examined the effect of federal insurance. The plaintiff argued that *Weaver* excludes certificates of deposit from federal securities regulation only to the monetary extent that such instruments are actually federally insured. The *Brockton* court rejected this argument, stating that language in *Weaver* regarding the protection given to depositors by federal insurance referred only to the fact that depositors in FDIC banks have always been paid in full.

[62] 577 F. Supp. 1281 (D. Mass. 1983). See generally Steinberg & Kaulbach, *The Supreme Court and the Definition of "Security": The "Context" Clause, "Investment Contract" Analysis, and Their Ramifications*, 40 Vand. L. Rev. 489 (1987).

CHAPTER 3

ISSUER EXEMPTIONS FROM REGISTRATION

§ 3.01 Exempt Securities From Registration

The general rule is that, absent an exemption, all offers or sales of securities must be registered pursuant to Section 5 of the Securities Act of 1933 ("Securities Act" or "1933 Act"). Note, importantly, that the securities law antifraud provisions apply irrespective of whether an exemption from registration exists. There are two general types of registration exemptions: transactional exemptions and securities exempt from registration. The latter covers specific securities or categories of securities which are never required to be registered under Section 5, largely due to the intrinsic character or nature of the issuer itself. These exempt securities include, for example, certain short-term promissory notes or bills of exchange, securities issued or guaranteed by municipalities, state or federal governments, and securities issued by nonprofit, religious, educational or charitable organizations.[1]

Moreover, some securities, although exempt from the 1933 Act's registration requirements, come under the supervision of another federal or state governmental authority. For example, with respect to securities issued by national banks, the Comptroller of the Currency has developed a regulatory framework somewhat similar, yet many feel not as rigorous, as that developed by the Securities and Exchange Commission ("SEC"). On the other hand, the securities of bank holding companies are not exempt securities from registration under the federal securities laws.[2]

Significantly, it is the transactional exemptions from registration which play the important role in this context. As a consequence, the chapter will focus on these exemptions.

§ 3.02 Why Perfect a Transactional Exemption?

As stated above, unless an exemption from registration is available, all offers or sales must be registered pursuant to Section 5 of the Securities Act. Given this consequence, one may ask "why perfect a transactional exemption from registration rather than registering the offer or sale under Section 5 of the 1933 Act?"

---

[1] See Sections 3(a)(2)-3(a)(8), 15 U.S.C. §§ 77c(a)(2)-(a)(8), for a listing of the securities exempt from registration.

[2] See generally L. Loss, *Securities Regulation* 559-641 (2d ed. 1961, Supp. 1969).

The answer to the above question contains several reasons why a transactional exemption often is the preferred route. Keep in mind that the following discussion somewhat simplifies the pertinent requirements. Generally, in order to register an offer or sale under Section 5 and have what is called a "public offering" or "to go public,"[3] a registration statement must be filed with the Securities and Exchange Commission. In addition, the statutory prospectus, which is part of the registration statement, must be provided to the purchaser at the time that the security is delivered or at the time the confirmation of the sale is received, whichever occurs earlier. The registration statement (the prospectus which is a part thereof) is no ordinary document. The disclosures required are detailed and complex, the document's length is massive, and the costs of preparing the registration statement, including accountant, attorney, investment banker and printer fees, can easily run into the hundreds of thousands of dollars.

The costs and nature of the registration statement are due largely to Section 11 of the 1933 Act which, in practical effect, imposes a "due diligence" requirement upon certain parties, including the issuer's directors and certain executive officers, the underwriters, and the experts, including the accountants (with respect to those portions of the registration statement which an accountant has "expertised"). Attorneys, unless they act as experts,[4] are not subject to Section 11 liability. Counsel, nonetheless, is integrally involved in the registration process. He or she frequently is delegated by the issuer, underwriter, or other parties potentially liable under Section 11 to perform the requisite "due diligence" on their behalf. Other fundamental aspects of counsel's role in this process involve the drafting of the language contained in the registration statement, advising whether certain disclosures should or must be made, and acting as informal mediator between the various parties involved.

The concept of "due diligence," its significance, and the steps that must be taken to fulfill this mandate are addressed in Chapter 6, *infra*. In theory, "due diligence" is a defense that may be asserted by the subject party rather than an affirmative obligation. It is certainly true that if the statements made in the registration statement are true or if no lawsuit is ultimately brought, no liability will be incurred for failure to exercise due diligence. If an action is instituted and a material misstatement or omission is shown, however, liability often may be avoided under Section 11 only by proving the

---

[3] The terms "public offering" and "going public" are often not synonymous. In short, the initial public offering ("IPO") made by an enterprise constitutes "going public." On the other hand, a successful corporation which has gone public decades ago may make public offerings of its securities on a periodic basis.

[4] Counsel acts as an expert, for example, if he or she proffers an opinion contained or referred to in the registration statement regarding the pertinent ramifications under the tax laws. An accountant, by certifying financial statements contained in the registration statement, is the party who normally is sued as an expert under Section 11.

performance of due diligence. In the realities of corporate practice, therefore, due diligence is a necessity rather than a discretionary function.

Hence, the "due diligence" requirement is given "teeth" by the liability consequences. In general, if there is a material misrepresentation or nondisclosure in the nonexpertised portion of the registration statement, parties subject to Section 11 liability, except experts and the issuer (which is strictly liable), can avoid such liability only by showing that they had conducted a reasonable investigation and, after such investigation, had no reason to believe and did not believe that the registration statement contained any materially false or misleading statement. With respect to expertised portions of the registration statement, nonexperts are not required to investigate. They need show only that they had no reason to believe and did not believe that the expertised portions of the registration statement contained any materially false or misleading statements. Moreover, experts are potentially liable under Section 11 only for those portions of the registration statement which they "expertised." They can avoid Section 11 liability by showing that, with respect to the expertised portions of the registration statement, they had conducted a reasonable investigation and, after such investigation, had no reason to believe and did not believe that such expertised portions of the registration statement contained any materially false or misleading statement.

While the issuer is the only party which has no "due diligence" defense under Section 11 and is subject to strict liability, it may well be insolvent. The result is that aggrieved plaintiffs seek redress against the "deep pockets," frequently the underwriters and the accountants. Because of the severe financial ramifications that can amount to several million dollars, parties potentially subject to Section 11 liability seek to ensure that abundant due diligence is performed and extensive disclosure made, including the potentially negative consequences and risks of the venture.

Hence, the costs of having a "registered" offering under the Securities Act frequently will be substantial. For a start-up venture or a business in severe financial difficulty, the costs of a public offering normally will prove prohibitive. Moreover, it is next to impossible to successfully consummate a registered offering unless receptive investment bankers can be retained to underwrite the offering and the financial markets are favorable. These conditions are exacerbated in cases where enterprises with little or no previous earnings history seek to "go public." As some of the "high-tech" and "research" companies have shown (*e.g.*, Apple Computer and Genentech), however, these problems are not insurmountable.

Even if a financially successful registered offering can be made, it may be advisable for the client nonetheless to perfect a transactional exemption. By refraining from "going public," the enterprise essentially is keeping its financial affairs and related matters private among its various participants. By "going public," however, the enterprise, pursuant to the disclosure requirements of the securities laws, will be hanging its dirty linen out for public viewing.[5] The enterprise, pursuant to certain provisions of the

---

[5] *Cf. Schlick v. Penn-Dixie Cement Corp.*, 507 F.2d 374, 384 (2d Cir. 1974).

Securities Exchange Act, such as Section 15(d), will be required to file annual, quarterly, and other periodic reports with the SEC as well as to provide periodic reports to its shareholders and the pertinent self-regulatory organizations. Moreover, other sections of the Exchange Act, such as Section 13(b)'s recordkeeping and internal accounting control provisions, will become applicable. Hence, the enterprise, by having a registered offering, will be faced not only with public scrutiny but saddled with high accounting and legal fees as well as the persistent threat of litigation due to the consequences of public disclosure.

For the above reasons as well as others (such as, by taking the corporation public, the insiders may potentially risk loss of control through a hostile takeover), it may well be advisable and indeed necessary, to procure a transactional exemption from registration. It should not be surprising that, given the above, the vast majority of offerings are made under a transactional exemption rather than by a registered offering pursuant to Section 5 of the Securities Act. In many instances, therefore, counsel will seek the viability of a transactional exemption before advising that a registered offering go forward. Hence, an examination of the offering process begins with the transactional exemptions.

§ 3.03 Transactional Exemptions — Introductory Points

Prior to turning to a discussion of the transactional exemptions from 1933 Act registration, certain introductory points should be made:

First, the following material in this chapter addresses exemptions from Securities Act registration that are transactionally based. Thus, for each separate *transaction* an exemption from registration must be perfected.

Second, the relevant parties for the purposes of this chapter who are seeking to come within the transactional exemptions are primary issuers of securities. For example, a corporation issuing authorized but unissued stock or a limited partnership issuing interests to its participants would each be viewed as a primary issuer while a shareholder who seeks to transfer his or her shares to another would not be.

Third, accordingly, individuals reselling their stock must register any offer or sale unless they perfect an exemption. The exemption that normally would be invoked in this context is Section 4(1) of the Securities Act which exempts from the registration requirements of Section 5 offers or sales made by any person "other than an issuer, underwriter, or dealer." The subject of resales is addressed in Chapter 5, *infra*.

Fourth, the party seeking the exemption has the burden of proving that it has perfected the exemption by establishing that it has satisfied the necessary conditions for invoking the exemption. Failure to carry this burden signifies that no transactional exemption has been perfected, resulting in liability under the Securities Act for failure to register the offer or sale in question.

Such failure to register gives rise to SEC, and perhaps criminal, liability for violation of Section 5 and to private recovery under Section 12(1) of the 1933 Act. Generally, Section 12(1) grants to the purchaser the right to rescind the transaction in an action brought against the seller for violation of Section 5. In effect, the provision imposes strict liability upon the seller for failure to comply with Section 5's registration requirements.

Fifth, consistent with the federal securities laws in general, the interstate commerce requirement must be met in order for federal jurisdiction to be invoked in the transactional exemption context. This requirement normally is shown without difficulty. Use of the mail or any means or instrumentality of interstate commerce is sufficient. An intrastate telephone call, for example, satisfies the federal jurisdictional requirement.

Sixth, even if a transactional exemption has been perfected, thereby obviating the need to register the offering, the antifraud provisions of the securities acts nonetheless fully apply. The antifraud provisions most frequently invoked are Section 17(a) of the Securities Act, Section 10(b) of the Exchange Act, and Rule 10b-5 promulgated by the SEC pursuant to its Section 10(b) rulemaking authority.

Seventh, as a final important point, federal law is not the only source of regulation in this setting. The state "blue sky" laws also apply and present additional dilemmas for the corporate practitioner and his or her client. In practical effect, to perfect an exemption, in addition to satisfying the requirements of federal law, the securities regulations of *each* state where *any* offer or sale is made also must be satisfied. To the credit of the SEC and the states, significant progress has been made in coordinating the federal and state transactional exemption scheme, thereby alleviating much of the burden in complying with this multi-faceted regulatory framework.

§ 3.04 The SEC "No-Action Letter"

Although not specifically related to transactional exemptions from registration, this is a good point to mention the SEC "no-action" letter process. Under this process, counsel advises the SEC staff in writing of his or her client's contemplated conduct. Such contemplated conduct may involve, for example, questions related to a Regulation D offering, resales of stock, or proxy statements. The staff responds by either issuing a no-action letter or by refusing to issue such a letter. Refusal by the staff to approve a no-action request normally results in the affected parties not engaging in the contemplated conduct. Even if the staff issues a no-action letter, however, that does not ensure that the client's conduct will not be challenged. Private parties are not bound by an SEC no-action letter and may sue irrespective of the issuance of such a letter. Moreover, although highly unlikely to happen, the SEC retains its discretion to institute an enforcement action even though its staff has issued a no-action letter covering the very same conduct.[6]

---

[6] See generally Lemke, *The SEC No-Action Letter Process*, 42 Bus. Law. 1019 (1987).

§ 3.05 The Section 4(2) Private Offering Exemption

Section 4(2) of the Securities Act exempts from the registration requirements "transactions by an issuer not involving any public offering." There is no monetary limit to the amount of funds that can be raised under this exemption. The provision's legislative history expresses Congress' intent to exempt those transactions from registration "where there is no practical need for [such] application . . . [or] where the public benefits are too remote."[7] As subsequently construed, courts have looked to a number of factors in determining the availability of the Section 4(2) private offering exemption.

A good starting point in ascertaining the requirements of the Section 4(2) private offering exemption is the Supreme Court's decision in *Securities and Exchange Commission v. Ralston Purina Co.*[8] In that case, the company made asserted private offerings to scores of "key" employees, many of whom held non-managerial positions. The Supreme Court, observing that the burden of proving the perfection of an exemption from registration is upon the party relying upon the availability of such an exemption, held that the company had not satisfied this burden. The availability of the Section 4(2) private offering exemption, according to the Court, should turn upon "whether the particular class of persons affected need the protection of the [Securities] Act."[9] Accordingly, the private offering exemption, among other things, requires that all persons to whom offers are made are to be provided with or are to have access to the type of information that would be contained in a registration statement.[10]

The lower federal courts, subsequent to *Ralston Purina*, have had numerous occasions to construe the Section 4(2) exemption.[11] Although the principles emerging from these cases are not crystal clear, the following points can be made:

First, the Section 4(2) exemption turns on whether *all offers* (rather than actual purchases) are made in accordance with the exemption. A single noncomplying offer may invalidate the entire offering. For example, the Fifth Circuit has stated: "[W]e have held that the defendant must establish that each and every offeree either had the same information that would have been available in a registration statement or had access to such information."[12]

Second, although the courts and the SEC have not placed a finite number on how many offers can be permissibly made under the Section

[7] H.R. Rep. No. 85, 73rd Cong., 1st Sess. 5 (1933).

[8] 346 U.S. 119 (1953).

[9] *Id.* at 124.

[10] *Id.* at 124-27.

[11] See, *e.g.*, *SEC v. Murphy*, 626 F.2d 633 (9th Cir. 1980); *Swenson v. Engelstad*, 626 F.2d 421 (5th Cir. 1980); *Lawler v. Gilliam*, 569 F.2d 1283 (4th Cir. 1978).

[12] *Swenson v. Engelstad*, 626 F.2d 421, 425-26 (5th Cir. 1980).

4(2) exemption, it is clear that certain limits, depending on the circumstances, apply.[13]

Third, related to the above point, is that, pursuant to the exemption, the issuer cannot engage in general solicitation or advertising. The precise limits of what conduct constitutes general solicitation so as to make unavailable the Section 4(2) exemption (as well as the Rule 506 of Regulation D exemption) are unclear. A seminar held for an offering where thirty-five existing clients of adequate sophistication attend should be permitted while a seminar for a particular offering open to all clients of a broker-dealer (*e.g.*, Merrill Lynch or Prudential-Bache) should be deemed general solicitation.[14]

Fourth, an issuer should take certain precautions against resales, including obtaining written commitments by purchasers that they are acquiring for investment purposes (called an investment letter), placing appropriate legends on the certificates, and issuing stop transfer instructions. These procedures help the issuer to perfect the Section 4(2) exemption in the event that purchasers subsequently resell their stock. It may well be, however, that the absence of these steps does not nullify an otherwise valid Section 4(2) exemption if no distribution in fact takes place.[15]

Fifth, all offerees must be financially sophisticated or be advised by someone who has the requisite acumen (called an offeree representative). Under case law, individual wealth does not make one sophisticated for Section 4(2) private placement purposes.[16]

Sixth, irrespective of whether an offeree (or offeree representative) has financial acumen, "[s]ophistication is not a substitute for access to the information that a registration statement would disclose."[17] In short, if offerees have not received information that registration would elicit, they cannot bring any alleged "sophistication" to bear in deciding whether or not to invest.[18] Hence, all offerees must be provided with the type of information (not necessarily identical) that would be contained in a registration statement or have access to such information.

---

[13] See *Ralston Purina*, 346 U.S. at 125.

[14] The SEC has issued no-action letters in this context. See § 3.04, *supra*. See also Cohn, *Securities Markets for Small Issuers: The Barrier of Federal Solicitation and Advertising Prohibitions*, 38 U. Fla. L. Rev. 1 (1986).

[15] See *Livens v. William D. Witter, Inc.*, 374 F. Supp. 1104, 1110 (D. Mass. 1974); Schneider, *The Statutory Law of Private Placements*, 14 Rev. Sec. Reg. 870, 881 (1981).

[16] See *Doran v. Petroleum Management Corp.*, 545 F.2d 893, 903 (5th Cir. 1977).

[17] *Id.* at 902; *United States v. Custer Channel Wing Corp.*, 376 F.2d 675, 678 (4th Cir. 1967).

[18] See *Hill York Corp. v. American International Franchises, Inc.*, 448 F.2d 680, 690 (5th Cir. 1971).

Ascertaining which offerees have "access" to registration-type information may be difficult. Relevant factors include promoter or high level executive status in the enterprise, family ties, a privileged relationship based upon prior business dealings between the parties, and economic bargaining power that enables an offeree effectively to obtain the registration-type information.[19]

As a final comment, some courts have looked to two additional factors in determining whether the Section 4(2) exemption has been perfected: the number of units offered and the size of the offering.[20] These factors, however, often are irrelevant. For example, the offer and sale by an issuer of one million corporate debentures for $300 million to five sophisticated institutional investors (such as insurance companies) who had effective access to registration-type information normally should be within the Section 4(2) private offering exemption.

§ 3.06 Rule 506 of Regulation D

As seen from the preceding discussion, perfecting a Section 4(2) exemption is no easy matter. In addition, the alleged vagueness of judicial decisions, setting forth relevant Section 4(2) criteria, resulted in the securities bar clamoring for an SEC "safe harbor" rule. In 1974, the Commission responded by adopting Rule 146. As stated by the SEC in a subsequent release:

> Section 4(2) of the Securities Act of 1933 provides that offers and sales of securities by an issuer not involving any public offering are exempt from the registration provisions of the Act. Rule 146 provides objective standards for determining when the exemption is available. The main conditions of the rule require that (1) there be no general advertising or soliciting in connection with the offering; (2) offers be made only to persons the issuer reasonably believes have the requisite knowledge and experience in financial and business matters or who can bear the economic risk; (3) sales be made only to persons as described above except that persons meeting the economic risk test must also have an offeree representative capable of providing the requisite knowledge and experience; (4) offerees have access to or be provided information comparable to that elicited through registration; (5) there be no more than 35 purchasers in the offering; and (6) reasonable care be taken to ensure that the securities are not resold in violation of the Act's registration provisions.[21]

Rule 146 was severely criticized by the securities bar. Indeed, the rule evidently was more restrictive than the case law construing the Section 4(2)

---

[19] See *Doran v. Petroleum Management Corp.*, 545 F.2d 893, 903 (5th Cir. 1977); Schneider, *supra* note 15, at 877.

[20] See, *e.g.*, *SEC v. Continental Tobacco Co.*, 463 F.2d 137, 158 (5th Cir. 1978).

[21] *Securities Act Release* No. 5913 (1978).

statutory exemption.[22] Responding to this criticism and in an effort to facilitate capital formation, the SEC promulgated Regulation D in 1982. Rule 506, one of the rules promulgated by the Commission pursuant to Regulation D, is a "safe harbor" to the Section 4(2) exemption and supersedes Rule 146. Compliance with Rule 506 thus may be viewed as an alternative method to perfect the Section 4(2) private offering exemption.

Generally, Rule 506 is available to any issuer. There is no limit to the aggregate price of the securities offered. Although Rule 506 does not limit the number of offerees, no advertising or general solicitation is permitted. Hence, offers to a large number of offerees may be viewed as general solicitation, resulting in loss of the exemption.[23] The number of purchasers is limited to thirty-five plus an unlimited number of accredited investors. If any of the purchasers are not accredited, then specified disclosure must be made to all purchasers (see chart in § 3.08, *infra*).

Unlike prior Rule 146, there is no requirement under Rule 506 that the issuer determine that the purchaser can bear the economic risk of the investment. Suitability determinations, however, must be made for nonaccredited purchasers. Except for accredited investors, the issuer prior to sale must "reasonably believe" that each purchaser either alone or with his or her "purchaser" representative has such knowledge and experience in financial and business matters that he or she is capable of evaluating the merits and risks of the prospective investment. Moreover, the issuer must take certain actions to guard against resales (*e.g.*, obtaining purchaser investment letters)[24] in order to help ensure that a "distribution" does not occur.[25] And, as discussed in § 3.11, *infra*, principles of "integration of offerings" generally apply to Regulation D offerings.

An important concept under Rule 506 (as well as under Rule 505) is that of an "accredited investor." Under Regulation D, accredited investors are deemed to have access to registration-type information and to possess investment sophistication. Under Rule 501, accredited investors include not only certain institutional investors but also "fat cat" individual investors. These persons include those whose net worth at the time of the purchase exceeds $1 million, and those who had an individual income exceeding $200,000 in each of the two most recent years (or $300,000 joint income with one's spouse) and who reasonably anticipate such an income for the current year.[26] Significantly, if a Rule 505 or 506 offering is made solely to accredited investors, there is no mandated delivery of information as Regulation D presumes that such investors can fend for themselves.

---

[22] See, *e.g.*, *Woolf v. S.D. Cohen & Co.*, 515 F.2d 591, 612 n.14 (5th Cir. 1975), *vacated and remanded on other grounds*, 426 U.S. 944 (1976).

[23] See *supra* note 14 and accompanying text.

[24] See *supra* note 15 and accompanying text.

[25] See *Securities Act Release* Nos. 6389 (1982), 6758 (1988). See generally J.W. Hicks, *Limited Offering Exemptions: Regulation D* (1987).

[26] See SEC *Release* note 25, *supra*.

It is noteworthy that Rule 506 expands the Section 4(2) private offering exemption in at least two ways. First, unlike Section 4(2) which applies to both offers and sales, Rule 506 focuses on purchaser (rather than offeree) qualification. Thus, for example, Rule 506, unlike Section 4(2), requires that only purchasers meet the sophistication standards. Second, institutions and wealthy individuals are deemed under Regulation D to be sophisticated and to have access to the type of information that a registration statement would provide. Case law under Section 4(2), particularly with respect to wealthy individual investors, disagrees with the SEC's position.[27]

Thus, it is quite possible that Rule 506, the "safe harbor" to Section 4(2), actually exceeds the scope of the private placement statute, namely Section 4(2), upon which it is based. If this is indeed the case, because an administrative rule's scope cannot exceed that given by Congress to its statutory source,[28] Rule 506 may be invalid. It seems unlikely, however, that a determination in this regard will be made. That is because Section 19(a) of the Securities Act provides a defense for those who rely in good faith on an SEC rule that is subsequently invalidated. Hence, there is little incentive for one to challenge the rule's validity.

§ 3.07 The Limited Offering Exemptions

The statutory limited offering exemptions are contained in Sections 3(b) and 4(6) of the Securities Act. These exemptions reflect Congressional concern that small enterprises should not be unduly burdened in raising capital.

[A] The Section 4(6) Exemption

Generally, Section 4(6) exempts from registration under the 1933 Act offers and sales by any issuer solely to one or more "accredited investors" if the total offering price does not exceed the amount permitted under Section 3(b) of the Act (currently $5 million). No advertising or public solicitation is permitted in connection with a Section 4(6) offering, and the issuer must file a notice of such sales made pursuant to the exemption with the SEC.[29]

[B] The Section 3(b) Exemption

Generally, Section 3(b) contains an exemption for small offerings, empowering the Commission to exempt from registration any offering of securities

[27] See M. Steinberg, *Corporate Internal Affairs — A Corporate and Securities Law Perspective* 44-49 (1983). But see Kripke, *Has the SEC Taken All the Dead Wood Out of Its Disclosure System?*, 38 Bus. Law. 833 (1983).

[28] See *Ernst & Ernst v. Hochfelder*, 425 U.S. 185 (1976) (concluding that despite the language of Rule 10b-5, which could be construed as not requiring scienter, the language of § 10(b) controlled and thereby required scienter).

[29] See *Securities Act Release* No. 6256 (1980).

where the aggregate amount of such offering does not exceed $5,000,000. The most significant rules that the SEC has promulgated pursuant to this authority are Regulation A and Rules 504, 505, and 701 of Regulation D.

[1] Rule 504

The SEC adopted Rule 504 to facilitate the capital raising needs for the small start-up company. The exemption is not available for investment companies and reporting entities under the Exchange Act (*i.e.*, those registrants which must file periodic reports with the SEC). In such an offering, the issuer need not determine whether the purchaser is sophisticated nor need the issuer provide a purchaser representative for the unsophisticated. There are no specified federal disclosure requirements in a Rule 504 offering and there is no express limit on the number of offerees and purchasers.

In fact, if the Rule 504 offering is made in states that require registration and the delivery of a disclosure document prior to sale (and the issuer complies with these requirements), then the issuer may conduct, in essence, a "mini-public" offering where the general limitations on the manner of offering and on resale do not apply. This is true even if the offering takes place in states that do not provide for a registration procedure so long as the offering also is made in a state which has such a procedure. Offerings made pursuant to the Rule 504 exemption (in aggregation with all other securities sold in reliance on any exemption under Section 3(b) or in violation of Section 5) during any twelve-month period have a ceiling of $1 million, provided that no more than $500,000 of securities are offered and sold without registration under states' securities laws.[30]

Thus, except for a few qualifying conditions, Rule 504 generally may be viewed as a blanket federal exemption from registration for offerings not exceeding $1 million. The SEC believes that the remedial provisions of the federal securities laws, in conjunction with state regulation, are sufficient protection in these smaller offerings.

[2] Rule 505

Rule 505 provides any issuer that is not an investment company with an exemption from registration under Section 3(b) of the Securities Act for sales of securities to (what the issuer reasonably believes are) not more than thirty-five purchasers and to an unlimited number of accredited investors. In aggregation with other offerings made pursuant to exemptions available under Section 3(b) (or sold in violation of Section 5), an issuer pursuant to Rule 505 may raise up to $5 million during any twelve-month period. In a Rule 505 offering, there may be no general solicitation or advertising and restrictions on resale apply.[31]

---

[30] See *Securities Act Release* Nos. 6389 (1982), 6758 (1988).

[31] See *Securities Act Release* No. 6389 (1982). See *supra* note 15 and accompanying text.

The availability of the Rule 505 exemption is conditioned upon the disclosure of specified information to all purchasers, if any of the purchasers are nonaccredited investors. Unlike Rule 506, however, the issuer need not make a determination that the purchaser is sophisticated. If unsophisticated, there is no requirement that the investor have a purchaser representative.[32] Finally, the Rule 505 exemption is unavailable to issuers that have engaged in certain misconduct ("bad boy" disqualifiers). For example, an issuer subject to an SEC injunction within the previous five years may not avail itself of the Rule 505 exemption.[33]

[3] Rule 701

In 1988, the SEC adopted Rule 701 pursuant to Section 3(b) of the 1933 Act. The new rule, which is part of Regulation D, provides an exemption from registration for offers and sales of securities for certain compensation benefit plans and written contracts adopted for the participation of employees, officers, directors, consultants, and advisers of an eligible company. Companies eligible to use the exemption must not be subject to the periodic reporting requirements of the Exchange Act. As a preliminary note to the rule makes clear, Rule 701 is designed to facilitate the issuance of securities for compensation. As a consequence, the rule does not exempt offers and sales which are intended to raise capital.[34]

So long as the offering is made solely to eligible purchasers, Rule 701 permits such offerings to be public in nature, thereby permitting general solicitation. In a Rule 701 offering, there are no specific disclosure requirements. Limitations on resales, however, do apply. The monetary amount of securities that can be offered and sold pursuant to Rule 701 during any twelve-month period is based upon the following:

> Under the rule, the amount of securities that may be subject to outstanding offers in reliance on Rule 701 plus the amount of securities sold in the preceding 12 months in reliance on Rule 701 may not exceed the greater of $500,000 or amounts determined under two different formulas. One formula limits this amount to 15% of the issuer's total assets measured at the end of the issuer's last fiscal year. The second formula restricts the amount to no more than 15% of the outstanding securities of the class being offered. In any case, the aggregate offering price of securities subject to outstanding offers and sold in the preceding 12 months may not exceed $5 million.[35]

Importantly, because of the exemption's compensatory (rather than capital raising) purpose, offerings made pursuant to Rule 701 are not aggregated with

---

[32] For further discussion on this point see Warren, *A Review of Regulation D: The Present Exemption Regimen for Limited Offerings Under the Securities Act of 1933*, 33 Am. U. L. Rev. 355 (1984).

[33] For a complete listing of the disqualifiers see Rules 252(c), (d), (e), and (f) of Regulation A, 17 C.F.R. §§ 230.252(c), (d), (e), (f).

[34] See *Securities Act Release* No. 6768 (1988).

[35] *Id.*

offerings made pursuant to the other Section 3(b) exemptions. Nor are the monetary ceilings for other offerings made pursuant to the other Section 3(b) exemptions affected by Rule 701 offers and sales. Moreover, "integration of offering" problems are minimized because Rule 701

> specifically state[s] that all offers and sales pursuant to its rubric are deemed to be a part of a single, discrete offering; consequently, Rule 701 transactions need not be integrated into any other offering made by the issuer or vice versa.

As a final point, Rules 702 and 703 require the filing and annual amendment with the SEC of Form 701 if aggregate sales under the Rule 701 exemption exceed $100,000. Failure by an issuer to file the Form 701 does not invalidate the exemption but does disqualify such issuer's future use of Rule 701 (unless the SEC elects to waive such disqualification).[36]

[4] Regulation A

The use of Regulation A, in view of recently adopted alternative means of raising capital, such as Rules 504, 505 and 701 of Regulation D, is becoming more limited. Although Regulation A is an exemption from registration, it in fact permits generalized interstate public offerings of up to $1.5 million during any twelve-month period. The Regulation imposes no limit on the number of offerees or purchasers and, under certain conditions, authorizes the use of broker-dealers to advertise and distribute the securities. Principles of aggregation and integration apply. Importantly, purchasers of securities acquired in a Regulation A offering generally may resell such securities without being subject to restrictions on resale imposed by such SEC rules as Rules 147, 504-506, and 701.

An offering pursuant to Regulation A may very much resemble a "mini-public" offering. Indeed, the filing with the SEC of an "offering statement" (like a registration statement in a registered offering) is required. There, however, are some important differences, including:

(1) Because Regulation A offerings are exempt from registration, there is no Section 11 liability (for materially false or misleading statements contained in a registration statement) and no requirement for the issuer to file with the SEC periodic reports under the Exchange Act.

(2) Regulation A filings are made in the appropriate SEC regional office rather than at the Commission's headquarters in Washington, D.C. This may prove quite useful for the issuer and counsel who may be able to communicate better with the regional office staff, situated in their locale.

(3) The Regulation A exemption is not available for any issuer if it or its affiliated persons, executive officers, or other like persons have been subject to certain discipline during the previous five years, including a

---

[36] *Id.* For restrictions on resales regarding securities issued in Rule 701 offerings, see Chapter 5, *infra*.

criminal conviction relating to the sale of securities and the imposition of an SEC injunction ("bad boy" disqualifications).

(4) The information required to be contained in a Regulation A offering statement is not as extensive as that mandated in a registration statement. In particular, (a) the textual information concerning such subjects as legal proceedings, remuneration of executive officers, and description of business is less detailed; and (b) unless certified financial statements are already being filed with the SEC, they are not required.[37]

[5] 1989 Amendments to Regulation D

When this text was in the printing process, the SEC adopted amendments to Regulation D.* As stated by the SEC in the adopting Release:

> The Commission announces the adoption of an amendment to the definition of "accredited investor" for purposes of the Section 4(6) and Regulation D exemptions from the registration requirements of the Securities Act of 1933 (The "Securities Act") to include those plans established and maintained by the governments of the states and their political subdivisions, as well as their agencies and instrumentalities for the benefit of their employees, that have total assets in excess of $5 million. Additional amendments to Regulation D also have been made. While the filing of Form D has been retained, it will no longer be a condition to any exemption under Regulation D. New Rule 507 will disqualify any issuer found to have violated the From D filing requirement from future use of Regulation D. New Rule 508 provides that an exemption from the registration requirements will be available for an offer or sale to a particular individual or entity, despite failure to comply with a requirement of Regulation D, if the requirement is not designed to protect specifically the complaining person; the failure to comply is insignificant to the offering as a whole; and there has been a good faith and reasonable attempt to comply with all requirements of the regulation. Rule 508 specifices that the provisions of Regulation D relating to general solicitation, the dollar limits of Rules 504 and 505, and the limits on non-accredited investors in Rules 505 and 506 are deemed significant to every offering and therefore not subject to the Rule 508 defense. Further, the rule specifies that any failure to comply with a provision of Regulation D is actionable by the Commission under the Securities Act.

§ 3.08 Comparative Chart

Given the complexity of the various requirements for perfecting the issuer transactional exemptions from registration discussed in §§ 3.05-3.07, the

---

[37] See *Securities Act Release* No. 6275 (1980); Sonsoni, *Regulation A*, 16 Rev. Sec. Reg. 781 (1983).

* *Securities Act Release* No. 6825 (1989).

following chart may prove helpful. Remember, however, that the chart may simplify certain of the requirements. Reference should be made to the pertinent SEC rules, releases, and the preceding discussion in this chapter.

Item	Rule 504	Rule 505	Rule 506	Rule 701	Reg. A	§ 4(2)	§ 4(6)
Aggregate Offering Price Limitation	$1,000,000 (12 mos.)	$5,000,000 (12 mos.)	Unlimited	Depending on certain factors, between $500,000 and $5,000,000 (12 mos.)	$1,500,000 (12 mos.)	Unlimited	$5,000,000 (12 mos.)
Number of investors	Unlimited	35 plus an unlimited number of accredited investors	35 plus an unlimited number of accredited investors	Unlimited but must be an eligible purchaser	Unlimited	Uncertain but evidently a finite number of offerees depending on the circumstances	An unlimited number of accredited investors only
Investor Qualification	None required	Accredited or none required	Purchaser must be sophisticated (alone or with representative); Accredited investors presumed to be qualified	Purchaser must be employee, officer, director, consultant or adviser of an eligible company who has acquired the securities as compensation	None required	Exact requirements uncertain; offeree must receive or have access to the type of information that registration would disclose; also, sophistication standards apply -- offeree must be financially sophisticated (alone or with representative)	Accredited investors only

Item	Rule 504	Rule 505	Rule 506	Rule 701	Reg. A	§4(2)	§4(6)
Commissions	Permitted	Permitted	Permitted	Permitted	Permitted	Permitted	Permitted
Limitations on Manner of Offering	No general solicitation or advertising permitted unless registered in a state that requires registration and delivery of a disclosure document	No general solicitation or advertising permitted	No general solicitation or advertising permitted	No such limitations if offering made solely to eligible purchasers	General solicitation and advertising permitted under certain circumstances	No general solicitation or advertising permitted	No general solicitation or advertising permitted
Limitations on Resale	Restricted unless registered in a state that requires registration and delivery of a disclosure document	Restricted	Restricted	Restricted	Not Restricted	Restricted	Restricted
Issuer Qualifications	No reporting or investment companies	No investment companies or issuers disqualified under Regulation A	None	No reporting companies	None except for "bad boy" disqualifiers	None	None
Notice of Sales	Form D required but not as a condition of exemption	Form D required but not as a condition of exemption	Form D required but not as a condition of exemption	Form 701 required where aggregate Rule 701 sales are over $100,000 but not as a condition of exemption	No notice of sales required	No notice of sales required	Form 4(6) required as a condition of exemption

Item	Rule 504	Rule 505	Rule 506	Rule 701	Reg. A	§4(2)	§4(6)
Information Requirements	No information specified	In either a Rule 505 or 506 offering: 1. If purchased solely by accredited investors, no information specified. 2. If purchased by any non-accredited investor(s), a. non-reporting companies must furnish i. offerings up to $2,000,000 - information required in Regulation A offering if issuer provides investors with a certified balance sheet within 120 days of the offering's commencement ii. offerings between $2,000,000 and $5,000,000 - information in Part I of Form S-18 or available registration, 2 years of financials, 1 year audited -- if undue effort or expense, issuers other than limited partnerships only balance sheet as of 120 days before offering must be audited -- if limited partnership and undue effort or expense, financials may be tax basis iii. offerings over $5,000,000 -- information in Part I of available registration -- if undue effort or expense, issuers other than limited partnerships only balance sheet as of 120 days before offering must be audited -- if limited partnership and undue effort or expense, financials may be tax basis		No information specified	Information specified in Regulation A	Investors receive or have access to the type of information that registration would disclose	No information specified

<u>Rule 505</u> <u>Rule 506</u>

b. reporting companies must furnish

i. Rule 14a-3 annual report to shareholders, definitive proxy statement and Form 10-K, if requested, plus subsequent reports and other updating information or

ii. information in most recent Form S-1 or Form 10 or Form 10-K plus subsequent reports and other updating information

c. issuers must make available prior to sale

i. exhibits

ii. written information given to accredited investors

iii. opportunity to ask questions and receive answers

§ 3.09 Intrastate Offerings

Section 3(a)(11) of the Securities Act provides an exemption from registration with respect to

> [a]ny security which is a part of an issue offered and sold only to persons resident within a single State or Territory, where the issuer of such security is a person resident and doing business, or, if a corporation, incorporated by and doing business within, such State or Territory.

The rationale underlying the intrastate offering exemption is based on

> the probability that investors in local enterprises will have adequate familiarity with [such enterprises] and an acknowledgment that [local] issuers will be relatively small and thus less able to bear the burden of federal registration,[38]

thereby leaving the respective states as the principal regulators in such offerings. In 1974, the SEC, in order to establish more definitive standards regarding the intrastate exemption, promulgated Rule 147 to serve as a safe harbor.[39] If the conditions of the rule have not been met, the party still may assert the availability of the Section 3(a)(11) statutory exemption. Unlike the exemption provided by Rule 147 and unlike those exemptions provided by Sections 3(b) and 4(2) of the Securities Act which are available only to the issuer, the Section 3(a)(11) exemption may also be used under certain circumstances by shareholders seeking to resell their stock.

[A] The Section 3(a)(11) Exemption

The Section 3(a)(11) exemption, like the Section 3(a)(9) and Section 3(a)(10) exemptions addressed in § 3.10, *infra*, are categorized in the Securities Act as exempt securities rather than transactional exemptions from registration. In practical effect, however, these exemptions come into play only where there is a transaction which meets the criteria of the applicable exemption. For example, the Section 3(a)(11) exemption, concerning securities which are offered and sold pursuant to an intrastate offering, is invoked only where there is an offering (*e.g.*, a transaction) which meets the exemptive requirements of the statute.

Generally, the principal issues that come into play concerning the Section 3(a)(11) exemption deal with the concepts of "resident," "doing business within the state," and restrictions on resale. For purposes of the statutory intrastate exemption, offers can only be made to persons "resident" in a single state or territory. An offer to a single nonresident voids the exemption, thereby giving rise to liability if no other exemption is perfected. Moreover, the SEC historically has defined "residence" to be similar to that of

---

[38] Deaktor, *Integration of Securities Offerings*, 31 U. Fla. L. Rev. 465, 481 (1979).

[39] See *Securities Act Release* No. 5450 (1974).

"domicile" which looks to the state of mind of the offeree. This subjective standard has been criticized for its uncertainty.[40]

Second, under the Section 3(a)(11) exemption, the issuer must be a person resident and "doing business" within the state in which the offering takes place. From the statutory definition, it is clear that the issuer must be incorporated in that state. Generally, the term "doing business" has been interpreted to mean that a "substantial," though not necessarily "exclusive," portion of the issuer's business must be conducted in that state. How much business is sufficiently substantial to validate use of the exemption seems unclear.[41]

With respect to restrictions on resale, a purchaser of securities offered under either the Section 3(a)(11) or Rule 147 exemption may resell without restriction to another bona fide resident. For an offer or sale by a purchaser to a nonresident to be permitted, however, the issue of the securities offered must have "come to rest." While the SEC is said to have taken the position that a one-year holding period normally is necessary under Section 3(a)(11) before there is a resale to a nonresident,[42] courts may adopt a shorter resale period. In this regard, one court held that a seven-month holding period, although not within the Rule 147 safe harbor, nonetheless was of sufficient duration for Section 3(a)(11) purposes:

> The Court is of the opinion that the seven month period from the time of initial sale to the time of resale [to an out-of-state resident] is sufficient for the offering to come to rest. Plaintiffs argue that Rule 147 requires nine months before a resale can be made. The Court concludes that Rule 147 provides only a safe harbor [to the Section 3(a)(11) exemption]; compliance with [Rule 147's] provisions ensures that the SEC will take no action. But it does not follow that, as plaintiffs argue, non-compliance necessarily means that the statute and its policies have been violated. . . . Accordingly, defendants havc complied with Section 3(a)(11). . . .[43]

[B] Rule 147

In an effort to minimize the uncertainty surrounding the scope of the Section 3(a)(11) intrastate exemption, the SEC promulgated Rule 147 as a safe harbor. In the release adopting Rule 147, the Commission stated:

---

[40] See *Securities Act Release* Nos. 4434 (1961), 5450 (1974); Thomforde, *Exemptions from SEC Registration for Small Businesses*, 47 Tenn. L. Rev. 1, 28-29 (1979).

[41] See, *e.g.*, *Chapman v. Dunn*, 414 F.2d 153 (6th Cir. 1969); Thomforde, *supra* note 40, at 29.

[42] See *In re Brooklyn Manhattan Transit Corp.*, 1 S.E.C. 147 (1935); Thomforde, *supra* note 40, at 29-30.

[43] *Busch v. Carpenter*, [1984-1985 Transfer Binder] Fed. Sec. L. Rep. (CCH) ¶ 91,810 (D. Utah 1984).

> Section 3(a)(11) was intended to allow issuers with localized operations to sell securities as part of a plan of local financing. Congress apparently believed that a company whose operations are restricted to one area should be able to raise money from investors in the immediate vicinity without having to register the securities with a federal agency. In theory, the investors would be protected both by their proximity to the issuer and by state regulation. Rule 147 reflects this Congressional intent and is limited in its application to transactions where state regulation will be most effective. The Commission has consistently taken the position that the exemption applies only to local financing provided by local investors for local companies. To satisfy the exemption, the entire issue must be offered and sold exclusively to residents of the state in which the issuer is resident and doing business. An offer or sale of part of the issue to a single non-resident will destroy the exemption for the entire issue.[44]

Rule 147 sets forth more objective criteria in defining the parameters of the intrastate exemption. Similar to Section 3(a)(11), Rule 147 has no monetary ceiling on the amount of funds that can be raised or on the number of offerees or purchasers. Offers and sales can only be made to residents of the state where the offering occurs. A single offering to a non-resident invalidates the exemption. Rule 147 defines "residence" to mean principal residence at the point in time that the offer and sale occur, thereby rejecting the subjective concept of "domicile."

With respect to the issuer's qualifications to use Rule 147, the enterprise must be incorporated or organized in the offering state and must be "doing business" within that state. The rule enumerates four specific criteria for defining the term "doing business within a state:" (1) the enterprise must have its principal office within that state, (2) the enterprise must derive at least eighty percent of its gross revenues "from the operation of a business . . . or from the rendering of services within such state," (3) the enterprise must have at least eighty percent of its assets situated within the state, and (4) the enterprise must use at least eighty percent of the funds raised by the offering for operations within the state.[45]

To come within Rule 147's safe harbor, while resales to residents can immediately be transacted, a period of nine months from the date of the last sale by the issuer must transpire before resales to non-residents are permitted. Issuers must take certain precautions to guard against illicit resales. These measures include disclosing in writing the resale limitations to all offerees, placing legends on the certificates describing the resale limitations, issuing stop transfer instructions to the transfer agent, and receiving a written representation from each purchaser declaring bona fide residence in the state of the offering.[46]

---

[44] *Securities Act Release* No. 5450 (1974).

[45] *Id.* See Thomforde, *supra* note 40, at 31-32.

[46] See Rule 147(f), 17 C.F.R. § 230.147(f).

[C] ALI Federal Securities Code

It has been asserted that the Section 3(a)(11) and Rule 147 intrastate exemptions are unduly restrictive. If so, criticism should be directed toward Congress and not the Commission which is bound by Section 3(a)(11)'s scope when adopting a safe harbor rule pursuant to that statute. The approach taken by the American Law Institute's (ALI) *Federal Securities Code* may be more appropriate. The ALI Code labels such offerings "local offerings" and does not confine them to a single state (§ 514). Section 514 of the ALI Code focuses solely on purchasers of securities rather than offerees. State lines under Section 514 no longer are necessarily controlling as the SEC is given authority, after evaluating economic characteristics and population, to define contiguous areas encompassing a number of states or a state and a contiguous foreign country. Moreover, Section 514 permits up to five percent of the securities in such an offering to be sold to no more than five percent of all purchasers who neither work nor reside in the localized area.

Prior to consultation with and determination by the SEC to support the ALI Code, Section 514 permitted up to twenty percent of the securities in a "local offering" to be sold to no more than five percent of "non-local" purchasers. In view of the provision's objective of facilitating local financing for local business, the SEC believed that the percent of securities sold "non-locally" should be decreased. The change to five percent was subsequently made.

In 1980 the SEC announced its support for congressional enactment of the ALI Code, provided that revisions it sought and obtained from the ALI Reporter and his group of advisers were not significantly amended during the legislative process.[47] The ALI Code, however, has not been introduced in either the U.S. House of Representatives or the Senate and its prospects for enactment are dim.

§ 3.10 The Section 3(a)(9) and Section 3(a)(10) Exemptions

Section 3(a)(9) of the Securities Act exempts from the registration requirements certain bona fide recapitalizations, namely,

> [a]ny security exchanged by the issuer with its existing security holders exclusively where no commission or other remuneration is paid or given directly or indirectly for soliciting such exchange.

Section 3(a)(10) generally exempts from registration securities which are issued in exchange for bona fide legal claims, securities, or property interests when a court or other specified tribunal, after conducting an adversary proceeding on the transaction's fairness, grants such approval. Traditionally, the Section 3(a)(10) exemption has been invoked in three situations: (1) settlement of private lawsuits; (2) reorganization of insolvent business

---

[47] See *Securities Act Release* No. 6242 (1980).

organizations outside of bankruptcy litigation; and (3) reorganization of solvent business organizations.[48]

While both the Section 3(a)(9) and Section 3(a)(10) exemptions reflect Congress' concern for the financially troubled enterprise which seeks internal readjustment without having to comply with the 1933 Act's costs of registration, an issuer may have a number of motives for utilizing these exemptions. Indeed, the financial status of an issuer does not affect the availability of these exemptions. For example, in practice the Section 3(a)(10) exemption "has been availed of almost exclusively by financially sound issuers involved in reorganization or other exchanges for a variety of legitimate ongoing business purposes."[49]

§ 3.11 Integration of Offerings

Under the concept of integration of offerings, what apparently may seem to be separate offerings instead are construed as one integrated offering. Because of the fairly distinct requirements for each exemption, otherwise exempt offerings are unlikely to qualify for an exemption once they are integrated, thereby resulting in a violation of the Securities Act's registration requirements. Moreover, if a purported exempt offering is integrated with a registered offering, the exemption will be destroyed, again resulting in liability.

Rule 152 is an exception to the above general principle, providing that the Section 4(2) exemption is still available, "although subsequently . . . the issuer decides to make a public offering and/or files a registration statement." The purpose of the rule is to permit

> those who have contemplated or begun to undertake a private offering to register securities without incurring any risk of liability as a consequence of having first contemplated or begun to undertake a private offering.[50]

In determining whether offers and/or sales should be integrated, the SEC has set forth a five factor analysis:

---

[48] See generally J. W. Hicks, *Exempted Transactions Under the Securities Act of 1933* § 3.02 (rev. ed. 1981); Glanzer, Schiffman & Packman, *Settlement of Securities Litigation Through the Issuance of Securities Without Registration: The Use of Section 3(a)(10) in SEC Enforcement Proceedings*, 50 Fordham L. Rev. 533 (1981); Mann, *The Section 3(a)(10) Exemption: Recent Interpretations*, 22 U.C.L.A. L. Rev. 1247 (1975).

[49] Ash, *Reorganizations and Other Exchanges Under Section 3(a)(10) of the Securities Act of 1933*, 75 Nw. U.L. Rev. 1, 10 (1980). See Hicks, *Recapitalizations Under Section 3(a)(9) of the Securities Act of 1933*, 61 Va. L. Rev. 1057, 1060-61 (1975).

[50] *Securities Act Release* No. 305 (1935). See also, *Securities Act Release* No. 4761 (1965).

(1) Whether the offerings are part of a single plan of financing;

(2) Whether the offerings involve issuance of the same class of securities;

(3) Whether the offerings have been made at or about the same time;

(4) Whether the same type of consideration is received; and

(5) Whether the offerings are made for the same general purposes.[51]

The SEC and the courts continue to apply this analysis.[52]

In order to provide greater certainty for issuers, the SEC, pursuant to its rulemaking authority, has adopted integration "safe harbor" rules. For example, Rule 502(a) of Regulation D in part provides:

> Offers and sales that are made more than six months before the start of a Regulation D offering or are made more than six months after completion of a Regulation D offering will not be considered part of that Regulation D offering, so long as during those six month periods there are no offers or sales of securities by or for the issuer that are of the same or a similar class as those offered or sold under Regulation D. . . .[53]

Rule 147(b)(2), as another example, has a similar "safe harbor" from integration with respect to the intrastate offering exemption.

Remember that Rules 147(b)(2) and 502(a) are "safe harbor" provisions. If the issuer engages in offers or sales during the six month period prior to commencement or after completion of the purportedly exempt offerings, the five factor analysis outlined above will be applied to determine whether the apparently separate offerings should be integrated.[54]

As a final point, the principle of *integration* of offerings must be distinguished from that of *aggregation* of offering price used for purposes of the Section 3(b) exemptions. The following example provided by the SEC serves aptly to distinguish the two concepts:

> The Commission is aware that in computing the aggregate offering price [for offerings made pursuant to the Section 3(b) exemptions] issuers frequently misunderstand the interaction of the concepts of aggregation and integration as applicable under Rules 504(b)(2)(i) and 505(b)(2)(i). Aggregation is the principle by which an issuer determines the dollar worth of exempt sales available directly under Section 3(b) of the Securities Act. Integration is a principle under which an issuer deter-

---

[51] *Securities Act Release* No. 4552 (1962).

[52] See, *e.g., SEC v. Murphy*, 626 F.2d 633 (9th Cir. 1980).

[53] See also discussion of integration of offerings with respect to Rule 701 in § 3.07[B][3], *supra.*

[54] See generally Deaktor, *Integration of Offerings*, 31 U. Fla. L. Rev. 465 (1979); Morrissey, *Integration of Securities Offerings — the ABA's "Indiscrete" Proposal,* 26 Ariz. L. Rev. 41 (1984); Shapiro & Sachs, *Integration Under the Securities Act: Once an Exemption, Not Always. . . .*, 31 Md. L. Rev. 3 (1971).

mines overall characteristics of its offering. The following examples illustrate the application of these concepts. An issuer that has conducted an offering under Rule 505 in May 1982 must aggregate the proceeds from that offering with the proceeds of a Rule 505 offering conducted in December 1982. [On the other hand] if the May offering had been under Rule 506 [which is a "safe harbor" to the § 4(2) exemption], it would not need to be aggregated with the December offering. In either case, the May offering should be exempt from principles of integration by virtue of the safe harbor provision in Rule 502(a). If a Rule 506 offering had been conducted in July 1982, the integration safe harbor would not be available as to a subsequent Rule 505 offering in December. Although the proceeds from the July [Rule] 506 offering would not be added to the December [Rule] 505 aggregate offering price under aggregation principles, they would have to be included if the two offerings [were] integrated. Assuming the two offerings were integrated, then the issuer would have to evaluate all characteristics of the combined transactions, *e.g.*, number of investors, aggregate offering price, etc., when determining the availability of an exemption.[55]

§ 3.12 State "Blue Sky" Law Exemptions

Generally, unless an exemption is perfected, any offer or sale within a particular state must be registered. The result is that perfecting a federal exemption from registration may be only half the battle. Exemptions must also be found on the state level in any state where the security is offered or sold. Until recently, there was little uniformity between the federal and state exemption framework. The promulgation of the Uniform Limited Offering Exemption (ULOE) by the North American Securities Administrators Association (NASAA) and its subsequent adoption (in whole or substantial part) by several states has significantly eased this uniformity problem. With some qualifications, the Uniform Limited Offering Exemption exempts offerings sold in compliance with Rules 501-503 and 505-506 of Regulation D. Rule 504, discussed in § 3.07[B][1], *supra*, leaves solely to the individual states the authority to prescribe disclosure of specified information and certain other requirements with respect to offerings made pursuant to that exemption.

Significantly, however, certain states adopting their respective version of ULOE have been more protective of investor interests than the SEC was in adopting Regulation D. For example, unlike the SEC's Regulation D, a number of states have applied investor "sophistication" requirements in ULOE Rule 505-type offerings and impose "bad boy" disqualifiers in ULOE Rule 506-type offerings.[56]

---

[55] *Securities Act Release* No. 6389 (1982). For further discussion, see §§ 3.05-3.07, *supra*.

[56] See generally Rossi, *The Uniform Limited Offering Exemption*, 16 Rev. Sec. Reg. 875 (1983); Sargent, *State Limited and Private Offering Exemptions: The Maryland Experience in a National Perspective*, 13 U. Balt. L. Rev. 496 (1984).

CHAPTER 4

THE REGISTRATION PROCESS

§ 4.01 Overview

In order adequately to protect investors and the integrity of the securities markets, the Securities Act of 1933 has two basic objectives: (1) to provide investors with adequate and accurate material information concerning securities offered for sale and (2) to prohibit fraudulent practices in the offer or sale of securities. The registration framework of the Act seeks to meet these goals by imposing certain obligations and limitations upon persons engaged in the offer or sale of securities. Pursuant to Section 5, a public offering of securities requires that a registration statement be filed with the Securities and Exchange Commission (SEC). As a general matter, before the registration statement is filed, there can be no offers to sell or offers to buy the securities in question. After the filing of the registration statement, with certain exceptions, only oral offers and written offers by means of a Section 10 prospectus are permissible. Until the registration statement becomes effective, however, there can be no sale of the securities. For the Securities Act's registration framework to apply, the interstate commerce requirement must be met. This normally is satisfied without difficulty.

The main purpose of registration is to provide adequate and accurate disclosure of material information concerning the issuer (as well as affiliated and certain other parties) and the securities the issuer proposes to offer. The disclosure of this information, in the form of a Section 10 prospectus, enables investors to evaluate the securities offered and thus make informed investment decisions.

The registration of a securities offering with the SEC does not mean that the offering is considered to be a good risk. The Commission does not have the authority to prevent an offering from going to market because it considers the investment to be of a speculative nature. Rather, the main role of the federal securities laws in this setting is to require the accurate disclosure of material information.

The SEC does not verify the truthfulness of the disclosures made in the registration statement. That a registration statement becomes effective in no way vouches for the veracity of the information contained therein. In this regard, the Securities Act prohibits materially false and misleading statements, with civil and criminal remedies available to redress such violations. For example, as discussed in Chapter 6, *infra*, Section 11 of the 1933 Act imposes civil monetary liability against certain persons who fail to establish "due diligence" (except the issuer which is strictly liable) for any misstatement or omission of a material fact contained in a registration statement; Section 12(1) provides that a purchaser may rescind, or alternatively, recover damages against any person who offers or sells a security in violation of Section 5; Section 12(2) likewise grants the purchaser the right to rescind or to recover damages against any person who sells a security by means of a prospectus or oral communication, which includes a materially false or misleading statement if such person fails to show the exercise of reasonable care; Section 17(a), as addressed in Chapter 8, *infra*, provides a remedy to the SEC and perhaps to private parties as well for redressing any fraudulent or deceptive conduct committed in the offer or sale of securities; and Section 24 of the Securities Act provides for criminal penalties for the willful violation of any provision of the Securities Act or any rule or regulation promulgated by the SEC thereunder. Moreover, as discussed in Chapter 7, *infra*, suit under certain circumstances may be brought under Section 10(b) of the Securities Exchange Act for any materially false or misleading statement contained in a registration statement.

Section 5 of the Securities Act may be viewed as the central provision of the registration framework. Subject to certain exceptions, the provision prohibits any person from using the mails or any means of interstate commerce to offer a subject security for sale unless a registration statement has been filed with the SEC and, with respect to any written communication, unless such communication meets the requirements in Section 10.[1] Section 5 also has the effect of prohibiting any sales of the subject securities unless a registration statement is effective and a statutory (Section 10(a)) prospectus has been sent or given to the investor. The terms "offer to sell" and "sale" are defined broadly in Section 2(3).[2] The term "prospectus" is defined expansively in Section 2(10). The information required to be contained in a registration statement is specified in Section 7; and Section 10 details the contents of the prospectus (remember that the statutory prospectus is part of the registration statement).

Pursuant to the requirements of Section 5(b)(1), a prospectus must meet the requirements of Section 10. Because the term "prospectus" is defined broadly in Section 2(10), a person engaged in the offering process should be wary. Pursuant to Section 2(10), a prospectus generally includes any written communication that is used to sell securities. Such written communications include confirmations, letters, brochures, circulars, notices, and advertise-

[1] There are a number of exceptions to this general principle. See § 2(10) of the Securities Act. For example, one exception occurs in the post-effective period where the "communication" is accompanied or preceded by the sending or giving of a statutory § 10(a) prospectus to the investor. In that case, the separate "communication" need not meet the requirements of § 10.

[2] See *Rubin v. United States*, 449 U.S. 424 (1981) (a pledge of stock as collateral for a loan is an "offer or sale" of a security under § 17(a) of the Securities Act).

ments which offer securities for sale. Hence, in general, with certain exceptions, any written communication to potential investors offering the subject securities for sale will constitute a prospectus, irrespective of whether such communication occurs before or after the effective date of the registration statement.

Generally, a Section 10 prospectus describes the issuer, affiliated persons, and the securities to be offered. The prospectus, among other things, may be viewed as being both a selling and a disclosure document. As a selling document, it is used by underwriters and dealers for the purpose of helping to persuade investors to purchase the securities. A more commonly-held view, however, is that the prospectus, as a disclosure document, serves to protect the various parties from liability. From this perspective, information placed in the prospectus traditionally has been conservative, focusing on historically-based information and clearly warning prospective investors of any risks involved. The SEC's promulgation of Rule 175, discussed later in this chapter, which provides a safe harbor for forward-looking statements if made with a reasonable basis and in good faith, may signal the beginning of a new era in the type of information disclosed.

§ 4.02 Framework of Section 5

When speaking of making a public offering, the concept of "in registration" is sometimes heard. Generally, the term refers to the entire registration period, commencing at least from the time that the issuer reaches an understanding with the managing underwriter prior to the filing of the registration statement to the time that the prospectus delivery requirements terminate in the post-effective period.

From a structural perspective having legal ramifications, Section 5 covers three basic time periods for making offers and sales of securities during a registered offering: (1) the pre-filing period, (2) the waiting period, and (3) the post-effective period. The following discussion will address each of these time periods.

[A] The Pre-Filing Period

[1] Overview

The *pre-filing* period is the time period before a registration statement has been filed with the Commission. During this time period, among other prohibitions, Section 5(c) prohibits the use of the mails or any means of interstate commerce to offer to sell or offer to buy the securities offered.[3]

Certain activities, however, are not deemed to be an offer to sell or an offer to buy. For example, Section 2(3) exempts negotiations and agreements

[3] For example § 5(a) prohibits the use of the mails or any instrument or means of interstate commerce to sell or to deliver securities for purposes of sale before the effective date of the registration statement.

between the issuer and any underwriter or among underwriters who are or will be in privity of contract with the issuer. Rule 135 permits an issuer to make an announcement of a proposed public offering, provided that only the information specified in the rule is released. Moreover, pursuant to Rules 137-139, dealers may publish certain information about specified issuers in the pre-filing period (as well as in the waiting and post-effective periods).

As a general proposition, however, during the pre-filing period, the concept of "offering" for sale is given a broad interpretation. Publication of information about the issuer or its securities, prior to the filing of a registration statement, may be considered to constitute an "offer to sell." Although the publication is not an express offer, it may be viewed as conditioning the public market or stimulating interest in the securities to be registered (more colorfully referred to as "gun-jumping"). Hence, during the pre-filing period, the issuer and other participants must be cautious regarding the publication of information.

[2] Conditioning the Market ("Gun-Jumping")

A major concern in the pre-filing period is that statements made by the issuer and others will be construed as "conditioning the market" ("gun-jumping"), and, hence, constitute an "offer to sell" in violation of Section 5(c). The SEC has issued a number of releases on this issue. In this regard, the Commission has asserted that

> the publication of information and statements, and publicity efforts, made in advance of a proposed financing which have the effect of conditioning the public mind or arousing public interest in the issuer or in its securities constitutes an offer in violation of the Act.[4]

Nonetheless, the SEC takes the position that, particularly if a current practice, the flow of *factual* information to shareholders and the marketplace should be encouraged. Hence, according to the Commission, issuers should:

(1) Continue to advertise products and services.

(2) Continue to send out customary quarterly, annual and other periodic reports to stockholders.

(3) Continue to publish proxy statements and send out dividend notices.

(4) Continue to make announcements to the press with respect to factual business and financial developments; *i.e.*, receipt of a contract, the settlement of a strike, the opening of a plant, or similar events of interest to the community in which the business operates.

(5) Answer unsolicited telephone inquiries from stockholders, financial analysts, the press and others concerning factual information.

---

[4] *Securities Act Release* No. 5180 (1971).

(6) Observe an "open door" policy in responding to unsolicited inquiries concerning factual matters from securities analysts, financial analysts, security holders, and participants in the communications field who have a legitimate interest in the corporation's affairs.

(7) Continue to hold stockholder meetings as scheduled and to answer shareholders' inquiries at stockholder meetings relating to factual matters.[5]

On the other hand, newly implemented practices or increased activity of existing practices (*e.g.*, increasing the company's advertising in the mass media) should be avoided when the issuer's securities are "in registration." Moreover, during this time the issuer and its personnel should not provide opinions concerning values.

An interesting issue is the effect of Rule 175 on "gun-jumping." As discussed in § 4.07[B], *infra*, Rule 175 permits an issuer under certain conditions to make forward-looking statements in registration statements, annual reports, and certain other documents filed with the SEC. Although the Commission has advised issuers to avoid making such forecasts or projections when its securities are in registration,[6] this position was taken prior to the SEC's adoption of Rule 175. As a result, Rule 175 by its terms arguably permits an issuer to make predictive statements in its annual report even though it contemplates filing a registration statement in the near future, such as within the next two weeks. Given the SEC's concerns with "gun-jumping," however, an issuer should not find undue comfort in Rule 175 in this context, particularly if the issuer has not made forward-looking statements in its SEC-filed documents on a regular basis.

[3] Effect of Rule 135

Under Rule 135, a notice given by an issuer in the pre-filing period that complies with the provisions of the rule is not deemed an "offer to sell," and hence may be released without violating Section 5(c). Generally, a Rule 135 notice, in addition to containing only certain specified information, states that the issuer intends to make a public offering of securities and that such offering will be made only by means of a prospectus. Note that the rule prohibits the underwriters from being named in the notice and that judicial authority has interpreted the rule to prohibit valuations from being contained in the notice.[7] The purpose of these prohibitions

> is . . . to prevent an issuer from arousing investor interest before a registration statement covering the securities proposed to be offered has

---

[5] *Id.*

[6] *Id.* See also *Securities Act Release* Nos. 4697 (1964), 3844 (1957).

[7] See *Chris-Craft Industries, Inc. v. Bangor Punta Corporation*, 426 F.2d 569 (2d Cir. 1970) (*en banc*).

been filed; investors are intended to have an opportunity to evaluate the disclosures there contained.[8]

The Second Circuit in its seminal decision in *Chris-Craft Industries, Inc. v. Bangor Punta Corporation*[9] construed Rule 135 as setting forth an exclusive list. Issuer notices that go beyond Rule 135 and which are not otherwise required by another SEC regulation constitute "an offer to sell," thereby violating Section 5(c). The Second Circuit in *Chris-Craft* reasoned:

> When it is announced that securities will be sold at some date in the future and, in addition, an attractive description of these securities and of the issuer is furnished, it seems clear that such an announcement provides much the same kind of information as that contained in a prospectus. Doubtless the line drawn between an announcement containing sufficient information to constitute an offer and one which does not must be to some extent arbitrary. A checklist of features that may be included in an announcement which does not also constitute an offer to sell serves to guide the financial community and the courts far better than any judicially formulated "rule of reason" as to what is or is not an offer. Rule 135 provides just such a checklist, and if the Rule is not construed as setting forth an exclusive list, then much of its value as a guide is lost.[10]

On the other hand, in certain situations, such as a tender offeror making an exchange offer and thereby becoming subject to the SEC's tender offer rules (see items 3(b) and 5(a) of Schedule 14D-1 which call for disclosure of any negotiations with the subject company and of any proposed merger), an issuer is required to disclose information that goes beyond the specified Rule 135 list. In such situations, it appears that Section 5 is not violated in the pre-filing period where disclosure of the pertinent information is required by a specific SEC rule and the issuer's purpose in making the disclosure is not to "condition the market" for the securities "in registration."[11]

[4] Transactions Between Market Professionals

In addition to Rule 135, certain other actions are exempt from constituting an offer to sell or an offer to buy, and, hence, are permitted in the pre-filing period. For example, negotiations and agreements between the underwriter and the issuer or among underwriters who are (or will be) in privity with the issuer are allowed in the pre-filing period.

Importantly, unless otherwise exempted, the prohibitions of Section 5 apply to transactions and discussions between market professionals. In this regard, an "offer to buy" in the pre-filing period by a dealer not in privity

---

[8] Letter from the SEC to Judge Lasker, dated January 6, 1978, quoted in *Sheinberg v. Fluor Corp.*, 514 F. Supp. 133, 139-40 (S.D.N.Y. 1981). The court in *Sheinberg* adopted this position.

[9] 426 F.2d 569 (2d Cir. 1970) (*en banc*).

[10] *Id.* at 574 (citation omitted).

[11] See *Sheinberg v. Fluor Corp.*, 514 F. Supp. 133 (S.D.N.Y. 1981), note 8, *supra*.

with the issuer to an underwriter who is in privity with the issuer constitutes a violation of Section 5(c). Likewise, an "offer to sell" in the pre-filing period by an underwriter in privity with the issuer to a dealer who is not violates Section 5(c). The prohibitions of Section 5 in the waiting and post-effective periods also apply to transactions and discussions between market professionals, unless otherwise exempted.[12]

Turning to another point, an individual investor who contacts his or her broker-dealer in the pre-filing period to buy a few shares of a start-up company's stock which is "in registration" probably does not violate Section 5 (see Chapter 5, *infra*). That is because the individual, unless he or she is deemed to be engaged in a "distribution," has the Section 4(1) exemption which exempts from the Section 5 registration requirements "transactions by any person other than an issuer, underwriter, or dealer." On the other hand, the broker-dealer's offer to sell to the investor in the pre-filing period the start-up company's stock to be issued in the initial public offering (IPO) would violate Section 5(c). Unlike the investor, the broker-dealer does not enjoy the Section 4(1) exemption nor can it invoke any other exemption in this context.

[5] Rules 137, 138, and 139

Rules 137, 138, and 139 permit broker-dealers to engage in specified "safe harbor" activities in the pre-filing period without violating Section 5. Rules 137-139 apply as well to the waiting and post-effective periods. For a broker-dealer to invoke these rules, the issuer must be an Exchange Act reporting entity having its securities registered on Form S-2 or S-3 (or F-2 or F-3 which are for foreign issuers), discussed in § 4.06[A], *infra.*[13]

Generally, Rules 137-139 establish standards for ascertaining the circumstances under which broker-dealers, without violating Section 5, may publish information concerning an S-2 or S-3 issuer which proposes to conduct a registered public offering.

Rule 137 is directed at broker-dealers who are not participating in the public offering — in other words, those dealers who are not in privity of contract with the issuer or with any underwriter of the offering. Generally, Rule 137 allows a nonparticipating dealer in its regular course of business to publish and distribute information, recommendations, and opinions concerning securities of an Exchange Act reporting company which has filed or intends to file a 1933 Act registration statement.

Turning to Rule 138, that rule "permits a broker-dealer participating in an offering of non-convertible senior securities registered on Form [S-2 or S-3] to publish opinions or recommendations concerning the issuer's common stock, and vice versa."[14]

---

[12] See *Byrnes v. Faulknes, Dawkins & Sullivan*, 550 F.2d 1303 (2d Cir. 1977).

[13] All references will hereafter be made only to U.S. issuers who register their Securities Act offering on such Forms as S-1, S-2, or S-3.

[14] *Securities Act Release* No. 5101 (1970).

Rule 139 is directed at those broker-dealers who publish research reports containing information, recommendations, or opinions and who are or will be "participants" in the issuer's public offering. In its amendment of the rule, the SEC elected to distinguish between S-2 and S-3 companies (discussed in § 4.06[A], *infra*). Although both S-2 and S-3 issuers are subject to the periodic reporting obligations of the Exchange Act, the S-3 issuers, being larger than their S-2 counterparts, have a wider market following, thereby ensuring adequate dissemination of information regarding such issuers. Consequently, broker-dealers research reports under the Rule 139 safe harbor are less regulated for S-3 issuers than for S-2 issuers.

Generally, for S-2 issuers, Rule 139 requires that information, opinions, or recommendations regarding such issuers be contained in a publication that is published at regular intervals in the normal course of business. The publication must consist of a comprehensive list of securities or include similar information concerning a substantial number of enterprises in the issuer's "sub-industry." Any opinion or recommendation contained in the publication may not be given greater space or prominence than that given to other securities (or companies) and may not be more favorable than the last previous opinion or recommendation published by the broker-dealer prior to its participation in the offering.

With respect to S-3 issuers, Rule 139 extends its safe harbor to require only that broker-dealer research reports that include information, recommendations, or opinions regarding such issuers be distributed with reasonable regularity in the normal course of business. In distinguishing between S-2 and S-3 issuers, the Commission reasoned:

> Amending Rule 139 will enhance the efficiency of the markets by allowing a greater number of research reports to provide a continuous flow of essential corporate information into the marketplace. The amended Rule is structured to differentiate between companies eligible to use Form S-3 (and Form F-3) and other registrants. This structure facilitates the functioning of the integrated disclosure system by increasing the flow of information most broadly as to S-3/F-3 companies, those companies whose marketplace following is relied upon to replace reiteration of all company-oriented information in the prospectus. Moreover, the marketplace following provides the basis for allowing more research as to S-3/F-3 companies to come within a Section 5 safe harbor because it lessens the opportunity to condition the market for such companies' securities.[15]

A question may be raised whether in adopting amendments to Rule 139 the SEC has gone too far to accommodate large (*i.e.*, S-3) issuers and participating dealers at the expense of the investing public. Arguably, the rule permits participating dealers to more easily condition the market for S-3 issuers. For example, a participating dealer may publish with reasonable

---

[15] *Securities Act Release* No. 6550 (1984).

regularity and in the normal course of business research reports highly recommending the purchase of the securities of an S-3 issuer whose registration statement for a prospective public offering will be filed with the SEC in the near future. On the other hand, it may be asserted that, even if this conduct is permitted by Rule 139, and hence not a violation of Section 5, the antifraud provisions, such as Section 10(b) of the Exchange Act (and Rules 10b-5 and 10b-6), still apply.

The Commission's amendments to Rule 139 with respect to S-3 issuers may raise certain inconsistencies with some of the other rules. For example, under Rule 135, as discussed in § 4.02[A][2], *supra*, issuers are quite limited in what they can say in a notice released in the pre-filing period; for example, the underwriters for the offering cannot be named. Yet, under Rule 139, dealers wishing to participate in the offering (although they cannot make "offers to buy" in the pre-filing period), can make highly favorable recommendations without violating Section 5 in the pre-filing period for the purchase of the S-3 company's securities. A question certainly can be asked whether this distinction makes sense. The inconsistency in the Commission's administrative framework with respect to the registration process may well be due to its hodge-podge adoption and amendment of various rules rather than making a concerted effort to scrutinize the entire process.

[B] The Waiting Period

[1] Overview

After the registration statement is filed with the Commission, the *waiting period* commences. In this time period, subsections (a) and (b) of Section 5 are applicable. Section 5(b)(1) prohibits the use of the mails or any means of interstate commerce to transmit any prospectus, unless such prospectus meets the requirements of Section 10. Since Section 2(10) defines a prospectus to include any written offer, there is no bar against verbal offers during the waiting period. However, the contents and the form of written offers are limited by Section 2(10) and Section 10.

During the waiting period (as well as the post-effective period), no written offers may be made except by means of a Section 10 prospectus. Pursuant to Section 5(a), the securities may not be sold nor may offers to buy be accepted unless the registration statement has become effective. The "tombstone ad" and the Rule 134 "identifying statement," both of which are not deemed to be prospectuses under Section 2(10), may be published during the waiting period (as well as during the post-effective period). These devices are used to ascertain what parties are interested in the securities and the extent of such interest.

During the waiting period, no written sales literature, namely, so-called "free writing," is allowed. Hence, during this period, written offering materials may not be used, other than a Section 10 prospectus (see Rules 430 and 431), a tombstone ad, or an identifying statement. Normally, through the use of oral communications and Section 10 prospectuses (Rule 431 summary and Rule 430 preliminary prospectuses), underwriters and dealers solicit indications of interest from prospective purchasers during this period.

[2] SEC's Power of Acceleration

Under Section 8(a) of the Securities Act, a registration statement becomes effective the twentieth day after it is filed with the SEC. Significantly, the filing of any amendment commences the twenty day waiting period anew. Pursuant to Section 8(a), however, the Commission has the power of acceleration, meaning, for example, that it can determine to have the registration statement become effective immediately after the last amendment is filed. In practice, this power may give the Commission a good deal of leverage. Imagine if an issuer, after filing its last amendment, would have to wait twenty days before being able to have the registered securities sold. In some cases, given the volatile nature of the financial markets, the offering, twenty days later, no longer may find a receptive audience. The end result is that the Commission staff may be able to "persuade" the issuer and other affiliated parties to disclose more information than it otherwise would consider.

In May 1987, the SEC adopted Rule 430A. Under Rule 430A, issuers engaging in offerings of securities for cash no longer are required to file a pre-effective "pricing" amendment (*i.e.*, information relating to price and the underwriting syndicate). The information omitted in reliance on the rule either must be contained in the final prospectus which will be deemed a part of the registration statement if filed with the SEC within five business days after the registration statement's effective date or in a post-effective amendment to the registration statement. In the *Release* adopting Rule 430A, the SEC pointed out that the rule does not alter an issuer's disclosure obligations. According to the Commission, Rule 430A is intended to

> minimize the risk of disruption of a registrant's marketing schedule caused by the need to file a pricing amendment and wait until the registration statement is declared effective.[16]

Moreover, as a condition to granting acceleration, the SEC may require the respective parties to undertake certain actions. For example, in order that market professionals can adequately advise their customers, particularly in an initial public offering, the Commission under Rule 460

> will not accelerate the effective date of a registration statement unless the preliminary prospectus . . . is distributed to underwriters and dealers who it is reasonably anticipated will be invited to participate in the distribution of the security to be offered or sold.[17]

Also, in determining whether to accelerate a registration statement's effective date, the Commission will consider, particularly for a nonreporting company under the Exchange Act, whether reasonable steps have been taken to furnish

---

[16] *Securities Act Release* No. 6714 (1987).

[17] *Securities Act Release* No. 4968 (1969).

preliminary Rule 430 prospectuses to prospective purchasers.[18] As a final example, under Item 512(i) of Regulation S-K the issuer, in order to request acceleration of the effective date of the registration statement, must disclose, *inter alia*, any arrangement to indemnify any director, officer or controlling person of the issuer against liabilities arising under the Securities Act. The issuer, pursuant to Item 512(i), also must disclose that such indemnification with respect to a director, officer, or controlling person of the issuer, "in the opinion of the Securities and Exchange Commission . . . is against public policy as expressed in the [Securities] Act and is, therefore, unenforceable."

[C] The Post-Effective Period

[1] Overview

After the registration statement becomes effective, the *post-effective* period commences. Sales of the subject securities may now be made. Written offers continue to be regulated by Section 5(b) as in the waiting period. Under Section 2(10)(a), "free writing" is permitted in the post-effective period. Hence, without violating Section 5, subject parties during this period may distribute any written material so long as the literature is accompanied or preceded by a statutory Section 10(a) prospectus. Remember, however, that the antifraud and other remedial provisions apply to statements made in such written materials, including Section 17(a) of the Securities Act and Section 10(b) of the Exchange Act.

The contents of the statutory prospectus are specified in Section 10(a). Unlike the preliminary prospectus which is used in the waiting period (see Rule 430), the statutory prospectus is used only after the registration statement becomes effective. This is because the preliminary prospectus has certain incomplete information.

During the post-effective period, Section 5 has the effect of requiring that a Section 10(a) statutory prospectus be sent or given to purchasers of securities. Note, however, that a Section 10(b) summary prospectus (see Rule 431) may continue to be used by certain issuers in the post-effective period for solicitation purposes only. This is because a summary prospectus meets the requirements of Section 10, and, thus, is permitted under Section 5(b)(1). If there is "free writing" (including a confirmation of sale), however, a statutory Section 10(a) prospectus must be transmitted. Otherwise, such "free writing" constitutes a separate prospectus under Section 2(10), thereby resulting in a violation of Section 5(b)(1). Moreover, if the securities are mailed to the customer for purposes of sale, Section 5(b)(2) requires that such securities must be accompanied or preceded by a Section 10(a) prospectus.

[2] Dealer Prospectus Delivery Requirements

In the post-effective period, dealers are subject to the prospectus delivery requirements, noncompliance with which results in a violation of Section 5(b). In order to help ensure that there is adequate information disseminated

---

[18] *Id.*

to the investing public, Section 4(3), as modified by SEC Rule 174 pursuant to the Commission's rulemaking authority under that statute, generally requires that either a participating or nonparticipating dealer must provide a Section 10(a) statutory prospectus for sale purposes in the following circumstances:

(1) Pursuant to Section 4(3), if the issuer has not previously sold its securities pursuant to an earlier effective registration statement, a dealer must provide a statutory prospectus up to ninety days after the effectiveness of the registration statement or after the securities have been bona fide offered to the public, whichever is later.

In April 1988, the SEC amended Rule 174 to modify the above. The Commission reduced the prospectus delivery requirement for dealers, other than participating dealers selling any unsold allotment, to twenty-five days after the effectiveness of the registration statement or twenty-five days after the securities were bona fide offered to the public, whichever is later. The amended rule applies to issuers who were not previously reporting companies and whose securities are now exchange-listed or traded in the National Association of Securities Dealers Automated Quotation System (NASDAQ). On the other hand, for offerings by previously non-reporting issuers whose stock is quoted in the "pink sheets" (and not traded on an exchange or NASDAQ), the prospectus delivery requirement of ninety days is retained.[19]

(2) If the issuer has previously sold its securities pursuant to an earlier effective registration statement, Section 4(3) provides that a dealer must provide a prospectus up to forty days after the public offering has commenced. Rule 174, in effect, nullifies this aspect of Section 4(3), however, by providing that a dealer generally is not subject to the prospectus delivery requirements if the issuer is a reporting company under the Exchange Act.

(3) Irrespective of the time period expired, either under Section 4(3) or Rule 174, a participating dealer selling part of its unsold allotment must adhere to the prospectus delivery requirements.

[3] The Section 4(4) Exemption

A word also needs to be said about Section 4(4). That provision exempts from the prospectus delivery requirements unsolicited brokers' transactions (as opposed to a "distribution" — see Chapter 5, *infra*, for discussion of this distinction) executed on an exchange or in the over-the-counter market. Note here that the intermediary must be effecting the transaction for "the account of others" (see § 3(4) of the Exchange Act) and not for its own account. If the amount of securities sold is deemed large enough to constitute a "distribution," however, the Section 4(4) exemption is unavailable (as it applies only to "transactions"). Moreover, the transaction must be at the customer's behest and must take place on an exchange or in the over-the-counter market.

---

[19] See *Securities Act Release* No. 0763 (1988).

[4] Loophole?

An argument can be made that there is a loophole in the prospectus delivery framework. For example, a participating dealer may telephone a customer in either the waiting or post-effective period to inquire whether the investor is interested in purchasing securities pursuant to the registered offering. After the customer expresses his or her desire to buy the stock, the dealer in the post-effective period mails the customer a confirmation of sale accompanied by a statutory Section 10(a) prospectus. The statutory prospectus thus is the first written communication that the investor receives. The dealer's conduct is permitted provided that the issuer is a reporting company under the Exchange Act. If the issuer is not a reporting company, however, SEC Exchange Act Rule 15c2-8(b) deems it a violation of the rule (not of Section 5 of the Securities Act) for a broker or dealer to fail to "deliver a copy of the preliminary prospectus to any person who is expected to receive a confirmation of sale at least 48 hours prior to the mailing of such confirmation."

In any case, under Uniform Commercial Code (UCC) § 8-319(c), the investor may object to the sale if he or she sends a written objection to the dealer within ten days after receiving the confirmation. The UCC commentary states that the provision

> is particularly important in the relationship of broker . . . and customer. Normally a great volume of such business is done over the telephone. Orders are executed almost immediately and confirmed on the same or the next business day, usually on standard forms. . . . It is reasonable to require the customer to raise his objection, if any, within ten days after the confirmation has been received.

Many ordinary investors, however, lack knowledge of their rights under the UCC. As a result, insofar as Exchange Act reporting companies are concerned, it may be asserted that in practice the prospectus delivery requirements often may be an "empty gesture." Moreover, in part because the remedies provided for violation of Rule 15c2-8(b) are uncertain, it may be the case that investors who purchase stock in initial public offerings are all too often doing so without receiving the preliminary prospectus.

[D] Chart of Time Periods

The following chart hopefully will help clarify the conduct permitted as well as prohibited during the pre-filing, waiting, and post-effective periods.

Pre-Filing	Waiting	Post-Effective
Offers to sell as well as offers to buy are prohibited -- see §§ 2(3), 5(c).	Oral offers and written offers by means of a § 10 prospectus are permitted -- see §§ 2(10), 5(b)(1), 10(b), Rules 430, 431.	Sales can be made only if a statutory § 10(a) prospectus has been sent or given to the investor -- see §§ 2(10), 5(b), 10(a).
Sales are prohibited--see §§ 2(3), 5(a).	Securities may be sold and offers to buy may be accepted only in the post-effective period -- see §§ 2(3), 5(a).	§ 10 summary prospectus permitted to be used by certain issuers for solicitation purposes only -- see §§ 5(b)(1), 10(b), Rule 431. Preliminary § 10 prospectus not permitted during post-effective period -- see Rule 430.
Negotiations and agreements between the issuer and any underwriter or among underwriters who are or will be in privity with the issuer are permitted--see § 2(3).	Both the "tombstone ad" and the "identifying statement" may be used -- see § 2(10), Rule 134.	"Free-writing" permitted only in the post-effective period and only if such material accompanied or preceded by a statutory § 10(a) prospectus -- see §§ 2(10), 5(b)(1), 10(a).
Issuer may make an announcement of a proposed public offering in compliance with Rule 135.		Both the "tombstone ad" and the "identifying statement" may be used -- see § 2(10), Rule 134.
Pursuant to Rules 137-139, a broker or dealer may publish certain information about specified issuers. This is also the case in the waiting and post-effective periods.		Prospectus delivery requirements for dealers are subject to § 4(3) and Rule 174.
With respect to all three time periods, the interstate commerce requirement must be met in order for § 5 to apply.		Unsolicited brokers' transactions without prospectus delivery requirements permitted if transactions (as opposed to a "distribution") executed on an exchange or in the over-the-counter market -- see § 4(4).

§ 4.03 The "Misleading" Prospectus

In *SEC v. Manor Nursing Centers, Inc.*,[20] the Second Circuit considered whether material misrepresentations or nondisclosures contained in a statutory prospectus signified that, in addition to incurring antifraud liability, the prospectus failed to meet the requirements of Section 10(a) of the 1933 Act and, hence, violated Section 5(b)(2) of that Act. In that case, the violations were premised on the defendants' failure to amend or supplement the prospectus to reflect changes which occurred in the post-effective period that made the previous information furnished false and misleading. The Second Circuit held that Section 5(b)(2) had been violated, stating:

> We hold that implicit in the statutory provision that the prospectus contain certain information is the requirement that such information be true and correct. A prospectus does not meet the requirements of § 10(a), therefore, if information required to be disclosed is materially false and misleading. Appellants violated § 5(b)(2) by delivering Manor securities for sale accompanied by a prospectus which did not meet the requirements of § 10(a) in that the prospectus contained materially false and misleading statements with respect to information required by § 10(a) to be disclosed.[21]

The *Manor Nursing* analysis is subject to criticism because it imposes essentially strict liability, thereby nullifying the due diligence and reasonable care defenses contained in Sections 11 and 12(2) of the Securities Act (see Chapter 6, *infra*). For this reason, some courts have limited its holding to apply only where the prospectus or a like document is egregiously incomplete or permeated with misrepresentations.[22] Other courts, in analogous situations, have completely rejected *Manor Nursing*'s rationale.[23]

One such case is *SEC v. Southwest Coal & Energy Company*.[24] There, the SEC relied by analogy on *Manor Nursing*, arguing that the issuer had never properly qualified for a Regulation B exemption since its Schedule D offering sheets were false and misleading. Such materially defective offering sheets, the SEC asserted, did not meet Regulation B's initial filing requirements, thereby violating Sections 5(a) and 5(c). The Fifth Circuit rejected this contention, reasoning that such an interpretation would impose strict liability and vitiate the defenses available under other provisions of the securities laws (*e.g.*, Sections 11, 12(2), and 17(a) of the Securities Act and Section 10(b) of the Exchange Act). The court stated:

> That an offering sheet which formally complies with the disclosure requirements of Schedule D is misleading in some respect, should not

[20] 458 F.2d 1082 (2d Cir. 1972).

[21] *Id.* at 1098.

[22] See, *e.g.*, *Byrnes v. Faulknes, Dawkins & Sullivan*, 413 F. Supp. 453 (S.D.N.Y. 1976), *aff'd on other grounds*, 550 F.2d 1303 (2d Cir. 1977).

[23] See, *e.g.*, *SEC v. Blazon Corp.*, 609 F.2d 960 (9th Cir. 1979).

[24] 624 F.2d 1312 (5th Cir. 1980).

automatically render void *ab initio* a Regulation B exemption obtained on the basis of that offering. Rather, representations and material nondisclosures may be adequately dealt with under the pertinent antifraud provisions expressly designed for that purpose, instead of under § 5(a), (c) which is more appropriately focused upon failures to adhere to the prescribed formal mechanisms or procedures.[25]

The view expressed above, on balance, is correct. To hold that a Section 5 violation occurs whenever a security is sold pursuant to a materially false or misleading statement in the prospectus or like document, such as an offering circular, would negate the defenses otherwise available. Such a result is one that Congress could not have intended.

On the other hand, if the thrust of *Manor Nursing* is confined to issuers of registered offerings, then the decision may be viewed as compatible with Section 11. Hence, because Section 11 holds issuers strictly liable for making material misrepresentations or nondisclosures in a registration statement, the *Manor Nursing* rationale is consistent with the framework of Section 11, provided that it is limited only to issuers.[26]

§ 4.04 A Brief Look at the Process of a Public Offering

The advantages and disadvantages of going public are addressed in § 4.05, *infra*. In addition, the process of the initial public offering and the ramifications thereof are described in several law review articles.[27]

In brief, and put simplistically, the process of a public offering may be analogized to the sale of commercial goods. In a public offering, the distribution chain normally is as follows: Issuer — Underwriters — Participating Dealers — Investors/Purchasers (who may be individuals or institutions). Generally speaking, the larger in dollar size and the greater the geographical area where the selling activity takes place, a larger number of underwriters and dealers will comprise the distribution chain to effectuate the offering. Note the similarity to the sale of commercial goods: Manufacturer — Wholesalers — Retailers — Consumers. As with the sale of commercial goods where wholesalers may sell directly to the public, underwriters also may bypass the "dealer-link" and sell the securities directly to investors. This

[25] *Id.* at 1319 (citations omitted).

[26] In this regard the Commission has certain enforcement powers if the registration statement is materially false or misleading. The most significant such power is the "stop order" pursuant to § 8(d) of the Securities Act. See McLucas, *Stop Order Proceedings Under the Securities Act of 1933: A Current Assessment*, 40 Bus. Law. 515 (1980). See generally A. Bromberg & L. Lowenfels, *Securities Fraud and Commodities Fraud* § 6.11 (1988); M. Steinberg, *Securities Regulation: Liabilities and Remedies* § 5.02 (1989).

[27] See, *e.g.*, Schneider, Manko & Kant, *Going Public: Practice, Procedure, and Consequences*, 27 Vill. L. Rev. 1 (1981); Schneider & Shargel, *"Now That You Are Publicly Owned . . ."*, 36 Bus. Law. 1631 (1981).

may occur, for example, when an underwriter (such as Merrill Lynch or Prudential-Bache) has a national retail brokerage capacity with which to market the securities directly to investors.

Underwriting agreements for the most part are on a "firm commitment" basis. This means that the underwriters agree to purchase the securities from the issuer (at a discount) with the intent to resell them to participating dealers and/or investors. Although the underwriters incur the risk of "being stuck" with the securities if there is insufficient buyer interest, this risk is minimized in that, during the "waiting" period (when offers can be made), purchaser interest can be estimated with a fair degree of accuracy. Because the underwriters are not obligated until the "eve" of the offering's effective date when the underwriting agreement is finalized to, *inter alia*, determine the desired number of shares to be offered and fix the offering price per share, they have a strong indication of the market's likely response to the offering.

Another type of underwriting agreement is on a "best efforts" basis. In this situation, the underwriters act as agent for the issuer. Rather than purchasing the securities outright from the issuer and incurring the risk of a "bear" market, the underwriters, acting as agent for the issuer, locate buyers utilizing their "best efforts." These types of offerings may be used for start-up or financially troubled enterprises where there is a substantial degree of uncertainty regarding the offering's as well as the company's ultimate success. Because investors may wish some degree of comfort when they part with their money in these types of offerings, such offerings frequently are made on "an all or nothing" basis. This means that unless the requisite number of shares as stated in the registration statement have been sold to bona fide purchasers, all funds will be returned to the prospective investors.

A word should be said about the underwriting syndicate and dealer group. The syndicate is headed by the main underwriter or main underwriters (there, for example, may be three main underwriters in a fairly large offering). These underwriters generally are the ones to negotiate with the issuer and are delegated by the other underwriters in the syndicate to perform the due diligence functions. To effectuate the desired distribution, the main underwriter(s) will locate and bring in other underwriters which desire to take part in the offering. Generally, these "lower-tier" underwriters in the offering will purchase a significantly smaller number of shares from the issuer than the main underwriter(s). Although all underwriters are jointly and severally liable for material misstatements in the registration statement, Section 11(e) mitigates this potentially harsh effect somewhat by limiting an underwriter's damages to the dollar amount of the securities offered to the public by such underwriter. Moreover, Section 11(f) expressly permits a party to recover contribution.

Members of the dealer group ("participating" dealers), as discussed in § 4.02, *supra*, are not in privity with the issuer. These are broker-dealers who for one reason or another (such as inability or a conscious desire not to commit the necessary funds) are not members of the underwriting syndicate but who nonetheless deem it in their financial interests to become a "participant" in the offering. Hence, they purchase from underwriters an allocated number of shares offered and resell them to their customers, their profit being the difference between the purchase price from the underwriters and the resale price to their customers. Although dealers are not subject to Section 11 liability, they may incur liability for violation of the prospectus delivery requirements and for material misrepresentations (and omissions) contained in the prospectus or stated orally (see § 4.02[C], *supra*, and §§ 6.09 and 7.01, *infra*).

§ 4.05 "Going Public" — Pros and Cons

Briefly, the *advantages* of an enterprise going public and having its initial public offering (IPO) include:

1. The funds obtained from the offering may be used for capital formation purposes as well as for retiring existing indebtedness.

2. The insiders may sell a substantial portion of their stock and thereby become (if they aren't already) millionaires.

3. A public offering, by improving the company's financial position, will enable it to have access to capital on more favorable terms.

4. The funds desired from the offering may enable the company to expand by acquiring other businesses.

5. By offering stock remuneration packages tied to a public market, the enterprise will be in a better position to hire and retain quality personnel.

6. By having a public market for its stock, the company may become better known, thereby possibly resulting in improved profits.

On the other hand, perceived *disadvantages* of going public include:

1. The costs of an IPO, particularly when compared to other methods of procuring funds, are high.

2. Due to shareholder concern for the short-term, management may discount long-term strategies in order to put emphasis on the company's stock prices.

3. Management, through its sale of stock, may lose control of the enterprise and become subject to a hostile takeover.

4. By going public, the enterprise becomes a reporting company under the Securities Exchange Act. Such a consequence may be viewed as having several disadvantages to insiders, including:

a. The company now must file periodic and annual reports, comply with the internal accounting controls and recordkeeping mandates of the Foreign Corrupt Practices Act (even if all of the company's operations are domestic), and be subject to the federal proxy provisions, as well as a number of other requirements.

b. The expenses of complying with Exchange Act requirements will be substantial.

c. Insiders lose much of their privacy as their salaries, perquisites, and transactions with the issuer must be disclosed pursuant to SEC rules.

d. Due to such mandated disclosure, there is a greater risk of shareholder litigation.

e. Insiders are subject to the short-swing six-month trading provisions of Section 16 of the Exchange Act, thereby resulting in loss of liquidity and potential liability.

Given the above, the decision to go public may not be an easy one. Moreover, the registration process, including the planning, preparation, structuring, and timing of a public offering, is a major undertaking for all parties concerned.

§ 4.06 The Integrated Disclosure Framework

The SEC's integrated disclosure system was adopted to ameliorate the expenses and duplication that were prevalent as a result of two different reporting mandates under the 1933 Act and the 1934 Act. In seeking to make disclosure as uniform as practicable under the two Acts, the SEC promulgated Regulation S-K and Regulation S-X (accounting rules) which act as the key sources for ascertaining the disclosures required to be made. This is not to imply, however, that the disclosures contained in the various documents filed with the Commission are identical. For example, with respect to the annual report on Form 10-K and the annual report to shareholders, the SEC took the following position:

> The Commission has determined to require only portions of the Form 10-K and the annual report to security holders to have equivalent disclosure because these documents are not necessarily used in an identical manner. Disclosure requirements in annual reports evolved in the context of shareholders making voting decisions. The Form 10-K has traditionally confirmed information previously delivered to investors and other users making economic decisions about the company and, as a result, has been more detailed.[28]

Hence, under the Commission's integrated disclosure framework, registrant reporting has been simplified in three ways:

> (1) disclosure requirements are made uniform under the Securities Act and the Exchange Act; (2) Exchange Act periodic reporting is used to

[28] *Securities Act Release* No. 6231 (1980).

> satisfy much of the disclosure necessary in Securities Act registration statements; and (3) the use of informal shareholder communications is encouraged, but not required, to satisfy formal statutory requirements under both Acts.[29]

This emphasis on Exchange Act periodic disclosure under the integrated disclosure system induced the Commission to require that a majority of the registrant's directors sign the annual Form 10-K. Such a signature requirement was necessary, according to the Commission, in order to encourage directors

> to devote the needed attention in reviewing the Form 10-K and to seek the involvement of other professionals to the degree necessary to give themselves sufficient comfort.[30]

The integrated disclosure process, although calling for meaningful non-duplicative information, has evoked important liability concerns. These liability issues, related to the concept of "due diligence," will be addressed in Chapter 6, *infra.*

[A] Registration Forms

To implement the integrated disclosure system, the Commission adopted three new registration forms, Forms S-1, S-2, and S-3. These Forms serve as the basic framework for registered offerings under the Securities Act. Incorporation by reference from 1934 Act reports is permitted only as to Forms S-2 and S-3:

> The registration statement for the first category is Form S-1. It requires complete disclosure to be set forth in the prospectus and permits no incorporation by reference. Form S-1 is to be used by registrants in the Exchange Act reporting system for less than three years and also may be used by any registrants who choose to do so or for whom no other form is available.
>
> The second category of registration statement is Form S-2 which combines reliance on incorporating Exchange Act reports by reference with delivery to investors of streamlined information. Registrants in the Exchange Act reporting system for three years may use this Form, which allows them to choose to either: (1) Deliver a copy of their annual report to security holders along with the prospectus describing the offering or (2) present registrant-oriented information comparable to that of the annual report in the prospectus along with the description of the offering. In either case, the more complete information in the Form 10-K is incorporated by reference into the prospectus.
>
> Form S-3, in reliance on the efficient market theory, allows maximum use of incorporation by reference of Exchange Act reports and requires

[29] *Securities Act Release* No. 6331 (1981).

[30] *Securities Act Release* No. 6231 (1980).

> the least disclosure to be presented in the prospectus and delivered to investors. Generally, the Form S-3 prospectus [which can be used in certain equity offerings by issuers which have $150 million of voting stock outstanding held by non-affiliates ("float") or have at least a $100 million float and 3 million share annual trading volume] will present the same transaction-specific information as will be presented in a Form S-1 or S-2 prospectus. Information concerning the registrant will be incorporated by reference from Exchange Act reports. The prospectus will not be required to present any information concerning the registrant unless there has been a material change in the registrant's affairs which has not been reported in an Exchange Act filing or the Exchange Act reports incorporated by reference do not reflect certain restated financial statements or other financial information.[31]

The rationale largely underlying incorporation by reference of Exchange Act reports into 1933 Act registration statements is that information regularly furnished to the securities markets through 1934 Act periodic reports is digested by the marketplace and reflected in the price of the issuer's securities, thereby eliminating the need to reiterate such information in the public offering context. Hence, this theory postulates that the securities markets, by analyzing the available information and accurately valuing the information in the price set for a security, are efficient. The efficient market theory has received Supreme Court approbation with respect to the issue of "reliance" in Section 10(b) litigation, discussed in Chapter 7, *infra.*[32]

One other registration form is worthy of comment at this stage, the S-18. Generally, the S-18 is a less demanding registration statement that may be utilized (instead of the Form S-1) by issuers going public when the amount to be raised by the offering doesnot exceed $7.5 million. Like the Regulation A offering circular for exempt offerings, the Form S-18 may be filed in an SEC regional office rather than in Washington, D.C. By filing the Form S-18 near to home, counsel may be in a better position to facilitate the SEC review process. It should be emphasized, however, that unlike the Regulation A offering circular, the Form S-18 is a registration statement. As a consequence, the various parties must be cognizant of the Section 5 prohibitions as well as the potential Section 11 and other liability. In addition, an issuer offering securities under Form S-18 will become subject to the periodic reporting and other mandates of the Exchange Act.

For mergers and certain other reorganizations, the Form S-4 registration statement may be used. This Form is discussed in Chapter 5, *infra.*

[B] Shelf Registration

One of the Commission's significant actions with respect to the integrated disclosure framework was its adoption of Rule 415, the "shelf" registration

---

[31] *Securities Act Release* No. 6383 (1982).

[32] See *Basic, Inc. v. Levinson*, 108 S. Ct. 978 (1988).

rule.[33] Generally, Rule 415 concerns the Securities Act registration of securities to be offered or sold on a delayed or continuous basis in the future. Significantly, the rule allows Form S-3 issuers to file primary-at-the-market offerings of equity securities which they plan to offer within two years of the effective date of the registration statement. As will be addressed in Chapter 6, *infra*, Rule 415 raises significant liability questions.

§ 4.07 The Mandatory Disclosure System

This Section addresses three timely issues in the securities regulation field: (1) the debate surrounding the securities acts' mandatory disclosure system, (2) issuer disclosure of forward-looking information, and (3) issuer disclosure of qualitative, in addition to quantitative, information.

[A] The Disclosure Debate

The propriety of Congress' enactment of a mandatory securities law disclosure system has generated much debate over the last two decades. As discussed throughout this chapter, issuers must disclose certain material and other specified information when publicly offering securities pursuant to the Securities Act's registration framework. Moreover, once an issuer engages in a public offering, it is required under the Exchange Act to provide the SEC and its shareholders with annual and other periodic reports. Whether such a mandatory disclosure system is appropriate and the type of information that should be subject to compelled disclosure have been subject to debate.

Critics of the mandatory disclosure system argue that the system produces considerable costs yet few benefits.[34] The quality of disclosure, according to critics, yields little useful information. Professor Kripke, for example, has opined:

> [T]he Commission's disclosure system cannot be given high marks either for performance or on a cost/benefit basis during its first forty years. The system was founded not on disclosure of "all material facts," but on disclosure of events in the past which the Commission could objectively verify. This historical perspective was assumed for the inefficient purpose of preventing blatant securities fraud and for the less apparent purpose of protecting the Commission from criticism for issues that turn sour. In recent years, while the Commission has shown commendable willingness to try to modernize the system, developments and economic theory have outrun adaptation of the system.[35]

---

[33] *Securities Act Release* No. 6499 (1983). See Banoff, *Regulatory Subsidies, Efficient Markets, and Shelf Registration: An Analysis of Rule 415*, 70 Va. L. Rev. 135 (1984).

[34] See, *e.g.*, Berston, H. Manne, *Inside Trading on the Stock Market* (1966); *The Valve of the SEC's Accounting Disclosure Requirements*, 44 Acct. Rev. 515 (1969); Stigler, *Public Regulation of the Securities Markets*, 37 J. Bus. 117 (1964).

[35] Kripke, *Fifty Years of Securities Regulation in Search of a Purpose*, 21 San Diego L. Rev. 257 (1984).

Proponents of a mandatory disclosure system assert that, in the absence of such a system: (1) some registrants would engage in fraudulent disclosure practices, (2) insider perquisites and salaries as well as underwriter costs would be excessive, (3) current state laws and self-regulatory oversight by themselves would be inadequate for enforcement purposes, (4) the threat of civil and criminal actions would not induce the appropriate level of disclosure, and (5) investors would lose confidence in the integrity of the securities markets.[36]

A point that should be raised is the role that disclosure under the federal securities laws has on normative corporate conduct. As this author has stated:

> Although the rationale underlying disclosure is not based primarily on influencing corporate internal affairs but rather on providing shareholders and the marketplace with sufficient information to make intelligent decisions and to be apprised of significant developments, there is little question that disclosure has a substantial impact on the normative conduct of corporations. In this regard, the Commission's disclosure policies . . . have not only had an effect of deterring unlawful or questionable conduct but have played a positive role in influencing the establishment of improved standards of conduct.[37]

[B] Disclosure of "Forward-Looking" Information

Although continuing to support strongly the need for a mandatory disclosure system, the Commission has responded to Professor Kripke and other critics by taking certain actions. The most important was the adoption of the integrated disclosure system. A second was the Commission's promulgation of Securities Act Rule 175 (and Exchange Act Rule 3b-6) which provides a "safe harbor" for projections.[38] In this regard, the area encompassing issuer affirmative disclosure obligations (including such subjects as disclosure of "soft" information, merger negotiations, and "bad" news) is addressed at length in Chapter 9, *infra.*

---

[36] See Seligman, *The Historical Need for a Mandatory Corporate Disclosure System*, 9 J. Corp. L. 1, 9 (1979). See generally Coffee, *Market Failure and the Economic Case for a Mandatory Disclosure System*, 70 Va. L. Rev. 717 (1984); Easterbrook & Fischel, *Mandatory Disclosure and the Protection of Investors*, 70 Va. L. Rev. 669 (1984).

[37] M. Steinberg, *Corporate Internal Affairs: A Corporate and Securities Law Perspective* 29 (1983). See R. Stevenson, *Corporations and Information — Secrecy, Access and Disclosure* 81-82 (1980) ("Today the disclosure requirements of the securities laws are used, in a variety of ways, for the explicit purpose of influencing a wide range of corporate primary behavior. . . ."); Weiss, *Disclosure and Corporate Accountability*, 34 Bus. Law. 575 (1979) ("one of the central themes of the system by which large corporations are governed [is] that corporate decision-making be regulated through mandatory disclosure requirements than direct government intervention").

[38] See *Securities Act Release* No. 6084 (1979).

Whereas "hard" information emphasizes historical data, "soft" information often focuses on forward-looking statements, such as projections, forecasts, and predictions. Until the mid-1970s, the SEC and the courts discouraged and even prohibited the disclosure of soft information. The major concern had been that investors, particularly the unsophisticated, might attach too much significance to information that is of questionable reliability.[39]

With the adoption of Rule 175, the SEC recognized that the flow of "soft" information to the marketplace may enable more informed investment decisions to be made. Generally, Rule 175 (as well as Rule 3b-6) encourages issuer use of financial projections in 1933 Act registration statements, Exchange Act reports, annual reports to shareholders, and other documents filed with the SEC. The rule establishes a "safe harbor" for parties who invoke the rule.

Under Rule 175,

> a safe harbor [is created] from the applicable liability provisions of the federal securities laws for statements relating to or containing (1) projections of reserves, income (loss), earnings (loss) per share or other financial items, such as capital expenditures, dividends, or capital structure, (2) management plans and objectives for future company operations, and (3) future economic performance included in management's statements.[40]

In providing this "safe harbor," Rule 175 precludes liability for the making of issuer forward-looking statements unless the plaintiff establishes that any such statement was made or reaffirmed without a reasonable basis or was disclosed other than in good faith.

It may be argued that the SEC went too far in permitting first-time public issuers to include "safe harbor" projections in their registration statements. This assertion is even more meritorious given that under Rule 175 the burden of proof is placed upon the plaintiff. Unlike reporting companies, many first-time issuers are start-up companies with no previous substantial earnings history. Moreover, in any event, most first-time issuers have not been followed in the market. Hence, the SEC may have thrown its normal caution to the wind for the sake of encouraging projections. It can be argued, however, that, if such first-time issuers make projections with no previous earnings history, such projections are not within Rule 175's "safe harbor" because they are not made in "good faith" and "with a reasonable basis."[41]

---

[39] See, *e.g.*, *Gerstle v. Gamble-Skogmo, Inc.*, 478 F.2d 1281, 1294 (2d Cir. 1973).

[40] *Securities Act Release* No. 6084 (1979).

[41] See generally Fiflis, *Soft Information: The SEC's Former Exogenous Zone*, 26 U.C.L.A. L. Rev. 95 (1978); Comment, *The Safe Harbor for Forecasts — A Step in the Right Direction?*, 1980 Duke L.J. 607; Note, *Disclosure of Future-Oriented Information Under the Securities Laws*, 88 Yale L.J. 338 (1978).

[C] Disclosure of "Qualitative" Information

Purely qualitative information, unlike quantitative information, does not impact significantly on the earnings, assets, or economic viability of the registrant. Rather, such information more directly relates to the integrity and competency of corporate management. Under the Commission's rules and judicial decisions, disclosure is required, for example, of certain self-dealing transactions engaged in by management as well as adjudicated illegalities and certain other events (such as the imposition of an SEC injunction).[42] Absent self-dealing, an adjudicated illegality, a pending criminal (and, in some situations, a pending civil) proceeding, or mandated disclosure called for by a specific SEC rule, courts are reluctant to require an issuer to disclose qualitative information that is not economically material.[43]

In this context, as well as others, where liability is premised on the failure to disclose, the information omitted in order to be actionable must be material (or called for by an SEC rule) and there must exist a disclosure obligation. For example, in the insider trading context, the Supreme Court has made it clear that silence when trading on material nonpublic information is not actionable under Section 10(b) of the Exchange Act unless there exists a duty to disclose such information.[44]

In the 1933 Act registration setting, the duty to disclose is present from two sources. First, because the issuer is itself selling securities, a fiduciary duty triggering a disclosure obligation arises between the issuer and purchasers of the securities.[45] Second, Rule 408 of SEC Regulation C provides:

> In addition to the information expressly required to be included in a registration statement, there shall be added such further material information, if any, as may be necessary to make the required statements, in the light of the circumstances under which they are made, not misleading.

The end result is that in the 1933 Act registration setting, if the information is material, it must be disclosed.

§ 4.08 State "Blue Sky" Law

Generally, under state Blue Sky law, as under the federal securities laws, every security offered to be sold in the applicable state must be registered or

---

[42] See, *e.g.*, *Maldonado v. Flynn*, 597 F.2d 789 (2d Cir. 1979); Items 401(f), 402, 404 of Regulation S-K.

[43] See, *e.g.*, *Gaines v. Haughton*, 645 F.2d 761 (9th Cir. 1981), *cert. denied*, 454 U.S. 1145 (1982). See generally Ferrara, Starr & Steinberg, *Disclosure of Information Bearing on Management Integrity and Competency*, 76 Nw. U.L. Rev. 555 (1981).

[44] See *Dirks v. SEC*, 463 U.S. 646 (1983); *Chiarella v. United States*, 445 U.S. 222 (1980).

[45] *Chiarella v. United States*, 445 U.S. 222, 230 (1980).

exempt from registration. The first type of registration, registration by coordination, is available to the issuer when a registered offering is being made under the Securities Act of 1933. This method of registration only requires the filing of three copies of the current federal prospectus as well as any additional information required by the state securities administrator. A second type of registration, registration by notification, requires the filing of a short-form registration statement and is available generally only when an issuer and its predecessors have had a seasoned business history for at least five years (*e.g.*, no default and average net earnings). The third type of registration, registration by qualification, goes further than mandating full disclosure and authorizes the state securities administrator to engage in merit regulation. Under merit regulation, the state securities administrator can prevent an offering from going forward because it is not "fair, just and equitable."[46]

A number of states have adopted a merit regulation approach. In these states, full and fair disclosure alone is not enough. Rather, the offering also must be deemed "fair, just, and equitable." The debate over merit regulation generally has focused on whether full disclosure of material information concerning an offering is sufficient to protect investors, the propriety of paternalistic government regulation, and the economic costs versus benefits of such a system of regulation. Generally, merit regulation is used to describe the securities laws of those states which,

> in addition to requiring full disclosure, have granted their administrators power to analyze the securities to be offered, the terms of the offering, and the business of the issuer for purposes of determining, according to certain formal and informal rules, whether the securities are too speculative for public sale.[47]

---

[46] See T. Hazen, *The Law of Securities Regulation* § 8.2 (1985). See generally J. Long, *Blue Sky Law* (1987).

[47] J. Mofsky, *Blue Sky Restrictions on New Business Promotions* 7-8 (1971). See generally Sargent, *The Challenge to Merit Regulation*, 12 Sec. Reg. L.J. 276, 367 (1984); Tyler, *More About Blue Sky*, 39 Wash. & Lee L. Rev. 899 (1982).

CHAPTER 5

RESALES AND REORGANIZATIONS

§ 5.01 Introduction

As seen from the foregoing materials, the Securities Act of 1933 was enacted in large part to help promote the dissemination of adequate and reliable information to the investing public in the distribution process. To achieve this objective, Section 5 requires registration for any offer or sale of a security unless such offer or sale is exempt from the registration provisions.

We have examined the exemptions for issuers in Chapter 3, *supra*. Attention now turns to exemptions for resales by persons other than an issuer. We begin by addressing Section 4(1) which provides the most important exemption in this context. By its terms, Section 4(1) exempts from the registration requirements of Section 5 "transactions by any person other than an issuer, underwriter or dealer." Hence, the Section 4(1) exemption permits individual investors to resell their securities without registration, provided such resales are viewed as "transactions" rather than a "distribution." Because Section 4(3) and Section 4(4) exempt most transactions by broker-dealers, the problems that arise under Section 4(1) generally involve underwriters. Underwriter status necessarily renders the Section 4(1) exemption unavailable.

§ 5.02 The Concept of "Underwriter"

The concept of underwriter is fundamental to the framework of the 1933 Act. Congress contemplated that underwriters would play an integral role in both the initial and secondary distribution process. Underwriter status subjects applicable parties to the provisions of Section 5 and aids in determining the scope of individuals who may be held liable for material misrepresentations and nondisclosures contained in the registration statement.

Section 2(11) of the Securities Act defines an "underwriter" as

> any person who has purchased from an issuer with a view to, or offers or sells for an issuer in connection with, the distribution of any security, or participates or has a direct or indirect participation in any such undertaking, or participates or has a participation in the direct or indirect underwriting of any such undertaking, but such term shall not include a person whose interest is limited to a commission from an

underwriter or dealer not in excess of the usual and customary distributors' or sellers' commission.[1]

For the purposes of Section 2(11) only (*i.e.*, who should be regarded as an "underwriter"), the term "issuer" is defined to include a person or party who controls the issuer. Rule 405 defines control as "the possession, direct or indirect, of the power to direct or cause the direction of the management and policies of a person, whether through the ownership of voting securities, by contract, or otherwise." Significantly, the inclusion of control persons within the definition of "issuer" for Section 2(11) purposes signifies that sales by directors and executive officers create the risk that some party involved in the transaction is an "underwriter."

An examination of Section 2(11) reveals that a party can become an underwriter in the following ways:

(1) By purchasing from the issuer with a view towards distribution;

(2) By offering or selling for an issuer in connection with a distribution;

(3) By participating, directly or indirectly, in the underwriting effort; and

(4) By selling securities of the issuer on behalf of a control person.

If a person falls within one of these categories, he or she will be deemed an underwriter. Note the lack of guidance Section 2(11) provides to counsel. For example: What evidence shows intent to "distribute"? What circumstances constitute "participation"? What power must a person possess to be "in control"? The answers to these questions are necessarily based on the individual circumstances of each case. Judicial decisions are fairly scarce and, not surprisingly, have not eliminated fears of inadvertent underwriter status. Moreover, beyond Rule 144 (which will be examined in § 5.05, *infra*), the SEC has promulgated few rules or regulations in this area.

A word should be said regarding Rules 141 and 142. In effect, these rules exclude from underwriter status (1) distributors and dealers who receive a commission from an underwriter or dealer not in excess of the usual and customary distributors' or sellers' commissions (Rule 141), and (2) those persons who, under the circumstances delineated in the rule, purchase for investment purposes all or a specified portion of the securities remaining unsold after the lapse of a specified period of time (Rule 142).

[A] The Presumptive Underwriter Doctrine

In an offering of securities registered pursuant to the Securities Act, an individual, a few investors, or an institution may purchase a substantial portion of the offering and thereafter resell the securities to the public. At least two problems may arise: The purchasers may hold the securities until the information in the registration statement becomes outdated; or the

---

[1] 15 U.S.C. § 77b(11).

purchasers, perhaps seeking to take advantage of the rapid price increase normally associated with a "hot issue" (that is, an issue that, shortly after the registration statement has gone effective, is trading in the aftermarket at a substantially higher price than the registered offering price), may sell large quantities of the subject securities (for substantial profit) within a short time period. If the Section 4(1) exemption were to apply, these sales would be free of the registration requirements, including, of course, the prospectus delivery obligation. Concerned with the lack of disclosure in this context, the SEC formulated the presumptive underwriter doctrine.[2]

Under the presumptive underwriter doctrine, one who purchases more than 10% of the securities offered in a registered offering may be deemed an underwriter unless such person establishes sufficient investment intent. The doctrine was subject to criticism by pension and employee benefit plans managed by life insurance companies and similar institutional investors. In fear of the doctrine, a number of institutional investors significantly limited their purchases of securities in registered public offerings.

Perhaps as a result, the SEC staff has abandoned the presumptive underwriter doctrine. The Commission's Director of the Division of Corporation Finance stated in 1986:

> For many years, a concept known as the "presumptive underwriter" doctrine existed. That doctrine assumed that a purchaser of a relatively large amount of securities covered by a registration statement (at one point 10 percent) was buying with a view to distribution and, therefore, should be deemed a statutory underwriter. The theory was most subjective, most difficult of explanation, and presented considerable problems both in compliance, as well as administration. In 1983, in the American Council of Life Insurance letter, the "presumptive underwriter" doctrine was for all intents and purposes abandoned. . . . Nothing in the Securities Act compelled the view that a person acquiring a substantial part of an offering should be treated differently from any other investor with a large position in the issuer, unless the purchaser becomes an affiliate as a result of the purchases.[3]

[B] Participating in the Underwriting Effort

From the Second Circuit's decision in *SEC v. Chinese Consolidated Benevolent Association*,[4] the making of continual solicitations resulting in a distribution of securities normally confers underwriter status, irrespective of

---

[2] See Ahrenholz & Van Valkenberg, *The Presumptive Underwriter Doctrine: Statutory Underwriter Status for Investors Purchasing a Substantial Portion of a Registered Offering*, 1973 Utah L. Rev. 773.

[3] Address by Linda C. Quinn, Esq., before the ABA's Federal Regulation of Securities Committee (Nov. 22, 1986), discussed in Barron, *The SEC Staff Finally Abandons the "Presumptive Underwriter" Doctrine*, 15 Sec. Reg. L.J. 296 (1987).

[4] 120 F.2d 738 (2d Cir. 1941).

a party's motive or relationship with the issuer. This is so even if the party is a volunteer and receives no compensation for its efforts.

The above principle is not always literally applied, creating uncertainty in this area. For example, in one case, the court found that the defendant bank purchased shares on behalf of its customers in a public offering, acted as an important link in the chain of distribution, and issued reports touting the shares to its customers at the time it was buying and selling securities for its customers' accounts. Nevertheless, the court found that, as a matter of law, the bank was not an underwriter. It reasoned that

> in no manner did [the bank] have a relationship with [the issuer], [the principal underwriter], or the underwriting itself. Plaintiff, therefore, must properly plead some greater nexus between the investment management department of [defendant] Bankers Trust and this underwriting of securities before such liability can attach.[5]

§ 5.03 Distributions by Controlling Persons or Affiliates

The concept of "control" is crucial to the understanding of secondary distributions. For the purposes of determining who is an "underwriter," Section 2(11) defines the term "issuer" to include a controlling person. Therefore, underwriter status may be accorded to any person who sells securities on behalf of a controlling person. The possibility of inadvertent underwriter status is ever present because of the ambiguities associated with the meaning of "control." Moreover, the inclusion of control persons within the definition of "issuer" for Section 2(11) purposes signifies that sales of securities by directors and executive officers create the risk that some party involved in the transaction is an "underwriter," irrespective of whether the securities are restricted or unrestricted. Because directors and executive officers frequently are shareholders, this problem of potential underwriter status is a very practical and widespread one.

The lack of a precise definition for control frustrates counselors and corporate planners.[6] The Commission, in an effort to alleviate some of the uncertainty, promulgated Rule 405 which defines "control" as

> the possession, direct or indirect, of the power to direct or cause the direction of the management and policies of a person, whether through the ownership of voting securities, by contract, or otherwise.

Rule 405 focuses on a person's ability to direct the management and policies of the corporation. Use of Rule 405 to define control in the Section 2(11) context, however, has been criticized by commentators. These commentators suggest that an appropriate definition of control should stress a person's ability to compel the issuer to register an offering. They assert that Congress

---

[5] *Zicklin v. Breuer*, 534 F. Supp. 745, 747 (S.D.N.Y. 1982).

[6] See Sommer, *Who's "In Control"? — S.E.C.*, 21 Bus. Law. 559 (1966).

never intended a person to be deemed an issuer in this context when that person did not possess the power to compel registration. Moreover, they argue that the SEC's use of Rule 405 to define control fails to relieve uncertainty.[7]

[A] Effecting a "Distribution"

The Securities Act does not explicitly hold the conduct of controlling persons illegal when they effect a distribution of unregistered shares through an underwriter. Of course, what a statute fails expressly to do, a court can accomplish through construing the statute's pertinent language, legislative history, and policy rationales. In *United States v. Wolfson,*[8] the Second Circuit held that a group of controlling persons, Wolfson and his cohorts, violated Section 5 because they effected an unregistered distribution of securities through several unwitting brokerage houses. As the court observed, Section 4(1) "by its terms exempts only transactions." Hence, because Wolfson and his cronies were effecting a "distribution," they could not avail themselves of the Section 4(1) exemption. As the Seventh Circuit more recently stated:

> Section 4(1) provides an exemption for transactions, not individuals. It was created to exempt routine trading transactions with respect to securities already issued and not to exempt distributions by issuers or acts of others who engage in steps necessary to such distributions.[9]

With respect to the six brokerage houses involved in *Wolfson,* they were not subject to the Section 5 requirements because of the Section 4(4) exemption. This was due to the court's conclusion that each of the unwitting brokerage houses effected only "transactions" (unaware of the "distribution"), the "transactions" were solicited by Wolfson, and the "transactions" were executed in the over-the-counter market.

An earlier case, *Ira Haupt & Co.,*[10] had the effect of making brokers wary of selling a controlling person's shares. There, an individual, Schulte, controlled Park & Tilford, Inc. He gave a series of sell orders, involving around 200 shares per order, to his broker Haupt. During a six-month period, 93,000 shares were sold pursuant to these orders. Haupt was charged with violating Section 5 for its role in effecting the unregistered offering. Haupt offered two defenses. First, Haupt argued that its sales of Park & Tilford shares were not a "distribution" because there was no plan to sell a specified number of shares. The Commission rejected this defense, finding that the facts and circumstances clearly put Haupt on notice that a distribution was

---

[7] See 7B J.W. Hicks, *Exempted Transactions Under the Securities Act of 1933* § 10.03[2][a] at 10-167-171 (1985); Campbell, *Defining Control in Secondary Distributions,* 18 B.C. Ind. & Comm. L. Rev. 37 (1976).

[8] 405 F.2d 779 (2d. Cir. 1968).

[9] *SEC v. Holschuh*, 694 F.2d 130, 137-38 (7th Cir. 1982). *Accord SEC v. Murphy*, 626 F.2d 633, 648 (9th Cir. 1980).

[10] 23 S.E.C. 589 (1946).

anticipated. Second, Haupt claimed the Section 4(4) exemption, which, *inter alia*, exempts "brokers' transactions executed upon customers' orders on any exchange. . . ." In rejecting this defense, the SEC reasoned that the Section 4(4) exemption does not exempt brokers from Section 5 when they act as underwriters in a "distribution." Here Haupt was effecting a "distribution" rather than engaging in a "transaction." As will be discussed later in the chapter, to alleviate some of the concern generated by the *Haupt* decision, the SEC promulgated Rule 154 and thereafter Rule 144.

[B] Secondary Offerings

As the foregoing discussion suggests, in order to effect a "distribution," a registered offering must take place. Irrespective of whether the offering is on behalf of an issuer or for the benefit of a control person, only the issuer can register a public offering. This consequence is not unduly onerous, according to proponents, because a controlling person has the leverage for inducing the issuer to file a registration statement and to elicit adequate disclosure on the part of such an issuer. Because of the ambiguities associated with the concept of control, a person who may be viewed as an affiliate may contract with the issuer when he or she acquires the stock for the right of demand registration, thereby granting the control person the contractual right to demand that the issuer file a 1933 Act registration statement when the person wishes to dispose of his or her stock. If the purported "control person" does not have such leverage, he or she may settle for the right of "piggy-back" registration. This right, looking to the terms of the covenant negotiated, authorizes the control person to "piggy-back" his or her stock or a portion thereof at the time that the issuer elects to file a registration statement.

Even where the control person in a secondary distribution induces the issuer to file a registration statement, there remain significant pitfalls. One particular concern is disclosure. For example, where all or a part of the proceeds of the offering will be paid to selling shareholders rather than to the issuer, the registration statement must carefully disclose this consequence.[11] Another problem is that shareholders effecting a secondary registered offering may be tempted to manipulate the price of the stock. The SEC, aware of the potential for abuse, has brought enforcement actions in this context and has promulgated a number of rules designed to curtail such manipulative activity.[12]

---

[11] See, *e.g.*, Item 507 of SEC Regulation S-K; *In the Matter of Universal Camera Corp.*, 19 S.E.C. 648 (1945).

[12] See, *e.g.*, SEC Rules 10b-6, 10b-7, 10b-8, 10b-13; *In the Matter of Hazel Bishop, Inc.*, 40 S.E.C. 718 (1961).

§ 5.04 Purchasing From an Issuer with a View Towards Distribution

A person who has acquired "restricted securities" from an issuer often has obtained the securities pursuant to Section 4(2) of the Securities Act which exempts from the registration requirements "transactions by an issuer not involving any public offering," or pursuant to Rules 505, 506, or 701 of Regulation D. One problem is that when an issuer sells unregistered securities to one or more persons in a non-public transaction, it is possible that the transfer is in reality a public offering in disguise — a two-step, indirect distribution in which the transferees function as "underwriters" for the issuer. An affiliate of the issuer selling either restricted or nonrestricted securities faces a similar problem — because of his or her close connection with the issuer, an affiliate, absent the exercise of utmost care, may be unable to invoke the Section 4(1) exemption in any resale transaction involving securities of the issuer.

As discussed earlier in this chapter, if a person is deemed to be an "underwriter," he or she cannot rely on the exemption from registration provided by Section 4(1) of the Act to protect the resale transaction. Generally, although Section 4(1) exempts ordinary transactions such as a private resale of securities, it does so only with respect to "transactions by any person other than an issuer, *underwriter*, or dealer." The dilemma for persons holding restricted securities of an issuer and for affiliates of an issuer comes into focus upon examining the statutory definition of "underwriter." Section 2(11) of the Act defines an "underwriter" to include any person who "has purchased" securities from the issuer "with a view to . . . the distribution of any security."

Section 2(11) does not provide an objective standard for determining whether a person acquiring securities from an issuer is taking with a view toward investment or with a view toward resale. For a non-affiliate holding restricted securities, a resale in purported reliance upon Section 4(1) carries the risk that the seller will be deemed to be an "underwriter" within the meaning of Section 2(11), and therefore, unable to claim the desired exemption. For an affiliate who intends to sell any securities of the issuer, restricted or not, the same risk is present. As will be discussed in § 5.05, *infra*, provided that the requirements of Rule 144 are met, the Rule provides a safe-harbor to persons holding restricted securities of an issuer and to affiliates of an issuer who seek to resell either restricted or nonrestricted securities.[13]

[A] Holding Period

In determining whether a person has purchased from the issuer with a view to distribution, the amount of time that the person held the security prior to resale is deemed a relevant factor. In this regard, a "rule of thumb" for the

[13] See J.W. Hicks, *supra* note 7, at § 10.01[1].

Section 4(1) exemption is that the SEC normally should not initiate an enforcement action against a party who is not a "control" person and who held the securities for at least two years prior to resale. On the other hand, because affiliates (or control persons) may be engaged in a distribution (rather than a transaction) when they resell their securities, such parties may not be able to avail themselves of the Section 4(1) exemption, irrespective of their stock holding period.[14]

[B] Restrictive Legends — Change in Circumstances

Restrictive legends normally are placed on securities acquired in an unregistered (*e.g.*, private) offering. Subject parties may claim that these restrictive legends establish their investment intent at the time of purchase. Not surprisingly, the courts have rejected this contention, holding that the purchase of stock from an issuer under an investment restriction is by no means a conclusive defense to underwriter status.[15] In certain situations, however, "change in circumstances" may serve as a valid defense to such status. When invoking the change in circumstances doctrine, the subject party asserts that he or she bought the stock with investment intent but that subsequent unforeseen changes compelled the earlier than planned sale of the stock.[16]

When the SEC adopted Rule 144 (discussed in § 5.05, *infra*), the Commission stated that

> the "change in circumstances" concept should no longer be considered as one of the factors in determining whether a person is an underwriter . . . since the circumstances of the seller are unrelated to the need of investors for the protections afforded by the registration [requirement] and other provisions of the Act.[17]

Hence, at least according to the SEC, the change in circumstances doctrine no longer retains its validity. On the other hand, it may be asserted that, to the extent that the change in circumstances defense is a valid test in terms of the statutory definition of one who purchases with an intent to redistribute, the Commission cannot by administrative fiat change the meaning of the statute.[18]

[C] Sales by Pledgees

The problem of assuming underwriter status, thereby rendering the Section 4(1) exemption unavailable, also arises in connection with sales by pledgees

[14] See *United States v. Sherwood*, 175 F. Supp. 480 (S.D.N.Y. 1959).

[15] See *G. Eugene England Foundation v. First Federal Corporation*, [1976-1977 Transfer Binder] Fed. Sec. L. Rep. (CCH) ¶ 95,837 (10th Cir. 1973); *Gilligan, Will & Co. v. SEC*, 267 F.2d 461 (2d Cir. 1959).

[16] See, *e.g.*, *Lectmor v. VTR, Inc.*, [1969-1970 Transfer Binder] Fed. Sec. L. Rep. (CCH) ¶ 92,707 (S.D.N.Y. 1970).

[17] *Securities Act Release* No. 5223 (1972).

[18] See T. Hazen, *The Law of Securities Regulation* 147 (1985).

(*e.g.*, banks) of securities pledged by control persons.[19] If the pledgor control person defaults on that debt (*e.g.*, a loan) secured by the pledge, can the pledgee (*e.g.*, a bank) sell the securities pledged without being deemed an underwriter? In *SEC v. Guild Films Co.*,[20] the pledgor, a controlling shareholder, pledged as collateral for a loan from a bank a substantial block of securities which bore a restrictive legend on the face of the securities. After the shareholder defaulted on the loan, the bank, knowing of the restrictive legend, sold some of the securities without a registration statement being filed. The Second Circuit held that the bank was an underwriter. Even though the bank may have taken the securities as collateral and had not directly dealt with the issuer, "the bank knew that [it] had been given unregistered stock and that the issuer had specifically forbidden that the stock be sold." Hence, to avoid Section 5 liability, the bank had to retain the securities pledged, invoke an exemption (*e.g.*, Section "4(1-1/2)" or Rule 144), or induce the issuer to file a registration statement.

Language contained in the *Guild Films* case may be criticized as being unduly onerous upon good faith pledgees. By asserting that a good faith pledgee participates in a distribution or takes with the view to distribute whenever a pledgor defaults, it may be asserted that the Second Circuit's rationale unfairly hampers legitimate commercial activity. On the other hand, it may be argued that the key issue is not the pledgee's culpability in facilitating the sale of unregistered securities to the investing public but rather whether such sales constituting a "distribution" should be permitted by the pledgee where the effect is to place into the hands of uninformed investors securities which have never been part of a registered offering. To purchasers of such securities who have not received adequate disclosure, the pledgee's good faith is of little solace.[21]

In this regard, the potentially harsh result of the *Guild Films* decision on legitimate commercial activity may be mitigated in practice by a pledgee bank's use of: (1) a covenant by the pledgor to effect registration of the securities ("a registration covenant") in the event of the pledgor's default (in all likelihood, such a covenant would not be worth the paper it was written on); (2) the invocation of the Section "4(1-1/2)" exemption (see § 5.06, *infra*); and (3) a more circumspect approach to accepting pledgor securities as collateral.

The thrust of the *Guild Films* decision evidently remains good law. The continued vitality of the court's broad language as it relates to good faith pledgees, however, is open to question. As the First Circuit opined, "[t]here is considerable support for the . . . view that a good faith pledgee who sells

---

[19] Note that a "pledge" is itself a "sale" under the Securities Act. See *Rubin v. United States*, 449 U.S. 424 (1981).

[20] 279 F.2d 485 (2d Cir.), *cert. denied*, 364 U.S. 819 (1960).

[21] See generally Rice, *The Effects of Registration on the Disposition of Pledged Securities*, 21 Stan. L. Rev. 1607 (1969); Sargent, *Pledgees and Foreclosure Rights Under the Securities Act of 1933*, 45 Va. L. Rev. 885 (1959).

unregistered shares at a foreclosure sale is not an 'underwriter.'"[22] Nonetheless, the SEC continues to adhere to the view that, under certain circumstances, the pledgee's sale of the securities pledged creates underwriter status.[23]

§ 5.05 Rule 144

[A] Background

Historically, that a non-affiliate acquired securities pursuant to a Section 4(2) private placement exemption did not thereafter preclude such person from reselling the securities. For example, as discussed earlier, a non-affiliate holding restricted securities normally could resell such securities after a substantial holding period, such as two or three years. Moreover, in certain situations, such non-affiliates, who acquired restricted securities allegedly for investment, could resell them pursuant to Section 4(1), notwithstanding a relatively recent acquisition date, if the seller could demonstrate a "change of circumstances." Nonetheless, given that the burden of proving the perfection of an exemption is upon the seller,[24] prudent parties exercised utmost caution when disposing of their securities without registration.

The situation for affiliates, and broker-dealers that executed orders to sell securities for the account of affiliates, was even more onerous. As a result of the SEC's 1946 administrative proceeding in *Ira Haupt,*[25] discussed in § 5.03[A], *supra*, it was difficult for the broker to determine whether an affiliate, when disposing of stock, was engaging in a "distribution" of the issuer's securities. The confusion that broker-dealers faced in attempting to determine whether a distribution would occur led the SEC to adopt Rule 154 in 1951.[26] Unfortunately, Rule 154 was of limited value because it was designed for brokers, but offered no protection to those persons on behalf of whom the sale was executed.[27]

After extensive analysis, the *Wheat Report* was issued in 1969.[28] The Report recommended a series of rules that sought to clarify the circumstances under which an affiliate or a non-affiliate could rely upon Section 4(1) for resale transactions. In 1970, the SEC substituted a single proposed rule as an

---

[22] *A.D.M. Corporation v. Thompson*, [1982-1983 Transfer Binder] Fed. Sec. L. Rep. (CCH) ¶ 99,206 (1st Cir. 1983) (and SEC "no-action" letters cited therein).

[23] See SEC Rule 144(d)(4)(D); T. Hazen, *supra* note 18, at 144-45; Hueter, *The Plight of the Pledgee Under Rule 144*, 3 Sec. Reg. L.J. 111 (1975).

[24] See, *e.g.*, *SEC v. Ralston Purina Co.*, 346 U.S. 119 (1953).

[25] 23 S.E.C. 589 (1946).

[26] See *Securities Act Release* No. 3421 (1951) *as amended by Securities Act Release* No. 3525 (1954).

[27] See S. Goldberg, *Private Placements and Restricted Securities* § 7.1 (1979); J.W. Hicks, *supra* note 7, at § 10.02[1].

[28] See *Disclosure to Investors — A Reappraisal of Federal Administrative Policies Under the '33 and '34 Acts* (1969) (*Wheat Report*).

alternative to the series recommended by the *Wheat Report.*[29] It was called Proposed Rule 144 and was designed to continue the SEC's efforts towards providing objective standards with respect to the availability of the Section 4(1) exemption. Finally, after lively debate and extensive public comments and suggestions, the final version of Rule 144 was adopted in 1972.[30]

Generally, subject to certain caveats, where adequate current information regarding an issuer is publicly available, Rule 144 acts as a safe harbor from liability under the registration provisions of the Securities Act, thereby permitting the public sale in ordinary trading transactions of limited amounts of securities owned by persons controlling, controlled by, or under common control with the issuer (*i.e.*, "affiliates"), and by other persons who have acquired "restricted securities" of the issuer. By confining its safe harbor in this manner, the Rule has the effect of limiting the development of public markets in securities of issuers where adequate public information is not available.

Hence, Rule 144 protects certain resale transactions from the Securities Act's registration mandates engaged in by: (1) persons who have acquired securities from either the issuer or an affiliate of the issuer in a transaction not involving a public offering ("restricted securities"), (2) persons who are deemed to be "affiliates" of the issuer at the time they propose to resell any securities of the issuer, and (3) brokers who effect transactions in compliance with the Rule. The safe harbor derived from Rule 144 is vitally important to the functioning of the securities markets. Absent the availability of an exemption, all offers or sales of securities must be registered under Section 5 of the Act. The exemptions normally available in the resale context are Section 4(1) for sellers and Section 4(4) for brokers. Their application under a given set of conditions, however, may be problematic. By creating a safe harbor for perfecting these exemptions, Rule 144 seeks to provide greater clarity in this area, without sacrificing investor protection.[31]

[B] Provisions of the Rule — Overview

Since its adoption in 1972, Rule 144 has been amended several times and substantially liberalized. The basic purpose of Rule 144, however, has remained the same. Generally, Rule 144 provides a safe harbor to both investors (*e.g.*, institutional as well as individual investors) who are selling their restricted or unrestricted securities without registration, and to brokers who are selling such securities on behalf of controlling persons. Rule 144 provides this safe harbor through an objective set of provisions, premised on the rationale that some relaxation of Securities Act disclosure and registration

---

[29] See *Securities Act Release* No. 5087 (1970).

[30] *Securities Act Release* No. 5223 (1972). See J.W. Hicks, *supra* note 7, at § 10.02[2].

[31] See M. Pollock, *Resale of Restricted Securities*, Corporate Practice Series (BNA) No. 46 (1986); Fogelson, *Rule 144 — A Summary Overview*, 37 Bus. Law. 1519 (1981).

requirements is appropriate with respect to relatively small secondary transactions. If the investor and the broker make the sales in compliance with the conditions set forth in Rule 144, they will neither be deemed underwriters nor engaged in a "distribution."[32]

An understanding of certain terms is crucial to an understanding of Rule 144. Rule 144 defines an affiliate of an issuer as a

> person that directly, or indirectly through one or more intermediaries, controls, or is controlled by, or is under common control with, such an issuer.

In addition, Rule 144 defines "restricted" securities as those

> securities that are acquired directly or indirectly from the issuer, or from an affiliate of the issuer, in a transaction or chain of transactions not involving any public offering, or securities acquired from the issuer that are subject to the resale limitations of Regulation D under the Act, or securities that are subject to the resale limitations of Regulation D and are acquired in a transaction or chain of transactions not involving any public offering.

These definitions are important. In certain situations, Rule 144 treats affiliates and non-affiliates differently. For example, only non-affiliates can resell restricted securities free of Rule 144 requirements after holding the securities for three years (see Rule 144(k)). In addition, Rule 144's holding requirements pertain only to restricted securities.

In order to utilize Rule 144 a person must meet five general requirements, some of which have been eliminated or substantially modified by the SEC in certain circumstances. First, there must be adequate current information concerning the issuer (see Rule 144(c)). This requirement is in accord with the underlying policy of the Securities Act which is to protect investors through adequate and fair disclosure. The information requirement can be satisfied in either of two ways: (1) the issuer can be subject to and be currently complying with the reporting requirements of the Exchange Act, or (2) the issuer, pursuant to Exchange Act Rule 15c2-11, can make publicly available information comparable to that required in Exchange Act reports.

A second requirement is that the person seeking to sell restricted securities (*e.g.*, stock acquired in a private offering) must meet the two-year holding period established by Rule 144 (see Rule 144(d)). The holding period ensures that the person assumed an investment stake in the prior purchase(s) and has not acted merely as the issuer's conduit for the sale to the public of unregistered securities.

Third, Rule 144 places restrictions on the amount of sales a person can make during a given time period in reliance on the Rule (see Rule 144(e)).

---

[32] See D. Goldwasser, *A Guide to Rule 144* (2d ed. 1978); Ash in 11 H. Sowards, *Federal Securities Act* § 6B.01 (1984); Gilroy & Kaufmann in 3 A.A. Sommer, *Securities Law Techniques* § 38.01 (1987).

This requirement is designed to ensure that a "distribution" does not take place and to lessen the impact of these sales on the trading markets. Generally, with certain exceptions (see Rule 144(k) discussed later in this section), sales of securities by a person under Rule 144 during any three-month period cannot exceed the greater of (i) 1% of the shares of that class outstanding as shown by the most recent statement of the issuer or (ii) the average weekly trading volume reported on all exchanges (and/or through NASDAQ or the consolidated transaction reporting system) for the four weeks preceding the filing of notice as specified in Rule 144(h).

The fourth requirement a prospective seller must meet to use Rule 144 is that the securities must be sold in brokerage transactions or in transactions directly with a market maker, without solicitation. Hence, a seller seeking to rely on Rule 144 must not "solicit or arrange for the solicitation of orders to buy securities in anticipation of or in connection with such transaction[s]."[33] Moreover, the broker must receive no more than the usual and customary broker's commission. Finally, notice of each sale must be filed with the SEC.

The "brokers' transactions" requirement referred to above (see Rule 144(f)) must be distinguished from the requirements with the same name in Rule 144(g). Rule 144(f) is one of the conditions that must be met by a seller intending to rely on the Rule. The broker also must find an exemption for its role in the transaction. Rule 144(g), by defining the terms "brokers' transactions" and by delineating aspects of "reasonable inquiry" to be conducted by the broker, greatly assists the broker in meeting Rule 144's safe harbor and to thereby perfect the Section 4(4) exemption.[34]

In order to invoke the exemption from Securities Act registration provided by Rule 144, all conditions of the Rule must be satisfied. Rule 144 is a "safe harbor" and, hence, is nonexclusive. Accordingly, even though a person has not met the conditions of Rule 144, he or she still may seek to invoke another exemption, such as the statutory Section 4(1) exemption. As the SEC, however, has stated in this regard:

> [P]ersons who offer or sell restricted securities without complying with Rule 144 are hereby put on notice by the Commission that in view of the broad remedial purposes of the Act and of public policy which strongly supports registration, they will have a substantial burden of proof in establishing that an exemption from registration is available for such offers or sales. . . . [S]uch persons and the brokers and other persons who participate in [such] transactions do so at their risk.[35]

---

[33] Rule 144(f), 17 C.F.R. § 230.144(f).

[34] See *Securities Act Release* Nos. 4445 (1962), 5168 (1972); J.W. Hicks, *supra* note 7, at § 10.11.

[35] *Securities Act Release* No. 5223 (1972).

[C] Certain Sales by Non-Affiliates

[1] Restricted Stock

Paragraph (k) of Rule 144 eliminates the current public information, volume limitation, manner of sale, and notice requirements for certain non-affiliates who have not been affiliated with the issuer for the preceding three months and who have beneficially owned the restricted securities for at least three years prior to the resale. Thus, Rule 144(k) effectively removes all restrictions for non-affiliates who have held restricted securities for three years and allows such non-affiliates to resell the securities as if they were nonrestricted securities. Rule 144(k) was designed to ease some of the burdens that the Rule places on the liquidity of restricted securities.

The SEC revised paragraph (k) of Rule 144 in 1983 to include current public information requirements among its exceptions.[36] Hence, as Rule 144 now stands, a person, who is not an affiliate and who has held the restricted securities for three years, can sell such securities to the public in any manner without any information whatsoever being available concerning the issuer. Consider this result with the SEC's assertion when it adopted Rule 144 in 1972:

> [T]he purpose and underlying policy of the [Securities] Act to protect investors requires . . . that there be *adequate current information concerning the issuer*, whether the resales of securities by persons result in a distribution or are effected in trading transactions. Accordingly, the availability of [Rule 144] is conditioned on the existence of adequate current public information.[37]

The SEC, with its amendments to Rule 144, essentially nullified the above rationale. One justification proffered is the deregulatory assertion that "[t]he purpose of the amendments is to relax restrictions on resales of securities that are more burdensome than necessary."[38] But nowhere does the Commission adequately explain why such restrictions are "more burdensome than necessary," particularly in view of the investor protection concerns which are highlighted throughout the 1972 Rule 144 adopting release. Hence, Rule 144, as revised, may be viewed as inconsistent with a major objective of the 1933 Act, which is to protect investors by ensuring that their decisions are informed, and also as incompatible with a fundamental premise underlying the Rule's adoption.

There is, of course, another side to this issue. In order to promote capital formation and induce investors to take a stake in start-up and similar enterprises, a non-affiliate who holds restricted securities must have a way to resell those securities if he or she chooses. Rule 144(k) now provides such shareholders with an opportunity to resell their securities after holding them

---

[36] See *Securities Act Release* No. 6488 (1983).

[37] *Securities Act Release* No. 5223 (1972) (emphasis supplied).

[38] *Securities Act Release* No. 6286 (1981). See *Securities Act Release* No. 6488 (1983).

for three years. In this way, the revised Rule meets prospective investor expectations and facilitates the flow of venture capital into the economy. The prospective purchaser is adequately protected, it may be asserted, by the application of the antifraud provisions. Moreover, a prospective buyer is not compelled to purchase the restricted securities. The determination whether to acquire such securities without adequate issuer current information being available should be left to the prospective purchaser, and not foreclosed by government intervention. As a final point, a non-affiliate who has held restricted stock for three years should come within the Section 4(1) exemption, provided that the sales taking place are transactions rather than a distribution. A three-year holding period should preclude a finding of underwriter status.

It may be asserted, however, that the 1983 revision to Rule 144 goes too far in liberalizing certain restrictions, while other overly burdensome limitations of the Rule have been virtually ignored by the SEC. If adequate information is not available concerning the issuer, a prospective non-affiliated seller should not be permitted to unload unlimited quantities of restricted securities into the market. The prospective seller should only be allowed to resell the restricted securities in limited volumes over a period of time. In this way, the prospective seller will not have to rely on the unwilling, nonreporting issuer for public information and will not be locked into the investment, while at the same time, he or she will not be able to dump large amounts of restricted securities into the market. In other words, paragraph (k) should permit a prospective non-affiliated seller to avoid the information requirements of Rule 144(c) only if that seller is willing to conform to the volume limitation restrictions of paragraph (e) of the Rule.

By promulgating paragraph (k), the SEC appears to take the position that the unloading of all of a non-affiliate's stock after a three-year holding period will never constitute a "distribution." Such a position is questionable. Given the substantial amount of restricted stock that a non-affiliate can unload in the marketplace under certain conditions, the SEC's blanket exemption spreads too far. A more sensible approach that would accommodate the competing interests would be to require a non-affiliate to adhere to the volume limitations of Rule 144(e).

Moreover, the Commission's amendments to Rule 144 are inconsistent with the disclosure approach to Rules 505 and 506 of Regulation D. If the Commission's objective is to ensure the providing of adequate information to "unsophisticated" investors of restricted securities, it should be irrelevant whether the investor purchased the securities from the issuer (pursuant to Regulation D) or from a shareholder who is not affiliated with the issuer (by means of Rule 144). In either case, the prospective purchaser's need for sufficient information to make an intelligent investment decision remains the same. Only in the Rule 505 or 506 Regulation D offering context, however, is the investor entitled to such information.[39] In the Rule 144 setting, by

[39] See discussion in §§ 3.06, 3.07[B][2], *supra*.

contrast, there is no mandated disclosure when the investor purchases restricted securities from a non-affiliated party (who has held the stock for at least three years) of an issuer which fails to provide current public information.

[2] Nonrestricted Stock

Rule 144 does not expressly cover a non-affiliate's disposition of nonrestricted stock. Nonetheless, the SEC, by its promulgation of Rule 144(k), appears to take the position that the sale of a non-affiliate's stock is not a separate distribution. Moreover, the assumption of underwriter status may no longer be a pitfall for non-affiliates selling nonrestricted stock due to the SEC staff's apparent abandonment of the presumptive underwriter doctrine. These developments may lead to the conclusion that a non-affiliate can freely resell nonrestricted stock without limitation pursuant to the Section 4(1) exemption. The Commission, however, has declined to expressly address this issue.

If the above represents the SEC's position, it is misplaced. In certain circumstances, a non-affiliate can hold a substantial percentage of nonrestricted stock. Permitting such nonaffiliates to freely liquidate their positions conflicts with both the definition of underwriter under Section 2(11) and the rationale underlying the Section 4(1) transactional exemption. In short, persons who dispose of large percentages of securities are, in actuality, engaging in a distribution rather than a transaction and, when they do so after a short holding period, are purchasing from an issuer with a view towards distribution. Support for this assertion may be premised on the fact that, if a substantial security holder were an affiliate, he or she would be subject to the volume limitation requirements of Rule 144(e). Yet, status as an affiliate in this context should not be determinative. At times, an affiliate may have more leverage to induce the issuer to file a registration statement for the securities the affiliate wishes to sell. Nevertheless, the detrimental effect on the capital trading markets and the investing public are identical, irrespective of whether one has affiliate status when reselling large quantities of stock.

The foregoing assertions are reinforced by the following scenario: Company X, for investment purposes, purchases 19% of Company Y's "unrestricted" stock on the open market. Insiders of Company Y, who still retain 51% ownership of the public company's stock and are able to elect the entire board of directors, have no desire to share control. Company X, pleased with its investment, increases its ownership interest in Company Y's "unrestricted" stock during a five-year period to 26%. One year later, after the insiders reject Company X's request to have a seat on Company Y's board of directors, Company X elects to sell all of its stock in Company Y on the open market during a thirty-day period.

Under the above scenario, Company X is not an "affiliate" of Company Y. It is neither in a "control" relationship nor can it compel Company Y to file a registration statement. Being a non-affiliate, its sales, by analogy to Rule 144(k), do not constitute a "distribution." Moreover, again in reference to Rules 144(d) and (k), a six-year holding period, as reflected in the illustration, indicates that Company X, not being a control person, acquired and held the securities with investment intent, hence mitigating against the assumption of underwriter status. The policies of the Securities Act, however, demand that Company X, absent registration, should not be able to unload its securities on the investing public.

With the promulgation of Rule 144(k) and the apparent abandonment of the presumptive underwriter doctrine, the SEC appears to have given the impression that non-affiliates can resell nonrestricted stock without limitation. Non-affiliates and their counsel, however, should not act with the same certainty as other parties and transactions that clearly come within Rule 144's scope. Because unlimited sales by non-affiliates should not be permitted for the reasons provided, the SEC should prescribe a safe harbor volume limitation under the Section 4(1) exemption for non-affiliates selling nonrestricted stock. This pronouncement may be effected either by amending Rule 144 or by promulgating a separate rule.[40]

[D] Chart

The following chart seeks to clarify the various requirements that a seller must comply with in order to come within the Rule 144 safe harbor. Remember, however, that the chart may simplify some of the pertinent requirements. Attention therefore should be directed to the relevant SEC releases, the discussion contained herein, and the text of the Rule itself.

---

[40] For further discussion, see Steinberg & Kempler, *The Application and Effectiveness of SEC Rule 144*, 49 Ohio State L.J. 473 (1988).

RULE 144

REQUIREMENTS FOR AFFILIATES AND NONAFFILIATES OF THE ISSUER

	Affiliate Selling Non-Restricted Securities	Affiliate Selling Restricted Securities	Nonaffiliate (Securities Are Restricted)	Nonaffiliate Selling Restricted Securities Who Complies With Three Year Holding Requirement of Rule 144(k)
Rule 144(c) -- Current Public Information	Must Comply	Must Comply	Must Comply	No Compliance Necessary
Rule 144(d) -- Holding Period for Restricted Securities	No Compliance Necessary	Must Comply	Must Comply	Must hold Restricted Securities for Three Years
Rule 144(e) -- Limitation on Amount of Securities Sold	Must Comply	Must Comply	Must Comply	No Compliance Necessary
Rule 144(f) -- Manner of Sale	Must Comply	Must Comply	Must Comply	No Compliance Necessary
Rules 144(h) and (i)-- Notice of Proposed Sale and Intention to Sell	Must Comply	Must Comply	Must Comply	No Compliance Necessary
Rule 144(j) -- Non-Exclusion of the Rule	Applicable	Applicable	Applicable	Applicable

§ 5.06 The Section "4(1-1/2)" Exemption

One exemption thus far not discussed is the so-called Section "4(1-1/2)" exemption. This exemption, based largely on SEC no-action letters and other SEC pronouncements, seeks to fill a gap in the statutory exemptive scheme. Upon examining this framework, it appears that none of the statutory or regulatory exemptions expressly cover unlimited sales of securities by affiliates (as well as sales of restricted securities by non-affiliates) who desire to sell such securities in a routine private transaction after a short holding period. By way of example, Rule 144 neither helps a "control" person who wishes to sell all of his or her stock in a private transaction nor a non-affiliate who has not held restricted securities for a sufficient time period to invoke the Rule. Such sales frequently occur and the SEC, provided that certain conditions are met, appears not to be especially troubled by their presence. In this respect, the Commission has stated:

> In making such private sales, the affiliates presumably would rely on the so-called "Section 4(1-1/2)" exemption. This is a hybrid exemption not specifically provided for in the 1933 Act but clearly within its intended purpose. The exemption basically would permit affiliates to make private sales of securities held by them so long as some of the established criteria for sales under both Section 4(1) and Section 4(2) of the Act are satisfied.[41]

Unfortunately, the Commission hasdeclined to identify the pertinent "established criteria" of Section 4(1) and Section 4(2) which must be satisfied in order for a party successfully to invoke the Section "4(1-1/2)" exemption. However, certain criteria relevant for perfecting the exemption may be as follows:

> — While the source of the Section "4(1-1/2)" exemption is Section 4(1), the determination of appropriate standards to govern the exemption is primarily derived from Section 4(2) authority.
>
> — Advertising and general solicitation are not permitted.
>
> — Although no finite number has been established, there is some limit (*e.g.*, thirty-five) on the number of purchasers.
>
> — Whether the prospective seller must hold the securities for a certain length of time (*e.g.*, two years) is uncertain. The holding point may be more relevant where there is no public information available concerning the issuer or where a large number of shares are sought to be sold.
>
> — The purchasers' access to registration-type information (or the actual providing of such information) as well as purchaser sophistication are relevant factors.[42]

---

[41] *Securities Act Release* No. 6188 (1980).

[42] See Olander & Jacks, *The Section 4(1-1/2) Exemption — Reading Between the Lines of the Securities Act of 1933*, 15 Sec. Reg. L.J. 339 (1988), also published in *Contemporary Issues in Securities Regulation* 151 (M. Steinberg ed. 1988);

§ 5.07 Corporate Reorganizations

[A] In General

Corporations as well as other entities frequently engage in reorganizations. State corporation statutes, corporate charters, and similar controlling instruments normally require shareholder approval or consent of mergers, consolidations, transfer of assets and reclassifications of stock. These reorganizations normally result in the exchange of shares or the issuance of new stock. Rule 145(a) makes it clear that when such plans of reorganization are submitted to shareholders for approval, the corporation makes an "offer to sell" within the meaning of Section 2(3). Rule 145, therefore, has several ramifications.

[B] Rule 145 — Ramifications

An offer to sell securities pursuant to Rule 145 triggers the registration requirements of Section 5, as well as due diligence obligations (including the rigorous culpability standards of Section 11). Rule 145 transactions may be registered pursuant to the Securities Act on Form S-4. Form S-4 improves the effectiveness of the business reorganization prospectus by requiring that information be presented in a more accessible and meaningful format.[43]

By triggering the registration requirements, Rule 145 also triggers Section 5's "gun-jumping" prohibition.[44] Thus, communications designed to influence shareholders' votes may be viewed as constituting offers to sell in the pre-filing period and, hence, violations of Section 5(c). Rule 145(b) provides certain exceptions in this respect, authorizing the corporation to communicate basic information, including the issuer's name, a brief description of the business of the parties, and a brief description of the transaction. Compliance with the provisions of Rule 145(b) has the effect of protecting the communication from constituting an "offer to sell" under Section 2(3) or from being deemed a "prospectus" under Section 2(10). In this regard, the pre-filing publicity notice permitted under Rule 135 is also available for such transactions.[45]

[C] "Downstream Sales"

The ramifications of Rule 145 do not end after the shareholders approve a plan of reorganization. Rule 145(c) addresses the problem of "downstream sales." Parties to a Rule 145 transaction who publicly sell or publicly offer to

---

Schneider, *Section 4(1-1/2) — Private Resales of Restricted or Control Securities*, 49 Ohio State L.J. 501 (1988); ABA Committee Report, *The Section "4(1-1/2)" Phenomenon: Private Resales of "Restricted" Securities*, 34 Bus. Law. 1961 (1979).

[43] See *Securities Act Release* No. 6578 (1985). See generally Campbell, *Rule 145: Mergers, Acquisitions and Recapitalizations Under the Securities Act of 1933*, 56 Fordham L. Rev. 277 (1987).

[44] For discussion on conditioning the market ("gun-jumping"), see § 4.02[A][2], *supra*.

[45] Rule 135 is addressed in § 4.02[A][3], *supra*.

sell their securities may be deemed to be engaged in a distribution and may therefore be underwriters within the meaning of Section 2(11). These parties can avoid underwriter status, however, by meeting the criteria contained in Rule 145(d).

As an initial point, for parties who are neither affiliates of the acquired company nor affiliates of the acquiring company, the securities received in a Rule 145 transaction are nonrestricted securities, thereby having no restrictions on resale.

In regard to parties who are affiliates of an entity *acquired* pursuant to a Rule 145 transaction, the SEC in 1984, consistent with its Rule 144 modifications, substantially relaxed the "resale" provisions of Rule 145. As a result, such parties (who are affiliates of the acquired, but not of the acquiring, entity) have much greater leeway (than pre-1984) in reselling their securities without fear of assuming underwriter status. Today, such parties receiving securities in registered business combinations and who subsequently transfer such securities will not be deemed underwriters if:

i. The securities are sold in compliance with the provisions of paragraphs (c), (e), (f), and (g) of Rule 144; or

ii. The party is a non-affiliate of the issuer (*i.e.*, a non-affiliate of the acquiring company), has held the securities for at least a two-year period, and the issuer has complied with the current public reporting requirement of Rule 144(c) (by either being an Exchange Act reporting company or by making adequate information available); or

iii. The party is a non-affiliate of the issuer and has held the securities for at least three years.[46]

Note the effect of the SEC's amendments to Rule 145 (with respect to persons who were affiliates of an entity acquired in a Rule 145 transaction and who are non-affiliates of the acquiring entity). First, such non-affiliates of the issuer (*i.e.*, non-affiliates of the acquiring company) can dispose of all of their securities after two years if the issuer has maintained adequate current public information. Second, such non-affiliates, after a three-year holding period, can sell all their shares even if the issuer is not making adequate current information available.

The public policy assessments made by the Commission in adopting these revisions can be questioned on much the same basis as was made with respect to the amendments to Rule 144 (see § 5.05[C], *supra*). Undoubtedly, the Commission's amendments to Rule 145 are a victory for deregulation and capital formation. Some may claim, however, that the costs are too great: By permitting non-affiliates of the issuer to "dump" their securities on the investing public with no information being available about the issuer deals a blow to two fundamental purposes underlying the federal securities laws, namely, to ensure the integrity of the financial marketplace and to enable

---

[46] See *Securities Act Release* No. 6508 (1984).

investors to have adequate information before them so that they can make informed investment decisions.

[D] "Spin-Offs"

A word also should be said about "spin-offs." A "spin-off" occurs, for example, when a parent corporation (either with or without a bona fide business purpose) distributes shares of a privately-held subsidiary as a stock dividend to its shareholders. In such event, it is only a matter of time before these shares become publicly traded. Absent the availability of an exemption, "spin-offs" thereby have the effect of evading the registration requirements. Due to this concern, the SEC and the courts have held that this technique, absent the availability of an exemption, calls for 1933 Act registration. Moreover, parent corporations that cause their subsidiaries to engage in such practices are deemed to be "underwriters."[47]

Defendants, charged with failing to register a "spin-off" offering, have asserted that the stock dividend distributed to shareholders was not an "offer to sell" or "sale" within the meaning of Section 2(3) of the Securities Act because it was not "for value," and hence, was not in violation of Section 5. The courts have rejected this argument, reasoning that the creation of a public market for the spun-off securities constitutes value to the parent corporation when the stockholders dispose of these securities. Moreover, SEC Rule 15c2-11 effectively thwarts public trading of securities acquired in unregistered spin-offs by prohibiting broker-dealers from either initiating or continuing to provide price quotations for a security unless adequate public information is available with respect to both the issuer and the security.[48]

---

[47] See *SEC v. Datronics Engineers, Inc.*, 490 F.2d 250 (4th Cir. 1973), *cert. denied*, 416 U.S. 937 (1974); *SEC v. Harwyn Industries Corp.*, 326 F. Supp. 943 (S.D.N.Y. 1971).

[48] See T. Hazen, *supra* note 18, at 170-72; Bloomenthal, *Market-Makers, Manipulators and Shell Games*, 45 St. John's L. Rev. 597 (1971); Long, *Control of the Spin-Off Device Under the Securities Act of 1933*, 25 Okla. L. Rev. 317 (1972); Lorne, *The Portfolio Spin-off and Securities Registration*, 52 Texas L. Rev. 918 (1974); Note, *Registration of Stock Spin-offs Under the Securities Act of 1933*, 1980 Duke L.J. 965; cases cited *supra* note 47.

CHAPTER 6

DUE DILIGENCE AND SECURITIES ACT LIABILITY

§ 6.01 Introduction

This chapter addresses the concept of due diligence, liability consequences, and other ramifications in both registered and unregistered offerings. The chapter begins with a discussion of Section 11's statutory framework. A number of key concepts under the statute are reviewed, including persons subject to liability under Section 11, requirements for invoking the right of action, defenses (particularly the due diligence defenses), damages, contribution, and indemnification.

Concerning due diligence in the registered offering context, the *BarChris* case[1] still serves as the most appropriate vehicle for focusing on this concept. As *BarChris* illustrates, although technically a defense, due diligence is a necessary function to be performed. The discussion thereafter addresses the various parties who may assert the due diligence defense and the degree of investigation required for each such party, including: directors ("inside" as well as "outside"), signatories of the registration statement, attorneys (who are not liable under Section 11 unless they "expertise" a portion of the registration statement, serve as a director, or in some other capacity that brings them within the provision's reach), accountants (who serve as "experts"), and underwriters.

After analyzing *BarChris* and its ramifications, the chapter discusses the controversial issue, particularly for underwriters, of due diligence in the integrated disclosure framework. These concerns, as the materials in § 6.07, *infra*, point out, are accentuated in the shelf-registration context. Many critics claim that the SEC's response, principally the adoption of Rule 176, is wholly inadequate. On the other hand, the Securities Industry Association's (SIA's) solution may be viewed as too self-interested. The ultimate resolution reached must take care of the legitimate concerns of underwriters yet be consistent with investor protection.

The last portion of the chapter focuses on Section 12(2) of the Securities Act which contains a "reasonable care" defense that, depending on the circumstances, may be similar to Section 11's "due diligence" defense. Importantly, Section 12(2) is Section 11's remedial counterpart in the *unregistered* offering context. Of course, Section 12(2) also may be invoked

---

[1] *Escott v. BarChris Construction Corporation*, 283 F. Supp. 643 (S.D.N.Y. 1968).

in connection with oral communications made and prospectuses used in registered offerings. Moreover, in either the registered or unregistered offering setting, plaintiffs always can seek to invoke Section 10(b) of the Securities Exchange Act.[2]

§ 6.02 The Registered Offering — Framework of Section 11

As discussed in the foregoing materials (you may wish to review the discussion in §§ 3.01 and 4.01, *supra*, at this time), a registered offering under the Securities Act requires that a registration statement be utilized. A key policy underlying this requirement is to enable prospective purchasers to make informed investment decisions based upon the disclosure of adequate and truthful information regarding the issuer, its associated persons, and the offering. This policy is frustrated when a registration statement (including the prospectus which comprises part of the registration statement) contains materially false or misleading statements.

In view of the above, investors under certain conditions may recover their losses if they purchase securities pursuant to a registration statement which contains a material misrepresentation or nondisclosure. The provision most likely to be invoked in this context is Section 11 of the Securities Act.

[A] Parties Subject to Section 11 Liability

Section 11(a) of the Securities Act specifies the classes of persons who may be subject to liability for material misstatements or omissions contained in the registration statement (including the prospectus which is part of the registration statement). Parties subject to Section 11 liability include: (1) all persons who sign the registration statement (including, pursuant to Section 6(a), the "issuer, its principal executive officer or officers, its principal financial officer, its controller or principal accounting officer, and the majority of its board of directors or persons performing similar functions"), (2) every director (or person performing similar functions) or partner of the issuer, (3) every person named with his or her consent in the registration statement as being or about to become a person stated in (2) above, (4) every expert "who has with his consent been named as having prepared or certified any part of the registration statement, or as having prepared or certified any report or valuation which is used in connection with the registration statement, with respect to the statement in such registration statement, report, or valuation which purports to have been prepared or certified by him," (5) every underwriter of the offering, and (6) pursuant to Section 15, every control person of the issuer.

Due to the exhaustive enumeration of those parties subject to suit under Section 11, the courts have refused to impose "aiding and abetting" liability

[2] See *Herman & MacLean v. Huddleston*, 459 U.S. 375 (1983), discussed in § 7.06, *infra*.

pursuant to that provision. For example, in *In re Equity Funding Corp. of America Securities Litigation*,[3] the court observed:

> [W]here a statute specifically limits those who may be held liable for the conduct described by the statute, the courts cannot extend liability, under a theory of aiding and abetting, to those who do not fall within the categories of potential defendants described by the statute.[4]

[B] Elements of Right of Action

Generally, providing that the interstate commerce requirement has been met, a private action for damages under Section 11(a) may be brought by "any person acquiring such security" unless it can be shown that, at the time of purchase, the purchaser knew of the misstatement or omission. Privity between the purchaser and the defendant is not required for recovery. Moreover, the Section 11 right of action is available in the initial offering setting as well as when those shares are subsequently traded in the aftermarket. In practical effect, however, the "tracing" requirement often may have the effect of nullifying the Section 11 right of action in the aftermarket context. For example, in *Kirkwood v. Taylor*,[5] stockholders purchasing in the aftermarket were held to lack standing under Section 11 with respect to those shares that they were unable affirmatively to establish were purchased in the public offering. Hence, pursuant to the tracing requirement, plaintiffs must show not that they "might" have purchased shares by means of a deficient registration statement in a particular offering, but that they in fact did purchase such shares pursuant to that specific offering (and registration statement). Given the practical difficulties of "tracing," this requirement is a burdensome one for "aftermarket" Section 11 plaintiffs.[6]

In addition, a plaintiff bringing suit under Section 11 normally need not show reliance upon the misstatement or omission. In fact, he or she need not even have read the prospectus. Pursuant to Section 11(a), however, where the plaintiff acquired the securities more than twelve months after the effective date of the registration statement and if the issuer has made generally available an "earnings statement" covering this twelve-month period, he or she must prove reliance on the misstatement or omission. Such reliance may be shown by means other than the actual reading of the prospectus.[7]

Another important point is that a plaintiff seeking to recover under Section 11 need not prove that the material misrepresentation or nondisclosure

---

[3] 416 F. Supp. 161 (D.C. Cal. 1976).

[4] *Id.* at 181.

[5] [1984-1985 Transfer Binder] Fed. Sec. L. Rep. (CCH) ¶ 91,877 (D. Minn. 1984).

[6] See *Barnes v. Osofky*, 373 F.2d 269 (2d Cir. 1967); *McFarland v. Memorex Corp.*, 493 F. Supp. 631 (N.D. Cal. 1980).

[7] See SEC Rule 158 (defining the terms: "earning statement," "made generally available to its security holders," and "effective date of the registration statement," for the purposes of the reliance requirement as set forth in the final paragraph of § 11(a)).

"caused" the loss. In this regard, however, Section 11(e), supported by case law, permits the defendant to reduce (either in part or totally) the plaintiff's monetary recovery by showing that the loss (or portion thereof) was attributable to factors other than the material misrepresentation(s) or nondisclosure(s) contained in the registration statement.[8]

Section 11's seemingly broad express right of action also is limited by the relatively short statute of limitations. Section 13 of the Securities Act essentially provides that an action pursuant to Section 11 must be brought

> within one year after the discovery of the untrue statement or the omission, or after such discovery should have been made by the exercise of reasonable diligence . . . [but] in no event shall any such action be brought . . . more than three years after the security was offered to the public.

To recap, under Section 11, *a plaintiff*:

— must have purchased the security where a means or instrumentality of interstate commerce was used in connection with the offer or sale;

— at the time of purchase, must not have known of the misrepresentation or nondisclosure;

— must show that the misrepresentation or nondisclosure was "material," meaning that reasonable investors would have considered the pertinent information important in making their investment decisions;

— need not establish privity;

— can recover for aftermarket purchases, subject to the difficult "tracing" requirement;

— normally need not show reliance upon the misrepresentation or nondisclosure;

— need not prove that the misrepresentation or nondisclosure "caused" the loss (in other words, causation is presumed once a material misstatement or nondisclosure has been shown to exist);

— must bring the action within the time period set forth by Section 13's statute of limitations.

[C] Defenses

[1] General

Section 11(b) provides a number of due diligence defenses for persons other than the issuer. Generally, the only defenses available to the issuer, who otherwise is strictly liable, are the purchaser's knowledge of the misstatement or omission, lack of materiality, lack of causation, and expiration of the

[8] See, *e.g.*, *Akerman v. Orxy Communications, Inc.*, [1984 Transfer Binder] Fed. Sec. L. Rep. (CCH) ¶ 91,680 (S.D.N.Y. 1984), *aff'd*, 810 F.2d 344 (2d Cir. 1987).

statute of limitations. These defenses, of course, are available to any defendant.

In addition to the above defenses and the "due diligence" defense (which will be addressed shortly), a non-issuer defendant, who discovers a material misstatement or omission in the registration statement, may avoid liability by taking the action specified in Section 11(b)(1) or (2), namely:

(1) *Before* the effective date of the registration statement or part thereof in question, he or she (1) resigns from or takes such steps as are permitted by law to resign from, or ceases or refuses to act in, every office, capacity or relationship ascribed to him or her in the registration statement, and (2) advises the SEC and the issuer in writing of the action taken and disavowing responsibility for such part of the registration statement.

(2) *After* such part of the registration statement has become effective, (1) if he or she was unaware that it had become effective, and (2) upon becoming aware of such fact, acts forthwith, (3) advises the SEC in writing as set forth above, and (4) gives reasonable public notice that such part of the registration statement had become effective without his or her knowledge.

[2] Due Diligence — Overview

The "due diligence" defenses are contained in Section 11(b)(3). As regards the unexpertised portion of the registration statement, a defendant must show that, after reasonable investigation he or she had reason to believe and did believe at the time such part of the registration statement became effective, there were no material misstatements or omissions. As regards the "expertised" part, a defendant (other than the responsible expert) need show only that he or she had no reasonable ground to believe and did not believe that the expertised portion of the registration statement was defective. While a non-expert is not required to make an investigation of expertised information, he or she must "have no reasonable ground to believe" such information is inaccurate.[9] An expert, on the other hand, is required to show that after reasonable investigation, he or she had reasonable ground to believe and did believe his or her statement to be accurate. In other words, an expert is required to exercise the same standard of care regarding the part expertised by him or her as a non-expert is required to exercise regarding the non-expertised portion of the registration statement. Experts are not subject to liability for misstatements or omissions in the unexpertised part of the registration statement merely by reason of their involvement as experts.

[3] Due Diligence Standard

Section 11(c) provides that the standard of reasonableness by which the concept of "reasonable investigation" is to be measured is that required of "a

[9] The same standard applies under § 11(b)(3)(D) to statements in the registration statement purporting to have been made by a public official or purporting to be a copy or extract from a public official document.

prudent man in the management of his own property." In this regard, the "prudent man" standard applies not only to the reasonableness of one's investigation but also to the reasonableness of one's belief.

While opinions may differ as to whether the standard is unitary or elastic, the *BarChris* decision, which is discussed in § 6.04, *infra*, unequivocally indicates that the degree of responsibility, and *a fortiori* the extensiveness of the investigation required to establish due diligence, largely will depend upon the type of person and the nature of his or her relationship with the issuer. While *BarChris* let it be known that the statutory due diligence obligations are not to be treated lightly, the decision did not resolve many of the problems inherent in the vague "reasonable investigation" standard. In 1982 the SEC adopted Rule 176 which lists a number of factors to be taken into account as "circumstances affecting the determination of what constitutes reasonable investigation." These factors are:

(a) The type of issuer;

(b) The type of security;

(c) The type of person;

(d) The office held when the person is an officer;

(e) The presence or absence of another relationship to the issuer when the person is a director or proposed director;

(f) Reasonable reliance on officers, employees, and others whose duties should have given them knowledge of the particular facts (in light of the functions and responsibilities of the particular person with respect to the issuer and the filing);

(g) When the person is an underwriter, the type of underwriting arrangement, the role of the particular person as an underwriter and the availability of information with respect to the registrant; and

(h) Whether, with respect to a fact or document incorporated by reference, the particular person had any responsibility for the fact or document at the time of the filing from which it was incorporated.[10]

Critics contend that these guidelines do little to provide meaningful content to the "reasonable investigation" standard. Rule 176 and the ramifications of due diligence in the integrated disclosure framework will be addressed in §§ 6.05-6.07, *infra*.

§ 6.03 Contribution and Indemnification

Under the federal securities laws, violators are subject to joint and several liability. Accordingly, a plaintiff is entitled to recover the entire judgment

[10] 17 C.F.R. § 230.176.

against any violator. In order to distribute judgment and settlement costs among joint violators, the two common techniques used are contribution and indemnification. While indemnification involves a shifting of the entire loss from one defendant to another person, contribution involves a sharing of the damages among the tortfeasors.

Section 11(f) of the Securities Act clearly provides for a right to *contribution.* The provision, however, leaves unsettled the extent to which losses are to be shared among the parties. The traditional view is that the parties share the entire loss on a pro rata basis (*i.e.*, equally among the joint tortfeasors irrespective of individual fault). The emerging view is that apportionment of damages should be premised upon the relative culpability of the various parties.[11]

The right to *indemnification* is far less certain. Neither Section 11 nor any other provision of the securities laws provides for such a right. The SEC's position, as contained in Item 512(i) of Regulation S-K, is that indemnification of officers, directors, and controlling persons of the registrant for liability arising under the Securities Act is against public policy, and, hence, unenforceable. Interestingly, however, the SEC has no such hostility to the procurement of insurance. Rule 461(c) provides that normally

> [i]nsurance against liabilities arising under the [Securities] Act, whether the cost of insurance is borne by the registrant, the insured or some other person, will not be considered a bar to acceleration [of the effective date of the registration statement].[12]

A more troubling issue is whether the underwriter, pursuant to an indemnity contract with the issuer or its controlling persons, may thereby avoid liability. With respect to intentional securities law violations by the underwriter, the courts have denied indemnification. Generally, the courts reason that, permitting a party to avoid monetary liability for its own reckless or willful misconduct, is contrary to the securities acts' objective of inducing parties to be scrupulous about their disclosure obligations. Moreover, the issuer's indemnification of the underwriter is suspect in that the funds ultimately come out of the shareholders' pockets, the very individuals who were damaged by the misconduct.[13] The foregoing reasons also are applicable for prohibiting indemnification where the underwriter has been negligent.

---

[11] See Comment, *Apportioning Contribution Shares Under the Federal Securities Acts: A Suggested Approach for an Unsettled Area*, 50 Fordham L. Rev. 450 (1981) (and cases cited therein). See generally Block and Barton, *Contribution and Indemnification Under the Federal Securities Laws*, 11 Sec. Reg. L.J. 351 (1984); Ruder, *Multiple Defendants in Securities Law Fraud Cases: Aiding and Abetting, Conspiracy, In Pari Delicto, Indemnification and Contribution*, 120 U. Pa. L. Rev. 597 (1972).

[12] Item 512(i) of Regulation S-K; 17 C.F.R. § 230.461(c).

[13] See, *e.g., Globus v. Law Research Serv., Inc.*, 418 F.2d 1276 (2d Cir. 1969), *cert. denied*, 397 U.S. 913 (1970).

Some courts, however, may enforce an indemnity contract where the underwriter's culpability does not surpass that of negligence.[14]

§ 6.04 Due Diligence in the Registered Offering Context

As an initial matter, it should be pointed out (see § 3.01, *supra*) that, strictly speaking, due diligence is a defense that may be asserted by the subject party rather than an affirmative obligation. If the statements made in the registration statement are true or, alternatively, if no lawsuit is brought, no liability will be incurred for an individual's failure to exercise due diligence. On the other hand, if an action is instituted and a material misstatement or omission is shown, liability often may be avoided under Section 11 only by proving the performance of due diligence. For this reason, as a practical matter, due diligence is a necessity.

Although not a recent decision, the seminal case on due diligence in the Section 11 context is *Escott v. BarChris Construction Corporation.*[15] In *BarChris*, convertible debentures of BarChris Construction Corporation, the issuer, were sold to the public by means of a registration statement filed with the SEC. Plaintiffs, who were purchasers of these debentures, alleged that the registration statement contained material misstatements and omissions. Relief was sought against various defendants, including the directors, the persons who signed the registration statement, the underwriters, and the auditors. In imposing liability against the various parties, the *BarChris* court set forth several key principles.

[A] Directors

In analyzing the due diligence defense raised by the defendant directors, *BarChris* draws a distinction between inside and outside directors, and between directors based upon the extent of their knowledge of or access to the pertinent facts. Certainly one would expect a director who also serves as the principal executive officer to be required to perform more diligently than an outside director who otherwise has no relationship with the issuer. As another example, many corporations have established executive committees, comprised of two or three directors who, in many cases, make decisions that otherwise would be within the province of the entire board of directors. Depending upon the circumstances, an inordinate hardship would be imposed upon directors not serving on those committees if they were held to the same degree of responsibility.

---

[14] See Comment, *Allocation of Damages Under the Federal Securities Laws*, 60 Wash. U. L.Q. 211 (1982) (and cases cited therein). For discussion of contribution and indemnification under § 10(b) of the Securities Exchange Act, see § 7.01, *infra*.

[15] 283 F. Supp. 643 (S.D.N.Y. 1968). See also, *Feit v. Leasco Data Processing Equip. Corp.*, 332 F. Supp. 544 (E.D.N.Y. 1971), for an extensive discussion of liability under § 11 of the Securities Act.

BarChris indicates that, while less may be required of certain outside directors in order to meet their due diligence obligations, reasonable investigation still requires affirmative action. Hence, even outside directors must endeavor to make some type of an independent verification of the information contained in the registration statement. Clearly, a director who makes no effort to investigate will not be able to sustain his or her burden of establishing that he or she acted with due diligence. It may be argued that an outside director should: seek to attend board of director meetings regarding the offering; review the registration statement with care (probing relevant corporate personnel and counsel on the factual contents and representations made therein); review the Exchange Act filed documents that are incorporated by reference into the registration statement; have a familiarity of the company's major contracts; with the aid of competent advisers, assess the abilities of management as well as the company's reputation; ask questions and follow up if necessary. Although the performance of the foregoing actions may not guarantee absolution from liability, it should provide persuasive evidence that the outside director met his or her due diligence obligations.

[B] Signatories

Persons who sign the registration statement (normally inside directors and officers of the issuer) may be held to stringent due diligence obligations. This is despite the fact that, had they not signed, their respective duties of investigation, particularly in the case of officers not holding directorships, may have differed. The rationale for holding signatories, particularly those who are inside directors or who otherwise hold principal corporate offices (even if not directors), to a strict standard of due diligence is that prospective investors reasonably may assume that, by signing the registration statement, the signatories represent that it is an accurate statement of the information contained therein.

To a large extent, *BarChris* may be viewed as treating "inside" signatories in effect as guarantors of the accuracy of the registration statement (indeed the court may have said as much). Interestingly, however, Congress specifically rejected a proposal that would have made directors guarantors in this context. On the other hand, it may be said that *BarChris* "does not deny the [due diligence] defense [to such inside signatories], but recognizes the obvious difficulty of establishing it."[16]

[C] Attorneys

Due diligence is a concern for lawyers who are involved in a registered offering. For example, counsel may: (1) serve as a director of the issuer, (2) act as an expert within the meaning of Section 11(a)(4) (*e.g.*, by rendering a

---

[16] Folk, *Civil Liabilities Under the Federal Securities Acts: The BarChris Case*, 55 Va. L. Rev. 1, 22 (1969). See H.R. Rep. No. 85, 73rd Cong., 1st Sess. 5 (1933); H.R. Rep. No. 152, 73rd Cong., 1st Sess. 26 (1933); Landis, *The Legislative History of the Securities Act of 1933*, 28 Geo. Wash. L. Rev. 29, 48 (1959).

tax opinion that is contained in the registration statement), and (3) perform due diligence investigations on behalf of a client in its stead.

With respect to assuming "expert" status, it is clear that an attorney who renders legal advice or assists in the preparation of the registration statement does not thereby become an expert within the meaning of Section 11. Further, because Section 11 limits the class of potential defendants, attorneys cannot be held liable under Section 11 on an aiding and abetting theory.[17] They evidently can be held liable, however, as aiders and abettors under Section 10(b) of the Securities Exchange Act (or perhaps under Section 12(2) of the Securities Act).

In *BarChris*, the young attorney, Birnbaum, while not a director at the time the registration statement originally was filed, was a director when he signed the later amendments. He thereby subjected himself to Section 11 liability as a director and as a signatory. Unfortunately, Birnbaum made no investigation whatsoever and relied on the statements of others. The court noted that, while Birnbaum was not an executive officer in any real sense, he was named as such in the prospectus. Further, by virtue of his duties as in-house counsel and keeper of the corporate minutes, he had considerable information about the corporation's affairs. While not aware of many of the inaccuracies in the prospectus, as a lawyer he must have appreciated some of them. He should have known his statutory obligations and made a reasonable investigation.

The court's opinion indicates that, even if he were not a signatory to the registration statement, Birnbaum would have been subject to Section 11 liability. In this regard, note that his liability would have been based upon his status as a director and not as an attorney. However, the fact that Birnbaum was an attorney was taken into consideration in determining whether he conducted a reasonable investigation.

Grant, the issuer's outside counsel, was liable both as a director and as a signatory. The court took into account his role of being primarily responsible for drafting the registration statement, reasoning that "more was required of him in the way of reasonable investigation than could fairly be expected of a director who had no connection with this work."[18] The court indicated that, by its holding, it was not seeking to establish an unduly onerous standard for outside counsel who also serves as a director. Rather, each case must turn on its own facts. Here, even taking into account that BarChris' officers had misled Grant, "there . . . [were] too many instances in which Grant failed to make an inquiry which, if pursued, would have put him on his guard."[19]

As noted above, counsel who renders a formal legal opinion which is included in the registration statement with his or her consent is considered an "expert" within the ambit of Section 11. For example, counsel may proffer an opinion that (1) the company and its subsidiaries are duly incorporated,

[17] See *Herman & McLean v. Huddleston*, 459 U.S. 375, 386 n.22 (1983).
[18] 283 F. Supp. at 690.
[19] *Id.* at 692.

(2) licenses are in order, (3) the company's securities are validly issued under state law and are non-assessable, and (4) there has been no default under material contracts. Such opinions rarely are problematic. More difficult issues arise when counsel proffers an opinion that is critical to the "deal," such as an opinion by tax counsel concerning the federal tax implications.

A different question is presented where an attorney, acting as counsel for either the issuer or the underwriter, furnishes a "comfort opinion." A comfort opinion essentially is a statement that, based on counsel's participation in the preparation of the registration statement and conferences with representatives of the issuer, underwriters and public accountants, he or she has no reason to believe that the registration statement violates Section 11. In order not to be subject to Section 11 liability, counsel should ensure that neither the opinion nor its contents appear in the registration statement.

In practice, the issuer, directors and underwriters frequently delegate their due diligence investigations to counsel. Such delegation, as *BarChris* makes clear, is appropriate. In effect, while counsel seeks to perform an adequate investigation on behalf of his or her client, it is the client, and not counsel, who will be held liable under Section 11 if counsel fails to meet the requisite standard of care. In such instances, however, counsel may well be faced with a legal malpractice suit.

When counsel performs due diligence on behalf of a client, counsel, at a minimum, must stand in the client's "shoes." The scope of the due diligence obligation depends on such factors as the client's position, its relationship with the issuer, and its involvement in the preparation of the registration statement. The extensiveness of the investigation appropriate may range from that required of an outside director who has no other affiliation with the issuer to the extensive verification required of underwriters in the traditional public offering setting.[20]

[D] Underwriters

The court in *BarChris* imposed a rigorous due diligence degree of investigation upon the underwriters. The court reasoned that the underwriters to a public offering are uniquely situated to verify the accuracy of the registration statement's contents. Underwriters not only have access to the necessary information; they have the leverage in the traditional registration context to compel the issuer to fulfill its disclosure duties. Moreover, the investing public relies upon the underwriters' reputations and upon their participation in the offering as an endorsement of the registration statement's accuracy.

Nonetheless, an underwriter is not expected to have the intimate knowledge of corporate affairs that inside directors would possess, and consequently its duty to investigate should be considered in view of its more limited

---

[20] See Spanner, *A Litigation Perspective on the Prospectus Preparation Process for an Initial Public Offering*, 16 Sec. Reg. L.J. 115 (1988).

access. The *BarChris* court emphasized, nonetheless, that an underwriter is expected to exercise a high degree of care in the course of its investigation. Not only must underwriters make an independent verification of management's representations, they must play the devil's advocate.[21] As discussed in depth later in this chapter, in recognition of possible limitations on the underwriter's ability to investigate in certain circumstances, the SEC adopted Rule 176.[22]

[E] Accountants

When the court in *BarChris* turned to consider the liability of the accountants, it did so with respect to that "part of the registration statement purporting to be made upon the authority of [the accountant] as an expert."[23] The only part of the registration statement made on the authority of the accountants in *BarChris* was, as is usually the case, the financial statements. In considering the defense that the accountants acted with due diligence, the court stated that this defense must be assessed at the time that the part of the registration statement containing the allegedly false and misleading financial statements became effective. To accomplish this task, the court scrutinized the audit as well as the accountants' review of events which occurred after the date of the certified balance sheet contained in the registration statement but before the effective date of the registration statement.

The most blatant error found by the court was the accountants' failure to discover that a bowling alley constructed by the registrant, which had been recorded on the books as having been sold, had not been sold. In determining whether the accountants should be held liable for the resulting misstatements in the financial statements, the court carefully considered the various internal documentary evidence examined by the accountants during the course of their audit. In addition, the court considered certain accounting records which had not been examined but which, if examined, would have put the accountants on notice of the impropriety. After reviewing the audit procedures in this context, the court concluded that the accountants failed to prove that they had conducted a reasonable investigation and, consequently, their ignorance of the true facts was unjustified.

In this aspect of the case, it is unclear whether the court's conclusion was based on the finding that the accountants failed to examine certain records which would have put them on notice of the impropriety, or whether the

---

[21] See also *Feit v. Leasco Data Processing Equipment Corp.*, 332 F. Supp. 544, 581-82 (E.D.N.Y. 1971).

[22] See generally T. Hazen, *The Law of Securities Regulation* 186-200 (1985); Fortenbaugh, *Underwriters' Due Diligence*, 14 Rev. Sec. Reg. 799 (1981); Greene, *Determining the Responsibilities of Underwriters Distributing Securities Within an Integrated Disclosure System*, 56 Notre Dame Lawyer 755 (1981).

[23] 283 F. Supp. at 698. See *SEC v. Arthur Young & Co.*, 590 F.2d 785 (9th Cir. 1979); *Hochfelder v. Ernst & Ernst*, 503 F.2d 1100 (7th Cir. 1974), *rev'd on other grounds*, 425 U.S. 185 (1976).

documents examined put them on notice and they failed to follow up. The facts suggest the latter: Once put on notice of an impropriety, an accountant should be required to diligently unearth sufficient information to establish a complete understanding of the matter if he or she is to render an audit opinion on the financial statements.[24]

In scrutinizing the accountants' review of events subsequent to the date of the certified financial statements but prior to the effective date of the registration statement, the court concluded that the written work program utilized for the review conformed to generally accepted auditing standards (GAAS) and would have provided the accountants with the due diligence defense had it been complied with. The program, with limited exceptions, only required a cursory review of the financial statements and certain specific accounts. Significantly, however, the court criticized the accountants for obtaining answers which they considered satisfactory without attempting to verify them. Thus, while limited review procedures may suffice as to "subsequent events," the court added the gloss that information obtained and examined in the course of such a review must be independently verified.

From an overall perspective, the court in *BarChris* believed that accountants "should not be held to a standard higher than that recognized in their profession."[25] Presumably then, according to *BarChris*, proof of compliance with GAAS is sufficient to establish a due diligence defense. In addition, in conducting a subsequent events review, an accountant need not perform a complete audit, but any danger signals must be pursued and answers must be verified.[26]

The Seventh Circuit's decision in *Hochfelder v. Ernst & Ernst*[27] is instructive on the standards by which an accountant's audit must be judged. The court, essentially agreeing with *BarChris*, held that accountants generally "are required to meet only the standard of care expected of persons holding themselves out as skilled accountants."[28] The Seventh Circuit, however, relying on Judge Learned Hand's opinion in *The T.J. Hooper*,[29] went on to assert that compliance with GAAS (Generally Accepted Auditing Standards) does not provide automatic insulation from liability. As the court pointed out, a determination must be made whether the prevailing professional practice constitutes reasonable prudence. Hence, while compliance with GAAS may strongly suggest that the requisite standard of care has been met, "[c]ourts must in the end say what is required; there are precautions so imperative that even their universal disregard will not excuse their omission."[30]

---

[24] See 283 F. Supp. at 703. See also *United States v. Benjamin*, 328 F.2d 854 (2d Cir.), *cert. denied*, 377 U.S. 953 (1964).

[25] 283 F. Supp. at 703.

[26] *Id.* at 700-03. See cases cited note 23, *supra*.

[27] 503 F.2d 1100 (7th Cir. 1974), *rev'd on other grounds*, 425 U.S. 185 (1976).

[28] *Id.* at 1108.

[29] 60 F.2d 737 (2d Cir. 1932).

[30] 503 F.2d at 1113 n.16 (quoting *The T.J. Hooper*, 60 F.2d at 740).

Generally, with respect to accountants' liability under Section 11 (as well as under other provisions of the federal securities laws), the lead of *BarChris* concerning the proper standard of care has been followed. Accordingly, it appears that compliance with GAAS normally will provide a shield to charges of carelessness. Note, however, that:

> It is vitally important to point out that this shield only relates to an accountant's care in obtaining essential underlying facts. Compliance with GAAS will not be a shield to liability where an unreasonable judgment is made on the basis of adequate information properly obtained. The decisions scrutinizing accountants' audit procedures have at the same time considered the reasonableness of the judgments made on the basis of the information unearthed during the audit.
>
> In addition, compliance with GAAS will not act as a shield from liability for misleading presentation of information obtained during the course of a properly conducted audit. In other words, the "investigative" portion of the audit, in which the accountant obtains evidential matter to support the information ultimately presented in financial statements is only the first step in the evaluation of liability. The next step is to scrutinize the judgments made by the accountant on the basis of the information obtained, and the final step is to scrutinize the fairness of the financial statements taken as a whole. When financial statements are alleged to be false or misleading, carelessness at any of the three levels can lead to liability.
>
> It is in the last of the three steps, *i.e.*, presentation of the financial statements, that generally accepted accounting principles (GAAP) come into play. GAAP deals with the proper reflection of economic events in comprehensible financial statements. Thus, while an accountant may comply with GAAS in an audit, the failure to comply with GAAP in the presentation of financial statements may be a basis for liability. [Moreover, as compared to GAAS], compliance with GAAP in financial statement presentation will not necessarily absolve an accountant of liability.[31]

§ 6.05 Impact of the Integrated Disclosure System

At this point, you may wish to review the discussion on the SEC's integrated disclosure system in § 4.06, *supra*. Perhaps the most significant liability issue raised by the integrated disclosure system is that certain issuers

---

[31] Gruenbaum & Steinberg, *Accountants' Liability and Responsibility: Securities, Criminal and Common Law*, 13 Loyola L.A.L. Rev. 247, 260-61 (1980). See also Ebke, *In Search of Alternatives: Comparative Reflections on Corporate Governance and the Independent Auditor's Responsibilities*, 79 Nw. U.L. Rev. 663 (1984); Fiflis, *Current Problems of Accountant's Responsibilities to Third Parties*, 28 Vand. L. Rev. 31 (1975).

can incorporate by reference Exchange Act periodic reports into the registration statement. Such incorporation of 1934 Act reports may make it substantially more onerous for subject parties to satisfy Section 11's "due diligence" obligation (as well as Section 12(2)'s "reasonable care" standard), thus resulting in greater exposure to liability for, among others, directors, underwriters, and accountants.

The issue of *underwriter due diligence* in the integrated disclosure process has raised the most serious liability concerns. It has been argued that, given the practical realities, incorporation by reference severely hampers an underwriter's ability to perform the type of due diligence that was conducted in the *BarChris* era. The reasons underlying this assertion include: (1) underwriters will not generally participate in the drafting of the disclosures incorporated by reference from the 1934 Act periodic reports into the registration statement; (2) underwriters, due to management's reluctance to modify filed documents it has approved (irrespective of SEC Rule 412), will be unable to persuade management to improve the disclosures previously made; (3) by its nature, incorporation by reference drastically limits the time period during which such due diligence can be performed; and (4) adoption of the integrated disclosure system has come at a time of intense competition among underwriters.

Taking the above considerations into account, one may argue, that "it is inevitable that the role of the underwriter as a contributor to the registration process drastically recedes in importance."[32] In short, according to many in the securities industry, the SEC's integrated disclosure system has "rendered untenable the underwriter's traditional role and responsibilities in securities distributions."[33]

Due to these concerns, the Corporation Finance Committee of the Securities Industry Association (SIA) proposed in 1978 that an underwriter would have satisfied its due diligence obligations if it

> (1) had read the registration statement and all exhibits and incorporated documents; (2) had discussed the registration statement with the registrant's representatives; and (3) after such review and discussion, did not know of any material misstatement or omission.

The SIA proposal should not be adopted as it neglects established case law and SEC policy that the element of independent verification by the underwriter is essential for establishing due diligence. Instead, the Commission has opted for Rule 176 which basically codifies Section 1704(g) of the American Law Institute's *Federal Securities Code*. According to the SEC, the rule's basic focus is to permit each person who has potential Section 11 liability to

---

[32] Hovdesven & Wolfram, *Underwriter Liability in the Integrated Disclosure System*, Nat. L.J., July 5, 1982, at 14.

[33] Greene, *supra* note 22, at 797.

evaluate the surrounding facts, including the extent of his prior relationship with the issuer, and utilize techniques of investigation appropriate to the circumstances of the offering.[34]

Rule 176 provides:

> In determining whether or not the conduct of a person constitutes a reasonable investigation or a reasonable ground for belief meeting the standard set forth in Section 11(c), relevant circumstances include, with respect to a person other than the issuer,
>
> (a) The type of issuer;
>
> (b) The type of security;
>
> (c) The type of person;
>
> (d) The office held when the person is an officer;
>
> (e) The presence or absence of another relationship to the issuer when the person is a director or proposed director;
>
> (f) Reasonable reliance on officers, employees, and others whose duties should have given them knowledge of the particular facts (in the light of the functions and responsibilities of the particular person with respect to the issuer and the filing);
>
> (g) When the person is an underwriter, the type of underwriter, the type of underwriting arrangement, the role of the particular person as an underwriter and the availability of information with respect to the registrant; and
>
> (h) Whether, with respect to a fact or document incorporated by reference, the particular person had any responsibility for the fact or document at the time of the filing from which it was incorporated.[35]

As a general proposition, Rule 176 correctly recognizes the concepts of delegation and specialization for all potentially liable persons (except the issuer) under Section 11. Moreover, subsections (g) and (h) recognize, at least somewhat, the concerns of underwriters in the integrated disclosure system. Nonetheless, the SEC has been criticized for failing to recognize, in view of market realities, the difficult task that underwriters have to independently verify the information contained in the registration statement. This criticism becomes accentuated when applied to the shelf registration process (discussed in § 6.07, *infra*).

On the other hand, the traditional role and responsibilities of the underwriter in the distribution process remain necessary for investor protection, at least until an adequate alternative approach has been adopted. Although underwriters may, for good reason, fear increased liability, investor protection should not be lessened. As stated by the Second Circuit:

---

[34] *Securities Act Release* No. 6383 (1982).

[35] 17 C.F.R. § 230.176.

> No greater reliance in our self-regulatory system is placed on any single participant in the issuance of securities than upon the underwriter. . . . Prospective investors look to the underwriter — a fact well known to all concerned and especially to the underwriter — to pass on the soundness of the security and the correctness of the registration statement and prospectus.[36]

While the above statement certainly was valid in the pre-SEC integrated disclosure era, it may be argued that its dogmatic application in the era now present makes the underwriter, in essence, an insurer for others' defalcations. No doubt, a sensitive balance must be struck. Unfortunately, the competing interests at stake preclude, at least presently, such an accommodation from being reached.

§ 6.06 Director Signing of Form 10-K

As part of its integrated disclosure framework, the SEC has mandated that a majority of a registrant's directors sign the Form 10-K. In adopting this requirement, the Commission reasoned:

> [A] requirement for the signatures [on the Form 10-K] of a majority of a registrant's directors — in addition to those of its principal executive officer, its principal financial officer, and its controller or principal accounting officer — is an appropriate one under the circumstances. The Commission believes that just as its rules and the administrative focus of the Division of Corporation Finance are being realigned to reflect the shift in emphasis toward relying on periodic disclosure under the Exchange Act, so too the attention of the private sector, including management, directors, accountants, and attorneys, must also be refocused towards Exchange Act filings if a sufficient degree of discipline is to be instilled in the system to make it work. With an expanded signature requirement, the Commission anticipates that directors will be encouraged to devote the needed attention to reviewing the Form 10-K and to seek the involvement of other professionals to the degree necessary to give themselves sufficient comfort. In the Commission's view, this added measure of discipline is vital to the disclosure objectives of the federal securities laws, and outweighs the potential impact, if any, of the signature on legal liability.[37]

Concerns have been expressed that the director signature requirement for the Form 10-K may result in greater liability exposure. For example, the signing of the Form 10-K by a subject director arguably may signify that the director "caused" the filing, failed to act in "good faith," and/or acted with "scienter," thereby giving rise to a host of both SEC and private liability

---

[36] *Chris-Craft Industries, Inc. v. Piper Aircraft Corp.*, 480 F.2d 341, 380 (2d Cir.), *cert. denied*, 414 U.S. 910 (1973).

[37] *Securities Act Release* No. 6231 (1980).

concerns. Although it is premature to assess whether the signature requirement will alter existing legal liabilities, it appears that this requirement will induce directors to scrutinize the Form 10-K and to seek the advice of corporate counsel in this exercise to a much greater degree than previously was the practice.[38]

§ 6.07 Shelf Registration

At this point, you may wish to review the discussion on shelf registration contained in § 4.06[B], *supra*. Generally, Rule 415 governs the registration of securities to be offered and sold on a delayed basis in the future. Significantly, for the first time, the rule permits eligible issuers (namely, those offering securities which may be registered on Form S-3 or F-3) to engage in primary at-the-market offerings of equity securities which the issuer expects to offer within two years of the registration statement's effective date.

The Commission's decision to include equity offerings within Rule 415's scope drew a sharp dissent from Commissioner Thomas who asserted that the rule should be limited to debt offerings. She argued that Rule 415, when applied to equity offerings,

> (1) jeopardizes the liquidity and stability of our primary and secondary markets by encouraging greater concentration of underwriters, market-makers, and other financial intermediaries and by discouraging individual investor participation in the capital markets thereby furthering the trend toward institutionalization of securities holders, and (2) reduces the quality and timeliness of disclosure available to investors when making their investment decisions. Incurring these risks is antithetical to the statutory duty of the Commission to protect investors and to maintain the integrity of our capital markets.[39]

There is little question that underwriter due diligence obligations are accentuated in the shelf registration setting. In this setting, underwriters assert that they will have little, if any, time to perform any meaningful due diligence.[40] The SEC has responded by promulgating Rule 176 and by advising potential underwriters to acquire "in advance a reservoir of knowledge" about the issuer. It is arguable, however, that the SEC's position overlooks the manner in which the shelf rule has impacted on the role of underwriters. First, due to the competitive nature of the shelf registration process, the bargaining position of the underwriter to induce disclosure on the issuer's part has been greatly diminished. Second, potential underwriters have

---

[38] For a discussion of the director signature requirement on the Form 10-K and its potential liability ramifications, see M. Steinberg, *Securities Regulation: Liabilities and Remedies* § 5.04[3] (1989).

[39] See *Securities Act Release* No. 6499 (1983).

[40] See Ketels, *SEC Rule 415 — The New Experimental Procedures for Shelf Registration*, 10 Sec. Reg. L.J. 318, 335-36 (1982).

little incentive to develop "in advance a reservoir of knowledge," with its attendant costs, if there is only a possibility that they will be selected.[41] As a result, the shelf registration rule may well leave underwriters in a quandary with respect as to how to perform their due diligence functions in an adequate, yet cost efficient, manner. Nonetheless, this dilemma is being alleviated to a large extent by the issuer selecting a law firm to conduct due diligence on the prospective underwriters' behalf. Although this development poses conflict of interest concerns, at least it is a means by which continuous due diligence can be conducted by an underwriter or its designee.[42]

§ 6.08 Section 12(1)

Section 12(1) of the Securities Act gives teeth to Section 5 by providing the purchaser of securities with an express private right of action against his or her seller if such seller offers or sells a security in violation of Section 5.[43] In an action brought under Section 12(1), the purchaser may seek rescission or, if he or she no longer owns the securities, damages. Section 12(1) (as well as Section 12(2) discussed in § 6.09, *infra*) does not provide a plaintiff with a choice of remedies. As stated by the Second Circuit: "If [the] plaintiff owns the stock, he is entitled to rescission but not damages. If [the] plaintiff no longer owns the stock, he is entitled to damages but not rescission."[44]

If a violation of Section 5 has been committed by the seller, the purchaser ordinarily is entitled to recovery. In other words, strict liability is imposed against the seller. The exercise of reasonable care or bona fide but unsuccessful efforts to perfect an exemption from registration is irrelevant. Hence, upon the purchaser establishing a *prima facie* casc that the seller violated Section 5, a seller may avoid liability only, for example, by showing that the offering qualifies for an exemption from registration, that the plaintiff is *in pari delicto* (see § 7.08, *infra*), or that the statute of limitations has expired.

---

[41] See generally Banoff, *Regulatory Subsidies, Efficient Markets, and Shelf Registration: An Analysis of Rule 415*, 70 Va. L. Rev. 135, 180-81 (1984); Fox, *Shelf Registration, Integrated Disclosure, and Underwriter Due Diligence: An Economic Analysis*, 70 Va. L. Rev. 1005 (1984).

[42] See *Securities Act Release* No. 6499 (1983) ("The trend toward appointment of a single law firm to act as underwriters' counsel is a particularly significant development. . . . Registrants appoint the law firm to act as underwriters' counsel either with or without consulting the prospective participating underwriters."); Frerichs, *Underwriter Due Diligence Within the Integrated Disclosure System — If It Isn't Broken, Don't Fix It*, 16 Sec. Reg. L.J. 386 (1989); Nicholas, *The Integrated Disclosure System and Its Impact Upon Underwriters' Due Diligence: Will Investors Be Protected?*, 11 Sec. Reg. L.J. 3 (1983); Note, *The Impact of the SEC's Shelf Registration Rule on Underwriter's Due Diligence Investigations*, 51 Geo. Wash. L. Rev. 767 (1983).

[43] The definition of "seller" for § 12 purposes is addressed in § 6.09[B], *infra*.

[44] *Wigand v. Flo-Tek, Inc.*, 609 F.2d 1028, 1035 (2d Cir. 1979).

A key issue under Section 12 is the meaning of the term "seller." The Supreme Court's recent decision focusing on this issue is addressed in the ensuing discussion (see § 6.09[B], *infra*).

§ 6.09 Section 12(2)

[A] Overview

Aggrieved purchasers of securities acquired in an exempt offering (such as pursuant to Regulation D) may seek to invoke Section 12(2) of the Securities Act. Generally, Section 12(2) affords an express right of action to a purchaser against his or her seller for rescission, or damages if the securities have been disposed of, where the purchaser acquired the securities by means of a prospectus or oral communication which contained a material misstatement or omission. Proof of reliance is not required. Indeed, to recover under Section 12(2), "a plaintiff need not prove that he ever received the misleading prospectus."[45] Accordingly, Section 12(2)'s terms

> do not require that the particular sale to an individual plaintiff directly be by means of the prospectus alleged to be misleading. . . . It is enough that the seller sold by means of a misleading prospectus securities of which those purchased by the plaintiff were a part.[46]

It may be, however, that a different result might follow if only oral communications were present.[47]

Section 12(2) provides the seller with a "quasi due diligence" defense. Once the purchaser has established a *prima facie* case, the onus is shifted to the seller to establish that he or she did not know, and in the exercise of reasonable care could not have known, of the untruth or omission.

In general terms, an action under Section 12(2) differs from an action under Section 11 in a number of respects. For example, the action is afforded to purchasers of securities in both registered and exempt offerings, whereas Section 11 only applies to registered offerings. Also, Section 12(2) arguably is available to purchasers in the aftermarket because the provision encompasses "oral communications,"[48] whereas prospectuses (although broadly defined under Section 2(10)) most often are used in connection with primary offerings. That is not to say that Section 11 is not available to purchasers in the aftermarket, but only that it is unlikely to be successfully invoked (see § 6.02[B], *supra*).

---

[45] *Sanders v. John Nuveen & Co., Inc.*, 619 F.2d 1222, 1226 (7th Cir. 1980), *cert. denied*, 450 U.S. 1005 (1981).

[46] *Id.* at 1226-27.

[47] *Id.* at 1227 n.8.

[48] See *Wilko v. Swan*, 127 F. Supp. 55 (S.D.N.Y. 1955). But see *Ralph v. Prudential-Bache Securities, Inc.*, [1988-1989 Transfer Binder] Fed. Sec. L. Rep. (CCH) ¶ 93,964 (S.D. Fla. 1988) (§ 12(2) only applies in the offering context).

Moreover, in contrast to the specific categories of possible defendants listed in Section 11, Section 12(2) by its terms subjects only "sellers" to potential liability. In this respect, note that underwriters are not necessarily within the reach of Section 12(2). As the Eleventh Circuit has observed:

> Since § 12 does not provide for underwriter liability *per se*, an underwriter must also be a seller of the security in question to be liable under the section.[49]

A major issue, which will be examined in the materials which follow, is who is a "seller" within the meaning of Section 12(2). Another key issue pertaining to the scope of the remedy afforded to purchasers under Section 12(2) is whether persons other than a seller may be held liable on a secondary liability rationale, such as aiding and abetting. This question is interwoven with the public policy considerations underlying the federal securities laws in general and the concept of "seller" in particular.

Another distinction between Section 11 and Section 12(2) lies in the standard of care defense. Whereas Section 11 establishes an affirmative defense of "reasonable investigation," Section 12(2) provides that the seller exercise "reasonable care." This apparently lower standard of care is consistent with the general notion that sellers of securities may not be intimately involved with the offering and may not have the same access to information as do potential Section 11 defendants. However, as the Seventh Circuit's decision in *Sanders v. John Nuveen & Co., Inc.*[50] indicates, the degree of care to be exercised by sellers who are within the Section 12(2) inner circle may converge with the reasonable investigation standard of Section 11.

[B] The Meaning of "Seller"

Prior to the Supreme Court's recent decision in *Pinter v. Dahl*,[51] courts disagreed as to who may be regarded as a "seller" under Section 12(2) (as well as under Section 12(1)). While some courts imposed a strict privity requirement,[52] most courts relaxed the privity requirement to some extent. Liability was imposed by a number of courts upon persons as "sellers" for being integrally connected with, or substantially involved in, the transaction.[53]

---

[49] *Foster v. Jessup and Lamont Securities Co., Inc.*, 759 F.2d 838, 845 (11th Cir. 1985).

[50] 619 F.2d 1222 (7th Cir. 1982), *cert. denied*, 450 U.S. 1005 (1981).

[51] 108 S. Ct. 2063 (1988).

[52] See, *e.g.*, *Collins v. Signetics Corp.*, 605 F.2d 110 (3d Cir. 1979); *McFarland v. Memorex Corp.*, 493 F. Supp. 631 (N.D. Cal. 1980). See generally Abrams, *The Scope of Liability Under Section 12 of the Securities Act of 1933: "Participation" and the Pertinent Legislative Materials*, 15 Fordham Urban L.J. 877 (1987).

[53] See, *e.g.*, *Davis v. Avco Financial Services, Inc.*, 739 F.2d 1057 (6th Cir. 1984); *Croy v. Campbell*, 624 F.2d 709 (5th Cir. 1980).

In *Pinter*, the Supreme Court rejected both of the above approaches. While the decision expressly dealt with the definition of "seller" under Section 12(1), one may reasonably conclude that the Court's analysis applies as well to Section 12(2). In this regard, however, the Court stated:

> Decisions under § 12(2) addressing the "seller" question are . . . relevant to the issue presented to us in this case, and, to that extent, we discuss them here. Nevertheless, this case does not present, nor do we take a position on, the scope of a statutory seller for purposes of § 12(2).[54]

Nonetheless, given the statutory framework of Section 12, it is likely that the lower courts will apply the *Pinter* analysis to actions brought under either subsection (1) or (2) of Section 12.

In *Pinter*, the Supreme Court, looking at the language and purpose of Section 12(1), defined "seller" under that provision as extending to one

> who successfully solicits the purchase, motivated at least in part by a desire to serve his own financial interests or those of the securities owner.[55]

Hence, for purposes of Section 12(1), a "seller" includes: (1) one who owned the security sold to the purchaser, (2) an agent for a vendor (such as a broker) who successfully solicited the purchase, (3) one who solicited the purchase with the intent to personally benefit thereby, and (4) one who, without financial benefit to oneself, solicited the purchase to serve the owner's financial interests.

The Court's construction of "seller" generally permits at least two groups of "participants" to avoid Section 12(1) primary liability. First, those persons who gratuitously provide advice on investment matters to friends, family members, and acquaintances are not "sellers" so long as they are not motivated by a desire to benefit the securities owner or themselves. Second, securities professionals, such as accountants and lawyers, whose involvement is solely the performance of their professional services (*e.g.*, counsel rendering solely legal advice to a client), are not "sellers."[56]

[C] Secondary Liability

The Supreme Court in *Pinter* did not resolve whether secondary liability may be imposed under Section 12.[57] A few courts have approved of such liability based largely upon an aiding and abetting rationale.[58] For example,

---

[54] 108 S. Ct. at 2076 n.20.

[55] *Id.* at 2079.

[56] *Id.* at 2077-79. Compare *Junker v. Crory*, 650 F.2d 1349 (5th Cir. 1981) (attorney, whose participation was a substantial factor in causing the transaction to take place, deemed a seller for § 12(2) purposes).

[57] 108 S. Ct. at 2079 n.24.

[58] See, *e.g.*, *deBruin v. Andromeda Broadcasting Systems*, 465 F. Supp. 1276 (D. Nev. 1979); *In re Caesars Palace Sec. Lit.*, 360 F. Supp. 366 (S.D.N.Y. 1973).

the Second Circuit under certain circumstances permits Section 12(2) liability to be imposed upon collateral participants who are not "sellers." In such cases, *scienter* (knowing or intentional misconduct on the defendant's part) must be proven by the plaintiff (see § 7.03, *infra*).[59] On the other hand, a majority of courts have rejected the imposition of secondary liability as inappropriate under Section 12.[60]

[D] The Reasonable Care Defense

Under Section 12(2), the defendant can avoid liability by showing that he or she did not know, and in the exercise of reasonable care could not have known, of the material misstatement or omission. Whether this standard imposes Section 11-type due diligence obligations, has been met with mixed reaction.

In defining the meaning of "reasonable care" under Section 12(2), it is important to distinguish the responsibilities of a so-called traditional underwriter from those of a "mere" seller. For example, to require a "seller" in a small private offering to comply with Section 11 due diligence would arguably impose too harsh a standard. Moreover, in many private offerings, the underwriter is neither in the bargaining position to carry out a Section 11-type due diligence investigation nor is it intimately involved in the preparation of the prospectus.

On the other hand, where an unregistered offering has many of the characteristics frequently associated with an offering that must be registered, "the standard of 'reasonable care' under Section 12(2) may converge with the standard of 'reasonable investigation' prescribed under Section 11."[61] For example, in *Sanders v. John Nuveen & Co.*,[62] the Seventh Circuit held an underwriter liable under Section 12(2) for failing to make a reasonable investigation. Although stating that it is far from clear that Congress intended to impose a more rigorous standard of care under Section 11 than under Section 12(2), the court also opined:

> Since what constitutes reasonable care under § 12(2) depends upon the circumstances, we, of course, do not intimate that the duty of a seller

[59] See *Mayer v. Oil Field Sys. Corp.*, 803 F.2d 749, 756 (2d Cir. 1986); *Lanza v. Drexel & Co.*, 479 F.2d 1277, 1298 (2d Cir. 1973) (*en banc*).

[60] See, *e.g.*, *Davis v. Avco Financial Services*, 739 F.2d 1067 (6th Cir. 1984); *Hokama v. E.F. Hutton & Co.*, 566 F. Supp. 636 (C.D. Cal. 1983); *Hagert v. Glickman, Lurie, Eiger & Co.*, 520 F. Supp. 1028 (D. Minn. 1981). See generally O'Hara, *Erosion of the Privity Requirement in Section 12(2) of the Securities Act of 1933: The Expanded Meaning of Seller*, 31 U.C.L.A. L. Rev. 921 (1984); Schneider, *Section 12 of the Securities Act of 1933: The Privity Requirement in the Contemporary Securities Law Perspective*, 51 Tenn. L. Rev. 235 (1984).

[61] *Brief of the Solicitor General* at pages 7-8 in *Sanders v. John Nuveen & Co.*, 619 F.2d 1229 (7th Cir. 1980), *cert. denied*, 450 U.S. 1005 (1981), urging the Supreme Court to deny the petition for a *writ of certiorari*.

[62] 619 F.2d 1222 (7th Cir. 1980), *cert. denied*, 450 U.S. 1005 (1981).

> under § 12(2) is always the same as that of an underwriter in a registration offering under § 11.[63]

In sum, under the circumstances at bar, the Seventh Circuit held that Section 12(2)'s reasonable care standard required a reasonable investigation.

In a dissent from the denial of *certiorari* in *Sanders*, two Supreme Court Justices expressed concern that the Seventh Circuit's decision would

> be read as recognizing no distinction between the standards of care applicable under §§ 11 and 12(2), and particularly as casting doubt upon the reasonableness of relying upon the expertise of certified public accountants.[64]

Indeed, perhaps the most troubling aspect of the Seventh Circuit's analysis is that, by stating that the underwriter should have examined the company's audited financial statements, the lower court evidently required a higher investigative standard under Section 12(2) than under Section 11. As stated in the dissent:

> Even under § 11 of the Act, an underwriter is explicitly absolved of the duty to investigate with respect to "any part of the registration statement purporting to be made on the authority of an expert" such as a certified accountant if "he had no reasonable ground to believe and did not believe" that the information therein was misleading. This provision is in the Act because, almost by definition, it is reasonable to rely on financial statements certified by public accountants. Yet, in this case, the Court of Appeals nevertheless seems to have imposed the higher duty prescribed by § 11 to investigate, but denied petitioner the right to rely on "the authority of an expert" that also is provided by § 11.[65]

Sanders, although an important case, should not be read, particularly in view of the Supreme Court's dissenters, as requiring underwriters to undertake independent financial investigations. Rather, as in Section 11, such persons should be entitled to rely, absent reason otherwise, on the accuracy of the issuer's audited financial statements. Nonetheless, the decision is highly significant because it clearly conveys that underwriters of unregistered offerings have substantial responsibilities in complying with the "reasonable care" obligation contained in Section 12(2).[66]

---

[63] *Id.* at 1228.

[64] 450 U.S. 1005 (Powell, J., dissenting).

[65] *Id.* at 1009-10.

[66] See generally Comment, *"Reasonable Care" in Section 12(2) of the Securities Act of 1933*, 48 U. Chi. L. Rev. 372 (1981).

CHAPTER 7

SECTION 10(b) AND RELATED ISSUES

§ 7.01 Overview

This chapter explores developments under Section 10(b) of the Securities Exchange Act and Rule 10b-5 promulgated thereunder by the SEC (as well as certain related issues). Generally, the antifraud provisions of the securities acts were designed to protect investors, to assure fair dealing in the securities markets, and to promote ethical business practices. Consistent with these objectives, Section 10(b) makes it unlawful to employ deceptive or manipulative devices "in connection with the purchase or sale of any security." As enacted by Congress, Section 10(b) was designed to be a "catch-all" provision and, as such, it encompasses a broad range of practices.[1]

The language of Section 10(b) does not create an express private remedy for its violation. Neither does the legislative history reveal that Congress intended to create a private right of action under the statute at the time of its passage. Nonetheless, the federal courts have routinely recognized the existence of a private remedy under Section 10(b). As the Supreme Court recognized in a fairly recent decision, "[t]he existence of this implied remedy is simply beyond peradventure."[2]

In order to establish a successful claim under Section 10(b), a plaintiff must prove certain elements. Many of these elements are explored in depth in this chapter. These elements include that the plaintiff (by proof of the preponderance of the evidence):

(1) Establish the *requisite jurisdictional means*. This requirement is normally met without difficulty. For example, as one appellate court has pointed out, "proof of intrastate telephonic messages in connection with the employment of deceptive devices or contrivances is sufficient to confer jurisdiction in a § 10(b) and Rule 10b-5 action."[3]

(2) Have the status as a *purchaser or seller* of the securities.[4] Note that the defendant need not be a purchaser or seller.

---

[1] See A. Bromberg & L. Lowenfels, *Securities Fraud & Commodities Fraud* (1986).

[2] *Herman & MacLean v. Huddleston*, 459 U.S. 375, 380 (1983).

[3] *Loveridge v. Dreagoux*, 678 F.2d 870, 874 (10th Cir. 1982).

[4] See *Blue Chip Stamps v. Manor Drug Stores*, 421 U.S. 723 (1975); § 7.02, *infra*.

(3) Prove *"manipulation" or "deception"* and not "merely" breach of fiduciary duty.[5]

(4) Show that a misstatement or nondisclosure of fact is *material*, signifying that a reasonable investor would consider such information important in making an investment decision. The investor need not show that the misstatement or nondisclosure, if accurately disclosed, would have changed the investment decision. Hence, to satisfy the materiality requirement, "there must be a substantial likelihood that the disclosure of the omitted fact would have been viewed by the reasonable investor as having significantly altered the 'total mix' of information made available."[6] Moreover, in the merger context as well as other situations involving uncertain events, the probability/magnitude standard has been applied. Under this standard, the existence of materiality depends "at any given time upon a balancing of both the indicated probability that the event will occur and the anticipated magnitude of the event in light of the totality of the company activity."[7]

(5) Establish that the defendant acted with *"scienter."*[8]

(6) Prove that the manipulative or deceptive practice was *"in connection with"* the purchase or sale of a security. Generally, in order to meet this requirement, the proscribed conduct "must 'touch' and exist in reasonably close proximity to, the purchase or sale."[9]

(7) Where called for, show that the plaintiff *relied* and exercised *due diligence.*[10]

(8) Establish *causation* between the defendant's wrongful conduct and the plaintiff's loss.[11]

(9) Where liability is based upon *silence*, establish that the primary alleged violator had a *duty to disclose.*[12]

---

[5] See *Santa Fe Industries, Inc. v. Green*, 430 U.S. 462 (1977); § 7.04, *infra.*

[6] *Basic, Inc. v. Levinson*, 108 S.Ct. 978, 983 (1988), quoting *TSC Industries, Inc. v. Northway, Inc.*, 426 U.S. 438, 449 (1976).

[7] *SEC v. Texas Gulf Sulphur Co.*, 401 F.2d 833, 849 (2d Cir.) (*en banc*), *cert. denied*, 394 U.S. 976 (1969), quoted in *Basic, Inc. v. Levinson*, 108 S.Ct. 978, 983 (1988).

[8] See *Aaron v. SEC*, 446 U.S. 680 (1980); *Ernst & Ernst v. Hochfelder*, 425 U.S. 185 (1976); § 7.03, *infra.*

[9] *Valente v. Pepsico, Inc.*, 454 F. Supp. 1228, 1236 (D. Del. 1978), quoting *Superintendent of Life Insurance v. Bankers Life and Casualty Co.*, 404 U.S. 6 (1971). For what may be viewed as a fairly restrictive interpretation of the "in connection with" requirement, see *Chemical Bank v. Arthur Andersen & Co.*, 726 F.2d 390 (2d Cir. 1984).

[10] See *Basic, Inc. v. Levinson*, 108 S.Ct. 978 (1988); *Affiliated Ute Citizens v. United States*, 406 U.S. 128 (1972); § 7.05, *infra.*

[11] See 3 A. Bromberg & L. Lowenfels, *supra* note 1, at §§ 7.6, 8.7.

[12] See *Chiarella v. United States*, 445 U.S. 222 (1980), discussed in § 9.02[A], *infra.*

(10) Prove the extent of *damages* suffered.[13]

The *defendant* may assert a number of *defenses*, including *in pari delicto*, *laches*, and *waiver*. The *in pari delicto* defense is addressed later in the chapter.[14]

With respect to *indemnification*, because the Supreme Court has ruled that scienter (*e.g.*, deliberate or perhaps reckless misconduct) is required to state a successful Section 10(b) (and Rule 10b-5) claim under the Exchange Act, it appears that indemnification would frustrate the public policy as well as the statutory underpinnings of the Act and therefore is prohibited in this context.[15] The right to *contribution* under Section 10(b), however, has not been definitively resolved. Unlike Section 11 of the Securities Act, there is no express right to contribution under Section 10(b). Hence, if such a right is to be recognized, it must be implied. Although a number of courts have implied such a right, others have declined. Thus, the issue is far from settled.[16]

The Exchange Act does not provide for a *statute of limitations* with respect to actions brought for alleged violations of Section 10(b). Traditionally, federal courts have looked to the statute of the forum state (*i.e.*, that state where the plaintiff brings the action) which is most analogous to the Section 10(b) right of action. With wide disparities, the federal courts have chosen between the typically shorter forum state's Blue Sky securities statute or the generally longer common law fraud limitations period. In the more recent cases, the majority of courts apply the statute of limitations of the forum state's Blue Sky statute. On the other hand, the Third Circuit, departing from the above approaches, has held that the appropriate statute of limitations for Section 10(b) claims is that contained in the express limitation provisions of the Exchange Act.[17]

Under certain circumstances, by invoking the *equitable tolling doctrine*, the federal courts will suspend the running of the statute of limitations, thereby permitting the plaintiff to maintain a Section 10(b) action. As stated by one federal appellate court:

> Under federal law, the doctrine of fraudulent concealment operates to toll the statute of limitations "where the party injured by the fraud

---

[13] See Thompson, *The Measure of Recovery Under Rule 10b-5: A Restitution Alternative to Tort Damages*, 37 Vand. L. Rev. 349 (1984).

[14] See *Bateman Eichler, Hill Richards, Inc. v. Berner*, 472 U.S. 299 (1985); *Hecht v. Harris, Upham & Co.*, 430 F.2d 1202 (9th Cir. 1970); § 7.08, *infra*.

[15] See cases cited note 8, *supra*; § 6.03, *supra*; § 7.03, *infra*.

[16] See Adamski, *Contribution and Settlement in Multiparty Actions Under Rule 10b-5*, 66 Iowa L. Rev. 533 (1981); Loewenstein, *Implied Contribution Under the Federal Securities Laws: A Reassessment*, 1982 Duke L.J. 543, 577 (1982).

[17] See *In re Data Access Systems Securities Litigation*, 843 F.2d 1537 (3d Cir. 1988) (*en banc*) (Exchange Act statute of limitations for express rights of action generally is one year from discovery and no more than three years from the violation). See generally Barton & Bloch, *Toward A Uniform Statute of Limitations in Private Actions Under Section 10(b)*, 16 Sec. Reg. L.J. 297 (1988) (and cases cited therein).

remains in ignorance of it without any fault or want of diligence or care on his part . . . until the fraud is discovered, though there be no special circumstances or efforts on the part of the party committing the fraud to conceal it from the knowledge of the other party." Even without affirmative acts on the part of defendants, then, a federal cause of action will accrue at the time when plaintiff in the exercise of reasonable diligence discovered or should have discovered the fraud of which he complains.[18]

§ 7.02 Standing: The Purchaser-Seller Requirement

In *Blue Chip Stamps v. Manor Drug Stores*,[19] allegedly defrauded offerees asserted that had the defendant not deceived them, they would have purchased the securities offered. The Supreme Court ruled that the plaintiffs did not have standing to bring a Section 10(b) right of action because they were neither purchasers nor sellers. The Court premised its decision on a number of factors:

(1) The statutory language of Section 10(b) proscribes manipulation or deception "in connection with the purchase or sale" of securities. This language, along with the pertinent legislative history, indicated that Congress did not intend to grant standing to defrauded (but non-purchasing) offerees.

(2) Granting standing to offerees under the implied remedy of Section 10(b) would make the Section 10(b) remedy more expansive than the comparable express causes of action that Congress chose to delineate. Hence, granting offerees standing under Section 10(b) evidently would contravene Congress' intent.

(3) Looking to policy matters, the Court asserted that Section 10(b) litigation poses a greater danger of vexatiousness than litigation in general. According to the Court, this is due to the presence of "strike" suits, potential abuse of the liberal discovery provisions of the Federal Rules of Civil Procedure, and that "hazy issues of historical fact" will be adjudicated on the basis of "oral testimony."[20]

Hence, under the *Blue Chip* standing requirement, three principal types of potential plaintiffs are barred from instituting Section 10(b) litigation:

First are potential purchasers of shares, either in a new offering or on the Nation's post-distribution trading markets, who allege that they decided not to purchase because of an unduly gloomy representation or the

---

[18] *Cook v. Avien, Inc.*, 573 F.2d 685, 694-95 (1st Cir. 1978) (citations omitted). For a more liberal application of the equitable tolling doctrine, see, *e.g.*, *Trecker v. Scag*, 679 F.2d 703 (7th Cir. 1982).

[19] 421 U.S. 723 (1975), upholding the *Birnbaum* standing rule, *Birnbaum v. Newport Steel Corp.*, 193 F.2d 461 (2d Cir. 1952).

[20] 421 U.S. at 733-61.

> omission of favorable material which made the issuer appear to be a less favorable investment vehicle than it actually was. Second are actual shareholders in the issuer who allege that they decided not to sell their shares because of an unduly rosy representation or a failure to disclose unfavorable material. Third are shareholders, creditors, and perhaps others related to an issuer who suffered loss in the value of their investment due to corporate or insider activities in connection with the purchase or sale of securities which violate Rule 10b-5.[21]

In this regard, shareholders of the second and third categories above, although unable to bring a direct action, will be able to institute a derivative action on the issuer's behalf if such issuer is a purchaser or seller of its securities.

The *Blue Chip* standing requirement has been extended to plaintiffs seeking solely injunctive relief. Thus, when seeking injunctive relief under Section 10(b), the plaintiff must be a purchaser or seller of securities. The policy rationale is that *Blue Chip* applies to injunctive actions due to the need to deter strike suits and the rendering of hazy oral testimony.[22]

It is important to emphasize that, in order to bring a Section 10(b) cause of action, only the plaintiff (not the defendant) must be a "purchaser" or "seller." Moreover, applying the purchaser-seller requirement, the lower federal courts have recognized standing under Section 10(b) in a variety of circumstances, including: in a shareholder derivative action brought on behalf of a defrauded corporation where the corporation was a purchaser or seller of its securities; in a "forced" sale transaction, such as a share exchange or "freeze-out" merger (see, *e.g.*, SEC Rule 145, § 5.07, *supra*); where the plaintiff has "pledged" the securities; and where the plaintiff has entered into a contract to buy or sell the securities.[23]

§ 7.03 Requisite Culpability Level

[A] Private Damages Actions

The Supreme Court in *Ernst & Ernst v. Hochfelder*[24] held that in private actions for damages pursuant to Section 10(b) scienter must be proven. The decision was largely predicated on a strict linguistic interpretation of Section 10(b). The construction of Rule 10b-5 was confined to that given the statutory source upon which the administrative rule (Rule 10b-5) is based, namely, Section 10(b). The *Hochfelder* Court pointed out that (1) the 1933 Act's statutory provisions granting private redress for negligent conduct[25] are

[21] *Id.* at 737-38.

[22] See, *e.g.*, *Cowin v. Bresler*, 741 F.2d 410 (D.C. Cir. 1984).

[23] For further discussion see T. Hazen, *The Law of Securities Regulation* 450-57 (1985).

[24] 425 U.S. 185 (1976).

[25] See §§ 11, 12(2), and 15 of the Securities Act, 15 U.S.C. §§ 77k, l(2), o.

"subject to significant procedural restrictions not applicable under § 10(b)"[26] and (2) except for the "short-swing" trading prohibition of Exchange Act Section 16(b),[27] "[e]ach of the provisions of the 1934 Act that expressly create civil liability . . . contains a state of mind condition requiring something more than negligence."[28] Hence, extending Section 10(b) to include negligent conduct in private damages actions, the Court held, would "nullify the effectiveness of the carefully drawn procedural restrictions on these express actions."[29]

While the *Hochfelder* Court stated that the term "scienter" encompasses "a mental state embracing intent to deceive, manipulate, or defraud"[30] and may be shown by "knowing or intentional misconduct,"[31] the Court declined to resolve whether "recklessness" constitutes scienter.[32] This issue is discussed later in this section.

[B] SEC Actions for Injunctive Relief

After the Supreme Court's decision in *Hochfelder*, the question remained whether the SEC was required to establish scienter in an action for injunctive relief brought for violations of Section 10(b). Because the principal focus of an SEC injunctive proceeding "is to protect the public against harm, not to punish the offender,"[33] it was argued by some authorities that an SEC action under Section 10(b) could be premised on negligent conduct. Others, relying upon a statutory linguistic analysis, asserted that scienter had to be proven under Section 10(b), irrespective of the plaintiff's identity.

The Supreme Court resolved this issue in *Aaron v. SEC*.[34] Largely relying on the language of Section 10(b) and its legislative history, the Court concluded that "scienter is an element of § 10(b) and Rule 10b-5, regardless of the identity of the plaintiff or the nature of the relief sought."[35] From an SEC enforcement view, *Aaron* is an important case, further aspects of which are discussed in Chapters 8 and 11, *infra*.

[C] "Recklessness"

A question left open by both *Hochfelder* and *Aaron* is whether reckless conduct constitutes scienter for Section 10(b) purposes. Overwhelmingly, the

---

[26] 425 U.S. at 208-09.

[27] For discussion of Section 16(b) see § 9.02[F], *infra*.

[28] 425 U.S. at 209 n.28. See, *e.g.*, §§ 9(e), 18 and 20 of the Exchange Act, 15 U.S.C. §§ 78i(e), r, t.

[29] 425 U.S. at 210.

[30] *Id.* at 193 n.12.

[31] *Id.* at 197.

[32] *Id.* at 193 n.12.

[33] *SEC v. Coven*, 581 F.2d 1020, 1027-28 (2d Cir. 1978).

[34] 446 U.S. 680 (1980). With respect to the portion of the decision addressing § 17(a) of the Securities Act, see the discussion of § 17(a) in Chapters 8 and 11, *infra*.

[35] 446 U.S. at 691.

lower federal courts have concluded that recklessness satisfies the scienter requirement. There has been some disagreement, however, as to the meaning of the term. The majority of courts have construed reckless conduct to mean conduct which is "highly unreasonable" and which represents

> an extreme departure from the standards of ordinary care . . . to the extent that the danger was either known to the defendant or so obvious that the defendant must have been aware of it.[36]

Other courts have adopted somewhat more relaxed standards. For example, the Ninth Circuit in *Keirnan v. Homeland, Inc.*[37] stated that the defendants had acted recklessly

> if they had reasonable grounds to believe material facts existed that were misstated or omitted, but nonetheless failed to obtain and disclose such facts although they could have done so without extraordinary effort.[38]

A third standard, termed the "barely reckless" standard, deems actionable an allegation that the defendant "should have known," with the proviso that such conduct surpasses that of negligence.[39]

Moreover, with respect to secondary liability for aiding and abetting (see § 7.10[A], *infra*), some courts have concluded that reckless conduct satisfies the scienter requirement only when there exists a fiduciary duty between the alleged violator and the plaintiff.[40] Other courts have deemed recklessness to be sufficient where the defendant, although not having a fiduciary duty, had reason to foresee that the complainant would be relying on his or her conduct.[41] Still other courts have held recklessness to satisfy the Section 10(b) scienter requirement irrespective of the defendant's status as an aider and abettor.[42]

[D] State Court Reaction

Due to the Supreme Court's decisions in the federal securities law area which have had the effect of making a plaintiff's task in establishing a successful cause of action under Section 10(b) more difficult, counsel may deem it wise to consider bringing state common law or state securities law claims. In this regard, in construing their respective Blue Sky statutes, a few state courts have elected not to follow the Supreme Court's lead in *Hochfelder* and *Aaron*, hence holding that scienter is not required to be shown. State

---

[36] *Sanders v. John Nuveen & Co., Inc.*, 554 F.2d 790, 793 (7th Cir. 1977).

[37] 611 F.2d 785 (9th Cir. 1980).

[38] *Id.* at 788.

[39] See *Stern v. American Bankshares Corp.*, 429 F. Supp. 818 (E.D. Wis. 1977).

[40] See *Edwards & Hanly v. Wells Fargo Securities Clearance Corp.*, 602 F.2d 478 (2d Cir. 1979).

[41] See *Oleck v. Fischer*, [1979 Transfer Binder] Fed. Sec. L. Rep. (CCH) ¶ 96,896 (S.D.N.Y.), *aff'd on other grounds*, 623 F.2d 791 (2d Cir. 1980).

[42] See Steinberg & Gruenbaum, *Variations of Recklessness After Hochfelder and Aaron*, 8 Sec. Reg. L.J. 179 (1980) (and cases cited therein).

court decisions holding that negligence is sufficient culpability to impose liability have distinguished Section 10(b)'s language from that contained in the respective state statute and have found no legislative history in the state statute comparable to that underlying Section 10(b).[43]

§ 7.04 The "Deception" Requirement

[A] Breach of Fiduciary Duty Not Sufficient

Santa Fe Industries, Inc. v. Green[44] involved the merger of the Kirby Lumber Corporation into its parent, Santa Fe Industries, Inc., which owned ninety-five percent of Kirby's stock. Santa Fe availed itself of a simplified Delaware procedure known as a "short-form" merger, under which a parent that owns at least ninety percent of a subsidiary's outstanding stock can absorb the subsidiary without being required to obtain approval by the shareholders of either corporation.[45] The day after the merger became effective, Kirby's minority shareholders were informed that they would receive $150 in cash for each of their shares, and that, if dissatisfied, they could seek appraisal in the Delaware courts.[46]

Santa Fe also provided the Kirby shareholders with an information statement containing facts and figures that convinced one of the recipients that Kirby stock was actually worth at least $772 a share. Rather than alleging that these materials contained misrepresentations and nondisclosures, the plaintiff claimed that the gross undervaluation of his shares was itself a "fraud" within the meaning of Section 10(b) and Rule 10b-5.[47]

The Supreme Court rejected this argument, holding that the transaction "was neither deceptive nor manipulative and therefore did not violate either § 10(b) of the [Exchange] Act or Rule 10b-5."[48] The Court largely premised its decision on Section 10(b)'s language and the statute's legislative history, finding "no indication that Congress meant to prohibit any conduct not involving manipulation or deception."[49] Further support was found by examining the Exchange Act's fundamental purpose of implementing a philosophy of full and fair disclosure. Once adequate disclosure has taken place, the fairness of the transaction is at most a tangential concern of the

---

[43] See *Kittilson v. Ford*, 93 Wash. 2d 223, 608 P.2d 264 (1980). But see *Ohio v. American Equitel Corp.*, 60 Ohio Misc. 7, 395 N.E.2d 1355 (Ct. C.P. Ohio 1979) (requiring scienter to be shown). See generally M. Steinberg & R. Ferrara, *Securities Practice: Federal and State Enforcement* § 12:18 (1985).

[44] 430 U.S. 462 (1977).

[45] 8 Del. Code Ann. § 253.

[46] 430 U.S. at 466-67.

[47] *Id.* at 474.

[48] *Id.*

[49] *Id.* at 473.

Exchange Act. Therefore, claims challenging solely the fairness of transactions or internal corporate mismanagement are best relegated to state law.[50]

Santa Fe was scarcely a surprise after the Court's previous decisions in *Ernst & Ernst v. Hochfelder*[51] and *Cort v. Ash.*[52] *Hochfelder* held that there can be no implied private right of action for damages under Section 10(b) and Rule 10b-5, absent an allegation of scienter. The decision was largely predicated on a strict construction of Section 10(b). This approach to the language of the statute was expressly affirmed and adopted by the *Santa Fe* court. In *Cort*, the Court demonstrated its reluctance to imply federal causes of action in areas traditionally left to state law. There, the court observed that

> corporations are creatures of state law, and investors commit their funds to corporate directors on the understanding that, except where federal law *expressly* requires certain responsibilities of directors with respect to stockholders, state law will govern the internal affairs of the corporation.[53]

Both cases evidence the Court's contraction of the scope of the federal securities laws. *Santa Fe* combined the approaches of *Hochfelder* and *Cort*, employing a narrow approach to construction and stressing that the regulation of the internal management of corporations is within the ambit of state corporation law.

Santa Fe is perhaps the most important decision that the Supreme Court has handed down in the federal securities law area. Had the decision gone the other way, garden variety suits for breach of fiduciary duty (irrespective of whether there had been adequate disclosure) would have been actionable under Section 10(b). *Santa Fe* thus signifies that a federal claim under Section 10(b) must allege manipulation or deception. Although theoretically applicable, "manipulation" will seldom be invoked in the corporate mismanagement-nondisclosure setting since the Supreme Court has construed that word as a term of art encompassing market operations.

[B] Federal Claims Premised on Breach of Fiduciary Duty

The *Santa Fe* decision had a second aspect, arising from the Court's comment in footnote 14 of the opinion. In that footnote, the Court stated that the failure to provide the minority with advance notice of the merger was not a material nondisclosure because, as the plaintiffs conceded,

> under Delaware law [the plaintiffs] could not have enjoined the merger because an appraisal proceeding [was] their sole remedy in the Delaware courts for any alleged unfairness in the terms of the merger.[54]

---

[50] *Id.* at 477-80.
[51] 425 U.S. 185 (1976). See § 7.03[A], *supra.*
[52] 422 U.S. 66 (1975).
[53] *Id.* at 80 (emphasis in original).
[54] 430 U.S. at 474 n.14.

Today no plaintiff would make this concession in a *Santa Fe* situation.

[1] Post-*Santa Fe* State Court Decisions

Subsequent to *Santa Fe*, Delaware[55] and a number of other state courts[56] held that appraisal is not a shareholder's sole remedy when a merger is unfair. Based on these decisions, under certain circumstances, aggrieved shareholders may bring suit in state court to enjoin a merger that has not been consummated. For example, in Delaware, a shareholder is not relegated to the appraisal remedy and may seek to enjoin a merger where "fraud, misrepresentation, self-dealing, deliberate waste of corporate assets, or gross and palpable overreaching are involved."[57]

[2] Post-*Santa Fe* Federal Court Decisions

In view of these post-*Santa Fe* state court decisions, aggrieved shareholders not only may seek redress under state law, they also can institute a Section 10(b) right of action where the material misrepresentation(s) or omission(s), if there had been adequate disclosure, would have enabled shareholders to take corrective steps to avoid financial loss, such as procuring a state court injunction against the contemplated action ("the *Goldberg* line of cases").[58] Hence, to a certain extent, federal claims under Section 10(b) based partially on breach of fiduciary duty under state law still survive.

Stated differently, subject to certain caveats, minority shareholders are entitled to information needed to determine whether the board of directors has breached its fiduciary duty under state law. Failure to provide this information, according to a number of courts,[59] may be a material deception actionable under Section 10(b). This federal right to information extends well beyond the freeze-out merger situation. Indeed, subject to certain caveats, it encompasses every corporate transaction in securities that shareholders could have attacked under state law, had they known the facts.

[3] Caveats

There are a number of caveats to the foregoing. First, assuming that disclosure to shareholders is required, the board of directors need only disclose objective facts. There is no requirement for the board to engage in subjective revelation or characterize its actions with pejorative nouns or adjectives. As stated by one court,

---

[55] See *Weinberger v. UOP, Inc.*, 457 A.2d 701 (Del. 1983); *Singer v. Magnavox Co.*, 380 A.2d 969 (Del. 1977).

[56] See, *e.g., Alpert v. 28 Williams St. Corp.*, 63 N.Y.2d 557, 483 N.Y.S.2d 667, 473 N.E.2d 19 (1984); *Perl v. IU International Corp.*, 607 P.2d 1036 (Hawaii 1980). But see *Steinberg v. Amplica, Inc.*, 42 Cal. 3d 1198, 233 Cal. Rptr. 249, 729 P.2d 683 (1986) (appraisal sole remedy).

[57] *Weinberger v. UOP, Inc.*, 457 A.2d 701, 714 (Del. 1983).

[58] See, *e.g., Healey v. Catalyst Recovery, Inc.*, 616 F.2d 641 (3d Cir. 1980); *Alabama Farm Bureau Mutual Casualty Co. v. American Fidelity Life Insurance Co.*, 606 F.2d 602 (5th Cir. 1979); *Goldberg v. Meridor*, 567 F.2d 209 (2d Cir. 1977), *cert. denied*, 434 U.S. 1069 (1978).

[59] See cases cited in note 58, *supra*.

> [t]he unclean heart of a director is not actionable, whether or not it is "disclosed" unless the impurities are translated into actionable deeds or omissions both objective and external.[60]

Moreover, the courts consistently have required Rule 10b-5 claims to allege more than the bare availability of state court injunctive relief. In derivative actions, when shareholder approval of a transaction is not required, the courts have reasoned that disclosure to a disinterested board of directors is equivalent to disclosure to the shareholders. Stated differently, the knowledge of the disinterested board is attributed to the corporation, thereby precluding a finding of deception.[61] Of course, in nonderivative actions, where an individual shareholder is the purchaser or seller of securities, a Section 10(b) claim need only allege that the shareholder was deceived. In such cases, the deception requirement is satisfied by alleging that there was a material misrepresentation or nondisclosure in the flow of information between the majority and the individual shareholder that deprived the plaintiff of an opportunity under state law to enjoin the transaction.[62]

A troublesome issue in determining whether a corporation has been deceived is the proper definition of a "disinterested" director. A director's "financial stake" in the subject transaction would clearly render such person "interested." What is not so clear is whether the presence of some other disability, such as a director's desire to maintain his or her position irrespective of the corporation's best interests, or the perpetuation of improper influence or deception upon a director by a controlling person, including the failure to apprise a director of material facts, would likewise render the director "interested." Although some courts have stated that only the existence of a financial conflict disqualifies the director,[63] the better view is that other disabilities have the same effect.[64] The crucial criterion should be whether a director can exercise *independent judgment* on behalf of the corporation and its shareholders.

Based on the above, only if corporate action requires shareholder approval or if the directors are interested or not informed, will nondisclosure provide the basis for a claim of deception of a corporation in a derivative action under Section 10(b). Even in such cases, however, the bare allegation of nondisclosure will not suffice to state a federal claim. Another limitation imposed by *Santa Fe* is that the aggrieved shareholder must also allege that, had the corporate malfeasance been disclosed, state court remedies would have been available. In this vein, a question left unanswered after *Santa Fe* is whether the complainant must show not only that a suit in state court

---

[60] *Stedman v. Storer*, 308 F. Supp. 881, 887 (S.D.N.Y. 1969), quoted in *Biesenbach v. Guenther*, 588 F.2d 400, 402 (3d Cir. 1978). See *Goldberg v. Meridor*, 567 F.2d 209, 218 n.8 (2d Cir. 1977).

[61] See, *e.g., Maldonado v. Flynn*, 597 F.2d 789 (2d Cir. 1979).

[62] See, *e.g., Healey v. Catalyst Recovery Co.*, 616 F.2d 641 (3d Cir. 1980).

[63] See, *e.g., Tyco Labs., Inc. v. Kimball*, 444 F. Supp. 292 (E.D. Pa. 1977).

[64] See generally *Maldonado v. Flynn*, 597 F.2d 789 (2d Cir. 1979).

could have been brought, but also that such a suit would have been won. The courts are split on this issue. While some courts appear to require that the complainant show that he or she would have been awarded relief in the state court action,[65] others require the plaintiff to show a reasonable basis or probability of success.[66]

[4] Summation

Based on *Santa Fe* and its progeny, although unfairness alone is an insufficient basis for a federal claim, there are circumstances, subject to certain limitations, in which unfairness coupled with either a failure to disclose or an affirmative deception remains a firm foundation for a federal claim. Interestingly, the viability of any such Section 10(b) claim will present local law questions akin to those with which the federal judiciary grapples in diversity cases governed by the rule of *Erie Railroad Co. v. Tompkins.*[67] Significantly, however, unlike the *Erie* doctrine, under which federal courts apply state substantive law in order to recognize state created remedies and liabilities, *Santa Fe*'s footnote 14, as construed by the lower federal courts, conditions the existence of a *federal* right upon the applicable *state* law.[68]

§ 7.05 The Reliance Requirement

[A] Generally

Proof of reliance normally is required to prove the causal connection between the defendant's wrongdoing and the complainant's loss. Positive proof of reliance has not been demanded of the plaintiff where unnecessary to show causation. In such instances, upon demonstrating materiality (*e.g.*, of the nondisclosure), the complainant enjoys a presumption of reliance which the defendant can rebut (*e.g.*, by showing that the plaintiff would not have acted differently had he or she known of the nondisclosure). As the Supreme Court stated in *Affiliated Ute Citizens v. United States*:[69]

> Under the circumstances of this case involving primarily a failure to disclose, positive proof of reliance is not a prerequisite to recovery. All that is necessary is that the facts withheld be material in the sense that

---

[65] See, *e.g., Madison Consultants v. Federal Deposit Insurance Corp.*, [1982-1983 Transfer Binder] Fed. Sec. L. Rep. (CCH) ¶ 99,239 (2d Cir. 1983); *Kidwell ex rel. Penfold v. Meikle*, 597 F.2d 1273 (9th Cir. 1979).

[66] See, *e.g., Healey v. Catalyst Recovery, Inc.*, 616 F.2d 641 (3d Cir. 1980); *Alabama Farm Bureau Mutual Casualty Co. v. American Fidelity Life Insurance Co.*, 606 F.2d 602 (5th Cir. 1979).

[67] 304 U.S. 64 (1938).

[68] The *Goldberg*-line of cases has been subject to criticism. See, *e.g., Healey v. Catalyst Recovery Co.*, 616 F.2d 641, 651 (Aldisert, J., dissenting). See generally Ferrara & Steinberg, *A Reappraisal of Santa Fe: Rule 10b-5 and the New Federalism*, 129 U. Pa. L. Rev. 263 (1980).

[69] 406 U.S. 128 (1972).

> a reasonable investor [would] have considered them important in the making of this decision. . . . This obligation to disclose and this withholding of a material fact establish the requisite element of causation in fact.[70]

Hence, in cases involving primarily a failure to disclose, the plaintiff's reliance is presumed. Although a number of courts have recognized this presumption in omission as well as "half-truth" cases,[71] a few courts hold to the contrary. The Fifth Circuit, for example, has opined that the presumption of reliance extends only to situations involving

> primarily a failure to disclose, implicating the first or third subparagraph of . . . Rule [10b-5] [and not to cases involving] primarily a misstatement or failure to state a fact necessary to make those statements not misleading, classified under the second subparagraph of the Rule.[72]

[B] The "Fraud on the Market" Theory

Plaintiffs also may enjoy a presumption of reliance by invoking the "fraud on the market" theory. This theory postulates that investors assume that the market price of a security is determined by the available material information and that no unsuspected fraudulent conduct has affected the price. The use of this theory to apply a rebuttable presumption of reliance received Supreme Court approbation in *Basic, Inc. v. Levinson*.[73]

In *Basic*, the Court quoted from a lower court decision which explained the rationale of the fraud on the market theory in the following terms:

> In face-to-face transactions, the inquiry into an investor's reliance upon information is into the subjective pricing of that information by that investor. With the presence of a market, the market is interposed between seller and buyer and, ideally, transmits information to the investor in the processed form of a market price. Thus the market is performing a substantial part of the valuation process performed by the investor in a face-to-face transaction. The market is acting as the unpaid agent of the investor, informing him that given all the information available to it, the value of the stock is worth the market price.[74]

The Supreme Court's decision in *Basic* recognized the reality of the modern securities markets involving the trading of hundreds of millions of

---

[70] *Id.* at 153-54.

[71] See, *e.g., Holmes v. Bateson*, 583 F.2d 545, 558 (1st Cir. 1978).

[72] *Huddleston v. Herman & MacLean*, 640 F.2d 534, 548 (5th Cir. 1981), *aff'd on other grounds*, 459 U.S. 375 (1983). See M. Steinberg, *Securities Regulation: Liabilities and Remedies* § 7.05 (1989) (asserting that "pure nondisclosures and half-truths should be deemed equivalent for Rule 10b-5 presumption of reliance purposes").

[73] 108 S.Ct. 978 (1988). Other aspects of the *Basic* decision are addressed in § 9.03[C], *infra*.

[74] *Id.* at 990, quoting *In re LTV Securities Litigation*, 88 F.R.D. 134, 143 (N.D. Tex. 1980).

shares on a daily basis and that most ordinary investors do not read corporate reports or press releases. Acknowledging the presence of impersonal trading markets, the Court relied in part on economic theory and empirical studies to support its holding. In so ruling, the Court promoted the use of the class action to redress Section 10(b) violations. If the Court had required positive proof of individualized reliance from each plaintiff, individual issues may have predominated over the common ones, thereby precluding the pursuit of class actions in this context. Hence, the Court's decision looked to policy grounds as well to help ensure that ordinary investors have a viable recourse when they are defrauded in the impersonal trading markets.[75]

Accordingly, the Court concluded:

> An investor who buys or sells stock at the price set by the market does so in reliance on the integrity of that price. Because most publicly available information is reflected in market price, an investor's reliance on any public material misrepresentations, therefore, may be presumed for purposes of a Rule 10b-5 action.[76]

It should be observed that only six Justices took part in the *Basic* decision, with Chief Justice Rehnquist, Justice Scalia, and Justice Kennedy not participating. In a sharp dissent, Justice White, joined by Justice O'Connor, disagreed with the Court's embracement of the fraud on the market theory, asserting:

> [I]n adopting a "presumption of reliance," the Court *also* assumes that buyers and sellers rely—not just on the market price—but on the "*integrity*" of that price. It is this aspect of the fraud-on-the-market hypothesis which most mystifies me. . . .
>
> Even if securities had some "value"—knowable and distinct from the market price of a stock—investors do not always share the Court's presumption that a stock's price is a "reflection of [this] value." Indeed, "many investors purchase or sell stock because they believe the price *inaccurately* reflects the corporation's worth." If investors really believed that stock prices reflected a stock's "value," many sellers would never sell, and many buyers never buy. . . .[77]

In view of Justice White's dissent, it remains to be seen whether the Court will revisit this issue.

A more expansive version of the fraud-on-the-market theory applies the theory to the offering context where no active trading market exists for the issuer's stock. The leading case is *Shores v. Sklar*,[78] in which the Fifth Circuit

---

[75] 108 S.Ct. 989-92.

[76] *Id.* at 991-92.

[77] *Id.* at 995-96 (White, J., concurring in part and dissenting in part) (emphasis not supplied, citations omitted). See generally Stout, *The Unimportance of Being Efficient: An Economic Analysis of Stock Market Pricing and Securities Regulation*, 87 Mich. L. Rev. 613 (1988).

[78] 647 F.2d 462 (5th Cir. 1981) (*en banc*), *cert. denied*, 459 U.S. 1102 (1983).

sitting *en banc* adopted the theory, with ten judges dissenting. The Supreme Court has yet to rule on the theory's validity in this context.

In *Shores*, the plaintiff purchased bonds without reading the offering circular. He alleged in a Section 10(b) cause of action that the defendants had perpetrated a fraudulent scheme on the investment community by bringing unmarketable securities onto the open market. Invoking the fraud-on-the-market theory, the court held that an investor is entitled to rely on the integrity of the market to the extent that the securities offered for sale are entitled to be in the marketplace. To recover under this theory, the plaintiff must establish that the bonds would never have been issued or marketed. Proof that the bonds would have been offered at a lower price is not sufficient.[79] Thus,

> the fraudulent scheme [must be] so pervasive that without it the issuer would not have issued, the dealer could not have dealt in, and the buyer could not have bought [the securities], because they would not have been offered at any time.[80]

[C] Plaintiff Due Diligence

The plaintiff "due diligence" requirement has been equated by a number of courts with the requirement of justifiable reliance. The Tenth Circuit, upon reviewing pertinent case law, indicated that the following factors are relevant in determining whether the plaintiff's reliance was justifiable:

> (1) the sophistication and expertise of the plaintiff in financial and securities matters; (2) the existence of long standing business or personal relationships; (3) access to the relevant information; (4) the existence of a fiduciary relationship; (5) concealment of the fraud; (6) the opportunity to detect the fraud; (7) whether the plaintiff initiated the stock transaction or sought to expedite the transaction; and (8) the generality or specificity of the misrepresentations.[81]

Two policy rationales for the plaintiff due diligence requirement are:

> First, general principles of equity suggest that only those who have pursued their own interests with care and good faith should qualify for the judicially created private [Rule] 10b-5 remedies. Second, by requiring plaintiffs to invest carefully, the court promotes the anti-fraud policies of the Acts and engenders stability in the markets.[82]

In light of the Supreme Court's decision in *Hochfelder* requiring a plaintiff to prove the defendant's scienter in order to recover under Section 10(b),[83]

---

[79] *Id.* at 469-71.

[80] *Id.* at 464 n.2. See A. Bromberg & L. Lowenfels, *Securities Fraud and Commodities Fraud* § 8.6 (1986).

[81] *Zobrist v. Coal-X, Inc.*, 708 F.2d 1511, 1516 (10th Cir. 1983).

[82] *Dupuy v. Dupuy*, 551 F.2d 1005, 1014 (5th Cir. 1977). See generally Sachs, *The Relevance of Tort Law Doctrines to Rule 10b-5: Should Careless Plaintiffs Be Denied Recovery?*, 71 Cornell L. Rev. 96 (1985).

[83] See § 7.03[A], *supra*.

courts have altered the plaintiff's due diligence burden. Rather than mandating that the plaintiff establish due care, these courts now require that such plaintiff's burden simply is to negate that he or she acted recklessly when engaging in the securities transaction.[84]

§ 7.06 Cumulative Remedies

Under a cumulative interpretation of the securities laws, a party may invoke a remedy even though another statute may provide another remedy for the same conduct. In *Herman & MacLean v. Huddleston*,[85] the Supreme Court adopted a cumulative construction to Section 10(b), thereby recognizing an implied right of action for damages under Section 10(b) despite the apparent availability of an express cause of action under Section 11 of the 1933 Act. The Court reasoned that, unlike Section 11, Section 10(b) imposes a heavier burden on the plaintiff by mandating that the defendant's scienter be proven in order to recover. Moreover, while Section 11 applies solely in the registered offering context, Section 10(b) is a "catch-all" antifraud provision designed to reach manipulative or deceptive practices in connection with the purchase or sale of any security, whether traded in the primary or secondary markets.[86]

In adopting a cumulative construction, the Court also applied the *Curran* analysis[87] (discussed in § 8.02[C], *infra*). The *Huddleston* Court reasoned:

> [W]hen Congress comprehensively revised the securities laws in 1975, a consistent line of judicial decisions had permitted plaintiffs to sue under Section 10(b) regardless of the availability of express remedies. In 1975 Congress enacted the "most substantial and significant revision of this country's Federal securities laws since the passage of the Securities Exchange Act of 1934." . . . When Congress acted, federal courts had consistently and routinely permitted a plaintiff to proceed under Section 10(b) even where express remedies under Section 11 or other provisions were available. In light of this well-established judicial interpretation, Congress' decision to leave Section 10(b) intact suggests that Congress ratified the cumulative nature of the Section 10(b) action.[88]

Although the Court did not directly so hold, the above and certain other language in *Huddleston* strongly suggests that a cumulative approach between Section 10(b) and other express rights of action, such as Section 12(2) of the Securities Act[89] and Section 18(a) of the Exchange Act[90] is appropriate where

---

[84] *Mallis v. Bankers Trust Co.*, 615 F.2d 68, 79 (2d Cir. 1980). See *Landry v. All American Assurance Co.*, 688 F.2d 381, 392-93 (5th Cir. 1982).

[85] 459 U.S. 375 (1983).

[86] *Id.* at 380-84.

[87] *Merrill Lynch, Pierce, Fenner & Smith, Inc. v. Curran*, 456 U.S. 353 (1982).

[88] 459 U.S. at 384-86.

[89] Section 12(2) is addressed in § 6.09, *supra*.

[90] Section 18(a) provides an express right of action for damages when an investor purchases or sells a security in reliance upon a materially false or

the express remedy does not require the plaintiff to prove scienter. In other words, the various procedural restrictions that apply in actions invoking the express remedies (which restrictions are absent in suits brought under Section 10(b)) are counter-balanced by Section 10(b)'s scienter requirement. Based in large part on this rationale, the lower courts have adhered to a cumulative approach where the express remedy involved was Section 11 or 12(2) of the Securities Act or Section 18(a) of the Exchange Act.[91]

A more difficult issue is presented when a cumulative approach is sought to be invoked between Section 10(b) and Section 9 of the Exchange Act. Under Section 9 (which provides a private remedy for purchasers and sellers who have been victimized by stock manipulation), the plaintiff in order to recover must prove scienter, reliance, causation, and damages. Moreover, plaintiffs suing under Section 9 are subject to rigorous procedural limitations. As one court has observed:

> Section 9(e) contains a relatively short statute of limitations, permits the court to require security for costs, limits damages to losses sustained by reason of the unlawful price manipulation, provides for contribution by persons not joined as defendants in the original action, and permits the court to assess attorneys' fees against either party.[92]

Hence, due to the breadth of the Section 9 requirements, plaintiffs bringing suit under Section 10(b) are subject to no additional burdens. Indeed, when contrasted with the Section 9 express remedy, the Section 10(b) right of action is more attractive in practically every respect and is not less attractive in any respect.[93]

Nonetheless, cogent reasons exist for recognizing a cumulative remedy in this context. Perhaps the most persuasive is that an exclusive approach precluding a Section 10(b) right of action where a Section 9 express remedy is available would afford less protection to investors who trade on a national securities exchange than to those who trade in the over-the-counter market. It is beyond dispute that Section 9 applies by its terms only to transactions on a national securities exchange. To fill this vacuum, courts have uniformly held that such manipulative practices that occur in the over-the-counter market may be redressed by private claimants under Section 10(b).[94] Because

---

misleading statement that is contained in a document filed with the SEC pursuant to the Exchange Act, where such statement affects the price of the security. Because of Section 18(a)'s strict reliance and causation requirements, a suit based solely on Section 18(a) evidently has never succeeded.

[91] *E.g.*, *Berger v. Bishop Investment Corp.*, 695 F.2d 302 (8th Cir. 1982); *Wachovia Bank & Trust Co. v. National Student Marketing Corp.*, 650 F.2d 342 (D.C. Cir. 1980); *Ross v. A.H. Robins, Co.*, 607 F.2d 545 (2d Cir. 1979).

[92] *Wolgin v. Magic Marker Corp.*, 82 F.R.D. 168, 180 (E.D. Pa. 1979).

[93] See generally *Chemetron Corp. v. Business Funds, Inc.*, [1983-1984 Transfer Binder] Fed. Sec. L. Rep. (CCH) ¶ 99,541 (5th Cir. 1983), 682 F.2d 1149 (5th Cir. 1982).

[94] See, *e.g.*, *Wachovia Bank & Trust Co. v. National Student Marketing Co.*, 650 F.2d 342 (D.C. Cir. 1980).

these claimants are not saddled with the limitations of Section 9, they may successfully seek redress under Section 10(b) in situations in which injured investors who trade on a national securities exchange under an exclusive construction of remedies would be denied recovery.

Such a result is not only misplaced but is contrary to congressional intent. The Securities Acts Amendments of 1964 were the ultimate result of a congressionally-mandated special study conducted by the Securities and Exchange Commission.[95] The study recommended, *inter alia*, that Congress strengthen over-the-counter regulation. Congress followed this recommendation in order to provide, as much as practicable, equality of regulation between the national securities exchange and over-the-counter markets. At no time, however, did Congress intend to create greater rights on behalf of over-the-counter investors as compared to those given to investors who trade in stock exchange listed securities.

Thus, Congress' approach is sound and firmly rooted in the reality of the operations of the securities markets. In contrast, an exclusive construction of remedies fragmentizes the operational components of the securities markets and ignores that the markets operate as a unified whole where those desiring to buy or sell may do so with confidence. Denying private parties the use of Section 10(b) with respect to manipulative schemes in listed securities would insulate violators from monetary liability for practices repugnant to the notions of honesty and fairness. Such a construction goes far toward undermining the very interests the securities laws were designed to promote.[96]

§ 7.07 Measure of Damages

Much of the discussion that follows applies to damages under the securities laws in general. Because the proper measure of damages most often arises in Section 10(b) litigation, the subject will be treated here. For damages in insider trading cases, Chapter 9, *infra,* should be consulted.

Section 28(a) of the Exchange Act has been construed by the courts to prohibit recovery of punitive, as opposed to compensatory damages,[97] and to prevent double recovery by those who assert both state and federal claims which arise out of the same conduct.[98] The measures of compensatory damages adopted by the courts primarily include the out-of-pocket measure[99]

[95] *Report of Special Study of Securities Markets of the Securities and Exchange Commission*, H.R. Doc. No. 95, 88th Cong., 1st Sess. (1963).

[96] See Steinberg, *The Propriety and Scope of Cumulative Remedies Under the Federal Securities Laws*, 67 Cornell L. Rev. 557 (1982).

[97] See, *e.g., Gould v. American-Hawaiian Steamship Co.*, 535 F.2d 761, 781 (3d Cir. 1976).

[98] See, *e.g., Osofsky v. Zipf*, 645 F.2d 107, 111 (2d Cir. 1981). See also 3 L. Loss, *Securities Regulation* 1624 (2d ed. 1961).

[99] See, *e.g., Estate Counselling Service, Inc. v. Merrill Lynch, Pierce, Fenner & Smith, Inc.*, 303 F.2d 527, 533 (10th Cir. 1962) (defining the out-of-pocket measure

and, in some circumstances, the rescissionary[100] and benefit-of-the-bargain measures.[101] In this regard, however, "[t]he customary measure of damages in a Rule 10b-5 case is the out-of-pocket loss."[102]

Nonetheless, where the amount of damages can be determined with reasonable certainty, courts may well apply the benefit-of-the-bargain measure, particularly if such application is necessary to prevent unjust enrichment.[103] A number of courts, however, have refused to apply this measure in cases involving defrauded purchasers due to the asserted speculative nature of the damages which would otherwise be awarded.[104]

§ 7.08 *In Pari Delicto* Defense

Considerable debate has been generated regarding the propriety of the *in pari delicto* defense in securities litigation.[105] In the *Bateman Eichler* case,[106] the Supreme Court limited the availability of the defense in a civil damages action pursuant to Section 10(b) where corporate insiders and a broker allegedly conveyed false "inside" information. In so doing, the Court applied a two-part test to ascertain whether the *in pari delicto* defense should be permitted. First, it looked to the relative culpability of the parties to the action. Second, the Court examined public policy considerations. Hence, a Section 10(b) action for damages

> may be barred on the grounds of the plaintiff's own culpability only where (1) as a direct result of his own actions, the plaintiff bears at least substantially equal responsibility for the violations he seeks to redress, and (2) preclusion of suit would not significantly interfere with the effective enforcement of the securities laws and protection of the investing public.[107]

---

as "the difference between the contract price, or the price paid, and the real or actual value at the date of the sale, together with such outlays as are attributable to the defendant's conduct").

[100] See, *e.g.*, *Blackie v. Barrack*, 524 F.2d 891, 909 (9th Cir. 1975). See also *Randall v. Loftsgaarden*, 106 S.Ct. 3143 (1986).

[101] See, *e.g.*, *Osofsky v. Zipf*, 645 F.2d 107, 111-15 (2d Cir. 1981).

[102] *Hackbart v. Holmes*, 675 F.2d 1114, 1121 (10th Cir. 1982).

[103] *Id.* at 1122.

[104] See, *e.g.*, *Barrows v. Forest Laboratories, Inc.*, [1984 Transfer Binder] Fed. Sec. L. Rep. (CCH) ¶ 91,614 (2d Cir. 1984). See generally Easterbrook & Fischel, *Optimal Damages in Securities Cases*, 52 U. Chi. L. Rev. 611 (1985); Thompson, *The Measure of Recovery Under Rule 10b-5: A Restitution Alternative to Tort Damages*, 37 Vand. L. Rev. 349 (1984); Comment, *The Measure of Damages Under Section 10(b) and Rule 10b-5*, 46 Md. L. Rev. 1266 (1987).

[105] See, *e.g.*, Comment, *Rule 10b-5: The In Pari Delicto and Unclean Hands Defenses*, 58 Calif. L. Rev. 1149 (1970).

[106] *Bateman Eichler, Hill Richards, Inc. v. Berner*, 472 U.S. 299 (1985).

[107] *Id.* at 310-11.

Turning to the first prong, the *Bateman Eichler* Court found that the plaintiff "tippees" were less blameworthy than the defendant "tippers." As the Court stated,

> [i]n the context of insider trading, we do not believe that a person whose liability is solely derivative can be said to be as culpable as one whose breach of duty gave rise to that liability in the first place.[108]

Regarding the second prong, the Court asserted that permitting private suits for damages in this context would enhance the enforcement of the securities laws and would serve as a deterrent to the perpetration of insider trading. Moreover, by bringing such an action and exposing oneself to civil and criminal penalties, a tippee would not enjoy a "heads-I-win, tails-you-lose" scenario. Accordingly, public policy would be promoted by allowing such actions.[109]

Until recently, it was uncertain whether the Court's analysis in *Bateman Eichler* applied to the securities laws in general. The Court answered this question affirmatively in an action involving Section 12(1) of the Securities Act, *Pinter v. Dahl.*[110] In *Pinter*, the Court held that the *Bateman Eichler* standard "provides the appropriate test for allowance of the *in pari delicto* defense in a private action under any of the federal securities laws."[111] The Court reasoned that, irrespective of whether the substantive statute imposes liability for willful or negligent misconduct or even is one of strict liability (such as Section 12(1)), there may be occasions where the objective of deterring unlawful conduct is served better by precluding suit rather than by allowing recovery.[112]

Applying the *Bateman Eichler* standard to the Section 12(1) litigation at bar, the *Pinter* Court's analysis indicates that the *in pari delicto* defense will be rarely successful in this context. According to the Court, the defense can be used only when the plaintiff's role in the offer or sale of the securities is more that of a promoter than an investor. Whether a plaintiff primarily is an investor or a promoter depends on several factors, such as

> the extent of the plaintiff's financial involvement compared to that of third parties solicited by the plaintiff, the incidental nature of the plaintiff's promotional activities, the benefits received by the plaintiff from his promotional activities, and the extent of the plaintiff's involvement in the planning stages of the offering.[113]

Where the plaintiff is deemed to be primarily an investor, the *in pari delicto* defense is unavailable. This is true even if the plaintiff-investor actively participates in the distribution of unregistered securities. The *Pinter*

---

[108] *Id.* at 313, citing *Dirks v. SEC*, 463 U.S. 646 (1983).
[109] 472 U.S. at 315-16.
[110] 108 S.Ct. 2063 (1988). For discussion of Section 12(1), see § 6.08, *supra.*
[111] *Id.* at 2072.
[112] *Id.* at 2073-74.
[113] *Id.* at 2074 (citations omitted).

Court reasoned that a contrary holding would pose a significant obstacle to the effective enforcement of the Securities Act's registration provisions and to the goal of investor protection.[114]

§ 7.09 Special Concepts of Fraud for Broker-Dealers

Under Section 10(b) as well as under certain other provisions (such as Section 17(a) of the Securities Act), a number of principles have been developed to hold broker-dealers to a fairly strict standard of conduct. One such theory is the shingle theory which posits that by hanging out its "shingle," a broker-dealer impliedly represents that its conduct and the behavior of its employees will be fair and will comport with professional norms. As the Second Circuit has opined, "[a] securities dealer occupies a special relationship to the buyer of securities in that by his position he impliedly represents he has an adequate basis for the opinions he renders."[115] One aspect of this duty, labeled the suitability theory, recognizes an implied representation by the broker that it will recommend only those securities suitable for each customer's investment objectives and economic status.[116]

A number of other implied representations have been recognized as coming within the shingle theory, including:

(1) An implied representation of fair pricing, including any markup or markdown;

(2) An implied representation that the broker-dealer will execute only authorized transactions for its customers;

(3) An implied representation to disclose any special consideration that influences the broker-dealer's recommendation;

(4) An implied representation to execute promptly customers' orders; and

(5) An implied representation that any recommendation made by a broker-dealer to a customer has a reasonable basis.[117]

One may inquire, however, whether aspects of the shingle theory still provide the basis for a Section 10(b) action in light of the Supreme Court's holding in *Santa Fe* that deception or manipulation must be shown (see § 7.04, *supra*). A few courts have taken the position that certain components of the shingle theory are no longer viable. For example, in *Pross v. Baird, Patrick & Co., Inc.*,[118] a Section 10(b) claim based on unauthorized trading by

---

[114] *Id.* at 2074-75. See generally Klock, *Promoter Liability and In Pari Delicto Under Section 12(1): Pinter v. Dahl*, 17 Sec. Reg. L.J. 53 (1989).

[115] *Hanly v. SEC*, 415 F.2d 589, 596-97 (2d Cir. 1969).

[116] See generally Kerr, *Suitability Standards: A New Look at Economic Theory and Current SEC Disclosure Policy*, 16 Pac. L.J. 805 (1985).

[117] M. Steinberg & R. Ferrara, *Securities Practice: Federal and State Enforcement* § 2:17 (1985) (and authorities cited therein).

[118] [1983-1984 Transfer Binder] Fed. Sec. L. Rep. (CCH) ¶ 99,668 (S.D.N.Y. 1984).

a broker was dismissed. The court reasoned that the claim was in actuality one for breach of fiduciary duty not involving the element of deception necessary to invoke Section 10(b).[119]

Nonetheless, the shingle theory basically remains good law. Arguably, it should remain so in view of the investing public's reliance on broker-dealers, investment advisers, and other financial experts (and which may be called a "relational reliance" interest). The shingle theory is premised on the proposition that these experts make certain implied representations to their customers. Consequently, where a customer relies on a broker-dealer's fair dealing, the failure by such broker-dealer to disclose its noncompliance with the implied representations made constitutes deception for Section 10(b) purposes.[120]

§ 7.10 Secondary Liability

[A] Aiding and Abetting Liability

Although the Supreme Court has not addressed the propriety of aiding and abetting liability under the federal securities laws, virtually every lower federal court considering the issue has recognized the validity of such liability.[121] Generally, in order to impose aiding and abetting liability, there must be:

(1) the existence of a securities law violation by the primary (as opposed to the aiding and abetting) party;

(2) improper knowledge on the part of the aider and abettor; and

(3) "substantial assistance" by the aider and abettor in the achievement of the primary violation.[122]

With respect to the requisite "knowledge" for culpability purposes, scienter must be shown. While some courts generally have held that reckless conduct is sufficient in this context,[123] others have held that recklessness suffices only where an alleged aider and abettor owes a fiduciary duty to the plaintiff[124] or where such aider and abettor has reason to foresee that third parties are relying on its conduct.[125] In the absence of such a fiduciary relationship or

---

[119] *Id.* at 99,683.

[120] See Langevoort, *Fraud and Deception by Securities Professionals*, 61 Texas L. Rev. 1247, 1280-83 (1983).

[121] See, *e.g.*, *ITT v. Cornfeld*, 619 F.2d 909 (2d Cir. 1980).

[122] *Id.* at 922.

[123] See, *e.g.*, *Stern v. American Bankshares, Inc.*, 429 F. Supp. 818 (E.D. Wis. 1977).

[124] See, *e.g.*, *Rolf v. Blyth, Eastman Dillon & Co., Inc.*, 570 F.2d 38 (2d Cir.), *cert. denied*, 439 U.S. 1039 (1978).

[125] See, *e.g.*, *Oleck v. Fischer*, [1979 Transfer Binder] Fed. Sec. L. Rep. (CCH) ¶ 96,898 (S.D.N.Y. 1979), *aff'd on other grounds*, 623 F.2d 791 (2d Cir. 1980).

foreseeability of third party reliance, a number of courts will impose aider and abettor liability only if there is a showing of "something closer to an actual intent to aid in a fraud."[126]

An issue that remains problematic is under what circumstances liability may be imposed against an aider and abettor based on silence or inaction. In this regard, courts have found such liability "(1) when there is a conscious or reckless violation of an independent duty to act,"[127] or (2) if no such independent duty exists, then "only where it is shown that the silence of the accused aider and abettor was consciously intended to aid the securities law violation."[128]

[B] Controlling Person Liability

Section 15 of the Securities Act imposes joint and several liability on any person who controls a person liable under Section 11 or 12

> unless the controlling person had no knowledge of or reasonable grounds to believe in the existence of the facts by reason of which the liability of the controlled person is alleged to exist.

Section 20(a) of the Exchange Act provides that

> every person who . . . controls any person liable under any provision of this title . . . shall also be liable jointly and severally with and to the same extent as such controlled person to any person to whom such controlled person is liable, unless the controlling person acted in good faith and did not directly or indirectly induce the act or acts constituting the violation or cause of action.

As has been pointed out,

> [t]he reason for this difference in language is hard to fathom, especially since Section 15 of the 1933 Act was amended in the bill which enacted the 1934 Act, and harder still to interpret.[129]

The term "control" is not defined in the securities acts. Pursuant to Rule 405, however, the Commission has defined the term to encompass "the possession, direct or indirect, of the power to direct or cause the direction of the management and policies of a person."[130] The courts generally are in accord with this standard. For example, the Fifth Circuit has held that control was established when the defendant "had the requisite power to directly or indirectly control or influence corporate policy."[131]

---

[126] *Edwards & Hanly v. Wells Fargo Securities Clearance Corp.*, 602 F.2d 478, 485 (2d Cir. 1979).

[127] *ITT v. Cornfeld*, 619 F.2d 909, 927 (2d Cir. 1980).

[128] *SEC v. Coffey*, 493 F.2d 1304, 1317 (6th Cir. 1974). See for a more recent application *SEC v. Washington County Utility District*, 676 F.2d 218, 226-27 (6th Cir. 1982).

[129] See R. Jennings & H. Marsh, *Securities Regulation* 1163 (6th ed. 1987).

[130] 17 C.F.R. § 230.405.

[131] *G.A. Thompson & Co., Inc. v. Partridge*, 636 F.2d 945, 958 (5th Cir. 1981).

As stated above, Section 20(a) absolves the controlling person of liability if he or she acted in good faith and did not directly or indirectly induce the violation. The statutory language appears clear in placing the burden of proof on the controlling person to establish the good faith defense. This view has been overwhelmingly adopted.[132] With respect to the state of mind required to establish liability, the Supreme Court in *Hochfelder* stated that the controlling person provision "contains a state-of-mind condition requiring something more than negligence."[133]

The courts have not been consistent in applying this standard. For example, the Third Circuit has required "culpable participation," signifying that the defendant's inaction, such as lack of supervision, "was deliberate and done intentionally to further the fraud."[134] On the other hand, the Second Circuit, consistent with other courts, has opined that, in the brokerage house setting, the controlling person must show that "it has maintained and enforced a reasonable and proper system of supervision and internal control over sales personnel."[135]

What constitutes "good faith" and "noninducement" under Section 20(a) should depend on the particular facts and circumstances. Although negligence is not sufficient to impose liability, a more relaxed form of reckless conduct should suffice. In determining whether the controlling person acted "recklessly," one should look to customary industry practice and the realistic practicalities of the trade. For example, the failure of a broker-dealer to institute adequate (not necessarily sure-proof) supervisory and internal control procedures should be viewed as reckless conduct. Under such circumstances, by ignoring an obvious danger, the controlling person's failure to institute such mechanisms constitutes a significant departure from the standards of ordinary care.[136]

[C] *Respondeat Superior* Liability

A controversial issue involves whether the common law principle of *respondeat superior* is compatible with the federal securities laws. Under this theory, a principal (*e.g.*, a broker-dealer firm) is held liable for the securities law violations committed by its agent (*e.g.*, a broker) when such agent acts within the scope of his or her employment having actual or apparent authority.[137]

---

[132] See, *e.g.*, *Marbury Management, Inc. v. Kohn*, 629 F.2d 705, 716 (2d Cir. 1980). But see for the minority position *Sharp v. Coopers & Lybrand*, 649 F.2d 175, 185 (3d Cir. 1981).

[133] *Ernst & Ernst v. Hochfelder*, 425 U.S. 185, 209 (1976).

[134] *Sharp v. Coopers & Lybrand*, 649 F.2d 175, 185 (3d Cir. 1981).

[135] *Marbury Management, Inc. v. Kohn*, 629 F.2d 705, 716 (2d Cir. 1979).

[136] See M. Steinberg, *supra* note 72, at § 10.03; Note, *The Burden of Control: Derivative Liability Under Section 20(a) of the Securities Exchange Act of 1934*, 48 N.Y.U. L. Rev. 1019 (1973).

[137] See, *e.g.*, *Paul F. Newton & Co. v. Texas Commerce Bank*, 630 F.2d 1111 (5th Cir. 1980).

A number of courts have rejected in all cases the application of *respondeat superior* liability under the federal securities laws. To hold otherwise, these courts reason, in effect would negate the controlling person provisions. For example, one court has reasoned:

> Noteworthy in each [controlling person] provision is the inclusion of a defense from liability based on "good faith" or lack of knowledge or reasonable belief. When originally passed by Congress, § 15 of the 1933 Act held controlling persons absolutely liable for § 11 and § 12 violations by controlled persons. Congress, in passing the 1934 Act, amended § 15 of the earlier Act, adding the language beginning at "unless the controlling person had no knowledge of or reasonable ground to believe in the existence of facts by reason of which the liability of the controlled person is alleged to exist." Likewise, the controlling person provision in the 1934 Act, § 20(a), contained the "good faith" defense to liability. Clearly Congress had rejected an insurer's liability standard for controlling persons in favor of a fiduciary standard — a duty to take due care.[138]

On the other hand, a majority of courts generally hold that *respondeat superior* liability may be properly imposed under the federal securities laws (except, for example, under Section 20A of the Exchange Act where Congress has manifested its intent that the doctrine of *respondeat superior* does not apply in private rights of action brought by contemporaneous traders for alleged insider trading violations). Those courts favoring imposition of *respondeat superior* liability reason that the controlling person provisions were enacted by Congress to supplement common law agency principles in order to reach individuals (such as intermediate and upper-level supervisors) who have no agency or employment relationship with the primary violator. As to the entity, the imposition of respondeat superior liability is appropriate.[139]

In an *amicus curiae* brief before the Third Circuit, the SEC presented its arguments in favor of *respondeat superior* liability. A portion of the Commission's brief was devoted to policy considerations:

> Defendant asserts . . . that because "the standard of liability under Rule 10b-5 is one of culpability, not strict liability," application of agency principles here would be inappropriate. The culpability requirement under Rule 10b-5, however, is satisfied by the reckless or knowing conduct of the primary wrongdoer. Agency theories such as *respondeat superior* merely serve to identify those persons to be held responsible for the violation of the primary wrongdoer. [T]here is no valid policy reason why the societal judgment in the common law principle of allocating the burden of making payment for the plaintiff's injuries to the employer, which benefits from the activities of its employees and which can insure

---

[138] *Carpenter v. Harris, Upham & Co., Inc.*, 594 F.2d 388, 393 (4th Cir. 1979).

[139] See, *e.g.*, *Henricksen v. Henricksen*, 640 F.2d 880 (7th Cir. 1981).

against the risk of liability, should not equally apply in cases of Rule 10b-5 violations.[140]

§ 7.11 Extraterritorial Jurisdiction

Extraterritorial jurisdiction implicating the federal securities laws comes into play in a number of different contexts, including in civil litigation involving Section 10(b). For purposes of organization, this subject will be treated here.

[A] Transnational Fraud

The principal extraterritorial application of the federal securities laws has involved the area of transnational fraud. In an effort to protect American investors and to prevent this country from being employed as a base for deceptive conduct in transactions abroad affecting American or foreign investors, the U.S. courts have given broad extraterritorial application to the antifraud provisions of the federal securities laws. Under formulations to determine whether subject matter jurisdiction exists, two tests have developed: (1) the "conduct" test and (2) the "effects" test.

Under the *conduct* test, courts have applied Section 10(b) of the Exchange Act to foreign transactions occurring abroad when fraudulent conduct (for example, a misstatement causing an investor's acquisition of a security) or conduct integrally associated with a fraud (for example, the drafting of an inaccurate prospectus for selling stock) took place within the United States.[141] However, in situations in which conduct transpiring in the United States was merely preparatory to the fraud, courts generally have declined to find subject matter jurisdiction where the complainant was a foreign, rather than a United States, citizen.[142] The Second Circuit, however, has opined that subject matter jurisdiction would be appropriate in the case of a foreign plaintiff where the preparatory conduct transpiring in the United States, such as the drafting of a prospectus, directly caused the foreign investor's loss.[143]

Applying the "effects" test, courts have found subject matter jurisdiction when securities transactions outside of the United States had substantial and foreseeable injurious effects in this country. For example, fraudulent conduct

[140] SEC *Brief Amicus Curiae* in *Sharp v. Coopers & Lybrand*, 649 F.2d 175 (3d Cir. 1981). See generally Ferrara & Sanger, *Derivative Liability in Securities Law: Controlling Person Liability, Respondeat Superior, and Aiding and Abetting*, 40 Wash. & Lee L. Rev. 1007 (1983).

[141] See, *e.g., Leasco v. Data Processing Equipment Corp. v. Maxwell*, 468 F.2d 1326 (2d Cir. 1972).

[142] See, *e.g., Bersch v. Drexel Firestore, Inc.*, 519 F.2d 974 (2d Cir. 1978).

[143] See *ITT v. Cornfeld*, 619 F.2d 909 (2d Cir. 1980); Thomas, *Extraterritorial Application of the United States Securities Laws: The Need for a Balanced Policy*, 7 J. Corp. L. 189, 192 (1982). See generally T. Hazen, *The Law of Securities Regulation* 521 n.1 (1985) (and authorities cited therein).

undertaken abroad, which caused a decrease in the value of stock listed on a U.S. exchange, was viewed as coming within the ambit of the federal securities laws, irrespective that no conduct, preparatory or otherwise, took place in the United States in regard to the transaction abroad.[144] The number of defrauded U.S. residents compared to foreign residents also has been considered by U.S. courts under the effects test.[145]

[B] Securities Act Registration

The extraterritorial scope of the federal securities laws is even less predictable when antifraud issues are not implicated. A recurring issue involving foreign issuers and brokers is whether a foreign issuer would transgress the Securities Act's registration requirements if unregistered securities offered abroad were sold to American investors or were subsequently traded in the U.S. markets without registration. In a 1964 SEC *Release* interpreting this issue, the Commission stated that the registration provisions of the 1933 Act were designed principally to protect the U.S. investing public. Accordingly, an issuer in this country may elect to register an offering of stock abroad to foreign nationals under the condition that the offering was "reasonably designed to preclude distribution or redistribution of the securities within, or to nationals of, the United States."[146] Although this *Release* did not extend by its terms to foreign companies, the views set forth in the *Release* may well be applicable to foreign companies. In an attempt to clarify this area, the SEC recently has proposed regulations. Whether such regulations will be adopted, and in what form, remains to be seen.[147]

In an effort to orchestrate an offering "reasonably designed to preclude distribution or redistribution of securities within the United States or to U.S. investors," issuers have implemented a variety of methods. One common measure obligates participants in an offering, or purchasers of the securities, to refrain from selling securities to a United States investor or within this country until a specified period of time after the offering has lapsed (generally 90 days). This event is called the time the securities have "come to rest."[148]

[C] Tender Offers

Another area involving the extraterritorial application of the securities laws is tender offer regulation. Foreign issuers seeking to purchase the securities of other foreign issuers which have U.S. shareholders have been circumspect in

---

[144] See, *e.g., Schoenbaum v. Firstbrook*, 405 F.2d 200, *modified en banc*, 405 F.2d 215 (2d Cir. 1969).

[145] See, *e.g., IIT v. Vencap, Ltd.*, 519 F.2d 1001 (2d Cir. 1975); Thomas, *supra* note 143, at 192.

[146] *Securities Act Release* No. 4708 (1964).

[147] See *Securities Act Release* No. 6779 (1988) (SEC proposed regulations to clarify extraterritorial application of the Securities Act's registration provisions).

[148] See, *e.g., SEC No-Action Letter, Proctor & Gamble*, letter available Feb. 21, 1985.

restricting their public communications concerning the bid to avoid triggering the Williams Act as well as the SEC's tender offer rules. This approach may be successful in certain situations. In one such instance, for example, General Electric Company plc made an offer to acquire a number of shares of the Plessey Company plc. Both companies were doing business pursuant to Great Britain law. Plessey, however, had American Depository Receipts (ADRs) trading in the United States securities markets and had certain other Dollar Shares registered in this country. To avoid implicating the United States tender offer regimen, General Electric refrained from issuing any press releases to the American press concerning the bid, made it clear in its communications to the press that the bid was neither being made in the United States nor was for the Plessey ADRs or Dollar Shares, and took additional measures to help guarantee that shares would not be accepted from stockholders in the United States.[149]

A United States district court ruled that the federal tender offer regimen did not extend to the General Electric offer. The court opined that, as contrasted with the antifraud provisions, it was more appropriate under the tender offer provisions to assess considerations of comity and policy in this area. As such, the court, after evaluating relevant factors, declined to invoke extraterritorial jurisdiction.[150]

§ 7.12 Arbitration

In *Shearson/American Express, Inc. v. McMahon,*[151] the Supreme Court held that pre-dispute arbitration agreements between brokerage firms and their customers did not contravene the Securities Exchange Act and the Racketeer Influenced and Corrupt Organizations Act (RICO). Hence, such claims ordinarily are arbitrable consistent with the terms of the applicable arbitration agreement. The following discussion focuses on the validity of such pre-dispute arbitration agreements under the securities laws.

In *McMahon*, the Supreme Court relied in large part on the Federal Arbitration Act (FAA)[152] which establishes a "federal policy favoring arbitration."[153] This policy is prevalent even when a claim is based on a federal statutory right. As a consequence, the burden is on the party opposing the validity of the arbitration agreement to show that Congress intended to preserve the availability of a judicial forum, irrespective of the terms of an

[149] *The Plessey Company plc v. The General Electric Company plc*, 628 F. Supp. 477, 479-86 (D. Del. 1986).

[150] *Id.* at 494-97.

[151] 107 S.Ct. 2332 (1987).

[152] 9 U.S.C. § 1, *et seq.*

[153] *Moses H. Cone Memorial Hospital v. Mercury Construction Corp.*, 460 U.S. 1, 24 (1983).

arbitration agreement.[154] Accordingly, in order to preclude application of the FAA, according to the Court, the party seeking to avoid arbitration

> must demonstrate that Congress intended to make an exception to the Arbitration Act for claims arising under . . . the Exchange Act, an intention discernible from the text, history, or purposes of the statute.[155]

Upon examining Section 29(a) of the Exchange Act which renders void any stipulation whereby a person waives compliance with any 1934 Act provision, the Court opined that Section 29(a) only proscribes waiver of the Exchange Act's *substantive* obligations. By contrast, Section 29(a) does not preclude parties from waiving a judicial forum in favor of an arbitral tribunal.[156]

The Court's holding in *McMahon* takes a far different view of arbitration than the Court's 1953 decision in *Wilko v. Swan*.[157] In holding that pre-dispute arbitration agreements were not enforceable in actions brought pursuant to Section 12(2) of the Securities Act, the *Wilko* Court invoked the anti-waiver provision of the Securities Act, Section 14, which is Section 29(a)'s counterpart. Underlying the *Wilko* Court's holding was its hostility to the arbitration process. Succinctly put, the Court believed that arbitration would fail to protect the investor's substantive rights. As a consequence, a judicial forum was necessary to ensure that the statutory rights created by Section 12(2) would be adequately protected.[158]

Although declining to overrule *Wilko*,[159] the Supreme Court in *McMahon* asserted that, in view of the increased regulatory oversight of arbitration since *Wilko* was handed down, a party's 1934 Act substantive rights are not waived by enforcing a pre-dispute arbitration agreement. Pursuant to the 1975 Amendments to the 1934 Act, the SEC now

> has broad authority to oversee and to regulate the rules adopted by the [self-regulatory organizations] relating to customer disputes, including the power to mandate the adoption of any rules it deems necessary to ensure that arbitration procedures adequately protect statutory rights.[160]

---

[154] 107 S.Ct. at 2337, relying on *Mitsubishi Motors Corp. v. Soler Chrysler-Plymouth, Inc.*, 473 U.S. 614 (1985); *Dean Witter Reynolds, Inc. v. Byrd*, 470 U.S. 213 (1985); *Scherk v. Alberto-Culver Co.*, 417 U.S. 506 (1974).

[155] 107 S.Ct. at 2338.

[156] *Id.* at 2338-41.

[157] 346 U.S. 427 (1953).

[158] *Id.* at 432-37. See generally Brown, Shell & Tyson, *Arbitration of Customer-Broker Disputes Arising Under the Federal Securities Laws and RICO*, 15 Sec. Reg. L.J. 3 (1987); Comment, *Predispute Arbitration Agreements Between Brokers and Investors: The Extension of Wilko to Section 10(b) Claims*, 46 Md. L. Rev. 339 (1987).

[159] 107 S.Ct. at 2341 ("*[S]tare decisis* concerns may counsel against upsetting *Wilko's* contrary conclusion under the Securities Act.").

[160] *Id.*

Accordingly, the *McMahon* Court held:

> We conclude, therefore, that Congress did not intend for § 29(a) to bar enforcement of all predispute arbitration agreements. In this case, where the SEC has sufficient statutory authority to ensure that arbitration is adequate to vindicate Exchange Act rights, enforcement does not effect a waiver of "compliance with any provision" of the Exchange Act under § 29(a).[161]

Although the Supreme Court in *McMahon* did not overrule *Wilko*, a number of lower courts have upheld the enforceability of pre-dispute arbitration agreements involving 1933 Act claims. These courts reason that the rationale of *McMahon* favoring arbitration should be extended to claims arising under the Securities Act.[162] On a different front, the SEC has been working with the self-regulatory organizations concerning the adoption of arbitration rules that will instill greater confidence by the investing public in the arbitral process.[163]

---

[161] *Id.* at 2343. But see *id.* at 2346-59 (Blackmun, J., concurring in part and dissenting in part).

[162] See, *e.g.*, *Aronson v. Dean Witter Reynolds, Inc.*, 675 F. Supp. 1324 (S.D. Fla. 1987).

[163] See Shell, *Arbitration After the Crash*, Nat. L.J., March 21, 1988, at 13. See generally Fletcher, *Learning to Live with the Federal Arbitration Act — Securities Litigation in a Post-McMahon World*, 37 Emory L.J. 99 (1988).

CHAPTER 8

ALTERNATIVE REMEDIES

§ 8.01 Introduction

As Chapters 6 and 7 have discussed, Sections 11 and 12(2) of the Securities Act and Section 10(b) of the Exchange Act play an important role in securities litigation. These provisions, however, may be unavailable to a complainant for a number of reasons. For example, the securities may have been purchased in the aftermarket, hence making the Section 11 right of action unavailable (unless the plaintiff meets the onerous "tracing" requirement). Or, alternatively, the complainant may be unable to invoke the Section 10(b) remedy because he or she is not a "purchaser" or "seller" or cannot establish that the defendant acted with scienter. Under such circumstances, counsel should focus on the availability of alternative remedies, including the invocation of implied remedies.

Moreover, even where a right of action can be successfully established (such as under Section 10(b)), counsel, where appropriate, still should assess the viability of remedies afforded by other provisions. For example, Section 29(b) of the Exchange Act may provide an aggrieved party with the right to rescind the subject transaction. Another attractive remedy may be available under the Racketeer Influenced and Corrupt Organizations Act (RICO) which authorizes an award of attorneys' fees and treble damages to successful claimants.

As an additional point, counsel always should assess the advisability of seeking relief under the applicable state common and statutory (including "Blue Sky") laws.

§ 8.02 Implied Rights of Action — In General

[A] Pre-1975 Approach

Prior to 1975, the federal courts liberally recognized implied private rights of action, generally looking to whether the granting of an implied remedy would benefit the class sought to be protected by the statute. For example, in *J.I. Case Co. v. Borak,*[1] the Supreme Court recognized an implied right of action under Section 14(a) of the Exchange Act (the "proxy" provision),

[1] 377 U.S. 426 (1964).

reasoning that such an implied right would promote investor protection and serve as a necessary supplement to SEC enforcement action.

[B] The *Cort* Formulation

The liberal construction to implied rights of action halted with the Supreme Court's decision in *Cort v. Ash.*[2] There, the Court formulated a four-prong standard:

> First, is the plaintiff "one of the class for whose especial benefit the statute was enacted," — that is, does the statute create a federal right in favor of the plaintiff? Second, is there any indication of legislative intent, explicit or implicit, either to create such a remedy or to deny one? Third, is it consistent with the underlying purpose of the legislative scheme to imply such a remedy for the plaintiff? And finally, is the cause of action one traditionally relegated to state law, in an area basically the concern of the States, so that it would be inappropriate to infer a cause of action based solely on federal law?[3]

In subsequent decisions, the Court has embraced the *Cort* formulation with varying levels of enthusiasm.[4] Perhaps somewhat ironically (given the pre-1975 broad construction to implied rights), certain members of the Court have criticized the *Cort* standard as being "an open invitation to federal courts to legislate causes of action not authorized by Congress."[5]

The apparent demise of the *Cort* formulation was evidenced by *Transamerica Mortgage Advisors, Inc. v. Lewis,*[6] where the Supreme Court refused to imply a private right of action under the antifraud provision of the Investment Advisers Act, Section 206. There, the Court, relying on its prior decision in *Redington,*[7] stated that the central inquiry is to examine Congress' intent. Hence, the Court reasoned:

> The question whether a statute creates a cause of action, either expressly or by implication, is basically a matter of statutory construction. While some opinions of the Court have placed considerable emphasis upon the desirability of implying private rights of action in order to provide remedies thought to effectuate the purposes of a given statute, what must ultimately be determined is whether Congress intended to create the private remedy asserted, as our recent decisions have made clear. We

---

[2] 422 U.S. 66 (1975).

[3] *Id.* at 78.

[4] Compare *Cannon v. University of Chicago*, 441 U.S. 677 (1979), with *Touche Ross & Co. v. Redington*, 422 U.S. 560 (1979), discussed in Steinberg, *Implied Private Rights of Action Under Federal Law*, 55 Notre Dame Law. 33 (1979).

[5] See *Cannon v. University of Chicago*, 441 U.S. 677, 731 (1979) (Powell, J., dissenting).

[6] 444 U.S. 11 (1979).

[7] *Touche Ross & Co. v. Redington*, 442 U.S. 560 (1979) (holding that no implied private right of action exists under § 17(a) of the Exchange Act).

> accept this as the appropriate inquiry to be made in resolving the issue presented by the case before us.[8]

Thus, in *Lewis* the Court adhered to what has been viewed as a restrictive approach. More recent cases, however, indicate that the *Cort* formulation still survives. *California v. Sierra Club*,[9] a non-securities law case, highlights the disagreement on the Court concerning the continued viability of *Cort*. There, in declining to imply a right of action under the pertinent statute, the five-member majority adhered to the *Cort* formulation and asserted:

> Combined, these four factors present the relevant inquiries to pursue in answering the recurring question of implied causes of action. Cases subsequent to *Cort* have explained that the ultimate issue is whether Congress intended to create a private right of action, but the four factors specified in *Cort* remain the "criteria through which this intent could be discerned."[10]

Concurring in the judgment, Justice Rehnquist (joined by three other Justices) in a separate opinion believed that "the Court's opinion places somewhat more emphasis on *Cort v. Ash* than is warranted in light of several more recent 'implied right of action' decisions which limit it."[11]

[C] The Congressional Reenactment Theory

Also very relevant in the implied rights of action context is the "congressional reenactment theory." The Supreme Court adhered to this theory in *Merrill Lynch, Pierce, Fenner & Smith, Inc. v. Curran.*[12] There, even though the *Cort* formulation had not been met, the Court implied a right of action under the Commodity Exchange Act (CEA). In adopting the congressional reenactment theory, the Court reasoned that it must examine the "contemporary legal context" at the time the pertinent legislation was enacted:

> [W]e must examine Congress' perception of the law that it was shaping or reshaping. When Congress enacts new legislation, the question is whether Congress intended to create a private remedy as a supplement to the express enforcement provisions of the statute. When Congress acts in a statutory context in which an implied private remedy has already been recognized by the courts, however, the inquiry logically is different. Congress need not have intended to create a new remedy, since one already existed; the question is whether Congress intended to preserve the preexisting remedy.[13]

In deciding *Curran*, the Court focused on ascertaining Congress' intent in 1974 when it "comprehensively reexamined and strengthened" the CEA.

[8] 444 U.S. at 15-16.
[9] 451 U.S. 287 (1981).
[10] *Id.* at 293.
[11] *Id.* at 302 (Rehnquist, J., concurring in the judgment).
[12] 456 U.S. 353 (1982).
[13] *Id.* at 378-79.

Upon examining the case law, the Court concluded that the federal courts had "routinely and consistently" implied private rights under the CEA prior to the 1974 amendments.[14] Accordingly, the existence of these remedies was part of the "contemporary legal context" in which Congress enacted the 1974 amendments. The Court, therefore, concluded that Congress' decision not to alter the statutory provisions that had been construed to provide implied private rights of action was evidence that Congress affirmatively intended to preserve these preexisting implied remedies.[15]

The *Curran* Court recognized that the *Cort v. Ash* criteria for implying a private remedy had not been met with respect to certain of the plaintiffs' claims. The Court asserted, however, that it was not faced with such an inquiry. Rather than discerning Congress' intent when it enacts "new" legislation, the *Curran* situation required an inquiry concerning such intent when Congress legislates in a statutory setting in which implied rights had already been consistently and routinely recognized by the courts. Hence, the focus is on whether Congress intended to preserve the preexisting implied remedy.[16]

Accordingly, under the *Curran* rationale, if the federal courts had routinely and consistently recognized an implied right of action under a particular statute, then Congress' passage of substantial legislation which leaves intact the judiciary's implication of a remedy manifests Congress' intent to preserve such judicial interpretation. As discussed in Chapter 7 (§ 7.06, *supra*), this analysis was applied by the Supreme Court in *Huddleston*[17] which adhered to a cumulative construction of remedies approach between Section 11 of the Securities Act and Section 10(b) of the Exchange Act. For the most part, however, except for the cumulative remedy issue, the lower federal courts have generally found the *Curran* analysis unavailing in the federal securities law implied right of action context.[18]

§ 8.03 Availability of Implied Rights of Action Under Select Statutes

The federal courts have invoked the *Cort* four-prong formulation in order to ascertain whether a private right of action should be implied under certain provisions of the federal securities laws. A number of these provisions are discussed later in this chapter.

---

[14] *Id.* at 379.

[15] *Id.* at 381-82.

[16] *Id.*

[17] *Herman & MacLean v. Huddleston*, 459 U.S. 375 (1983).

[18] See, *e.g.*, *Walck v. American Stock Exchange, Inc.*, 687 F.2d 778 (3d Cir. 1982) (when Congress amended the securities acts in 1975, lower federal courts had not consistently and routinely recognized implied rights of action under §§ 6 and 7 of the Exchange Act).

Applying the *Cort* formulation, the federal courts, for example, have:

— Generally refused to recognize an implied right of action under Section 6 of the Exchange Act (i) against a national securities exchange based on the exchange's failure to enforce its own rules,[19] or (ii) against a broker-dealer, listed corporation, or other subject party based on a violation of exchange rules.[20]

— Declined to imply a private damages action under Section 7 of the Exchange Act on behalf of investors against financial institutions and brokers for violation of the margin requirements. In this regard, Section 7 authorizes the Federal Reserve Board to regulate margin transactions and prohibits violation of the Board's regulations. Generally, the regulations promulgated by the Board under the authority of Section 7 set the margin rate for securities purchased at 50%, meaning that the purchaser must advance the other 50% of the purchase price of the securities bought "on margin."[21] Declining to imply a Section 7 right of action, the Second Circuit reasoned:

> We . . . hold that no private right of action exists under section 7. First, . . . there is simply no evidence that in passing section 7 Congress intended to create a private action. . . . Second, section 7 was clearly not passed for the "especial benefit" of individual investors. The major reason for enacting section 7 was to control the excessive use of credit in securities transactions. . . . Finally, it is doubtful that allowing a private cause of action would be consistent with the underlying purposes of the legislative scheme. As stated above, the underlying purpose of section 7 is to regulate the use of credit in securities transactions. As the addition of section 7(f) makes clear, this regulation is aimed at both lenders and investors. While allowing a private cause of action could conceivably deter violations by lenders, it seems just as conceivable that it could encourage violations by investors seeking to shift the risk of loss.[22]

— In the tender offer setting, implied a private right of action for damages under the tender offer antifraud statute, Section 14(e) of the Exchange Act, on behalf of target corporation shareholders but not a damages remedy on behalf of an offeror.[23] With respect to the availability of *injunctive* (rather than

---

[19] See, *e.g., Walck v. American Stock Exchange, Inc.*, 687 F.2d 778 (3d Cir. 1982).

[20] See, *e.g., Jablon v. Dean Witter & Co.*, 613 F.2d 677 (9th Cir. 1980). But see for a more liberal construction *Buttrey v. Merrill Lynch, Pierce, Fenner & Smith, Inc.*, 410 F.2d 135 (7th Cir. 1979).

[21] See *Walck v. American Stock Exchange, Inc.*, 687 F.2d 778 (3d Cir. 1982); 2 L. Loss, *Securities Regulation* 1248 (2d ed. 1961).

[22] *Bennett v. United States Trust Company of New York*, 770 F.2d 308, 312 (2d Cir. 1985).

[23] See *Piper v. Chris-Craft Industries, Inc.*, 430 U.S. 1 (1977) (applying *Cort* defeated tender offeror does not have standing to bring an implied action for damages under § 14(e)); *Panter v. Marshall Field & Co.*, 646 F.2d 271 (7th Cir. 1981) (target shareholders sought relief under § 14(e)).

monetary) relief under Sections 13(d), 14(d), and 14(e) of the 1934 Act,[24] most courts recognize that an offeror has an implied right of action.[25]

— Implied private rights of action under certain provisions of the Investment Company Act[26] and the Trust Indenture Act.[27]

§ 8.04 Section 17(a) of the Securities Act

[A] Generally

Section 17(a) of the Securities Act provides:

> It shall be unlawful for any person in the offer or sale of any securities by the use of any means or instruments of transportation or communication in interstate commerce or by the use of the mails, directly or indirectly —
>
> (1) to employ any device, scheme, or artifice to defraud, or
>
> (2) to obtain money or property by means of any untrue statement of a material fact or any omission to state a material fact necessary in order to make the statements made, in the light of the circumstances under which they were made, not misleading, or
>
> (3) to engage in any transaction, practice, or course of business which operates or would operate as a fraud or deceit upon the purchaser.

Section 17(a), the 1933 Act's antifraud provision, applies only to the offer or sale of securities. Hence, the prohibitions of Section 17(a) do not reach fraud in the purchase of securities. Based upon the Supreme Court's decisions in *United States v. Naftalin*[28] and *Aaron v. SEC*,[29] Section 17(a) has emerged as an attractive enforcement weapon for the SEC.

[B] Supreme Court Decisions

The Supreme Court in *Naftalin* handed down three significant principles regarding Section 17(a). First, the protection afforded by Section 17(a)(1) extends beyond investors to encompass financial intermediaries such as

---

[24] These provisions were passed by Congress in 1968 as part of the Williams Act which, in effect, amended the Exchange Act. They are discussed in Chapter 10, *infra.*

[25] See, *e.g., Indiana National Corp. v. Rich*, 712 F.2d 1180 (7th Cir. 1983); *Mobil Corp. v. Marathon Oil Co.*, 669 F.2d 366 (6th Cir. 1981). But see *Polaroid Corp. v. Disney*, [1988-1989 Transfer Binder] Fed. Sec. L. Rep. (CCH) ¶ 94,095 (3d Cir. 1988). See also discussion in § 10.07, *infra.*

[26] See, *e.g., Fogel v. Chestnut*, 668 F.2d 100 (2d Cir. 1981).

[27] See, *e.g., Zeiffiro v. First Pennsylvania Banking and Trust Co.*, 623 F.2d 290 (3d Cir. 1980). See generally Johnson, *The "Forgotten" Securities Statute: Problems in the Trust Indenture Act*, 13 Toledo L. Rev. 92 (1981).

[28] 441 U.S. 768 (1979).

[29] 446 U.S. 680 (1980).

broker-dealers. Second, the language of Section 17(a) relating to the prohibition of fraud "in" the offer or sale of securities was sufficiently inclusive to cover Naftalin's misconduct. And third, Section 17(a) not only applies in the initial offering context but also extends to the secondary trading markets.[30] This last holding is particularly important. Prior to *Naftalin*, some authorities believed that, as part of the Securities Act which is directed at the regulation of initial offerings, Section 17(a) was likewise limited to the initial offering context. Hence, with respect to misconduct occurring in the aftermarket context involving the offer or sale of securities, *Naftalin*'s effect is to subject such misconduct to the prohibitions of both Section 17(a) and Section 10(b).[31]

The importance of *Naftalin* to the SEC became evident when the Supreme Court handed down its decision in *Aaron*. In *Aaron*, the Court, applying a linguistic analysis, held that in SEC actions seeking injunctive relief, scienter must be proven to establish a violation of Section 10(b) of the Exchange Act and Section 17(a)(1) of the Securities Act.[32] To show violations of Section 17(a)(2) and 17(a)(3), on the other hand, the SEC need only establish the defendant's negligence.[33]

Note the effect of *Aaron* when considered in light of *Naftalin*. Upon the making of a proper showing (*i.e.*, a reasonable likelihood that, absent the ordering of an injunction, future violations will occur), the SEC can invoke Section 17(a)(2) or 17(a)(3) to obtain injunctive relief based on a defendant's negligent misconduct which occurred in the offer or sale of securities in the secondary trading markets. In view of this consequence, Section 17(a) becomes a more appealing enforcement weapon to the SEC in the "offer or sale" context than the traditional antifraud provision, Section 10(b), which requires the Commission to prove scienter.

[C] Availability of Implied Right of Action

Based upon a linguistic analysis (as the Supreme Court applied in *Aaron*), the assertion has been made that, if a private damages action were implied under Section 17(a), the requisite culpability standard would be that of negligence.[34] On the other hand, the Supreme Court has stressed that it is inappropriate to imply a private right of action that is significantly more expansive than the provisions that Congress expressly chose to provide. Because Sections 11 and 12(2) of the Securities Act subject plaintiffs to certain procedural limitations and have a culpability standard resembling that of negligence, an argument can be made that liability should be imposed

---

[30] 441 U.S. at 773-78.

[31] For further discussion see Steinberg, *Section 17(a) of the Securities Act After Naftalin and Redington*, 68 Geo. L.J. 163 (1979).

[32] 446 U.S. at 696.

[33] *Id.* at 696-97. The *Aaron* decision also is discussed in § 7.03[B], *supra*, and § 11.05[A], *infra*.

[34] See *Landry v. All American Assurance Co.*, 688 F.2d 381, 387 (5th Cir. 1982).

pursuant to Section 17(a) only for actions that are more blameworthy, namely, for intentional or reckless misconduct.[35]

Hence, the most important issue that has not been resolved in regard to Section 17(a) is whether an implied private right of action exists. Although a number of courts have implied such a remedy,[36] the vast majority of the more recent decisions have declined to do so.[37] Applying the *Cort* four-prong formulation, these more recent cases have concluded that Congress did not intend to create a Section 17(a) private right of action. As stated by the Fifth Circuit:

> [I]t would appear that the *Cort* test as applied to § 17(a) of the Securities Act of 1933 points away from the implication of a private cause of action. This, together with the Supreme Court's conservative interpretation of the test in recent years, leads us to the conclusion that the district court correctly dismissed this theory of relief [thereby denying the existence of a § 17(a) private right of action].[38]

The Supreme Court's decision in *Curran* (discussed in § 8.02, *supra*) may support the recognition of an implied remedy under Section 17(a). Under *Curran's* rationale, when Congress significantly amended the securities acts in 1964, 1968, 1970, and 1975, the existence of an implied right of action under Section 17(a) had been consistently and routinely permitted. Indeed, as stated by Professor Loss, the existence of the Section 17(a) implied remedy "seems to be taken for granted."[39] According to the language of *Curran*, therefore,

> the fact that a comprehensive reexamination and significant amendment of the [federal securities laws] left intact the statutory provisions under which the federal courts had implied a cause of action is itself evidence that Congress affirmatively intended to preserve that remedy.[40]

Nonetheless, it may be argued that the *Curran* rationale is inapplicable in this context because some lower courts in the pre-1975 period had declined to find a private remedy under Section 17(a),[41] thereby arguably signifying that the remedy had not been "routinely and consistently" recognized. If this is indeed the case, then the Supreme Court's four-prong standard, as initially enunciated in *Cort v. Ash*, becomes the applicable guidepost. Applying this standard, as discussed above, most of the recent decisions have declined to recognize an implied right of action under Section 17(a).

---

[35] See *Ernst & Ernst v. Hochfelder*, 425 U.S. 185 (1976), discussed in § 7.03[A], *supra*.

[36] See, e.g., *Roth v. Bank of Commonwealth*, [1981-1982 Transfer Binder] Fed. Sec. L. Rep. (CCH) ¶ 98,627 (W.D.N.Y. 1981).

[37] See, *e.g., Krause v. Perryman*, 827 F.2d 346 (8th Cir. 1987).

[38] *Landry v. All American Assurance Co.*, 688 F.2d 381, 391 (5th Cir. 1982).

[39] 6 L. Loss, *Securities Regulation* 3913 (2d ed. 1969).

[40] 451 U.S. at 379.

[41] See, *e.g., Dyer v. Eastern Trust & Banking Co.*, 336 F. Supp. 890 (D. Me. 1971).

§ 8.05 Section 14(a) of the Exchange Act

Section 14(a) of the Securities Exchange Act and the SEC rules and regulations promulgated thereunder regulate the solicitation of proxies with respect to securities registered under Section 12 of the Exchange Act. Section 14(a)

> was intended to promote the free exercise of the voting rights of stockholders by ensuring that proxies would be solicited with explanation to the stockholder of the real nature of the questions for which authority to cast his vote is sought.[42]

[A] Meaning of "Solicitation"

In this regard, a proxy solicitation subject to Section 14(a) includes not only a request for a proxy but also any communication, whether written or oral, which under the circumstances is *reasonably calculated* to result in the procurement, withholding or revocation of a proxy.[43] As stated by the Second Circuit, the proxy rules

> apply not only to direct requests to furnish, revoke or withhold proxies, but also to communications which may indirectly accomplish such a result or constitute a step in a chain of communications ultimately to accomplish such a result.[44]

Although this standard may result in uncertain application, the breadth of the proxy provisions can be very wide to encompass such communications as letters to shareholders, press releases, speeches, and newspaper advertisements.[45]

[B] Elements of Private Right of Action

Due to the Supreme Court's decision in *J.I. Case v. Borak*,[46] it is clear that an implied private right of action exists under Section 14(a) and Rule 14a-9. Generally, Rule 14a-9 prohibits the solicitation of proxies which contain any materially false or misleading statement. The standard of materiality, as the Supreme Court held in *TSC Industries, Inc. v. Northway, Inc.*,[47] is that "there is a substantial likelihood that a reasonable shareholder would consider [such information] important in deciding how to vote."[48] Note that this standard does not require proof that accurate disclosure of the misrepresented or omitted fact would have caused a reasonable shareholder to change his or her

---

[42] *Mills v. Electric Auto-Lite Co.*, 396 U.S. 375, 381 (1970).

[43] Securities Exchange Act Rule 14a-1, 17 C.F.R. § 240.14a-1.

[44] *Long Island Lighting Company v. Barbash*, 779 F.2d 793, 796 (2d Cir. 1985).

[45] See generally E. Aranow & H. Einhorn, *Proxy Contests for Corporate Control* (1968); Cherno & Zelenty, *Solicitations in Proxy Contests*, 17 Rev. Sec. Reg. 965 (1984).

[46] 377 U.S. 426 (1964).

[47] 426 U.S. 438 (1976).

[48] *Id.* at 449.

vote but only that a substantial likelihood existed that accurate disclosure "would have been viewed by the reasonable investor as having altered the 'total mix' of information made available."[49]

The Supreme Court has eased a plaintiff's task in establishing reliance and causation in a Section 14(a) action. In *Mills v. Electric Auto-Lite Co.*,[50] the Court held that, provided that the misstatement or omission is material and thus had "a significant propensity to affect the voting process," a plaintiff in a derivative or class action under Section 14(a) and Rule 14a-9 is not required to show individual reliance on the misleading proxy solicitation. Thus, according to the Supreme Court in *Mills*, upon a finding of materiality,

> a shareholder has made a sufficient showing of causal relationship between the violation and the injury for which he seeks redress if . . . he proves that the proxy solicitation itself . . . was an essential link in the accomplishment of the transaction.[51]

Regarding the requisite state of mind for liability purposes, Section 14(a) and Rule 14a-9, unlike Section 10(b), do not by their terms require that deceptive or manipulative conduct be shown. As a consequence, where injunctive relief rather than damages is sought, some courts will order relief based upon the objective sufficiency of the disclosure.[52] Where damages are sought, most courts apply a negligence standard. For example, the Third Circuit has stated:

> The language of Section 14(a) and Rule 14a-9(a) contains no suggestion of a scienter requirement, merely establishing a quality standard for proxy material. The importance of the proxy provision to informed voting by shareholders has been stressed by the Supreme Court, which has emphasized the broad remedial purpose of the section, implying a need to impose a high standard of care on the individuals involved. And, unlike Sections 10(b) and 18 of the Act, which encompass activity in numerous and diverse areas of securities markets and corporate management, Section 14(a) is specially limited to materials used in soliciting proxies. Given all of these factors the imposition of a standard of due diligence as opposed to actual knowledge or gross negligence is quite appropriate.[53]

On the other hand, in *Adams v. Standard Knitting Mills*[54] the Sixth Circuit took the position that scienter is required in private damage actions against accountants for false and misleading audited financial statements contained in proxy materials. In taking this position, the Sixth Circuit noted, however, that other circuits had prescribed a negligence standard under Section 14(a)

---

[49] *Id.*

[50] 396 U.S. 375 (1970).

[51] *Id.* at 384-85.

[52] See, *e.g.*, *Ash v. LFE Corp.*, 525 F.2d 215 (3d Cir. 1975). But see *Plant Industries, Inc. v. Bregman*, 490 F. Supp. 265 (S.D.N.Y. 1980).

[53] *Gould v. American Hawaiian S.S. Co.*, 585 F.2d 761, 797-98 (3d Cir. 1976).

[54] 623 F.2d 422 (6th Cir. 1980).

when the defendant was a corporation issuing the proxy statement. The Sixth Circuit distinguished these cases, stating that scienter was required in the case at bar because accountants, among other things, are removed from the issuing corporation and do not stand to benefit from a misleading proxy statement.[55]

[C] Contexts Where Proxy Provisions Apply

Finally, it is important to point out that, while the areas covered by the proxy provisions are limited, the Section 14(a) right of action may be available in a variety of factual contexts. For example, the alleged failure to disclose in a proxy statement information material to the shareholders' assessment of management's integrity or competence implicates Section 14(a).[56] Moreover, certain breach of fiduciary duty claims, patterned after the *Goldberg* Section 10(b) line of cases (see § 7.04[B], *supra*), are actionable under Section 14(a), provided that there is a proxy solicitation and an inadequacy of disclosure.[57] The Section 14(a) remedy also comes into play in proxy fights for corporate control.[58] And, as a final example, Section 14(a) may be invoked in connection with merger transactions.[59] Interestingly, because Section 14(a) does not have a purchaser-seller standing requirement and because the requisite culpability standard may be that of negligence, plaintiffs may be successful in a Section 14(a) right of action where such relief would have been denied under Section 10(b).[60]

§ 8.06 Section 29(b) of the Exchange Act

Although rarely invoked since the Exchange Act's passage in 1934, Section 29(b) may serve as a powerful weapon for aggrieved litigants. Under the provision's language, every contract formed or performed in contravention of the 1934 Act or any rule or regulation prescribed thereunder "shall be void" as regards the rights of the violating party or his or her successor who takes with knowledge. This is the case even though the provision violated itself provides no private right of action. As the Supreme Court has stated, Section 29(b) impliedly "confers a 'right to rescind' a contract void under the criteria of the statute."[61]

---

[55] *Id.* at 428.

[56] See, *e.g.*, *Gaines v. Haughton*, 645 F.2d 761 (9th Cir. 1981).

[57] See, *e.g.*, *Weisberg v. Coastal States Gas Corp.*, 609 F.2d 650 (2d Cir. 1979).

[58] See, *e.g.*, *GAF Corporation v. Heyman*, 724 F.2d 727 (2d Cir. 1983); discussion in § 10.03, *infra*.

[59] See, *e.g.*, *Pavlidis v. New England Patriots Football Club, Inc.*, 737 F.2d 1227 (1st Cir. 1984).

[60] See generally Hazen, *Corporate Mismanagement and the Federal Securities Act's Antifraud Provisions: A Familiar Path with Some New Detours*, 20 B.C.L. Rev. 819 (1979); Steinberg, *Fiduciary Duties and Disclosure Obligations in Proxy and Tender Contests for Corporate Control*, 30 Emory L.J. 169 (1981).

[61] *Transamerica Mortgage Advisors, Inc. v. Lewis*, 444 U.S. 11, 17 (1979). See *Mills v. Electric Auto-Lite Co.*, 396 U.S. 375, 387-88 (1970).

Taken literally, Section 29(b)'s language, to quote Judge Friendly, is "[d]raconian."[62] Due to the "devastating meaning" of the provision's language, a number of courts have held that Section 29(b) merely codifies common law principles of illegal bargain in the application of the Exchange Act.[63]

Some courts, however, have construed Section 29(b) according to its language. In these decisions, the provision has been interpreted to provide plaintiffs with the relief sought, namely, the rescission of the subject transaction. For example, the Fifth Circuit has held that, pursuant to Section 29(b), a plaintiff can avoid a contract if it can be shown that: (1) the contract involved a "prohibited transaction," namely, that in the making or performance of the contract, there was perpetrated a violation of an Exchange Act provision or any rule or regulation prescribed thereunder, (2) there exists contractual privity between the plaintiff and the defendant, and (3) the plaintiff is in the class of persons the Exchange Act was designed to protect.[64] Once the plaintiff proves the above, the defendant may raise available equitable defenses, such as laches, estoppel, and "unclean hands."[65]

If the elements of the Section 29(b) right of action are satisfied, a plaintiff may rescind a contract, even after performance has been rendered. Given a remedial construction, Section 29(b) may subject every transaction, from an ordinary purchase of securities, to a complex merger, reorganization, proxy contest, or tender offer to which the Exchange Act applies, to its voidability provisions. Such an interpretation of Section 29(b), of course, is uncertain and awaits further judicial scrutiny.[66]

§ 8.07 The Racketeer Influenced and Corrupt Organizations Act (RICO)

A complainant seeking relief due to alleged securities law and related violations should assess the viability of instituting a RICO civil cause of action. Although RICO was enacted as a means to combat organized crime, a large number of civil RICO cases have been instituted against recognized,

---

[62] *Pearlstein v. Scudder & German*, 429 F.2d 1136, 1149 (2d Cir. 1970) (Friendly, J., dissenting).

[63] See, *e.g.*, *Occidental Life Insurance Co. v. Pat Ryan & Associates*, 496 F.2d 1255 (4th Cir. 1974).

[64] *Regional Properties, Inc. v. Financial and Real Estate Consulting Company*, 678 F.2d 552, 559 (5th Cir. 1982).

[65] *Id.* at 562-63.

[66] See Gruenbaum & Steinberg, *Section 29(b) of the Securities Exchange Act of 1934: A Viable Remedy Awakened*, 48 Geo. Wash. L. Rev. 1 (1979). See also, Scott, *A Broker-Dealer's Civil Liability to Investors for Fraud: An Implied Private Right of Action Under Section 15(c)(1) of the Securities Exchange Act of 1934*, 63 Ind. L.J. 687 (1988) (discussing the availability of an implied right of action under § 15(c)(1) as well as the application of the § 29(b) remedy).

legitimate businesses. In addition to providing an express right of action to redress fraud in the sale of securities (as well as mail and wire fraud), RICO plaintiffs are entitled to treble damages and attorneys' fees.[67]

[A] Elements of Civil RICO

In order to state a claim for damages under RICO, the complainant first must allege a violation of the substantive RICO statute,[68] commonly referred to as "criminal RICO." The constituent elements of criminal RICO, as set forth by the Second Circuit, are

> (1) that the defendant (2) through the commission of two or more acts (3) constituting a "pattern" (4) of "racketeering activity" (5) directly or indirectly invests in, or maintains an interest in, or participates in (6) an "enterprise" (7) the activities of which affect interstate or foreign commerce.[69]

After adequately alleging the foregoing, a private plaintiff, in order to invoke RICO's civil provisions for treble damages, attorneys' fees and costs, must satisfy a second burden, namely that he was "injured in his business or property *by reason of* a violation of Section 1962 [criminal RICO]."[70]

[B] Interpretive Issues

Not surprisingly, civil RICO's potential reach raises a number of interpretive issues. In *Sedima S.P.R.L. v. Imrex Co., Inc.*,[71] the Supreme Court, in a five to four decision, held that a prior criminal conviction is not required for the bringing of a RICO civil action and that no distinct "racketeering injury" is called for by the statute.[72] With respect to the former issue, the Court reasoned that there is no support for a prior conviction requirement in RICO's history, language, or in considerations of policy.[73]

---

[67] 18 U.S.C. § 1964(c). See generally Blakey & Gettings, *Racketeer Influenced and Corrupt Organizations (RICO): Basic Concepts — Criminal and Civil Remedies*, 53 Temple L.Q. 1009 (1980).

[68] 18 U.S.C. § 1962.

[69] *Moss v. Morgan Stanley, Inc.*, 719 F.2d 5, 17 (2d Cir. 1983). Criminal RICO, therefore, makes unlawful:

(1) using income derived from a pattern of racketeering activity to acquire an interest in an enterprise;

(2) acquiring or maintaining an interest in an enterprise through a pattern of racketeering activity or collection of an unlawful debt;

(3) conducting the affairs of an enterprise through a pattern of racketeering activity; and

(4) conspiring to commit any of these offenses.

18 U.S.C. § 1962(a)-(d).

[70] 18 U.S.C. § 1964(c)(emphasis added).

[71] 105 S.Ct. 3275 (1985).

[72] *Id.* at 3281-92.

[73] *Id.* at 3281-84.

With respect to the second holding, prior to *Sedima*, some courts had required a complainant to establish a commercial or competitive injury.[74] Others required the showing of a "racketeering enterprise injury," signifying that the harm suffered by the plaintiff was different from that resulting from the commission of the predicate offenses.[75] The *Sedima* Court rejected these interpretations, stating:

> If the defendant engages in a pattern of racketeering activity in a manner forbidden by [criminal RICO], and the racketeering activities injure the plaintiff in his business or property, the plaintiff has a claim under [civil RICO]. There is no room in the statutory language for an additional, amorphorous "racketeering injury" requirement.[76]

Another interpretive issue with respect to RICO is whether there must be a nexus between the defendant and "organized crime," as that term is traditionally understood. A small minority of courts have dismissed RICO claims on the basis that the defendants were not alleged to be "members" of "organized crime."[77] This interpretation has been a judicial attempt, somewhat similar to the lower court's effort in *Sedima*, to narrow the broad scope of RICO. The requirement of "an organized crime" nexus may possibly be inferred from the requirement of "a pattern of racketeering activity."[78]

Generally, RICO's primary objective is to develop more effective strategies to combat organized crime. Accordingly, the argument that RICO should apply only where a tie to organized crime is alleged is plausible, yet conflicts with the thrust of the Supreme Court's reasoning in *Sedima*. Although a few courts have used this limitation in dismissing private RICO cases, the majority of courts have concluded that such a judicially created affiliation with organized crime cannot be justified.[79] This latter view is consistent with *Sedima*. Although the Supreme Court did not address this issue, it pointed out that: (1) "Section 1962 . . . makes it unlawful for 'any person' — not just mobsters — to use money derived from a pattern of racketeering activity to invest in an enterprise, to acquire control of an enterprise through a pattern of racketeering activity, or to conduct an enterprise through a pattern of racketeering activity,"[80] and (2) the fact that RICO is applied in situations not expressly anticipated by Congress indicates breadth and not ambiguity.[81] Although the Court stated that "[i]t is true that private civil actions under the statute are being brought almost solely against such defendants [respected and

---

[74] See, *e.g.*, *Johnson v. Rogers*, 551 F. Supp. 281 (C.D. Cal. 1982).

[75] See, *e.g.*, *Landmark Savings & Loan v. Rhoades*, 527 F. Supp. 206 (E.D. Mich. 1981).

[76] 105 S.Ct. at 3285.

[77] See, *e.g.*, *Adair v. Hunt International Resources Corp.*, 526 F. Supp. 736 (N.D. Ill. 1981).

[78] See Bridges, *Private RICO Litigation Based Upon "Fraud in the Sale of Securities,"* 18 Ga. L. Rev. 43 (1983).

[79] See, *e.g.*, *Schact v. Brown*, 711 F.2d 1343 (7th Cir. 1983).

[80] 105 S.Ct. at 3285.

[81] *Id.* at 3287.

legitimate enterprises], rather than against the archetypal, intimidating mobster,[82] the majority concluded that, if this is a defect in the statute, finding a proper solution was the legislature's concern and not the Court's prerogative.[83]

Hence, although the lower courts have attempted to narrow the application of the RICO statute in the civil area, the Supreme Court in *Sedima* (with respect to the issues at bar) did not agree. Importantly, however, the Court's language on the necessity of establishing a "*pattern* of racketeering activity" may very well serve the same purpose. In this regard, a plaintiff under RICO must allege that the injury suffered was accomplished through a "pattern of racketeering activity."[84] This definition, as contained in the statute, states that a pattern "requires at least two acts of racketeering activity" within a ten-year period.[85] As the Supreme Court pointed out in *Sedima*, however, the applicable statute fails to define clearly whether the commission of two such acts must be related and continual or whether they are sufficient by themselves to constitute the requisite "pattern." Nonetheless, language in the opinion strongly implies that the acts must be sufficiently related and form a continuous course of conduct.[86] Thus, after *Sedima*, sporadic unrelated activity should be deemed insufficient to constitute a pattern of racketeering activity. At the very least, proof of a continuous and "common scheme, plan, or motive" connecting the racketeering acts to one another should be required.[87]

[C] Statutory and Policy Considerations

As a final point, given the relief afforded by civil RICO, it is not surprising that this remedy is frequently sought to be invoked in securities fraud cases. Irrespective of the Supreme Court's decision in *Sedima*, there is a legitimate question whether a RICO claim should be appropriate where relief under the federal securities laws is available. Because of the far greater recovery provided by RICO, a number of the remedial provisions of the securities laws may become meaningless, unless the private RICO cause of action is construed with practical limitations. Further, where the securities laws do not provide an express or implied private remedy, it appears imprudent to allow a private remedy under RICO for the same substantive conduct. Certain post-*Sedima* decisions reflect this concern. For example, in *International Data Bank v. Zepkin*,[88] the Fourth Circuit held that Section 10(b)'s purchaser-seller standing requirement (see § 7.02, *supra*) applied to civil RICO claims based on predicate offenses of securities fraud.

---

[82] *Id.*

[83] *Id.*

[84] 18 U.S.C. § 1961(5).

[85] *Id.*

[86] See 105 S.Ct. at 3285 n.14.

[87] See, *e.g.*, *Superior Oil v. Fulmar*, 785 F.2d 252 (8th Cir. 1986).

[88] 812 F.2d 149 (4th Cir. 1987).

Even though private plaintiffs have been somewhat successful in alleging civil RICO claims premised on securities law violations, strong factors weigh against broadly applying RICO in this context. As the dissent in *Sedima* pointed out, legislative history is lacking in support of the proposition that Congress intended a major change in this well-defined area of law. In addition, the absence of prosecutorial discretion in civil cases is a strong argument against the expansive application of RICO.[89] Thus, while congressional intent and persuasive policy considerations indicate that there should be a line drawn identifying those securities violations that fall within RICO's ambit, the problem, of course, is to determine where to draw such a line.

---

[89] 105 S.Ct. at 3294, 3296 (Marshall, J., dissenting). See generally Comment, *RICO and Securities Fraud: A Workable Limitation*, 83 Colum. L. Rev. 1513 (1983).

CHAPTER 9

SELECTED DISCLOSURE ISSUES

§ 9.01 Introduction

As addressed in prior chapters, the federal securities laws are fundamentally premised on the disclosure of adequate and truthful information. This chapter will examine selected disclosure and related issues which have not been specifically covered elsewhere in this reference text. The two major subjects treated here are insider trading and the duty of an issuer affirmatively to disclose material nonpublic information.

§ 9.02 Insider Trading

A fundamental tenet underlying the federal securities laws, at least since the SEC's decision in *Cady Roberts*,[1] is that "insiders" and, in certain circumstances, their tippees must either disclose material nonpublic information in their possession prior to trading or refrain from such trading. Unfortunately, although seemingly straightforward, the theoretical underpinnings for a duty to "disclose or abstain" from trading as well as its application to concrete factual situations and the persons to whom the duty should run have not always been clear.

[A] Supreme Court Decisions — *Chiarella & Dirks*

In *Chiarella v. United States*,[2] the Supreme Court held that under Section 10(b) of the Exchange Act and Rule 10b-5 promulgated thereunder, a financial printer, who purchased stock after deciphering information gleaned from confidential documents entrusted to his employer that certain companies were to be the subjects of mergers or tender offers, did not breach a duty to the investing public.[3] In so doing, the Court rejected the parity of information[4] and parity of access to information[5] principles that a number of lower courts had embraced. Hence, the Court held that silence, absent a duty

---

1 *In re Cady Roberts & Co.*, 40 S.E.C. 907 (1961).

2 445 U.S. 222 (1980).

3 *Id.* at 226-35.

4 See, *e.g.*, *SEC v. Texas Gulf Sulphur Co.*, 401 F.2d 833 (2d Cir. 1968) (*en banc*), *cert. denied*, 394 U.S. 976 (1969).

5 See, *e.g.*, *United States v. Chiarella*, 588 F.2d 1358 (2d Cir. 1978), *rev'd*, 445 U.S. 222 (1980).

to disclose, will not give rise to Section 10(b) liability. Such liability based on silence, the Court asserted, "is premised upon a duty to disclose arising from a relationship of trust and confidence between parties to a transaction."[6]

With respect to insiders, the *Chiarella* Court reinforced the principle, expanded upon in *Dirks v. SEC*,[7] that a duty to disclose or abstain from trading arises where such persons possess material nonpublic information.[8] Quoting from the SEC's decision in *Cady Roberts*, the *Chiarella* Court stated that the obligation to disclose or abstain from trading derives from

> an affirmative duty to disclose material information [which] has been traditionally imposed on corporate "insiders," particularly officers, directors, or controlling stockholders. We . . . have consistently held that insiders disclose material facts which are known to them by virtue of their position but which are not known to persons with whom they deal and which, if known, would affect their investment judgment.[9]

Significantly, the *Chiarella* Court did not address the issue of whether the financial printer could have been held liable on the misappropriation theory under Section 10(b) and Rule 10b-5. Had this theory been applied, as it subsequently has been by the lower federal courts,[10] Chiarella would have breached a duty to the acquiring corporation and to his employer when he traded on the basis of information he procured by virtue of his strategic position.

Turning to the Supreme Court's decision in *Dirks*, the Court held that the duty of tippees to disclose or abstain from trading depends on whether the tipper has himself breached a fiduciary duty to the corporation's shareholders by divulging the information to the tippee.

> Thus, the test is whether the insider personally will benefit, directly or indirectly, from his disclosure. Absent some personal gain, there has been no breach of duty to stockholders. And absent a breach by the insider, there is no derivative breach [by the tippee].[11]

Such personal benefit may be shown by the insider's receipt of pecuniary gain or reputational enhancement that will translate into future earnings.[12] Also,

---

[6] 445 U.S. at 230.

[7] 463 U.S. 646 (1983).

[8] 445 U.S. at 226-27.

[9] *Id.*, quoting *In re Cady Roberts & Co.*, 40 S.E.C. 907, 911 (1961). See generally Branson, *Discourse on the Supreme Court Approach to SEC Rule 10b-5 and Insider Trading*, 30 Emory L.J. 263 (1981); Langevoort, *Insider Trading and the Fiduciary Principle: A Post-Chiarella Restatement*, 70 Calif. L. Rev. 1 (1982); Wang, *Trading on Material Nonpublic Information on Impersonal Stock Markets: Who Is Harmed and Who Can Sue Whom Under SEC Rule 10b-5?*, 54 So. Cal. L. Rev. 1217 (1981).

[10] See, *e.g.*, *SEC v. Materia*, 745 F.2d 197 (2d Cir. 1984) (financial printer liable under § 10(b) under misappropriation theory).

[11] 463 U.S. at 662.

[12] *Id.* at 664.

the requisite showing of benefit may be made by the insider making a gift of confidential information to the tippee. In such circumstances, "[t]he tip and trade resemble trading by the insider himself followed by a gift of the profits to the recipient."[13] In order to hold the tippee liable under Section 10(b) for trading on the information conveyed by the insider, the tippee must or should have known that the insider breached his or her fiduciary duty by disclosing such confidential information to the tippee.[14]

By holding that (1) there must be a breach of the insider's fiduciary duty to the corporation's shareholders before the tippee inherits the duty to disclose or abstain and (2) by premising the existence of a breach on whether the insider will personally benefit from disclosing the information to the tippee, the Court in *Dirks* made it significantly more difficult for the SEC and private claimants to prove liability. By imposing a motivational requirement, the Court's holding arguably "excuses a knowing and intentional violation of an insider's duty to shareholders if the insider does not act from a motive of personal gain."[15] The task of proving such a motive in many cases must rest on circumstantial evidence and may be troublesome.[16] Moreover, the benefit apparently must be a personal one which, at least in most instances, must enrich the insider monetarily. Other types of benefits, such as an enhanced reputation which does not translate into future earnings, appear insufficient to find a breach. Liability also may not be imposed against the "loose-lipped" director or officer who divulges confidential corporate information to such persons as financial analysts, broker-dealers and golfing cronies without any intention to make a gift or personally benefit therefrom. This result appears to be a departure from prior lower court case law.[17]

Contrary to the generally restrictive nature of the holding, the Court in *Dirks* recognized the "quasi-insider" principle, stating:

> Under certain circumstances, such as where corporate information is revealed legitimately to an underwriter, accountant, lawyer, or consultant working for the corporation, these outsiders may become fiduciaries of the shareholders. The basis for recognizing this fiduciary duty is not simply that such persons acquired nonpublic corporate information, but rather that they have entered into a special confidential relationship in the conduct of the business of the enterprise and are given access to information solely for corporate purposes. . . . [W]hen such a person breaches his fiduciary relationship, he may be treated more properly as a tipper than as a tippee. . . . For such a duty to be imposed, however,

---

[13] *Id.*

[14] *Id.* at 660.

[15] *Id.* at 671-74 (Blackmun, J., dissenting).

[16] See, *e.g., SEC v. Switzer*, 590 F. Supp. 756 (W.D. Okla. 1984).

[17] See, *e.g., Elkind v. Liggett & Myers, Inc.*, 635 F.2d 156, 165 (2d Cir. 1980). See generally Hiler, *Dirks v. SEC — A Study in Cause and Effect*, 43 Md. L. Rev. 292 (1984); Phillips, *Insider Trading Liability After Dirks*, 16 Rev. Sec. Reg. 848 (1983).

> the corporation must expect the outsider to keep the non-public information confidential, and the relationship at least must imply such a duty.[18]

Hence, under this rationale, individuals enjoying a special relationship with the corporation, such as accountants, attorneys, consultants, and underwriters, may be viewed as insiders when they trade on material nonpublic information that they legitimately received during the course of that relationship.

[B] The Misappropriation Theory

In *Chiarella*, *Dirks*, and, most recently, *Carpenter*,[19] the Court left unresolved the viability of the misappropriation theory. Stated succinctly, this theory

> extends liability to persons possessing material nonpublic information who use the information in violation of a duty owed to someone other than the shareholders of the corporation whose securities were traded.[20]

After *Chiarella*, the SEC and the Justice Department successfully have invoked this rationale. In *United States v. Newman*,[21] for example, the Second Circuit upheld an indictment on the grounds that the defendants had allegedly misappropriated valuable nonpublic information entrusted to them in the utmost secrecy. The court found that the defendants had "sullied the reputations" of their employers, investment banks, "as safe repositories of client confidences" and had deceived the clients of these investment banks "whose takeover plans were keyed to target company stock prices fixed by market forces, not artificially inflated through purchases by purloiners of confidential information."[22]

After the Second Circuit's decision in *Newman*, the question remained whether purchasers and sellers of securities had a cause of action for monetary damages under Section 10(b) even though the defrauding parties who misappropriated the inside information owed them no fiduciary duty. In *Moss v. Morgan Stanley, Inc.*,[23] the Second Circuit held that in order to recover monetary damages under Section 10(b) it must be shown that the defendant breached a duty owed to the plaintiff. Relying on *Chiarella*, the court asserted that the relationship giving rise to a duty to disclose must be between the parties to the transaction. Thus, because the misappropriators in

---

[18] 463 U.S. at 677 n.14.

[19] *Carpenter v. United States*, 108 S.Ct. 316 (1987).

[20] Ferrara & Raul, *New "Insider Trading" Act Fails to Define Liability*, N.Y.L.J., Dec. 10, 1984, at 33, 42.

[21] 664 F.2d 12 (2d Cir. 1981).

[22] *Id.* at 17-18. See note 10, *supra*.

[23] 719 F.2d 5 (2d Cir. 1983).

Moss owed no fiduciary duty to the plaintiff, no Section 10(b) right of action was available.[24]

In legislation recently passed by Congress, the Second Circuit's decision in *Moss* has been nullified in this respect. In the Insider Trading and Securities Fraud Enforcement Act of 1988, Congress enacted Section 20A of the Exchange Act to provide an express right of action on behalf of "contemporaneous traders" who were trading the same class of securities on the opposite side of the transaction during the time that the allegedly illegal inside trade(s) occurred. Thus, to recover under this newly created express right of action, the plaintiff must be trading contemporaneously with and on the opposite side of the transaction from the inside trader. Moreover, the damages available in an action instituted under Section 20A on behalf of contemporaneous traders are limited to the profit gained or loss avoided by the defendant's illegal trades.[25]

Importantly, Section 20A does not limit a complainant's entitlement to private rights of action under other provisions of the Exchange Act, such as Section 10(b). In this regard, a private right of action under Section 10(b) may be available against inside traders (as well as their tippers) on behalf of certain noncontemporaneous traders. Such a situation may arise when, due to insider trading which has increased the price of the target company's stock, a bidder must pay more to acquire such stock. In the House Report accompanying the 1988 legislation, the Committee took the position that a Section 10(b) right of action exists in the above situation and that a plaintiff should be able to recover the full extent of any actual damages incurred.[26]

[C] Damages and Penalties

[1] Damages — Section 10(b) Actions

The measure of damages for insider trading in open market transactions under Section 10(b) has received diverse treatment from the few courts that have considered the issue. *Shapiro v. Merrill Lynch, Pierce, Fenner & Smith, Inc.*,[27] represents an expansive approach. There, the Second Circuit, relying on *Affiliated Ute Citizens v. United States,*[28] stated that

> [t]he proper test to determine whether causation in fact has been established in a nondisclosure case is "whether the plaintiff would have

[24] *Id.* at 15-16. But see *O'Connor & Associates v. Dean Witter Reynolds, Inc.*, 529 F. Supp. 1179 (S.D.N.Y. 1981) (right of action extended to options trader even though insiders owed such person no fiduciary duty).

[25] See H.R. Rep. No. 100-910 to accompany H.R. 5133, 100th Cong., 2d Sess. (1988); Fed. Sec. L. Rep. (CCH) No. 1309 (Oct. 26, 1988); 20 Sec. Reg. & L. Rep. (BNA) 1623 (1988); Ingersoll & Ricks, *Congress Clears Bill to Toughen Insider Penalties*, Wall St. J., Oct. 24, 1988, at A4.

[26] H.R. Rep. No. 100-910, *supra* note 25, at 28. But see *Wilson v. Comtech Telecommunications*, 648 F.2d 88, 94-95 (2d Cir. 1981).

[27] 495 F.2d 228 (2d Cir. 1974).

[28] 406 U.S. 128 (1972).

> been influenced to act differently than he did if the defendant had disclosed to him the undisclosed fact."[29]

After finding that causation in fact had been established (notwithstanding that all transactions occurred on a national securities exchange), the court formulated a potentially broad measure of damages:

> [W]e hold that defendants are liable in this private action for damages to plaintiffs who, during the same period that defendants traded in or recommended trading in Douglas common stock, purchased Douglas stock in the open market without knowledge of the material inside information which was in the possession of defendants.[30]

Having so held, the Second Circuit, however, left to the district court's discretion the proper measure of damages, noting its concern with the potential for draconian liability.[31]

In *Fridrich v. Bradford,*[32] the Sixth Circuit rejected the *Shapiro* analysis. Disagreeing with the Second Circuit, the *Fridrich* court found that the plaintiffs had failed to show that their loss was caused by the defendants' inside trading. The Sixth Circuit supported its holding by pointing out that an award of damages to contemporaneous traders in the open market would create a windfall for fortuitous investors while being essentially punitive. Although the court recognized that it could limit the amount of recovery to the defendants' profits, it declined to do so.[33]

Subsequently, in *Elkind v. Liggett & Myers, Inc.*,[34] the Second Circuit, although not expressly rejecting the *Shapiro* rationale, greatly limited the potential damages recovery. There, the court considered three alternative measures of damages: (1) out-of-pocket, (2) market-repercussion, and (3) disgorgement. Rejecting the out-of-pocket measure, the court pointed out that this measure is normally directed toward compensating a trader for damages which are directly traceable to the defendant's perpetration of a fraud upon the trader. In an impersonal open market, however, "uninformed traders . . . are not induced by representations on the part of the tipper or tippee to buy or sell."[35] Secondly, the Second Circuit observed that the out-of-pocket measure posed serious proof problems as the "value" of the stock traded during the period of nondisclosure can often be hypothetical. Lastly, the court concluded that the out-of-pocket measure had the potential for the imposition of "draconian, exorbitant damages, out of all proportion to the wrong committed."[36]

---

[29] 495 F.2d at 239.
[30] *Id.* at 241.
[31] *Id.*
[32] 542 F.2d 307 (6th Cir. 1976).
[33] *Id.* at 318-22.
[34] 635 F.2d 156 (2d Cir. 1980).
[35] *Id.* at 169.
[36] *Id.* at 170.

The *Elkind* court also rejected the direct market-repercussion theory of damages. This measure would allow recovery of damages caused by an increase or erosion of the stock's market price that is traceable to the defendant's wrongful trading. The rationale underlying the theory is that "if the market price is not affected by the [defendant's] trading, the uninformed investor is in the same position as he would have been had the insider abstained from trading." Upon analysis, the Second Circuit rejected this theory due to the difficult problems of proof it would impose on plaintiffs and that adoption of the theory would frequently preclude recovery for an insider's breach of his or her duty to disclose the confidential information prior to trading.[37]

The *Elkind* court thereupon adopted a third alternative, the disgorgement measure of damages. This measure also is the proper measure of damages under Section 20A for contemporaneous traders who trade on the opposite side of the transaction from the defendant.[38] Under the *Elkind* formulation, the measure of damages is as follows:

> (1) [T]o allow any uninformed investor, where a reasonable investor would either have delayed his purchase or not purchased at all if he had the benefit of the tipped information, to recover any post-purchase decline in market value of his shares up to a reasonable time after he learns of the tipped information or after there is a public disclosure of it but (2) limit his recovery to the amount gained by the tippee as a result of his selling at the earlier date rather than delaying his sale until the parties could trade on an equal informational basis. . . . Should the intervening buyers, because of the volume and price of their purchases, claim more than the tippee's gain, their recovery (limited to that gain) would be shared *pro rata*.[39]

[2] Penalties

A number of different parties may be subject to a variety of monetary penalties under the federal securities laws. These parties may include actual traders, their tippers, as well as broker-dealers and investment advisers (when they fail to take appropriate steps to prevent the insider trading violation(s) or fail to maintain and enforce policies and procedures reasonably designed to prevent the occurrence of such trading). Penalties that may be levied in this context are (1) requiring the subject party to "disgorge" the ill-gotten profits (or loss avoided) in an SEC enforcement action,[40] (2) subjecting the defendant to a maximum criminal fine of $1 million and ten years imprisonment,[41] and (3) in an SEC enforcement action, within a court's

---

[37] *Id.* at 171.

[38] See H.R. Rep. No. 100-910, note 25, *supra.*

[39] 635 F.2d at 172.

[40] See, *e.g., SEC v. Commonwealth Chemical Securities, Inc.*, 574 F.2d 90, 102-03 (2d Cir. 1978).

[41] See § 32(a) of the Exchange Act, 15 U.S.C. § 78ff(a) (as amended by the Insider Trading and Securities Fraud Enforcement Act of 1988).

discretion, ordering the subject party to pay into the United States Treasury a treble damages penalty amounting to three times the profits gained or loss avoided.[42] These penalties, together with the imposition of jail terms and the availability of civil damages, are intended to strongly deter insider trading. As an additional measure to combat insider trading, the SEC may award "bounties" (up to ten percent of the amount disgorged or monetary penalty imposed) to persons who provide information concerning insider trading violations.[43]

[D] Rule 14e-3

Subsequent to the Supreme Court's decision in *Chiarella*, the SEC, in an effort to regulate insider and tippee trading in the tender offer context, adopted Rule 14e-3 which establishes a "disclose or abstain from trading" rule under Section 14(e) of the Exchange Act. As adopted, with certain exceptions, Rule 14e-3 applies this disclose-or-abstain provision to the possession of material information relating to a tender offer where the person knows or has reason to know the information is nonpublic and was received directly or indirectly from the offeror, the subject corporation, any of their affiliated persons, or any person acting on behalf of either company. Moreover, the rule contains a broad anti-tipping provision and provides for certain exceptions pertaining to sales to the offeror and to certain activities by multiservice financial institutions.[44]

In the release adopting Rule 14e-3, the Commission asserted that *Chiarella* did not limit its authority under Section 14(e) to prescribe such a mandate regulating insider trading in the tender offer context. The Commission in the release also asserted the continued viability of the misappropriation rationale under Section 10(b).[45] Thus far, Rule 14e-3, as invoked by the SEC and private claimants, has been upheld by the courts.[46]

[E] The Mail and Wire Fraud Statutes

Although not available to the SEC, the mail and wire fraud statutes,[47] as seen from the Supreme Court's decision in *Carpenter v. United States*,[48] are

---

[42] See H.R. 559, S. 910, 98th Cong., 2d Sess. (1984). See generally Langevoort, *The Insider Trading Sanctions Act of 1984 and Its Effect on Existing Law*, 37 Vand. L. Rev. 1273 (1984).

[43] See H.R. Rep. No. 100-910, note 25, *supra*; Fed. Sec. L. Rep. (CCH) No. 1309 (Oct. 26, 1988).

[44] 17 C.F.R. § 240.14e-3.

[45] See *Securities Exchange Act Release* No. 17120 (1980).

[46] See *O'Connor & Associates v. Dean Witter Reynolds, Inc.*, 529 F. Supp. 1179, 1188-93 (S.D.N.Y. 1981). For commentary on Rule 14e-3, see, *e.g.*, Steinberg, *Securities Regulation: Liabilities and Remedies* § 3.06 (1989); Gruenbaum, *The New Disclose or Abstain From Trading Rule: Has the SEC Gone Too Far?*, 5 Corp. L. Rev. 350 (1981).

[47] 18 U.S.C. §§ 1341, 1343.

[48] 108 S.Ct. 316 (1987).

potent weapons in the U.S. Attorney's arsenal to combat alleged criminal offenses involving insider trading. Moreover, although a private right of action is unavailable under these statutes,[49] they do constitute predicate offenses under RICO.[50] As a result, plaintiffs who can satisfy the requisite elements for civil RICO may recover treble damages and attorneys' fees based on violations of the mail or wire fraud statute.

[F] Section 16 — "Short-Swing" Trading

[1] Overview

Section 16 of the Exchange Act applies to directors, officers, and beneficial owners of more than ten percent of any class of equity security of an issuer (other than an exempted security),[51] with such class of equity security having been registered pursuant to Section 12(b) or 12(g) of the Exchange Act.[52] The statute seeks to deter insider trading based on the use of material nonpublic information by such persons. Section 16 contains three key provisions in attempting to meet this objective.

1. Section 16(a) of the Exchange Act requires that, upon becoming an officer, director, or ten percent equity shareholder of a Section 12(b) or 12(g) issuer, such individual must file with the SEC (and with the self-regulatory organization (SRO) with which the stock is listed) a report disclosing the number of the corporation's shares beneficially owned. Thereafter, in any month where there is a change in beneficial ownership, a Form 4 Statement must be filed with the SEC and the SRO within ten days after the end of the month reflecting such change.

2. Section 16(c) prohibits such insiders from transacting short sales in their issuer's equity securities.

3. Generally, "Section 16(b) is designed to permit the corporation or a security holder bringing an action upon behalf of the corporation to recover for the benefit of the corporation short-swing profits arising from the purchase [and sale or sale and purchase] by insiders within any six-month period of equity securities of the company."[53]

Under Section 16(b), an irrebuttable presumption is created when "insiders" engage in such short-swing transactions. The profits that the insider

---

[49] See, *e.g., Sedima, S.P.R.L. v. Imrex Company, Inc.*, 473 U.S. 479, 505 (1985) (Marshall, J., dissenting).

[50] See 18 U.S.C. § 1961. RICO is discussed in § 8.07, *supra.*

[51] Exempt securities for purposes of Section 16 include, for example, municipal bonds, obligations of the United States, and securities issued in connection with certain employee benefit plans. See *Securities Exchange Act Release* No. 18114 (1981).

[52] Hence, these equity securities are either listed on a national securities exchange (§ 12(b)) or are securities of an issuer having at least 500 shareholders of record and $5 million in assets (§ 12(g)). See § 3.01, *supra.*

[53] H. Bloomenthal, *Securities Law* 365 (1966).

gained from the transaction(s) are recoverable by the issuer in a suit initiated by it, or if it declines to do so, in a properly instituted shareholder's suit expressly authorized by the statute. In view of the broad remedial nature of the statute, a strict formula for computing "profit realized" has been established. Such a formula is designed

> to squeeze all possible profits out of stock transactions, and thus to establish a standard so high as to prevent any conflict between the selfish interest of a fiduciary officer, director, or stockholder and the faithful performance of his duty.[54]

The formula established matches the lowest price "in" with the highest price "out," thus ensuring recovery of all possible profits. In fact, this formula can yield a profit when in actuality a loss has been suffered.[55]

Moreover, an insider's intent to profit under a transaction that falls within Section 16(b)'s scope need not be shown in order for there to be recovery. As the Seventh Circuit, as well as other courts, has stated, an insider is "deemed capable of structuring his dealings to avoid any possibility of taint and therefore must bear the risks of any inadvertent miscalculation."[56] In some situations, however, the courts, by finding that certain unorthodox transactions do not constitute the predicate purchase or sale, have displayed a judicial reluctance to impose liability under Section 16(b) where no congressional purpose would be served.[57]

[2] Relevant Issues

The issues dealing with the construction of Section 16(b), at times, are complex. The following discussion seeks to highlight the key concepts. For more extensive treatment, other sources should be consulted.[58]

[a] Beneficial Ownership and the Concept of Attribution

A significant problem that arises with respect to the concepts of attribution and beneficial ownership in the context of Section 16(b) is in attempting to determine whether, and the extent to which, a corporate insider will be liable for short-swing trading profits. This issue may arise, for example, within the context of family-related transactions, of a related trust, of a partnership in which the insider is a partner, or of a corporation in which the insider is an officer, director or shareholder. The question becomes one of the responsibili-

---

[54] *Smolowe v. Delendo Corp.*, 136 F.2d 231 (2d Cir. 1943).

[55] See *Morales v. Consolidated Oil & Gas, Inc.*, [1982 Transfer Binder] Fed. Sec. L. Rep. (CCH) ¶ 98,796 (S.D.N.Y. 1982).

[56] *Bershad v. McDonough*, 428 F.2d 693, 696 (7th Cir. 1970). See *Whiting v. Dow Chemical Co.*, 523 F.2d 680, 687 (2d Cir. 1975) ("[T]he unwary who fall within [§ 16(b's)] terms have no one but themselves to blame.").

[57] See, *e.g.*, *Kern County Land Co. v. Occidental Petroleum Corp.*, 411 U.S. 582 (1973).

[58] See, *e.g.*, M. Steinberg, *Securities Regulation: Liabilities and Remedies* § 4.01 *et seq.* (1989).

ty of the corporate insider for the acts of such parties and his or her relationship with these other parties.

The cases involving beneficial ownership and the concept of attribution have failed to provide clear standards. Nonetheless, two important factors are (1) whether the insider exercised control over the securities and (2) the insider's ability to benefit, directly or indirectly, from the profits generated from the short-swing transactions.[59] On the other hand, the Seventh Circuit has applied a more restrictive analysis. Rather than focusing on control over the securities, the court looked to whether the insider stood to receive a direct monetary benefit from the subject transactions. The court held that

> profit realized by a corporate insider [for purposes of Section 16(b)] means direct pecuniary benefit to the insider. . . . [I]t is not enough that ties of affinity and consanguinity between the . . . recipient and the insider make it likely that the insider will experience an enhanced sense of well-being as a result of the receipt, or will be led to reduce his gift-giving to the recipient.[60]

[b] Directors

Directors and any person performing similar functions (irrespective of whether the business organization is incorporated) are subject to Section 16(b). A key issue in this setting is whether a business organization can be viewed as a director of another entity by virtue of that organization having a representative on the latter entity's board of directors.

Generally, the courts have answered the above question affirmatively, holding that a corporation may "deputize" one of its directors or other person to serve on a second corporation's board. For example, the Second Circuit, in *Feder v. Martin Marietta Corp.,*[61] imposed liability based on the deputization theory. There, the court found that the president and chief executive officer of Martin Marietta had been "deputized by or represented" Martin Marietta during the time he served as a director of Sperry Rand. Therefore, the court concluded, Martin Marietta was in effect a director of Sperry Rand and was forced to disgorge the profits it acquired in the short-swing trading of Sperry Rand stock.[62]

[c] Officers

SEC Rule 3b-2 states that

> [t]he term "officer" means a president, vice president, secretary, treasurer or principal financial officer, comptroller or principal accounting officer, and any person routinely performing corresponding functions

---

[59] See, *e.g., Whitaker v. Whittaker Corp.*, 639 F.2d 516 (9th Cir. 1981); *Whiting v. Dow Chemical Co.*, 523 F.2d 680, 688 (2d Cir. 1975); *Altamil Corp. v. Pryor*, 405 F. Supp. 1222 (S.D. Ind. 1975).

[60] *CBI Industries, Inc. v. Horton*, 682 F.2d 643, 646 (7th Cir. 1982).

[61] 406 F.2d 260 (2d Cir. 1969).

[62] *Id.* at 262-66. See *Blau v. Lehman*, 368 U.S. 403 (1961).

> with respect to any organization whether incorporated or unincorporated.[63]

The focus of the inquiry in ascertaining who is an officer for purposes of Section 16 is upon an individual's functions and responsibilities within the organizational structure. This matter can arise in several different settings. Primarily, however, the issue is whether one, lacking in a title representing him or her as an officer, nevertheless in fact had that status, or, conversely, whether one having the title of officer, for example as vice president, had a role so devoid of decision-making functions that he or she could not in reality be called an officer within the meaning of Section 16.

While the courts and the SEC generally take the position that one holding a title coming within Rule 3b-2 is an officer for purposes of Section 16,[64] this inference can be overcome. For example, the Ninth Circuit has opined:

> [T]he title "Vice President" does no more than raise an inference that the person who holds the title has the executive duties and the opportunities for confidential information that the title implies. The inference can be overcome by proof that the title was merely honorary and did not carry with it any of the executive responsibilities that otherwise might be assumed.[65]

[d] Ten Percent Beneficial Owners

Unlike the situation for directors and officers, Section 16(b) imposes liability on a ten percent beneficial owner if that person had that status both when the securities were acquired and when they were sold or transferred. Hence, in *Foremost-McKesson, Inc. v. Providence Securities Co.,*[66] the Supreme Court held that "in a purchase-sale sequence, a beneficial owner must account for profits only if he was a beneficial owner before the purchase."[67] And, in *Reliance Electric Co. v. Emerson Electric Co.,*[68] the high Court ruled that liability pursuant to Section 16(b) normally cannot be based on a beneficial owner's sale of securities which takes place after his or her ownership has been reduced to less than ten percent. This is so, even if at the time when the seller owned more than ten percent of the stock, he or she deliberately structured two separate transactions so as to reduce the extent of liability. For example, the first such sale transaction could be arranged so as to result in the beneficial owner holding 9.9% of the issuer's stock. In the second transaction, the beneficial owner could sell the remaining shares. Provided that in such a two-stage transaction the sales are not "legally tied"

---

[63] 17 C.F.R. § 240.3b-2.

[64] See *Securities Exchange Act Release* No. 18114 (1981).

[65] *Merrill Lynch, Pierce, Fenner and Smith v. Livingston*, 566 F.2d 1119, 1122 (9th Cir. 1978).

[66] 423 U.S. 232 (1976).

[67] *Id.* at 250.

[68] 404 U.S. 418 (1972).

to one another,[69] the beneficial owner under *Reliance* is liable under Section 16(b) only as to the first transaction.[70]

[e] Objective v. Pragmatic Approach

Persons are subject to Section 16(b) liability only if they engage in a "purchase" and "sale" or "sale" and "purchase" of a subject security within a six-month period. As such, an insider's liability may turn upon whether there indeed has been a "purchase" and "sale" within Section 16(b)'s scope.

The traditional and still commonly used approach is objective. The "objective" approach works in a mechanical fashion. Courts applying it will not inquire into an insider's reasons in engaging in the transaction nor will they ascertain his or her access to or use of inside information. Consequently, any transaction that can be viewed as a "purchase" or "sale" and brought within the ambit of the statute will result in liability.[71]

Due to its unfair consequences in certain situations, the objective approach is subject to criticism. As a result, the "pragmatic" approach has been employed in certain "unorthodox" transactions, such as stock reclassifications, dealings in options, warrants, and rights, stock conversions, and exchanges pursuant to mergers. As stated by one commentator:

> The pragmatic approach involves a number of elements. First, and most important, it applies only in certain unusual circumstances. If these circumstances exist, then the transaction is characterized as "unorthodox." Unorthodox transactions are ill-defined, but they usually have peculiar features that either make it unfair to apply Section 16(b) or make it difficult to determine whether or when a purchase or sale has taken place.[72]

The pragmatic approach received Supreme Court approbation in *Kern County Land Co. v. Occidental Petroleum Corp.*[73] The Court reasoned:

> In deciding whether borderline transactions are within the reach of the statute, the courts have come to inquire whether the transaction may serve as a vehicle for the veil which Congress sought to prevent — the realization of short-swing profits based upon access to inside information — thereby endeavoring to implement Congressional objectives without extending the reach of the statute beyond its intended limits. . . . [T]he prevailing view is to apply the statute only when its application would serve its goals. . . . [I]n interpreting the terms "purchase" and "sale," courts have properly asked whether the particular type of transaction is one that gives rise to speculative abuse.[74]

---

[69] *Id.* at 421. See *Reece Corp. v. Walco National Corp.*, [1981-1982 Transfer Binder] Fed. Sec. L. Rep. (CCH) ¶ 98,289 (S.D.N.Y. 1981).

[70] 404 U.S. at 422-25.

[71] See, *e.g., Park and Tilford, Inc. v. Shulte*, 160 F.2d 984 (2d Cir. 1947).

[72] Tomlinson, *Section 16(b): A Single Analysis of Purchases and Sales — Merging the Objective and Pragmatic Analyses*, 1981 Duke L.J. 941, 947.

[73] 411 U.S. 582 (1973).

[74] *Id.* at 594-95 (citations omitted).

Several courts have employed the pragmatic approach in a variety of contexts. Using this approach, Section 16(b) liability has been imposed in some cases[75] but not in others.[76] From these cases as well as the scholarly commentary,[77] the key inquiries in applying the pragmatic approach include:

(1) Is the transaction in question of a type that may be characterized as unorthodox?

(2) Did the insider have control over the timing of the decision involved in the transaction?

(3) Did the insider have access to inside information, irrespective of whether that information was in fact used?[78]

§ 9.03 Issuer Affirmative Disclosure Obligations

[A] Generally

Cogent arguments have been made in favor of recognizing an issuer's affirmative duty to disclose material nonpublic information.[79] These include that first, by circulating a regular flow of information to the securities markets, a publicly-held company implicitly represents that information previously disclosed remains accurate. By failing to disclose, thereby inducing marketplace reliance that the previously disclosed information represents present conditions, the company has engaged in "deception" under Section 10(b).[80] Second, the "shingle" theory, currently applied to broker-dealers,[81] could be extended to encompass publicly-held companies. Such companies, the argument generally posits, have a duty to deal fairly with their

---

[75] See, *e.g.*, *Texas International Airlines v. National Airlines, Inc.*, 714 F.2d 533 (5th Cir. 1983).

[76] See, *e.g.*, *Heublein, Inc. v. General Cinema Corp.*, 722 F.2d 29 (2d Cir. 1983).

[77] See, *e.g.*, Ferber, *Short-Swing Transactions Under the Securities Exchange Act*, 16 Rev. Sec. Reg. 801 (1983); Hazen, *The New Pragmatism Under Section 16(b) of the Securities Exchange Act*, 54 N.C.L. Rev. 1 (1975); Wentz, *Refining a Crude Rule: The Pragmatic Approach to Section 16(b) of the Securities Exchange Act of 1934*, 70 Nw. U.L. Rev. 221 (1975); Note, *Insider Liability for Short-Swing Profits: The Substance and Function of the Pragmatic Approach*, 72 Mich. L. Rev. 592 (1974).

[78] M. Steinberg, *supra* note 58, at § 4.06 (and authorities cited therein). See R. Clark, *Corporate Law* § 8.7 (1986); Tomlinson, *supra* note 72, at 949.

[79] See, *e.g.*, Bauman, *Rule 10b-5 and the Corporation's Affirmative Duty to Disclose*, 67 Geo. L.J. 935 (1979). But see Sheffey, *Securities Law Responsibilities of Issuers to Respond to Rumors and Other Publicity: Reexamination of a Continuing Problem*, 57 Notre Dame Law. 755 (1982).

[80] See Note, *Disclosure of Material Inside Information: An Affirmative Corporate Duty?*, 1980 Ariz. St. L.J. 795, 801.

[81] See, *e.g.*, *Hanly v. SEC*, 415 F.2d 589 (2d Cir. 1969); discussion in § 7.09, *supra*.

shareholders and the securities markets, and the breach thereof constitutes "deception" under Section 10(b).[82]

Despite the above arguments, neither the courts nor the SEC are willing to recognize such a general mandate.[83] Affirmative disclosure obligations, however, clearly exist in a number of specific circumstances. For example, an issuer must affirmatively disclose when: (1) SEC rules and regulations require disclosure of specified information;[84] (2) the issuer is purchasing or selling its stock in the securities markets;[85] (3) the issuer previously has made a public statement that, although accurate when made, has become false or misleading as a result of subsequent events;[86] and (4) information has been leaked by, or rumors in the marketplace are attributable to, the issuer.[87] In other situations the law is less clear as to the existence and scope of an affirmative duty to disclose, such as in the case of merger negotiations, soft information, and bad financial news.

[B] Responding to Rumors

The circulation of rumors in the marketplace concerning a material development affecting a particular issuer (*e.g.*, being awarded a major contract or being the subject of a tender offer) is common. The question arises whether an issuer has a duty to respond to rumors under Section 10(b) when such rumors are not attributable to the corporation. The district court in the *Fluor* case opined that such a duty may exist where there are present widespread rumors, a substantial and rapid movement in the price of the subject corporation's stock, and the possession of a high degree of scienter.[88] On appeal, the Second Circuit construed this disclosure duty more narrowly, asserting that "[a] company has no duty to correct or verify rumors in the marketplace unless those rumors can be attributed to the company."[89]

Reading the district court and the Second Circuit decisions in *Fluor* somewhat differently, both opinions stated that the corporation had a justifiable business reason for delaying disclosure of the information. This is consistent with the accepted view that justifications for delaying disclosure by

---

[82] See Bauman, *supra* note 79, at 944-45. See generally M. Steinberg, *supra* note 58, at § 2.01, *et seq.*

[83] See, *e.g.*, *Greenfield v. Heublein, Inc.*, 742 F.2d 751 (3d Cir. 1984); SEC *Brief as Amicus Curiae* in *Levinson v. Basic, Inc.*, 786 F.2d 741 (6th Cir. 1986), *vacated and remanded*, 108 S.Ct. 978 (1988).

[84] See, *e.g.*, SEC Forms 10-K, 10-Q.

[85] See, *e.g.*, *Fridrich v. Bradford*, 542 F.2d 307, 318 (6th Cir. 1976).

[86] See, *e.g.*, *Ross v. A.H. Robins Co.*, 465 F. Supp. 904, 908 (S.D.N.Y.), *rev'd on other grounds*, 607 F.2d 545 (2d Cir. 1979).

[87] See, *e.g.*, *State Teachers Retirement Bd. v. Fluor Corp.*, 654 F.2d 843, 850 (2d Cir. 1981).

[88] *State Teachers Retirement Board v. Fluor Corp.*, 500 F. Supp. 278, 292-93 (S.D.N.Y. 1980).

[89] *State Teachers Retirement Board v. Fluor Corp.*, 654 F.2d 843, 850 (2d Cir. 1981).

an issuer of material nonpublic information generally fall into three categories:

> delay while corporate officials ascertain and verify information [until] it is "ripe for disclosure"; delay while a corporation pursues a business opportunity that would be jeopardized by immediate disclosure; and delay because disclosure would expose the corporation to undue and avoidable risk of loss.[90]

In certain circumstances, it is possible that an issuer may have a duty to seek a halt in the trading of its stock.[91] Moreover, the rules and other pronouncements of the self-regulatory organizations (SROs), including the New York and American Stock Exchanges, impose affirmative and timely disclosure requirements that are more rigorous than current Section 10(b) case law.[92] Violation of these rules, however, although perhaps resulting in SRO disciplinary action, do not provide investors with an implied right of action for damages.[93] This position may stem from the belief that, where there are no prior inadequate disclosures, no particular SEC disclosure requirements, nor the presence of "insider" trading, disclosure determinations and the timing of such disclosure generally are left best to the discretion of management. Moreover, if regulation is to have a role in this setting, such regulation should be conducted and enforced by the self-regulatory organizations without the threat of monetary liability.

[C] Disclosure of Merger Negotiations

With respect to disclosure of merger negotiations, the Supreme Court's decision in *Basic, Inc. v. Levinson*[94] provides guidance. There, the issuer on three separate occasions falsely denied that it was engaging in merger negotiations.[95] In assessing whether these misstatements were "material," the Supreme Court adopted the fact-specific inquiry of *Texas Gulf Sulphur*.[96] Under this standard, the materiality of merger negotiations

> depend[s] at any given time upon a balancing of both the indicated probability that the event will occur and the anticipated magnitude of the event in light of the totality of the company activity.[97]

In applying this fact-specific inquiry in a given situation, Justice Blackmun, writing for the Court, opined:

---

[90] Vaughn, *Timing of Disclosure*, 13 Rev. Sec. Reg. 911, 913 (1980).

[91] See 654 F.2d at 851 n.7.

[92] See, *e.g., New York Stock Exchange Company Manual* § A2, 2 Fed. Sec. L. Rep. (CCH) ¶ 23,121 (1981).

[93] See 654 F.2d at 852-53. See also § 8.03, *supra*.

[94] 108 S.Ct. 978 (1988). See generally Bagby & Ruhnka, *The Predictability of Materiality in Merger Negotiations Following Basic*, 16 Sec. Reg. L.J. 245 (1988).

[95] 108 S.Ct. at 981.

[96] *SEC v. Texas Gulf Sulphur Co.*, 401 F.2d 833 (2d Cir. 1968) (*en banc*).

[97] 108 S.Ct. at 987, quoting 401 F.2d at 849.

> Whether merger discussions in any particular case are material therefore depends on the facts. Generally, in order to assess the probability that the event will occur, a factfinder will need to look to indicia of interest in the transaction at the highest corporate levels. Without attempting to catalog all such possible factors, we note by way of example that board resolutions, instructions to investment bankers, and actual negotiations between principals or their intermediaries may serve as indicia of interest. To assess the magnitude of the transaction to the issuer of the securities allegedly manipulated, a factfinder will need to consider such facts as the size of the two corporate entities and of the potential premiums over market value. No particular event or factor short of closing the transaction need be either necessary or sufficient by itself to render merger discussions material.[98]

It is important to emphasize that the issuer in *Basic* elected to speak. Hence, the case neither involved the timing of disclosure nor an issuer's obligation to speak.[99] As a result, the decision may seem more expansive than, in actuality, it is. In this regard, absent the existence of certain triggering events, such as the presence of a competing tender offer where SEC Schedule 14D-9 requires disclosure of merger negotiations,[100] present law may not require the issuer affirmatively to disclose the existence of such negotiations, even if they are material. The SEC takes this position:

> In urging that merger negotiations may become material before there is certainty of an agreement, we are not suggesting that material merger negotiations therefore have to be disclosed to the public as a matter of course. We agree with the court below that corporations ordinarily have no duty to disclose even material merger negotiations.[101]

After the *Basic* decision, issuers may well be inclined to remain silent until an agreement as to price and structure are reached. Moreover, a "no comment" statement, according to language in *Basic*, is "generally the functional equivalent of silence."[102] Unfortunately, issuer silence, absent justifiable business reasons for maintaining secrecy, conflicts with the disclosure policies of the federal securities acts. Nonetheless, given the enormous liability potential, issuer silence (or "no comment") may be a practical policy to implement.

[D] Disclosure of "Soft" Information

Traditionally, the securities laws have required disclosure of "hard" information, that is, factual, objectively verifiable data.[103] "Soft" information,

---

[98] 108 S.Ct. at 987.

[99] *Id.* at 984-85.

[100] 17 C.F.R. § 240.14d-101, item 7 (calling for a subject company's management to disclose merger negotiations even though the potential offeror's identity need not be revealed if the negotiations are in a preliminary stage).

[101] See *Brief for the SEC*, *supra* note 83, at 7.

[102] 108 S.Ct. at 987 n.17.

[103] See generally *Securities Act Release* No. 6084 (1979).

on the other hand, predominantly focuses on forward-looking statements, such as projections, forecasts, and predictions.[104] Moreover, soft information need not necessarily relate to expectations regarding the future, but may include any statement that cannot be factually supported, whether due to a lack of substantiating data or because the information consists primarily of subjective evaluations or opinions.[105]

Until the mid-1970s the SEC and the courts discouraged and even prohibited the disclosure of soft information.[106] The major concern has been that investors, particularly the unsophisticated, might attach too much significance to information that is of questionable reliability.[107] On the other hand, the flow of soft information to the marketplace may enable sophisticated investors more intelligently to evaluate the total mix of information influencing their decisionmaking.[108]

Merger mania has brought the issue of disclosing soft information into current focus. For example, in a departure from its traditional view that forward-looking information is untrustworthy and, hence, discouraged, the SEC adopted Rule 175,[109] which encourages issuer use of financial projections and establishes a "safe harbor" for parties who invoke the rule.[110] While a number of courts have extended this position to require issuer disclosure of forward-looking statements in certain circumstances,[111] most courts continue to adhere to the traditional philosophical concerns as a basis for not imposing liability upon issuers who decline to disclose soft information.[112]

Hence, while soft information historically has been treated as immaterial as a matter of law, an emerging, although still minority, view clearly suggests that this is no longer so. The leading case for the proposition that there is an affirmative duty to disclose soft information when certain indicia of reliability are present is *Flynn v. Bass Brothers Enterprises.*[113] In that case the

---

[104] *Id.*

[105] See Schneider, *Nits, Grits, and Soft Information in SEC Filings*, 121 U. Pa. L. Rev. 254, 255 (1972).

[106] See, *e.g., Gerstle v. Gamble-Skogmo, Inc.*, 478 F.2d 1281, 1294 (2d Cir. 1973); *Securities Act Release* No. 5180 (1971).

[107] See, *e.g., South Coast Services Corp. v. Santa Ana Valley Irrigation Co.*, 699 F.2d 1265, 1271 (9th Cir. 1982).

[108] See generally Hiler, *The SEC and the Courts' Approach to Disclosure of Earnings Projections, Asset Appraisals, and Other Soft Information: Old Problems, Changing Views*, 46 Md. L. Rev. 1114 (1987); Kerr, *A Walk Through the Circuits: The Duty to Disclose Soft Information*, 46 Md. L. Rev. 1071 (1987).

[109] 17 C.F.R. § 230.175. See *Securities Act Release* No. 6084 (1979).

[110] Rule 175 is discussed in greater detail in § 4.07[B], *supra*. See generally Dennis, *Mandatory Disclosure Theory and Management Projections: A Law and Economics Perspective*, 46 Md. L. Rev. 1197 (1987).

[111] See, *e.g., Flynn v. Bass Brothers Enterprises, Inc.*, 744 F.2d 978 (3d Cir. 1984).

[112] See, *e.g., Starkman v. Marathon Oil Co.*, 772 F.2d 231 (6th Cir. 1985).

[113] 744 F.2d 978 (3d Cir. 1984).

Third Circuit canvassed the events marking what it considered to be the emergence of a new public policy favoring the disclosure of soft information, spawned "in response to developing corporate trends, such as the increase in mergers,"[114] and held:

> In order to give full effect to the evolution of the law of disclosure, . . . today we set forth the law for disclosure of soft information as it is to be applied from this date on. Henceforth, the law is not that asset appraisals are, as a matter of law, immaterial. Rather, in appropriate cases, such information must be disclosed. Courts should ascertain the duty to disclose asset valuations and other soft information on a case by case basis, by weighing the potential aid such information will give a shareholder against the potential harm, such as undue reliance, if the information is released with a proper cautionary note.
>
> The factors a court must consider in making such a determination are: the facts upon which the information is based; the qualifications of those who prepared or compiled it; the purpose for which the information was originally intended; its relevance to the stockholders' impending decision; the degree of subjectivity or bias reflected in its preparation; the degree to which the information in unique; and the availability to the investor of other more reliable sources of information.[115]

Sharply contrasting *Flynn* is the Sixth Circuit's approach in *Starkman v. Marathon Oil Co.*,[116] in which the court declined to recognize a mandatory obligation to disclose asset appraisals or financial projections, unless "the predictions underlying the appraisal or projection are substantially certain to hold."[117] Criticizing the Third Circuit's approach in *Flynn*, the Sixth Circuit reasoned:

> By its very nature . . . this sort of judicial cost-benefit analysis [referring to *Flynn*] is uncertain and unpredictable, and it moreover neglects the role of the market in providing shareholders with information regarding the target's value through competing tender offers. Our approach, which focuses on the certainty of the data underlying the appraisal or projection, ensures that the target company's shareholders will receive all essentially factual information, while preserving the target's discretion to disclose more uncertain information without the threat of liability, provided appropriate qualifications and explanations are made.[118]

Flynn represents an approach aimed at addressing investor concerns, whereas *Starkman* illustrates the disclosure concerns from an issuer's perspective. Both views have merit, but each is too one-sided. The cost-

---

[114] *Id.* at 986.
[115] *Id.* at 988.
[116] 772 F.2d 231 (6th Cir. 1985).
[117] *Id.* at 241.
[118] *Id.* at 242.

benefit analysis advocated by the Third Circuit does not promote certainty, because the approach calls for a court to determine the qualitative value of the enumerated factors with the benefit of hindsight and on an ad hoc basis. Under this approach, judicial guidelines may well have little stability, because the subjective nature of the inquiry is likely to result in the factors being applied differently under an ad hoc analysis. In addition, the Third Circuit's desire "to give full effect to the evolution in the law of disclosure"[119] overlooks the fact that, while the securities laws are designed to protect investors, they are not intended to impose undue hardship upon issuers. The issuer's duty to disclose should be based on what is fair and reasonable from both an investor's and an issuer's perspective.

On the other hand, the Sixth Circuit's approach in *Starkman* is too rigid. Disclosure, a key concept underlying the securities laws, is subordinated to the perceived need to avoid imposing liability in circumstances in which certainty cannot be assured. The *Starkman* court's concern is misplaced, because an important policy underlying the disclosure doctrine is issuer fair dealing through the sharing of information that is material to investor decisionmaking. Congress, the SEC, and the courts generally require issuers to make accurate and complete disclosure of specified information in order to enhance the level of investor decisionmaking and to ensure that the information disclosed is not materially misleading. All that should be required in the context of soft information is that the available material data be accurately disclosed; it need not be certain.

Clearly, there is a need for an approach that embraces both investor and issuer concerns. While an affirmative duty to disclose has been held to exist only in certain well-defined situations,[120] consistent application of the disclosure principle underlying the securities laws requires that, to ensure investor decisionmaking based on a flow of accurate information between the issuer and the financial markets, soft information must be affirmatively disclosed in certain circumstances. Hence, the following two-prong test should be adopted for establishing when an issuer has an affirmative duty to disclose soft information: (1) the information must be material and ripe for disclosure and (2) the failure to disclose must be fundamentally unfair to stockholders.[121]

[E] Duty to Disclose "Bad" News

"Bad news" usually refers to circumstances having an adverse financial impact upon the corporation, such as the loss of one or more major customers or valuable contracts, the initiation of a significant lawsuit or SEC enforcement action, or events giving rise to troubling liquidity problems, to

---

[119] 744 F.2d at 988.

[120] See *supra* text accompanying notes 84-87.

[121] For further discussion see Steinberg & Goldman, *Issuer Affirmative Disclosure Obligations — An Analytical Framework for Merger Negotiations, Soft Information and Bad News*, 46 Md. L. Rev. 923, 934-46 (1987).

mention but a few examples. Bad news also may refer to impending changes in corporate management, or the loss of access to or dismissal of special advisers upon whom corporate management has come to rely.

The reasons for issuer reluctance to disclose bad news concerning the company are axiomatic. Equally obvious is the significance of such information to investors. The periodic reports that issuers are required to file under the Exchange Act are comprehensive, and one generally cannot omit bad news without violating the securities laws. However, certain disclosure loopholes exist, because there is no specific SEC rule mandating disclosure of material adverse financial information between periodic reports.

Hence, the affirmative disclosure issue relating to adverse financial information normally arises during an interval in which the issuer is not required to file a periodic report with the SEC. Under the Exchange Act an issuer is required, *inter alia*, to file annual reports on Form 10-K, quarterly reports on Form 10-Q and current reports on Form 8-K. The regulations which mandate the filing of these reports are fairly specific as to what is required to be disclosed in the various line items. For example, Form 10-K requires, among other things, an extensive discussion of the issuer's business, audited financial statements, disclosures regarding certain legal proceedings, and a management discussion and analysis ("MD&A").[122] With respect to the MD&A, mandated disclosures include identifying "any known trends or any known demands, commitments, events, or uncertainties that will result in, or that are reasonably likely to result in, the registrant's liquidity increasing or decreasing in any material way" and a description of "any known trends or uncertainties that have had or that the registrant reasonably expects will have a material favorable or unfavorable impact on net sales or revenues or income from continuing operations."[123]

Quarterly reports (on Form 10-Q) also must contain an MD&A and other extensive disclosures, including unaudited interim financial information prepared in accordance with generally accepted accounting principles ("GAAP").[124] Moreover, periodic disclosure, on Form 8-K, is required to facilitate current disclosure of certain significant events. A key ingredient of the Form 8-K disclosure obligation is that it is mandatory only with respect to certain specified events.[125] Disclosure of other events is permissive.[126] Although the Commission has issued a number of releases urging corporate managements to review their disclosure policies "and endeavor to set up

[122] Form 10-K, Items 1-3, 6-9, 14, 17 C.F.R. § 249.310.

[123] Form 10-K, Item 7 (calling for information required by Item 303 of Regulation S-K).

[124] Form 10-Q, Part I, Items 1-2, 17 C.F.R. § 249.308a.

[125] 17 C.F.R. § 249.308. The following items are mandatory under Form 8-K: Changes in Control of Registrant (Item 1), Acquisition or Disposition of Assets (Item 2), Bankruptcy or Receivership (Item 3), Changes in Registrant's Certifying Accountant (Item 4), and Resignations of Registrant's Directors (Item 6).

[126] See Form 8-K, Item 5.

procedures which will insure that prompt disclosure be made of material corporate developments, both favorable and unfavorable, so that investor confidence can be maintained in an orderly and effective securities market,"[127] the Commission has refrained from promulgating rules which mandate affirmative disclosure of bad news arising between quarterly reports. In addition, there is a dearth of judicial authority on the issue. Hence, because there currently is no general affirmative duty to disclose even material information regarding the issuer except in certain specific circumstances,[128] the disinclination by issuers to make such disclosure is not surprising.

Accordingly, the central issue in this context is one of timing. Issuers understandably wish to delay disclosure of adverse news as long as possible. For example, during the interim when the next Form 10-Q must be filed, perhaps new major contracts can be procured to replace the ones that were terminated. Immediate disclosure, according to management, could have a "snowball" effect, depressing the company's business and the price of its stock in the securities markets.

Generally, there is little judicial authority to support an affirmative duty to disclose adverse news during the period between SEC required reports. Courts have held that the timing of disclosure is a matter of business judgment.[129] Under this concept, disclosure may be deferred until the information is ripe, or withheld if a valid business reason exists, such as where premature disclosure would jeopardize a contract. On the other hand, where the material information clearly is ripe and the business justifications proffered are not compelling, a plausible case exists for imposing liability for nondisclosure. A court should balance the potential impact of disclosing the bad news against the fiduciary duty owed to shareholders.[130]

It is not surprising that questions concerning issuer affirmative disclosure obligations raise difficult public policy issues. In seeking to set forth a proper balance, legitimate concerns of both issuers and investors should be addressed. On the one hand, issuers should be required to affirmatively disclose only if there are sufficiently clear guidelines in effect and only if legitimate business interests will not be impeded by such disclosure. On the other hand, investors and the marketplace should be entitled to all material financial information that is ripe for disclosure, in a manner which is not misleading to investors, and that does not impose an unduly rigorous burden upon issuers.[131]

---

[127] See *Securities Exchange Act Release* No. 18271 (1981).

[128] See *supra* text accompanying notes 84-87.

[129] See, *e.g., Billard v. Rockwell International Corp.*, 683 F.2d 51 (2d Cir. 1982).

[130] *Cf. Flynn v. Bass Brothers Enterprises, Inc.*, 744 F.2d 978 (3d Cir. 1984).

[131] For further discussion see Steinberg & Goldman, *supra* note 121, at 946-51.

CHAPTER 10

CORPORATE CONTROL ACQUISITIONS AND CONTESTS

§ 10.01 Introduction

This chapter addresses three types of corporate control acquisitions or contests: the proxy battle, the going-private transaction, and the hostile tender offer. Although state law is very relevant in these contexts, emphasis is placed (due to the subject matter covered in the course) on federal securities regulation.

In focusing on this chapter, one should keep in mind that hostile proxy and tender offer fights, by their nature, are contests for corporate control. In this way, they are quite similar. As Judge Friendly, in *Electronic Specialty Company v. International Controls Corp.*,[1] stated:

> The likeness of tender offers to proxy contests is not limited to the issue of standing. They are alike in the fundamental feature that they generally are contests. This means that the participants on both sides act, not "in the peace of a quiet chamber," but under the stresses of the marketplace. They act quickly, sometimes impulsively, often in angry response to what they consider, whether rightly or wrongly, to be low blows by the other side. Probably there will no more be a perfect tender offer than a perfect trial. Congress intended to assure basic honesty and fair dealing, not to impose an unrealistic requirement of laboratory conditions that might make the new statute a potent tool for incompetent management to protect its own interests against the desires and welfare of the stockholders. These considerations bear on the kind of judgment to be applied in testing conduct — on both sides — and also on the issue of materiality.[2]

§ 10.02 Going-Private Transactions

Generally, "[a] going-private transaction is a transaction or series of transactions instituted by the controlling shareholders of a publicly-held corporation and designed to eliminate or substantially reduce the corporation's outstanding equity, thereby returning the corporation to private

[1] 409 F.2d 937 (2d Cir. 1969).

[2] *Id.* at 948.

ownership."[3] Generally, these transactions often take the form of a cash-out (or more pejoratively "freeze-out" or "squeeze-out") merger and result in compelling the minority stockholders to exchange their shares for cash.[4]

[A] State Law

In *Singer v. Magnavox Co.*,[5] the Delaware Supreme Court held that, in order to comport with a controlling shareholder's fiduciary duties to the subsidiary corporation and its minority shareholders, a cash-out merger must have a proper business purpose and must be entirely fair to the minority. A number of states adhere to the *Singer* standards.[6] The Delaware high court itself, however, in *Weinberger v. UOP, Inc.*,[7] abandoned the business purpose test and confined its inquiry to the "entire fairness" standard. In so doing, the court formulated a more liberal approach to valuation, permitting such elements as premiums over market price offered in similar transactions and future earnings potential (so long as not speculative) to be considered. The *Weinberger* court's approach facilitates mergers and normally leaves a minority shareholder to the appraisal remedy. However, as stated by that court,

> [t]he appraisal remedy we approve may not be adequate in certain cases, particularly where fraud, misrepresentation, self-dealing, deliberate waste of corporate assets, or gross and palpable overreaching are involved.[8]

In such cases, injunctive relief may be awarded prior to the merger's consummation and breach of fiduciary duty actions seeking monetary damages may be invoked after the transaction has been accomplished (and cannot be "undone").[9]

It should be pointed out that a number of states do not follow *Singer* or *Weinberger*. For example, in some states, absent fraud or illegality, appraisal is a minority shareholder's sole remedy in a cash-out merger.[10] A few states accomplish this result by statute. A Minnesota statute, for instance, provides that corporations may merge "with or without a business purpose" and that the remedy for lack of "entire fairness" is appraisal.[11]

---

[3] Comment, *Regulating Going-Private Transactions: SEC Rule 13e-3*, 80 Colum. L. Rev. 782 (1980).

[4] *Id.*

[5] 380 A.2d 969 (Del. 1977).

[6] See, *e.g.*, *Alpert v. 28 Williams St. Corp.*, 63 N.Y.2d 557, 473 N.E.2d 19, 483 N.Y.S.2d 667 (1984); *Perl v. IU Int'l Corp.*, 61 Haw. 622, 607 P.2d 1036 (1980).

[7] 457 A.2d 701 (Del. 1983).

[8] *Id.* at 714.

[9] *Id.* See Weiss, *Balancing Interests in Cash-Out Mergers: The Promise of Weinberger v. UOP, Inc.*, 8 Del. J. Corp. L. 1 (1983).

[10] See, *e.g.*, *Steinberg v. Amplica, Inc.*, 42 Cal. 3d 1198, 233 Cal. Rptr. 249, 729 P.2d 683 (1986); *Yanow v. Teal Industries, Inc.*, 178 Conn. 262, 422 A.2d 311 (1979).

[11] Minn. Stat. Ann. § 302A.601.

Given the increased frequency of leveraged buy-outs where incumbent management takes a substantial equity position in the surviving entity, it remains to be seen whether the state courts will analyze such transactions on the same terms as cash-out mergers between parent-subsidiary corporations. Unlike cash-out mergers, leveraged buy-outs enable incumbent managements to put up little cash of their own and through the use of borrowed funds collateralized by corporate assets (the repayment of such funds to be made by means of future revenues or the sale of certain assets) eliminate the public shareholders and gain for themselves a substantial equity position. Critics view such transactions as implicating inherent conflicts of interest, calling for the application of heightened fiduciary duty standards. For example, it may be posited that, given the conflicts of interest and potential for abuse present, leveraged buy-out proposals benefitting incumbent management must be left open for a substantial period of time in order to enable unaffiliated third parties to make competing bids, thereby effectuating the "auction" process.[12]

[B] Federal Law

In addition to Section 10(b) of the Exchange Act, Sections 13e-3 and 13e-4 of the Exchange Act and the SEC rules promulgated thereunder (Rules 13e-3 and 13e-4) are the principal federal securities law provisions governing going-private transactions. Rule 13e-3 is a comprehensive rule that prohibits fraudulent, deceptive or manipulative practices in connection with going private transactions and sets forth filing, disclosure, and dissemination requirements.[13] Rule 13e-4 is narrower in scope and applies to an issuer's tender offer for its own securities ("self tenders"). It, like Rule 13e-3, is an antifraud provision and mandates extensive disclosure.[14] Moreover, the same procedural requirements that apply in third-party tender offers pursuant to Section 14(d) generally are extended by Rule 13e-4 to issuer self tenders.[15] Note that an issuer self tender which comes under Rule 13e-4 also may be a going-private transaction within Rule 13e-3's reach. Under such circumstances, both Rule 13e-3 and Rule 13e-4 apply.[16]

Rule 13e-3 calls for subject parties to disclose extensive information with respect to a going-private transaction by filing a Schedule 13E-3 with the SEC. The disclosures include: (1) a description of both the benefits and

---

[12] See, generally *MacAndrews & Forbes Holdings v. Revlon, Inc.*, 506 A.2d 173 (Del. 1986); DeMott, *Directors' Duties in Management Buyouts and Leveraged Recapitalizations*, 49 Ohio St. L.J. 517 (1988); Lowenstein, *Management Buyouts*, 85 Colum. L. Rev. 730 (1985); Morrissey, *Law, Ethics, and the Leveraged Buyout*, 65 U. Det. L. Rev. 403 (1988); Steinberg & Lindahl, *The New Law of Squeeze-Out Mergers*, 62 Wash. U.L.Q. 351 (1984).

[13] See *Securities Exchange Act Release* No. 16075 (1979).

[14] See *Securities Exchange Act Release* No. 16112 (1979).

[15] See [1985-1986 Transfer Binder] Fed. Sec. L. Rep. (CCH) ¶ 83,954 (SEC 1986).

[16] *Securities Exchange Act Release* No. 16112 (1979). See Manges, *SEC Regulation of Issuer and Third-Party Tender Offers*, 8 Sec. Reg. L.J. 275 (1981).

detriments of the transaction to the issuer as well as to affiliated and unaffiliated shareholders; (2) disclosure of any report, opinion, or appraisal received from an outside party concerning the going-private transaction; (3) disclosure of any plans by the issuer to merge, reorganize, sell assets or employ any other material change after the transaction; (4) disclosure of the source and total amount of funds for the transaction, an estimation of anticipated expenses, a summary of any loan agreements, and arrangements to finance and repay loans; and (5) disclosure of whether the subject parties reasonably believe that the transaction is fair to unaffialiated stockholders and the factors upon which they have that belief.[17]

As to the last disclosure listed above, some commentators assert that, by requiring that the subject parties disclose whether they "reasonably believe" that the going-private transaction is fair, the SEC is engaging in impermissible substantive regulation.[18] In this respect, the Supreme Court's decision in *Schreiber* (discussed in § 10.09[A], *infra*) is relevant.[19] There, the Supreme Court held that Section 14(e) of the Exchange Act is premised on the truthful disclosure of adequate information rather than on the substantive fairness of the transaction. Because both Sections 13(e) and 14(e) were enacted as part of the Williams Act in 1968 (as an amendment to the Exchange Act) and contain in part similar language, the assertion that Rule 13e-3's disclosure of "fairness" provision is invalid has an even stronger basis today. Nonetheless, an argument can be made that, in prescribing this requirement, the Commission has focused on its disclosure function rather than engaging principally in substantive regulation.[20] Note, moreover, that minority shareholders, if they can show a material misrepresentation or nondisclosure in connection with the going private transaction, often can avail themselves of the Section 10(b) right of action, provided, of course, that they satisfy the requirements necessary to recover under that provision.

§ 10.03 Proxy Contests

Under federal law, proxy contests principally are governed by Section 14(a) of the Exchange Act and SEC rules prescribed thereunder. In this regard, the legal standards underlying a private right of action under Section 14(a) are addressed in § 8.05, *supra*. That discussion should be reviewed at this point.

In recent years, it has been generally thought that the tender offer has replaced the proxy battle as the means for procuring corporate control or effecting a change in corporate policies.

This situation was attributed to the difficulty of ousting an incumbent management (unless it was demonstrably incompetent and the insurgents

---

[17] See Schedule 13E-3, 17 C.F.R. § 240.13e-100.

[18] See, *e.g.*, Note, *Rule 13e-3 and the Going-Private Dilemma: The SEC's Quest for a Substantive Fairness Doctrine*, 58 Wash. U.L.Q. 883 (1980).

[19] 472 U.S. 1 (1985).

[20] See generally A. Borden, *Going Private* (1980).

> had a large stock position), the significant amount of money and time consumed by a proxy fight, and the impossibility of recouping proxy fight costs if the insurgents failed to take control.[21]

To a degree, however, the proxy fight has seen a partial renaissance. While this renaissance arguably may be more in response to market conditions than to regulatory developments, it also reflects changes in the regulatory context. Indeed, with the proliferation of state takeover statutes, SEC tender offer regulations, and court battles, the costs of pursuing a hostile tender offer can be exorbitant (*e.g.*, costs of acquiring a controlling interest, attorney and investment banker fees, and, depending upon market conditions, high interest rates).

Nonetheless, proxy contests normally are viable today when economic benefits accrue to the shareholders. For example, as seen by the proxy contest involving GAF Corporation,[22] a number of these battles have had as the insurgents' main objective the sale or liquidation of certain assets of the corporation, particularly where the company's stock was trading at what was viewed as an unreasonably low price. The proceeds from the sale of assets then may be passed onto the shareholders as a cash distribution.

Given the "hurly-burly" of proxy contests, courts generally apply a standard of fair accuracy.[23] "[N]it-picking should not become the name of the game."[24] Nonetheless, as discussed in § 8.05[B], *supra*, an implied private right of action exists to redress violations of Section 14(a), particularly where materially false or misleading statements have been made.

Section 14(a) of the Exchange Act and Regulation 14A promulgated thereunder regulate the solicitation of proxies in regard to securities registered under Section 12 of the 1934 Act. Rules 14a-3 to 14a-10 of Regulation 14A prescribe certain filing, dissemination, disclosure and substantive requirements with respect to all proxy contests. Rule 14a-11 prescribes special requirements relating only to contested elections of directors.[25] Although the proxy rules have been subject to judicial and SEC interpretation, there remain pitfalls and unresolved issues. As a consequence, counsel may be presented with difficult questions in this setting.[26]

---

[21] Brown, *Changes in Offeror Strategy in Response to New Laws and Regulations*, 25 Case W. Res. L. Rev. 843, 865-66 (1978).

[22] See *GAF Corporation v. Heyman*, 724 F.2d 727 (2d Cir. 1983).

[23] See *General Time Corporation v. Talley Industries, Inc.*, 403 F.2d 159, 162 (2d Cir. 1968).

[24] *Kennecott Copper Corp. v. Curtiss-Wright Corp.*, 584 F.2d 1195, 1200 (2d Cir. 1978).

[25] See Schwartz & Steinberger, *Proxy Contests for Corporate Control*, appearing in *Proxy Contests for Corporate Control: How to Mount the Attack or Defend the Citadel* at 4-5 (1980).

[26] See generally E. Aranow & H. Einhorn, *Proxy Contests for Corporate Control* (1968); Schwartz & Tillman, *Proxy Contest Developments*, 16 Rev. Sec. Reg. 789 (1983); Steinberg, *Fiduciary Duties and Disclosure Obligations in Proxy and Tender Contests for Corporate Control*, 30 Emory L.J. 169 (1981).

§ 10.04 A Primer on the Williams Act

[A] Introduction

By the mid-1960's the frequency of cash tender offers had risen to levels that made many people uncomfortable. This discomfort was felt from the corridors of the Securities and Exchange Commission (SEC), where secret corporate control transactions that had somehow slipped between the regulatory cracks were viewed with great suspicion, to the boardrooms of many of the nation's corporations, where fear of being swallowed up by corporate raiders was spreading. The rate of tender offers, although small when compared to today's world of merger mania, had increased from 8, involving $200 million in 1960, to 107, involving $1 billion by 1966.[27]

There were many reasons for this takeover boom, not the least of which was a thriving economy that had left many corporations cash-rich and looking for investments. The perfect vehicle for investment in many cases proved to be the cash tender offer; there was little regulation compared to other control transaction devices (such as public exchange offers and proxy contests); results could be achieved swiftly and often with little resistance from the surprised incumbent managements.

Some viewed these new developments as a natural consequence of a pent-up economy that was showing signs of growth. Indeed, many saw the movement as a healthy signal of a mature, capitalist economy that promoted competition between managements as well as between products. In this kind of economy, most inefficient managements would gradually give way to those best able to accumulate and distribute earned profits to shareholders. Others were not quite as optimistic and feared that once-proud companies were falling prey to larger corporate raiders that would all too frequently victimize the smaller companies. In the process, shareholders, who had little understanding of these corporate maneuvers, would suffer.

The Williams Act of 1968,[28] which amended the Securities Exchange Act of 1934, was the legislative attempt at accommodating both of these viewpoints. The Act required offerors to disclose information that was material to a shareholder's decision whether to tender his or her shares, while, at the same time, not imposing too stringent regulations that would impede the efficacy of the cash tender offer vehicle.

The Williams Act, as adopted, was the ultimate product of the dialogue engendered by congressional proposals. The first attempt at legislation in this area came in 1965 when Senator Harrison Williams of New Jersey introduced S. 2731. Stories of giant corporate raiders swallowing or gutting small proud companies upset many members of Congress, particularly since this situation was due, at least in part, to a loophole in the securities laws.

---

[27] 113 Cong. Rec. S. 24,664 (daily ed. Aug. 30, 1967) (statement of Senator Williams).

[28] S. 510, Pub. L. 90-439, 82 Stat. 454 (1968).

Before the Williams Act's passage, an offeror could avoid federal filing, dissemination, and disclosure obligations by procuring control through a cash tender offer.[29] Corporations and individuals took advantage of another disclosure loophole by buying up shares of an acquisition prospect in the open market until they had gained control or had acquired a substantial percentage of the company's stock. This could be accomplished swiftly and secretly without the attendant regulation that accompanied other merger vehicles such as the public exchange offer or the proxy contest.[30]

Although the philosophy of the proposed 1965 legislation was attractive to some members, hearings were never held and the bill died. One reason for that bill's failure was the feeling that it was too favorable to the incumbents in a tender offer contest, and, hence, would stifle economically beneficial corporate combinations. For example, one provision of the bill would have required a bidder to give incumbent management twenty days notice of its intention to commence a tender offer. Many felt that this kind of notice would have effectively eliminated hostile cash tender offers because it would have allowed incumbent managements more time to implement various defensive tactics, thereby causing the defeat of the takeover bid.[31]

By 1967 proponents had refined their proposals. The major advocates for the legislation were the SEC and a coalition of corporate leaders who feared that, without some regulation, a detrimental tender offer fever would sweep the country, causing great harm to the American economy. These strange bedfellows provided a rather broad base of support for S. 510.

[B] Legislation

The legislation, as enacted in 1968, added Sections 13(d), (e), and 14(d), (e), and (f) to the Exchange Act. Many of the tender offer provisions in the Act are set forth in Section 14(d). That section principally contains disclosure mandates and provisions designed to give shareholders sufficient time in a noncoercive setting to make informed investment decisions. A number of these provisions have been modified by the SEC pursuant to its rulemaking powers.[32] Section 14(e) is a broad antifraud provision which makes it unlawful for any person to make false or misleading statements of material fact, or to engage in fraudulent, deceptive or manipulative acts or practices in connection with a tender offer. In 1970, Congress amended Section 14(e) to give the SEC broad rulemaking authority under that statute.

Some of the procedural provisions evidently did not provoke much debate. For example, Section 14(d)(5) allows a shareholder to withdraw his or her

---

[29] See *Piper v. Chris-Craft Industries, Inc.*, 430 U.S. 1, 22 (1977); R. Clark, *Corporate Law* § 13.3 (1986).

[30] See Cohen, *A Note on Takeover Bids and Corporate Purchases of Stock*, 22 Bus. Law. 149 (1966).

[31] See discussion in Brudney, *A Note on Chilling Tender Solicitations*, 21 Rutgers L. Rev. 609 (1967).

[32] See discussion in § 10.08, *infra*.

tendered shares within seven days after the offer commences and after sixty days following the commencement of the offer. This provision now has been expanded by Rule 14d-7 to permit a shareholder to withdraw the shares tendered during the entire period that the offer remains open. This withdrawal right changes the pre-Williams Act irrevocability of tendered shares, thereby enabling the shareholder to withdraw his or her shares and not be indefinitely held to a decision to tender that is not in one's best interest. Moreover, Section 14(d)(6) softens the "stampede" effect of coercing shareholders to rapidly tender their stock in first-come first-serve offers by providing for a pro rata purchase of all shares tendered within ten days of the initial offer. As with the withdrawal right, the SEC pursuant to Rule 14d-8 has expanded this right to proration to encompass the entire offering period.

The disclosure provisions of Sections 13(d)(1) and 14(d)(1) are what apparently caused the greatest stir in Congress and among the academics. Section 13(d)(1) requires disclosure within ten days from any person (or group) who becomes the direct, indirect, or beneficial owner of five percent of a company's outstanding stock. This post-transaction filing requirement is principally directed at providing notice to the marketplace where a potential shift in corporate control may take place.[33] Section 14(d)(1) governs the cash tender offer and mandates the filing by an offeror of essentially the same information as required by Section 13(d)(1). These disclosures include:

(1) the background and identity of the offeror;
(2) the source and amount of funds used;
(3) the purpose of the contemplated purchases;
(4) the number of shares owned;
(5) information regarding any special arrangements involving the offer; and
(6) such additional information as the SEC may prescribe.

A fundamental purpose of these disclosures is to protect incumbent shareholders from having to make hasty and uninformed decisions on whether or not it would be in their best interests to tender their shares for the offered price. Critics, on the other hand, believe that the information required to be disclosed is largely irrelevant to the shareholder's decision and that by, forcing disclosure, the economic incentive to embark on a takeover bid is needlessly impaired.[34]

Nonetheless, Section 13(d) has a significant loophole. Because the disclosures required by Section 13(d) need not be made until ten days after attaining five percent ownership, additional purchases may be made during this period so long as they do not constitute a "tender offer." This ten-day "window" permits potential acquirors to enhance their ownership level well

---

[33] See *Treadway Companies, Inc. v. Care Corp.*, 638 F.2d 357, 380 (2d Cir. 1980).

[34] See generally Brudney, *supra* note 31, at 617-20.

beyond that contemplated by Congress through means of open market purchases and privately negotiated transactions.

Another provision of the Williams Act, Section 14(e), is designed to protect incumbent shareholders from fraud, deception and manipulation in connection with tender offers. Prior to enactment of this legislation, shareholders had to rely on the reach of Section 10(b) which is directed at preventing such practices in connection with the purchase or sale of any security. The problem is that Section 10(b) does not reach far enough due to at least two reasons: (1) generally, in cases of nondisclosure (*i.e.*, silence), the statute is deemed not to be applicable unless there is a duty to disclose,[35] and (2) there must be a purchase or sale to trigger the statute's application.[36] In the pre-Williams Act era, therefore, unless a tender offer actually commenced and shares were purchased or sold, there was presumably no effective federal remedy for the SEC and private parties to invoke. Moreover, disclosure was not generally required until the offeror became a controlling shareholder with all the fiduciary duties that came with that status or unless the insurgent was receiving material nonpublic information derived from a corporate source.[37] Thus, Section 14(e) filled the need for legislation in this area and gave further substance to the disclosure requirements under Section 14(d).

As enacted, the legislation was designed to protect the valid interests of the target corporation's stockholders and to enable both the bidder and target managements to present their positions to the stockholders.[38] The neutral position taken by the Act was emphasized by its primary sponsor, Senator Williams: "We have taken extreme care to avoid tipping the scales either in favor of management or in favor of the person making the takeover bid."[39] Hence, the even-handed disclosure approach of the Act was adopted in an attempt to ensure that target corporation shareholders had sufficient information, and the time necessary, to make informed uncoerced investment decisions.[40]

---

[35] See *Chiarella v. United States*, 445 U.S. 222 (1980). See also Note, *The Regulation of Corporate Tender Offers Under Federal Securities Law: A New Challenge for Rule 10b-5*, 33 U. Chi. L. Rev. 359, 373 (1966).

[36] See *Blue Chip Stamps v. Manor Drug Stores*, 421 U.S. 723 (1975).

[37] See *SEC v. Texas Gulf Sulphur Co.*, 401 F.2d 833 (2d Cir. 1968) (*en banc*); *Diamond v. Oreamuno*, 24 N.Y.2d 494, 248 N.E.2d 910 (1969).

[38] See House Comm. on Interstate and Foreign Commerce, *Disclosure of Corporate Equity Ownership*, H.R. Rep. No. 1711, 90th Cong., 2d Sess. 4, reprinted in 1968 U.S. Code Cong. & Ad. News 2811, 2813; Senate Comm. on Banking and Currency, *Full Disclosure of Corporate Equity Ownership and in Corporate Takeover Bids*, S. Rep. No. 550, 90th Cong., 1st Sess. 3 (1967).

[39] 113 Cong. Rec. 24664 (1967).

[40] See Statement by Senator Kuchel, *Full Disclosure of Corporate Ownership and in Corporate Takeover Bids: Hearings on S. 510 Before the Senate Subcomm. on Securities of the Comm. on Banking and Currency*, 90th Cong., 1st Sess. 46 (1967); sources cited in notes 38-39, *supra*.

[C] Debate

The advocates of the legislation insisted that the disclosure provisions of the Williams Act were absolutely essential for protection of incumbent shareholders.[41] Critics, on the other hand, were convinced that the disclosure provisions were irrelevant to a shareholder's decision to tender his or her shares. They viewed with cynicism the motives of the proponents seeking legislation, arguing that the primary beneficiaries of the disclosure provisions were the potential target managements, not the shareholders.[42] As for the SEC, its interests were shareholder protection and maintaining the integrity of the securities markets. Irrespective of such warranted SEC concerns, critics felt that the requirement of disclosure was unjustifiable in light of the dampening effect it would have on the efficient combinations of businesses.[43] The ultimate issue therefore is whether the disclosure provisions designed to protect shareholders and the securities markets justify the alleged discouragement of business combinations.

Generally, critics took exception to the disclosure provisions for three alleged reasons: First, as mentioned above, the disclosure required was asserted to be irrelevant to a shareholder's decision on whether to tender the shares. Second, the legislation, at least in part, confused a free market philosophy with that of a distribution of wealth philosophy. And third, the practical effects of the legislation would destroy the climate for efficient business combinations.[44]

To the advocates, the disadvantages of the legislation were overwhelmingly outweighed by the advantages that would be gained from it. As one Senator put it, "[d]espite the sneers of a few cynics back in 1934, full disclosure has provided a strong stimulus to the American investor. Now is the time to eliminate the few areas where full disclosure is not available."[45] In other words, the protection of shareholders and the integrity of the market as a whole made any dampening effect on the efficient combination of business well worth it.

Despite the controversy stirred, there was relatively little opposition to the bill once it reached the floor of both Houses. In fact, it passed both the House and the Senate on a voice vote.[46] There may be a number of explanations accounting for this development. First, there was a broad consensus between the SEC and the corporate sector, which gave great impetus to the legislation. Second, the legislation was politically feasible to support since it was

---

[41] See Cohen, *supra* note 30, at 156-57.

[42] See Manne, *Cash Tender Offers for Shares — A Reply to Chairman Cohen*, 1967 Duke L.J. 231.

[43] *Id.* at 245.

[44] *Id.* at 245-53. See also Brudney, *supra* note 31, at 616-41.

[45] 111 Cong. Rec. S. 28,260 (daily ed. Oct. 22, 1965) (Statement of Senator Williams).

[46] S. 510, 90th Cong., 2d Sess., 114 Cong. Rec. H. 21,484 (daily ed. July 15, 1968), and 114 Cong. Rec. S. 21,954 (daily ed. July 18, 1968).

ostensibly aimed at protecting the securities markets and innocent shareholders of large publicly-held corporations. Also, as contrasted with today's attitudes, tender offers were viewed by many somehow as a sneaky, "ungentlemanly" way to conduct corporate transactions. Hence, the Williams Act's approach based on full disclosure, with no side purportedly having an unfair advantage over the other and the shareholder being the ultimate beneficiary, merited support.

§ 10.05 Definition of Tender Offer

The conventional tender offer generally is easily identified. Its characteristics frequently are a publicized bid to purchase shares of stock at a premium over market price made directly to the target corporation's shareholders with certain conditions attached, often including a time limit for the duration of the offer and a quantity limit on the total number of shares that the bidder is willing to acquire.[47] Tender offers, however, also may be unconventional. One such unconventional tender offer, for example, involved a bid made to approximately thirty sophisticated investors who owned 34% of the outstanding stock. Solicitors acting on behalf of the bidder followed a prearranged script, offered a premium over market price with no room for negotiation, and left the offer open for a short time period. Applying an eight-factor analysis discussed below, the court held that the solicitations constituted a tender offer under the Williams Act.[48]

The significance of the above holding is that conventional as well as unconventional tender offers trigger application of the Williams Act's regulatory framework. Unconventional tender offers are unlikely to meet the requirements of Section 14(d) and SEC rules thereunder, such as the twenty business day time period within which an offer remains open and the right of shareholders during the offer to withdraw their shares tendered. Moreover, an offeror must file a Schedule 14D-1 providing detailed disclosures.[49]

The unconventional tender offer today is a rare occurrence. That is because courts hold that (1) open market purchases on an exchange or in the over-the-counter market[50] as well as (2) privately negotiated transactions between an acquiror and sophisticated investors[51] normally do not constitute a tender offer. In making this determination, a number of courts apply the following eight-factor test:

---

[47] See *Hanson Trust PLC v. SCM Corporation*, 774 F.2d 47, 54-55 (2d Cir. 1985).

[48] *Wellman v. Dickinson*, 475 F. Supp. 783 (S.D.N.Y. 1979), *aff'd on other grounds*, 682 F.2d 355 (2d Cir. 1982).

[49] See § 10.08, *infra*, for further discussion on the SEC's tender offer rules.

[50] See, *e.g.*, *SEC v. Carter Hawley Hale Stores, Inc.*, 760 F.2d 945 (9th Cir. 1985).

[51] See, *e.g.*, *Brascan Ltd. v. Edper Equities, Ltd.*, 477 F. Supp. 773 (S.D.N.Y. 1979).

(1) active and widespread solicitation of public shareholders for the shares of an issuer;

(2) solicitation made for a substantial percentage of the issuer's stock;

(3) offer to purchase made at a premium over the prevailing market price;

(4) terms of the offer are firm rather than negotiable;

(5) offer contingent on the tender of a fixed number of shares, often subject to a fixed maximum number to be purchased;

(6) offer open only for a limited period of time;

(7) offeree subjected to pressure to sell the stock;

(8) public announcements of a purchasing program concerning the target company precede or accompany rapid accumulation of large amounts of the target company's securities.[52]

The eight-factor test, although flexible, is uncertain in its application. In any given situation, solicitations may constitute a tender offer even though some of the eight factors are not satisfied. Conversely, a tender offer may not exist even though many of the factors are present. Hence, the eight-factor test is akin to an ad hoc balancing test in which the various factors are weighed.[53]

Due to the uncertainty of the above standard, the Second Circuit has adopted a different formulation. In *Hanson Trust PLC v. SCM Corporation*,[54] a corporation withdrew its tender offer after being confronted with a competing offer and tactics engaged in by target management that favored the "white knight." After terminating its offer, the corporation, engaging in what is called a "market sweep," purchased shares from five arbitrageurs constituting about 25% of the target's stock. In ascertaining whether these solicitations were a tender offer, the court reasoned:

> [S]ince the purpose of § 14(d) is to protect the ill-informed solicitee, the question of whether a solicitation constitutes a "tender offer" within the meaning of § 14(d) turns on whether, viewing the transaction in the light of the totality of circumstances, there appears to be a likelihood that unless the pre-acquisition filing strictures of that statute are followed, there will be a substantial risk that solicitees will lack information needed to make a carefully considered appraisal of the proposal put before them.[55]

Looking at such factors as the small number of solicitees and the solicitees' high level of financial acumen, the Second Circuit held that a tender offer had not been made.[56]

---

[52] See *SEC v. Carter Hawley Hale Stores, Inc.*, 760 F.2d 945, 950 (9th Cir. 1985).

[53] See *id.* at 950-52.

[54] 774 F.2d 47 (2d Cir. 1985).

[55] *Id.* at 57.

[56] *Id.* at 57-58.

Critics assert that the Second Circuit's decision in *Hanson Trust* provides a means by which an acquiror can "sidestep" the Williams Act and SEC regulations thereunder. The *Wall Street Journal* evidently believes this to be the case and has reacted favorably to this perceived development. In an editorial entitled *A Happy Jig,* the *Journal* applauded the *Hanson Trust* decision as signaling the emergence of a "new deregulated takeover market" in which acquirors would no longer "hav[e] to worry about the costs and delays of securities regulations," hence resulting in "more simplified takeovers — and more profits for shareholders."[57] On the other hand, although full disclosure certainly is the principal objective of the Williams Act, it may be asserted that another purpose is to ensure the evenhanded treatment of all shareholders, including the small unsophisticated shareholder. "Market sweeps" discriminate against the ordinary investor and, arguably, should not be permitted. The SEC may share this position. In a possible effort to restrain the use of market sweeps, the Commission has proposed Rule 14d-11. That proposal, if adopted, would impose a cooling-off period for the purchase of a target's stock upon a party who has withdrawn a tender offer.[58]

§ 10.06 Constitutionality of State Takeover Statutes

In *Edgar v. MITE,*[59] the Supreme Court, in an opinion written by Justice White, declared the Illinois Business Takeover Act unconstitutional on interstate commerce grounds, reasoning that the burdens imposed on interstate commerce by the Act were excessive in relation to the local interests served. Another portion of Justice White's opinion, not joined in by the majority of the Court, asserted that the Illinois Act was unconstitutional under the Supremacy Clause.[60]

In the aftermath of the Supreme Court's decision in *MITE*, several state statutes, having provisions similar to the Illinois Act, were declared unconstitutional by the lower federal courts. Cognizant of the constitutional infirmities of their takeover statutes, several states responded by enacting "second generation" statutes which sought to pass constitutional scrutiny.[61]

---

[57] Editorial, *A Happy Jig,* Wall St. J., Oct. 7, 1985.

[58] See *Securities Exchange Act Release* No. 24976 (1987). See generally Tyson, *The Williams Act After Hanson Trust v. SCM Corporation: Post-Tender Offer Purchases by the Tender Offeror*, 61 Tulane L. Rev. 1 (1986).

[59] 457 U.S. 624 (1982).

[60] See generally Sargent, *On the Validity of State Takeover Regulation: State Responses to MITE and Kidwell,* 42 Ohio St. L.J. 689 (1981).

[61] See Goelzer & Cohen, *The Empire Strikes Back — Post-MITE Developments in State Antitakeover Regulation*, in *Tender Offers: Developments and Commentaries* 49 (M. Steinberg ed. 1985); Sargent, *Do The Second-Generation State Takeover Statutes Violate the Commerce Clause? A Preliminary Inquiry,* in *Tender Offers: Developments and Commentaries* 75 (M. Steinberg ed. 1985).

[A] The *CTS* Decision

In *CTS Corp. v. Dynamics Corp. of America*,[62] the Supreme Court upheld one version of the second-generation statutes. There, the Court held that the Control Share Acquisitions Chapter of the Indiana Business Corporation Law[63] does not violate the Constitution on either preemption or interstate commerce grounds. In brief, the Indiana statute, which applies to corporations chartered in Indiana and which have certain other connections with that state, focuses on the acquisition of "control shares" in such a corporation. Under the Act, a control share acquisition is one which, but for the operation of the Act, would raise the purchaser's voting power to or above any of three thresholds: (1) one-fifth and less than one-third, (2) one-third and less than a majority, or (3) above a majority. When a control share transaction occurs, the acquiring entity does not have voting rights with respect to those shares unless a majority of the disinterested shares[64] entitled to vote approves the transaction. Such vote must take place within fifty days if the acquiring entity so requests.[65]

Even though the fifty day period of the Indiana statute exceeds the minimum twenty business day period which a tender offer must remain open under the Williams Act, Justice Powell, writing for the Court, stated that this extra delay was permissible. Only unreasonable delays, Justice Powell asserted, are unconstitutional. Moreover, to preempt the Indiana Act, the Court felt, would bring into question the constitutionality of a wide variety of state corporate laws of hitherto unquestioned validity. Such statutes include permitting corporations to have cumulative voting and the staggering of director terms, which, like the Indiana statute, may delay or limit the exercise of control by a successful bidder. Thus, the Court concluded:

> In our view, the possibility that the Indiana Act will delay some tender offers is insufficient to require a conclusion that the Williams Act preempts the [Indiana] Act. The longstanding prevalence of state regulation in this area suggests that, if Congress had intended to pre-empt all State laws that delay the acquisition of voting control following a tender offer, it would have said so explicitly.[66]

Likewise, the *CTS* Court found that the Indiana statute does not offend the Commerce Clause. Upon examination, the Indiana Act, according to Justice Powell, neither discriminates against interstate commerce nor does it create

---

[62] 107 S.Ct. 1637 (1987).

[63] Ind. Code §§ 23-1-42-1 to 23-1-42-11.

[64] "Interested shares" are those beneficially controlled by the entity acquiring the corporation, an officer or an inside director of the subject corporation. *Id.* § 23-1-42-3.

[65] *Id.* § 23-1-42-7. Such a request must be made when the acquiror files an "acquiring person statement" with the corporation. The expenses of the meeting are to be paid by the acquiring person. *Id.* For further details of the Indiana Act see 107 S.Ct. at 1641.

[66] 107 S.Ct. at 1648.

an impermissible risk of inconsistent regulation by the various states. As a basis for its holding, the Court relied on the premise that a state's authority to regulate domestic corporations is a fundamental precept of corporate law. In its role as regulator of corporate governance, a state has an interest in facilitating stable relationships among the participants in its domestic corporations. Applying these principles, the Court stated:

> The primary purpose of the [Indiana] Act is to protect the shareholders of Indiana corporations. It does this by affording shareholders, when a takeover offer is made, an opportunity to decide collectively whether the resulting change in voting control of the corporation, as they perceive it, would be desirable. A change of management may have important effects on the shareholders' interest; it is well within the State's role as overseer of corporate governance to offer this opportunity.[67]

[B] The "Second-Generation" Statutes

After *CTS*, a number of different state "anti-takeover" types of statutes remain in force. Although their constitutionality has not been definitively resolved,[68] they play an integral role in the takeover process. Significantly, unlike the Illinois statute declared unconstitutional in *MITE*, these second-generation statutes do not directly impact upon an offeror making a tender offer for all shares outstanding. Nonetheless, aspects of these statutes may deter prospective offerors from engaging in takeover bids.

In addition to the control share acquisition type of statute upheld as constitutional in *CTS*, other types of statutes include:

> *"Fair Price" Statute* — This type of statute reaches fundamental "second step" transactions, such as mergers or sales of substantially all assets, which frequently follow a hostile tender offer for a bare majority of the target's shares. The statute basically provides that such a transaction can be undertaken only if: (1) a majority of the disinterested shares of the subject corporation approve or (2) the same price is paid in the second-step transaction as was paid in the first-step tender offer. There are a number of variations to this type of statute.[69]
>
> *"Right of Redemption" Statute* — With certain exceptions, this type of statute provides that once a person or group owns thirty percent of a class of voting shares registered under the Exchange Act, that person or group is deemed to be a controlling shareholder. Attainment of that

---

[67] *Id.* at 1651. See generally Langevoort, *The Supreme Court and the Politics of Corporate Takeovers: A Comment on CTS Corp. v. Dynamics Corp. of America*, 101 Harv. L. Rev. 96 (1987).

[68] The Delaware statute thus far has been upheld as constitutional by the courts which have examined the issue. See, *e.g., Black & Decker Corp. v. American Standard, Inc.*, [1987-1988 Transfer Binder] Fed. Sec. L. Rep. (CCH) ¶ 93,685 (D. Del. 1988).

[69] See generally Scriggins & Clarke, *Takeovers and the 1983 Maryland Fair Price Legislation*, 43 Md. L. Rev. 266 (1984).

status requires such shareholder to provide notice to the "minority" shareholders that they may obtain appraisal, namely, the "fair value" of their shares from such controlling shareholder. Fair value is to be measured by taking into account "all relevant factors, including an increment representing a proportion of any value payable for acquisition of control of the corporation."[70]

"Business Combination Restriction" Statute — This type of statute, codified in such states as Delaware, New Jersey, New York, and Pennsylvania, generally provides that, with certain exceptions, if a person acquires a certain percentage of stock (*e.g.*, 15% or more under the Delaware statute) without the approval of the board of directors of the subject corporation, that person becomes an interested shareholder and may not consummate a business combination (*e.g.*, a merger) with the subject corporation for a substantial period of time (three years under the Delaware statute and five years under the New York statute). As stated above, there are certain exceptions where the business combination restriction does not apply. One such exception under the Delaware statute is that the acquisition by a controlling shareholder of at least 85% of the voting stock[71] in a tender offer or other acquisition entitles the interested shareholder to engage in a merger without being subject to the three-year prohibition. Another exception occurs when the target's board of directors approves the contemplated business combination before the time that the prospective acquiror becomes an interested shareholder.[72]

[C] Need For Federal Preemption

To proponents of takeover activity, the *CTS* decision and the enactment of the state anti-takeover statutes signal a defeat for the American economy, market efficiency, and shareholder protection for at least three reasons. First, because there will be fewer tender offers, shareholders will be denied the opportunity to realize the full value of their stock, hence losing the opportunity for substantial profits. Second, inefficient managements will become more entrenched, thereby making their removal more difficult. This consequence harms not only shareholders but also the proficiency of American industry and our nation's quest to maintain its status as a world

[70] See Pa. Stat. Ann § 910(A). See generally Newlin & Gilmer, *The Pennsylvania Shareholder Protection Act: A New State Approach to Deflecting Corporate Takeover Bids*, 40 Bus. Law. 111 (1984); Steinberg, *The Pennsylvania Anti-Takeover Legislation*, 12 Sec. Reg. L.J. 184 (1984).

[71] Shares owned by the target's directors and officers are not counted when determining whether the interested shareholder attains 85% stock ownership. See 8 Del. Code Ann. § 203.

[72] See 8 Del. Code Ann. § 203; N.Y. Bus. Corp. Law § 912(b). See generally Pinto, *The Constitution and the Market for Corporate Control: State Takeover Statutes After CTS Corp.*, 29 Wm. & Mary L. Rev. 699 (1988); Romano, *The Political Economy of Takeover Statutes*, 73 Va. L. Rev. 111 (1987).

economic leader. Third, the efficient deployment of corporate assets to their most productive capacity will be impeded, again resulting in harm to shareholders, market efficiency, and our nation's economic proficiency.[73]

Given the adverse effect that the state anti-takeover statutes have on our nation's as well as the international securities markets, it is incumbent upon the Congress to preempt this area. The consequences of takeover activity present dilemmas of national and worldwide concern. They are not adequately debated and resolved by the respective states enacting legislation to protect their parochial interests. The time is now for Congress to act. As SEC Chairman David S. Ruder has remarked;

> Limitations on the free transferability of securities of corporations which are owned by shareholders nationwide diminish the efficiency, depth, and liquidity of the nation's securities markets. Accordingly, I believe that federal law should control in that area by preempting state statutes that unduly interfere with the free transferability of securities. I believe that corporations whose activities and ownership are national in scope should not be given protection against takeovers by the states where their primary production facilities are located. Just as I believe it to be imprudent for Congress to regulate internal corporate affairs through tender offer regulation, I believe it is imprudent for states to use their authority over matters of internal governance as a means of regulating the interstate market for corporate control.[74]

§ 10.07 Disclosure of Beneficial Ownership Interest

As discussed in § 10.04[B], *supra*, Section 13(d)(1) of the Exchange Act and Rule 13d-1 prescribed thereunder require any person or group of persons agreeing to act together who acquire beneficial ownership of more than five percent of a class of equity securities registered under Section 12 of the Act to disclose, within ten days, specific information by filing a Schedule 13D with the SEC and by sending copies to the issuer and to each exchange on which the security is traded. In short,

> Schedule 13D requires disclosure of the identity of the issuer and the security, the identity, background, and citizenship of the reporting persons, the source and amount of funds used to acquire the securities, the purpose of the transaction, the reporting person's interest in the securities including trading history for the last 60 days and any contracts,

---

[73] See Judge Posner's opinion in *CTS*, 794 F.2d 250 (7th Cir. 1986), *rev'd*, 107 S.Ct. 1637 (1987).

[74] *Federal Preemption of State Anti-takeover Legislation*, Remarks of David S. Ruder, Chairman, Securities and Exchange Commission, Before the 26th Annual Corporate Counsel Institute, at 8-9 (Chicago Oct. 7, 1987), reported in Fed. Sec. L. Rep. (CCH) No. 1256, at 8-9 (1987). See generally Coffee, *Regulating the Market for Corporate Control: A Critical Assessment of the Tender Offer's Role in Corporate Governance*, 84 Colum. L. Rev. 1145 (1984).

arrangements, understandings or relationships with respect to the securities to which the reporting person or group is a party.[75]

Importantly, the requirements of Section 13(d) apply irrespective of whether the person (or group) acquiring five percent beneficial ownership intends to make a tender offer. The objective of the statute is to alert the securities markets of potential shifts in corporate control.[76] Although courts have declined to recognize a damages remedy under Section 13(d),[77] a majority of courts have implied a private right of action for injunctive relief under Sections 13(d) and 14(e) on behalf of an issuer corporation.[78] The rationale is that, despite the Supreme Court's holding in *Piper v. Chris-Craft Industries*[79] that a defeated tender offeror does not have standing under Section 14(e) to bring an action for damages, the target company frequently may be the only willing party with the resources to maintain an injunctive action against a prospective bidder. In situations where the bidder's potential conduct may harm the company and its shareholders, granting standing to the target corporation to seek injunctive relief is therefore a practical approach to protecting shareholders and the marketplace.[80]

With respect to the type of relief awarded for a Section 13(d) violation, the usual remedy has been to require the violating party to amend its previous disclosures and to prohibit additional purchases until such corrective disclosure has been made. A few courts, however, have deemed such relief insufficient and have ordered disenfranchisement, divestiture, or rescission of shares acquired during the period that the misleading Section 13(d) disclosures were disseminated in the marketplace.[81] While some may applaud these measures, it also should be kept in mind that such actions for equitable relief under Section 13(d) may serve as a delaying tactic, thereby providing target management with sufficient time to develop and implement a successful defensive strategy to fend off the hostile offeror.

A major problem with Section 13(d) that has drawn attention is that a beneficial owner of more than five percent of a subject security need not disclose such ownership status until ten days after attaining that status. As a result, such parties may acquire additional shares through privately negotiat-

[75] Bialkin, Attora and D'Alimonte, *Why, When and How to Conduct a Proxy Battle for Corporate Control,* in *Proxy Contests and Battles for Corporate Control* at 87, 117 (1981). See Block & Rudoff, *Schedule 13D Problems Associated with Large Accumulations of Stock,* 10 Sec. Reg. L.J. 3 (1982).

[76] See *GAF Corp. v. Milstein,* 453 F.2d 709, 719 (2d Cir. 1971).

[77] See, *e.g., Stromfeld v. Great Atlantic and Pacific Tea Co., Inc.,* 484 F. Supp. 1264 (S.D.N.Y. 1980).

[78] See, *e.g., Indiana National Corp. v. Rich,* 712 F.2d 1180 (7th Cir. 1983). But see *Polaroid Corp. v. Disney,* [1988-1989 Transfer Binder] Fed. Sec. L. Rep. (CCH) ¶ 94,095 (3d Cir. 1988).

[79] 430 U.S. 1 (1977).

[80] See, *e.g., Mobil Corp. v. Marathon Oil Co.,* 669 F.2d 366, 371 (6th Cir. 1981).

[81] See, *e.g., Hanna Mining Co. v. Norcen Energy Resources Ltd.,* [1982 Transfer Binder] Fed. Sec. L. Rep. (CCH) ¶ 98,742 (S.D. Ohio 1982).

ed transactions and open market purchases during that ten-day "window" period so long as the acquisitions do not constitute a "tender offer." This loophole makes possible the accumulation of securities, representing a potential shift in corporate control, without adequate notification and disclosure of pertinent information to the marketplace. It has been proposed that Congress should close this loophole by either: (1) prohibiting additional accumulations above the five percent level unless there has been prior disclosure of the requisite information[82] or (2) deeming acquisition of more than twenty (or some other) percent of an equity security, with certain exceptions, to constitute a tender offer, thereby triggering the disclosure and dissemination requirements of the Williams Act.[83]

As a final comment, although outside the scope of this text, it should be pointed out that the Hart-Scott-Rodino Antitrust Improvements Act of 1976 generally imposes upon certain tender offerors and their targets in specified transactions pre-acquisition notification and disclosure requirements. Pursuant thereto, information relevant to the transaction must be furnished to the Antitrust Division of the Department of Justice and the Federal Trade Commission.[84]

§ 10.08 SEC Tender Offer Rules

During the recent past, the SEC has been fairly active in the tender offer rulemaking setting. The principal provisions of the current SEC rules and regulations were promulgated in 1979.[85] The rules are quite extensive, mandating, *inter alia*, that both the offeror and the subject (*i.e.*, target) corporation file detailed disclosure schedules. For example, Rule 14d-9 requires the subject company to file with the Commission a Schedule 14D-9 which calls for the disclosure of specified information. The SEC "believes that the disclosure elicited by the Schedule will assist security holders in making their investment decisions and in evaluating the merits of a solicitation/recommendation."[86] Such information includes, if material, a description of any arrangement or other understanding and conflicts of interest between, among others, the offeror, the subject corporation, and their

---

[82] See, *e.g.*, Advisory Comm. on Tender Offers, U.S. SEC, *Report of Recommendations* 21-22 (1983).

[83] *Id.* at 23-24. See Tender Offer Reform Act of 1987, H.R. 2172, 100th Cong., 1st Sess. (1987) (if enacted, would have prohibited, with certain exceptions, the acquisition of more than ten percent of a target's stock except by means of a tender offer). See generally Steinberg, *Tender Offer Regulation: The Need for Reform*, 23 Wake Forest L. Rev. 1 (1988).

[84] See generally S. Axinn, B. Fogg & N. Stoll, *Acquisitions Under the Hart-Scott-Rodino Antitrust Improvements Act* (1979); Easterbrook & Fischel, *Antitrust Suits by Targets of Tender Offers*, 80 Mich. L. Rev. 1155 (1982).

[85] *Securities Exchange Act Release* No. 16384 (1979).

[86] *Id.*

affiliates. Disclosure is also required in the Schedule of certain negotiations and transactions (*e.g.*, merger negotiations) undertaken by the target company in response to the tender offer.[87] Moreover, in order to adhere to the disclosure requirements of Rule 14e-2,[88] the subject company in the Schedule 14D-9 must advise shareholders of its position in regard to the tender offer and the reasons therefor.

The SEC's tender offer rules cover a number of other matters. Rule 14d-6(d), for instance, expressly requires an offeror to disclose promptly any material change in the information provided to shareholders. As another example, in an attempt to render invalid many of the state takeover statutes prior to the Supreme Court's decision in *MITE*, the SEC promulgated Rule 14d-2(b). This rule generally provides that the announcement of the number of shares sought to be acquired and the price to be offered triggers the commencement of a tender offer.

Since their adoption in 1979, the Commission periodically has revised its tender offer rules. One such rule, Rule 14d-8, extends the proration period from the previous ten-calendar-day period to the entire period that the offer remains open. Generally, Rule 14d-8 obligates a bidder in an oversubscribed partial tender offer "to take up and pay for" shares tendered on a pro rata basis "during the period such offer, request, or invitation remains open." The rule has precipitated comment on the extent of the Commission's rulemaking authority and on the broader question of its effect on the balance between the bidder and target in two-tier offers, particularly where the pressure on shareholders to tender is accentuated by a price differential between the tender offer and the proposed subsequent merger.[89]

Another key revision was the SEC's adoption of the "all holders" rule under Rules 13e-4 and 14d-10.[90] This rule adoption, in practical effect, nullifies the Delaware Supreme Court's decision in *Unocal v. Mesa Petroleum Co.*[91] In *Unocal*, the Delaware high court, applying a modified version of the business judgment rule, upheld the target management's use of a discriminatory issuer tender offer which excluded the hostile shareholder from participation. Under the SEC's "all holders" rule, by contrast, both issuer and third-party tender offers must be open to all shareholders and the best price paid to any tendering security holder must be paid to any other tendering security holder. Thus, the SEC's rule signifies that exclusionary tender offers for publicly-held companies no longer remain a viable defensive strategy.

---

[87] Compare this disclosure requirement with the duty affirmatively to disclose merger and similar negotiations in other contexts, discussed in § 9.03[C], *supra*.

[88] SEC Rule 14e-2, 17 C.F.R. § 240.14e-2 (Rule 14e-2 generally obligates the target company to transmit to its shareholders within ten business days of the commencement of the tender offer a statement of its position in regard thereto).

[89] See Brennan, *SEC Rule 14d-8 and Two-Tier Offers*, contained in *Tender Offers: Developments and Commentaries* at 109 (M. Steinberg ed. 1985).

[90] *Securities Exchange Act Release* No. 23421 (1986).

[91] 493 A.2d 946 (Del. 1985).

§ 10.09 Substantive Regulation of Defensive Tactics

[A] Federal Law

With respect to the legitimacy of defensive tactics under federal law, the key issue is whether Section 14(e), the antifraud provision of the Williams Act, regulates substantive conduct. In other words, is Section 14(e)'s purpose solely that of ensuring adequate and fair disclosure or does the statute have a broader reach? In adhering to the former approach, the Supreme Court definitively resolved this issue in *Schreiber v. Burlington Northern, Inc.*[92] The statutory analysis and policy implications of that decision merit attention.

Prior to the Supreme Court's decision in *Schreiber*, the Williams Act could have been applied in either of two ways to ensure that target shareholders normally had an opportunity to accept or reject a tender offer. First, conduct by management that deprived shareholders of an opportunity to tender could have been held to constitute "constructive fraud" within the meaning of Section 14(e) of the Williams Act. Although the Supreme Court held in *Santa Fe Industries v. Green*[93] that "mere" breaches of fiduciary duty not amounting to "manipulation" or "deception" do not violate Section 10(b) of the Exchange Act and Rule 10b-5 promulgated thereunder, Section 14(e) ought to be interpreted differently. Unlike Section 10(b), Section 14(e) by its terms prohibits "fraudulent" acts or practices. This difference in statutory language and the legislative history of Section 14(e) support giving it a broader reach than Section 10(b). Second, defensive tactics, the practical effect of which prevent shareholders from tendering in response to a bid, could have been viewed as "manipulative" under Section 14(e). Under this rationale, target management could be found to have engaged in "manipulative" practices proscribed by Section 14(e) when it artificially impedes the operation of a fair market for the corporation's stock by such tactics as granting options on valuable corporate assets to friendly third parties.[94]

Prior to *Schreiber*, a few courts held that certain defensive tactics engaged in by target management, even though fully disclosed, constituted "manipulation" under Section 14(e).[95] The Supreme Court in *Schreiber* rejected this

---

[92] 472 U.S. 1 (1985).

[93] 430 U.S. 462 (1977), discussed in § 7.04, *supra*.

[94] Steinberg, *supra* note 83, at 19-20. See Junewicz, *The Appropriate Limits of Section 14(e) of the Securities Exchange Act of 1934*, 62 Texas L. Rev. 1171 (1984); Levine, Lykos & Chafetz, *Application of the Federal Securities Laws to Defensive Tactics in Control Contests,* contained in *Tender Offers: Developments and Commentaries* at 193 (M. Steinberg ed. 1985); Loewenstein, *Section 14(e) of the Williams Act and the Rule 10b-5 Comparisons*, 71 Geo. L.J. 1311 (1983); Weiss, *Defensive Responses to Tender Offers and the Williams Act's Prohibition Against Manipulation*, 35 Vand. L. Rev. 1087 (1982).

[95] See, *e.g., Mobil Corp. v. Marathon Oil Co.*, 669 F.2d 366 (6th Cir. 1981) (target oil company's grant to competing tender offeror of certain options considered "manipulative" within meaning of § 14(e)); *Data Probe Acquisition Corp. v. Datatab, Inc.*, 568 F. Supp. 1538 (S.D.N.Y.) (self-serving grant of option

interpretation, holding that Section 14(e)'s reach is limited to that of disclosure. In assessing Section 14(e)'s scope, the Court stated: "All three species of misconduct listed in Section 14(e), *i.e.*, fraudulent, deceptive or manipulative . . ., are directed at failure to disclose."[96] Hence, the *Schreiber* decision clearly limits the availability of federal law remedies in a tender offer situation. In so doing, the Supreme Court echoed the rationale of *Santa Fe* and relegated the policing of the substantive fairness of tender offers to state corporation law. Consequently, after *Schreiber*, to support a Section 14(e) right of action, a plaintiff must allege either misrepresentation or nondisclosure.

The *Schreiber* Court's decision signifies that, with certain exceptions such as the "all holders rule,"[97] the legitimacy of takeover maneuvers employed in multibillion dollar tender offers having both national and international ramifications will be examined solely under state law. To proponents of corporate accountability and shareholder democracy, the states' continual "race for the bottom" signals that meritorious interests will be neglected.[98] The decision also means that the state of Delaware, being the predominant state of incorporation for publicly-held companies, may well have the principal voice in determining the validity of takeover tactics.[99]

[B] State Law

The following discussion succinctly treats the application of state law with respect to the legitimacy of takeover tactics engaged in by the target corporation's board of directors.

Generally, in a number of jurisdictions, so long as the target's board (relying upon outside directors and experts) adopts defensive tactics for the purpose of maintaining the company as an independent viable entity, the business judgment rule will apply to insulate those actions from successful challenge.[100] The business judgment rule basically provides that corporate

---

to purchase shares of target by target's management was "manipulative device"), *rev'd*, 722 F.2d 1 (2d Cir. 1983), *cert. denied*, 465 U.S. 1052 (1984).

[96] 472 U.S. at 8.

[97] See Rules 13e-4 and 14d-10 discussed in § 10.08, *supra*.

[98] See generally Cary, *Federalism and Corporate Law: Reflections Upon Delaware*, 83 Yale L.J. 663 (1974).

[99] See Fiflis, *Of Lollipops and Law — A Proposal for a National Policy Concerning Tender Offer Defenses*, 19 U.C. Davis L. Rev. 303, 306 (1986) ("One may properly ask whether it is appropriate for Delaware, which conceivably may not be the abode of a single Unocal shareholder, to fix national policy in an international securities market, while Congress and the federal courts, Nero-like, abdicate a policymaking role.").

[100] See, *e.g.*, *Panter v. Marshall Field & Co.*, 646 F.2d 271 (7th Cir. 1981) (applying Delaware law); *Moran v. Household International, Inc.*, 500 A.2d 1346 (Del. 1985); *Unocal Corp. v. Mesa Petroleum Co.*, 493 A.2d 946 (Del. 1985); *GAF Corp. v. Union Carbide Corp.*, [1985-1986 Transfer Binder] Fed. Sec. L. Rep. (CCH) ¶ 92,408 (S.D.N.Y. 1985) (applying New York law).

officers and directors will be shielded from judicial inquiry into the propriety of their decisions and from liability for harm to the corporation resulting from their decisions, so long as (1) the decision was within management's authority to make, and (2) such corporate fiduciaries (a) made reasonable inquiry and were informed with respect to the determination, (b) acted in good faith and had no disabling conflict of interest, and (c) had a rational basis for believing that the business judgment was in the corporation's best interests.[101] As the Supreme Court of Delaware has pointed out, the doctrine is an acknowledgment of the managerial perogatives of corporate directors under state law:

> It is a [rebuttable] presumption that in making a business decision the directors of a corporation acted on an informed basis, in good faith and in the honest belief that the action taken was in the best interests of the company.[102]

In ascertaining whether the business judgment rule will be applied in a given situation involving defensive tactics undertaken by the target's board of directors, a distinction has been made between defensive maneuvers employed to maintain the corporation as an independent, viable entity and those measures implemented to favor one bidder over another in an active bidding or "auction" setting. In the auction context, recent decisions have refused to apply the business judgment rule to target management's actions.[103] Where "lock-up" and "no-shop" clauses are extended to management's favored suitor in an active bidding situation, thereby precluding the auction process from ultimately resulting, the directors must demonstrate "some rationally related benefit accruing to the stockholders."[104]

Significantly, however, the apparent majority view is that the business judgment rule continues to be the prevalent standard when assessing target management's actions taken for the purpose of maintaining the company as an on-going independent entity.[105] This standard has been applied to show-stop tactics, such as the unilateral adoption by a board of directors of an anti-takeover "poison pill" amendment to the corporation's by-laws which, if

---

[101] *Principles of Corp. Governance and Structure: Analysis and Recommendations* § 4.01(d) (Text Draft No. 3, 1984).

[102] *Aronson v. Lewis*, 473 A.2d 805, 812 (Del. 1984).

[103] See, *e.g.*, *Edelman v. Fruehauf Corp.*, [1986-1987 Transfer Binder] Fed. Sec. L. Rep. (CCH) ¶ 92,863 (6th Cir. 1986) (applying Michigan law); *Hanson Trust v. ML SCM Acquisition, Inc.*, 781 F.2d 264 (2d Cir. 1986) (applying New York law); *MacAndrews & Forbes Holdings v. Revlon, Inc.*, 506 A.2d 173 (Del. 1986).

[104] *Revlon*, 506 A.2d at 182.

[105] See, *e.g.*, *Gearhart Indus. v. Smith Int'l*, 741 F.2d 707 (5th Cir. 1984) (applying Texas law); *Turner Broadcasting Sys. v. CBS*, 627 F. Supp. 901 (N.D. Ga. 1985) (applying New York law); *Moran v. Household Int'l*, 500 A.2d 1346 (Del. 1985). But see *Dynamics Corp. of Am. v. CTS Corp.*, 794 F.2d 250 (7th Cir. 1986) (applying Indiana law), *rev'd on other grounds*, 107 S.Ct. 1637 (1987); *Norlin Corp. v. Rooney, Pace, Inc.*, 744 F.2d 255 (2d Cir. 1984) (applying New York law).

triggered, would result in the entity's liquidation[106] and to corporate recapitalizations and restructurings, such as issuer self-tenders, dividend payouts, and related techniques.[107] Moreover, language in certain decisions indicates that the grant of a lock-up to a potential acquiring entity, when no other bidder is on the scene, is also protected by the business judgment rule.[108]

As a number of commentators have pointed out,[109] the Delaware Supreme Court, in its recent decisions, has not applied the business judgment rule in its traditional form. In *Unocal Corp. v. Mesa Petroleum Co.*,[110] the Delaware high court acknowledged that

> [b]ecause of the omnipresent specter that a board may be acting primarily in its own interests . . . there is an enhanced duty which calls for judicial examination at the threshold before the protections of the business judgment rule may be conferred.[111]

Hence, before the business judgment rule may be invoked, target management must show that there were "reasonable grounds for believing that a danger to corporate policy and effectiveness existed" and that the action taken was "reasonable in relation to the threat posed."[112]

It remains to be seen whether this modified application of the business judgment rule has major substantive impact. An interesting point is that, at least under Delaware law, by retaining outside advisors (such as investment brokers and lawyers) and relying extensively on outside directors, the board, in all probability, will be able to rebut assertions that the defensive maneuvers implemented were primarily motivated by entrenchment purposes, *i.e.*, a desire to retain control.[113] As a result, under Delaware law, if a breach were shown, it would be of the duty of care rather than of loyalty. Consequently, pursuant to the 1986 statutory amendments to Delaware law, the directors would be absolved from monetary liability unless their actions constituted bad faith or intentional misconduct.[114]

A minority of courts, on the other hand, have declined to invoke the business judgment rule to management's tactics that evidence an intention to

---

[106] *E.g.*, *Revlon*, 506 A.2d at 180.

[107] *E.g.*, *Unocal*, 493 A.2d at 954.

[108] See, *e.g.*, *Revlon*, 506 A.2d at 181.

[109] See, *e.g.*, Brennan, *New Cases on the Business Judgment Rule: Defending Defensive Tactics Becomes More Difficult*, 14 Sec. Reg. L.J. 245 (1986); Johnson, *Corporate Takeovers and Corporations: Who Are They For?*, 43 Wash. & Lee L. Rev. 781 (1986); Wander & LeCoque, *Boardroom Jitters: Corporate Control Transactions and Today's Business Judgment Rule*, 42 Bus. Law 29 (1986).

[110] 493 A.2d 946 (Del. 1985).

[111] *Id.* at 954.

[112] *Id.* at 955.

[113] *Revlon*, 506 A.2d at 181.

[114] See Delaware S. Bill 533, L. 1986, *amending*, Del. Code Ann. tit. 8, § 102. This comment presumes that the limitation on liability provision has been added to the corporation's articles of incorporation.

retain control.[115] Instead, in these situations, the burden is placed upon the board to "prove that the transaction was fair and reasonable to the corporation."[116] This standard is more protective of shareholder interests but its strict implementation has certain deficiencies. From a practical standpoint, it is undeniable that incumbent corporate management in nearly all hostile takeover bid situations wishes to retain control.[117] This attitude may be based on financial self-interest, prestige, or a sincere (but perhaps misguided) belief that the incumbent's continued stewardship is in the corporation's best interests. Hence, attention should focus on both the motive and effect of the directors' actions upon shareholder decisionmaking.

Unfortunately, vigorous application of a fairness standard may subject directors to astronomical monetary damages, totaling hundreds of millions, if not billions, of dollars.[118] The present director and officer insurance crisis would be exacerbated and outside directors would become even less inclined to serve on corporate boards. The consequence may be that courts would respond by making overly lenient factual determinations to whatever legal standard is applied in assessing alleged director misconduct, except perhaps in cases seeking exclusively injunctive relief. A better approach may be to: (1) recognize that takeovers deeply affect corporate constituencies in addition to shareholders, (2) permit management to take these non-investor interests into account in certain circumstances, (3) scrutinize defensive tactics by their effect on shareholder decisionmaking, (4) apply a fairly strict standard when assessing the legitimacy of "show-stopper" and similar maneuvers, and (5) implement a functional ceiling on damages that promotes the competing policies at stake.[119]

§ 10.10 Views of Commentators

Several commentators have expressed their opinions regarding the need for tender offer reform. The following summarizes a number of these divergent views.

---

[115] *E.g., Dynamics Corp. of Am. v. CTS Corp.*, 794 F.2d 250 (7th Cir. 1986) (applying Indiana law), *rev'd on other grounds*, 107 S.Ct. 1637 (1987); *Norlin Corp. v. Rooney, Pace, Inc.*, 744 F.2d 255 (2d Cir. 1984) (applying New York law); *Heckmann v. Ahmanson*, 168 Cal. App. 3d 119, 214 Cal. Rptr. 177 (1986).

[116] *Norlin*, 744 F.2d at 265.

[117] See *Johnson v. Trueblood*, 629 F.2d 287, 292-93 (3d Cir. 1980) (construing Delaware law).

[118] See *Panter v. Marshall Field & Co.*, 646 F.2d 271 (7th Cir. 1981) (applying Delaware law) (over $200 million in damages sought).

[119] For further discussion see Steinberg, note 83, *supra*. See also Lynch & Steinberg, *The Legitimacy of Defensive Tactics in Tender Offers*, 64 Cornell L. Rev. 901 (1979).

1. *Application of the Business Judgment Rule* — These commentators believe that the business judgment rule, if the requirements of the rule are met, should govern the legitimacy of defensive takeover tactics.[120]

2. *Reliance on Outside Directors* — This view posits that deference to defensive tactics undertaken by a target's board of directors should be given by courts only if the outside directors have a significant role in determining the target's response to the takeover bid.[121]

3. *"Fairness" Standard* — Under this standard, the business judgment rule would not apply in the takeover setting. Rather, target management would have the burden of establishing that the defensive actions taken were fair to the corporation and its shareholders.[122]

4. *"Freeze" Period* — This proposal would establish a "freeze" period in which a hostile tender offer would remain open for a substantial period of time, such as six months, in order to enable shareholders to make informed decisions. During this "freeze" period, any "structural" change in the company (for example, an option to sell the target's "crown jewel") would require shareholder approval.[123]

5. *"Modified Shareholder Choice"* — Pursuant to this proposal, target shareholders would have an unimpeded right to tender their shares to the hostile bidder, subject to the exception that target management may take appropriate steps to fend off a hostile bid if it affirmatively shows that the offeror constituted a clear threat to the target's business, including the equity interests of the shareholders.[124]

6. *"The Passivity Approach"* — Tender offers are viewed as beneficial to shareholders and the economy under this approach. They encourage managerial efficiency, competition, proficient use of corporate assets, and shareholder gain. As a result, when a tender offer is made, target management under this approach must remain totally passive and no defensive tactics are permitted.[125]

---

[120] See, *e.g.*, Lipton, *Takeover Bids in the Target's Boardroom,* 35 Bus. Law. 101 (1979); Steinbrink, *Management's Response to the Takeover Attempt*, 28 Case W. Res. L. Rev. 882 (1978).

[121] See, *e.g.*, Gelfond & Sebastian, *Reevaluating the Duties of Target Management in a Hostile Tender Offer*, 60 B.U.L. Rev. 403 (1980); Williams, *Role of Directors in Takeover Offers*, 13 Rev. Sec. Reg. 963 (1980).

[122] See generally Prentice, *Target Board Abuse of Defensive Tactics: Can Federal Law Be Mobilized to Overcome the Business Judgment Rule?*, 8 J. Corp. L. 337 (1983).

[123] See, *e.g.*, Goldberg, *Regulation of Hostile Tender Offers: A Dissenting View and Recommended Reforms*, 43 Md. L. Rev. 225 (1984); Lowenstein, *Pruning Deadwood in Hostile Takeovers: A Proposal for Legislation*, 83 Colum. L. Rev. 249 (1983).

[124] See, *e.g.*, Steinberg, note 83, *supra*; Steinberg, *Some Thoughts on Regulation of Tender Offers*, 43 Md. L. Rev. 240 (1984).

[125] See, *e.g.*, Easterbrook & Fischel, *The Proper Role of Target Management in Responding to a Tender Offer*, 94 Harv. L. Rev. 1161 (1981).

7. *"The Auction Model"* — This approach takes on a number of variations. Basically, this proposal entitles target management to communicate to shareholders regarding its position on the takeover bid but does not permit the use of significant defensive maneuvers. Moreover, target management may (or should or must depending on the particular approach) put the corporation up for "auction," seeking out more favorable bids from other prospective offerors.[126]

---

[126] See, *e.g.*, Bebchuck, *The Case for Facilitating Competing Tender Offers*, 95 Harv. L. Rev. 1028 (1982); Gilson, *A Structural Approach to Corporations: The Case Against Defensive Tactics in Tender Offers*, 33 Stan. L. Rev. 819 (1981); Oesterle, *Target Managers as Negotiating Agents for Shareholders in Tender Offers: A Reply to the Passivity Thesis*, 71 Cornell L. Rev. 53 (1985).

CHAPTER 11

SEC ENFORCEMENT

§ 11.01 Introduction

Congress enacted the federal securities laws in light of a perceived need to protect investors and the integrity of the marketplace. To help ensure that the purposes of the securities laws are fulfilled, Congress vested the SEC with broad investigatory and enforcement powers. As part of its investigatory authority, the Commission may subpoena witnesses and records. Once the Commission obtains sufficient information to believe that a violation of law has occurred, it may bring an enforcement action either administratively or in a federal district court.

The overwhelming percentage (about ninety percent) of SEC enforcement actions are settled pursuant to the consent negotiation process where the defendant neither admits nor denies the Commission's allegations. Parties generally consent rather than litigate due to a number of factors. These include that the SEC may have a strong case, the financial costs involved in litigating with the Commission, avoidance of adverse publicity that would be generated by prolonged litigation, disruption of normal operations that would otherwise result due to management's attention being diverted, and fear of offensive collateral estoppel should the SEC emerge victorious. With respect to this last factor, there is the concern that an adverse decision in an SEC contested matter may result in the initiation of private damages actions in which the claimants seek to estop the defendants from relitigating issues resolved against them in the prior SEC action.[1]

SEC enforcement practice raises a multitude of issues. A number of the key topics are discussed in this chapter. For more extensive treatment, other sources should be consulted.[2]

---

[1] See *Parklane Hosiery Co., Inc. v. Shore*, 439 U.S. 322 (1979); authorities cited note 2, *infra*.

[2] See, *e.g.*, 4 A. Bromberg & L. Lowenfels, *Securities Fraud & Commodities Fraud* (1988); H. Friedman, *Securities and Commodities Enforcement* (1981); M. Steinberg & R. Ferrara, *Securities Practice: Federal and State Enforcement* (1985) (and annual supplements).

§ 11.02 SEC Subpoena Power

[A] Overview

SEC investigations normally are nonpublic and may take the form of a preliminary inquiry or a formal investigation. Frequently, a substantial portion of the materials in the Commission's files is obtained in the informal stage through cooperation. However, if the SEC is unable to elicit the needed information informally, it must initiate a formal investigation and seek authorization from the courts to compel uncooperative sources to supply the desired information. An informal inquiry can be commenced by the SEC's enforcement division and does not involve the use of subpoenas. The formal investigation, on the other hand, requires Commission authorization and, when necessary, court enforcement as well.[3]

Pursuant to a formal order of investigation, which outlines the general scope of the Commission's inquiry, the SEC can issue subpoenas if it determines that the documents and witnesses ordered produced may be relevant. If the party to whom the subpoena is issued refuses to voluntarily produce the requested information, the Commission must petition a federal district court for an order that compels compliance with the subpoena.[4] Because the Commission's subpoena enforcement power constitutes a necessary element of its investigations, the courts frequently order enforcement.[5]

An SEC investigation serves to uncover facts that may reveal whether a violation of the securities laws has occurred.[6] Because such an investigation by itself carries no formal sanctions, judicial intervention may be necessary to enforce compliance with an SEC subpoena. Accordingly, the courts possess the power to hold a party in contempt for noncompliance with a subpoena they have ordered enforced.[7] A party commits civil contempt by disobeying a court order after knowledge that the order has been issued.[8]

[B] Supreme Court Standards

The Supreme Court has established standards that must be met by an administrative agency before a subpoena will be enforced by the lower courts. In *United States v. Powell*,[9] the Court determined that an agency seeking enforcement of a subpoena does not have the burden of establishing probable cause. Rather, the agency must show

---

[3] See SEC Rules of Practice, 17 C.F.R. § 202.5; *Securities Act Release* No. 6345 (1981).

[4] See, *e.g.*, § 21(b) of the Exchange Act, 15 U.S.C. § 78u(b).

[5] See, *e.g.*, *SEC v. Brigadoon Scotch Distributing Co.*, 480 F.2d 1047 (2d Cir. 1973).

[6] See, *e.g.*, *United States v. Morton Salt Co.*, 338 U.S. 632 (1950).

[7] See, *e.g.*, § 21(c) of the Exchange Act, 15 U.S.C. § 78u(c).

[8] See *Penfield Co. v. SEC*, 330 U.S. 585 (1947).

[9] 379 U.S. 48 (1964).

> that the investigation will be conducted pursuant to a legitimate purpose, that the inquiry may be relevant to the purpose, that the information sought is not already within the [agency's] possession, and that the administrative steps required by the [federal statutes] have been followed.[10]

If the Commission can establish these four elements, it will be deemed to have affirmatively established agency good faith, and the burden thereupon will shift to the opposing party to challenge on any appropriate ground.[11]

To procure enforcement under the *Powell* standards, the SEC is not required to provide evidence of probability of coverage under the securities statutes or the likelihood of a violation of these statutes.[12] Rather, the agency must demonstrate that the investigation falls within the mandate Congress granted to the SEC and that the documents sought are reasonably relevant to the inquiry.[13] The subpoena cannot be issued in bad faith,[14] its scope cannot be too indefinite,[15] and compliance with the subpoena cannot be too burdensome.[16]

Although demonstrating agency bad faith is difficult for those opposing enforcement of an SEC subpoena, this sometimes can be shown.[17] However, the other appropriate grounds for fending off enforcement of such a subpoena, including the assertion of First,[18] Fourth,[19] and Fifth[20] Amendment constitutional challenges, rarely succeed. Hence, although judicial enforcement of an SEC subpoena may not be automatic, such enforcement generally is likely if the purpose of the SEC's request is legitimate and if the information sought is relevant to that purpose.

[C] Notice to Third Parties

The formal order of investigation, to which the Commission's subpoena power attaches, ordinarily names the initial subject(s) of the SEC's inquiry. In practice, the Commission may not include the identification of all or even a substantial number of the parties who may be implicated in the investigation. Also, the formal order does not indicate the third parties to whom the

---

[10] *Id.* at 57-58.

[11] *Id.* at 58.

[12] *Id.* at 51-58.

[13] See *Oklahoma Press Publishing v. Walling*, 327 U.S. 186 (1946).

[14] 379 U.S. at 58.

[15] See *SEC v. Blackfoot Bituminous, Inc.*, 622 F.2d 512 (10th Cir. 1980).

[16] See *SEC v. Savage*, 513 F.2d 188 (7th Cir. 1975) (*per curiam*).

[17] See *SEC v. Wheeling-Pittsburgh Steel Corp.*, 648 F.2d 118 (3d Cir. 1981) (*en banc*). See generally Comment, *SEC v. Wheeling-Pittsburgh Steel Corp. — Informant Bad Faith Defense to Enforcement of an Administrative Subpoena*, 7 J. Corp. L. 121 (1984).

[18] See, *e.g.*, *SEC v. McGoff*, 647 F.2d 185 (D.C. Cir. 1981).

[19] See, *e.g.*, *See v. City of Seattle*, 387 U.S. 541 (1967).

[20] See, *e.g.*, *Couch v. United States*, 409 U.S. 322 (1973).

Commission may issue subpoenas. A target of an investigation, unless informed by a third party who receives a subpoena, may thus remain ignorant of the parties from whom the Commission seeks information.

In *SEC v. Jerry T. O'Brien, Inc.*,[21] the Supreme Court refused to require the Commission to provide notice to the targets of subpoenas issued to third parties in nonpublic investigations. In reaching its decision, the Court explored three sources from which such a requirement had to be derived if it were to be imposed upon the Commission:

> a consitutional provision; an understanding on the part of Congress, inferable from the structure of the securities laws, regarding how the SEC should conduct its inquiries; or the general standards governing judicial enforcement of administrative subpoenas enunciated in . . . *Powell.*[22]

The Court found that neither the Fourth, Fifth nor Sixth Amendment mandated that notice of third party subpoenas be given in order to protect the target's constitutional rights. The Fourth Amendment affords no support because a third party provides information to the Commission. Even though the target may have communicated the subpoenaed information to the third party in confidence, the target may not rely on the third party's Fourth Amendment protection to claim an unreasonable search or seizure when the third party relinquishes the information. Neither the Due Process Clause nor the Self-Incrimination Clause of the Fifth Amendment apply to the third party notice situation. The Due Process Clause under such circumstances does not apply because no adjudication of legal rights occurs in an administrative investigation. The Self-Incrimination Clause does not apply because a third party answers the subpoena; the target is not compelled to act as a witness against himself. Finally, the protection of the Sixth Amendment's Confrontation Clause arises only upon the initiation of criminal proceedings.[23]

The Court rejected the structural statutory argument for requiring notice because, rather than supporting the purpose of the securities laws, notice to targets of third party subpoenas undermines Congress' intent to provide the Commission with expansive power to issue and enforce subpoenas. The federal securities laws contain no specific provision relating to notice of third party subpoenas, and the Court found no evidence that Congress desired the Commission to adopt any procedures to implement the practice. Instead, the Court determined that "Congress intended to vest the SEC with considerable discretion in determining when and how to investigate possible violations of the statutes administered by the Commission."[24]

Finally, the Court considered the argument that the right to notice of third party subpoenas issued in an SEC investigation stems from the standards

---

[21] 467 U.S. 735 (1984).

[22] *Id.* at 741.

[23] *Id.* at 742-43.

[24] *Id.* at 745.

governing judicial enforcement of administrative subpoenas embraced in *Powell.* The Court rejected the argument on two bases: "[f]irst, administration of the notice requirement . . . would be highly burdensome for both the Commission and the courts;" and, "[s]econd, the imposition of a notice requirement on the SEC would substantially increase the ability of persons who have something to hide to impede legitimate investigations by the Commission."[25] In its holding, the Court recognized that, when the Commission initiates an investigation, it frequently does not know which parties will be "targets" of the investigation. To police the SEC's process of identification of targets, the district court would have to intervene by conducting a hearing "to determine the scope and thrust of the ongoing investigation." Moreover, if a target had notice of third party subpoenas, the target could delay the investigation by discouraging third parties from complying with the subpoenas.[26]

Of even more consequence, a target, by following the progress of the Commission's inquiry by knowing to whom subpoenas were issued, could destroy crucial evidence before the SEC could gain possession. The Court concluded that the SEC was not prohibited from notifying a target of any subpoenas it issues, but refused to impose a judicial mandate which would "curtail the Commission's discretion to determine when such notice would be appropriate and when it would not."[27]

§ 11.03 Parallel Proceedings

Parallel proceedings, that is, concurrent or successive civil proceedings by the SEC (or another administrative agency) and criminal investigation by the U.S. Attorney (or another prosecutorial entity) generally are constitutional. As stated by the Fifth Circuit: "There is no general federal constitutional, statutory, or common law rule barring the simultaneous prosecution of separate civil and criminal actions by different agencies against the same defendants involving the same transactions."[28]

Hence, parallel proceedings are restricted only in very limited circumstances.[29] A key issue that has arisen but is not yet resolved is whether SEC subpoenas issued pursuant to a Commission investigation may be enforced after a criminal indictment has been returned. One federal appellate court has framed this issue as follows:

> Other than where there is specific evidence of agency bad faith or malicious governmental tactics, the strongest case for deferring civil

[25] *Id.* at 748.

[26] *Id.* at 749-50.

[27] *Id.* at 750-51. For further discussion see Steinberg, *SEC Subpoena Enforcement Practice,* 11 J. Corp. L. 1 (1985).

[28] *SEC v. First Financial Group of Texas, Inc.*, 659 F.2d 660, 666 (5th Cir. 1980).

[29] See *United States v. Kordel,* 397 U.S. 1 (1970).

> proceedings until after completion of criminal proceedings is where a party under indictment for a serious offense is required to defend a civil or administrative action involving the same matter. The noncriminal proceeding, if not deferred, might undermine the party's Fifth Amendment privilege against self-incrimination, expand rights of criminal discovery beyond the limits of Federal Rule of Criminal Procedure 16(b), expose the basis of the defense to the prosecution in advance of criminal trial, or otherwise prejudice the case. If delay of the noncriminal proceeding would not seriously injure the public interest, a court may be justified in deferring it. In some such cases, however, the courts may adequately protect the government and the private party by merely deferring civil discovery or entering an appropriate protective order.[30]

In many such instances, the most feasible alternative may well be to place protective conditions on the exercise of the SEC's power to transmit information after return of an indictment. This approach would permit the Commission to pursue its civil enforcement functions, yet prevent undue expansion of discovery by prohibiting disclosure (of the information uncovered) between the SEC and the pertinent prosecuting entity.[31]

Today, the potential adverse ramifications incurred from parallel proceedings no longer are confined to SEC-Department of Justice referrals. As a number of episodes illustrate,[32] there is the distinct possibility that information transmitted to the SEC will be referred to other federal and state regulatory agencies. Moreover, pursuant to requests under the Freedom of Information Act,[33] the Commission may release documents and other information to private litigants involving matters that previously were subject to SEC scrutiny. Hence, in today's expanding world of parallel proceedings, the adverse consequences that may flow from providing information to the SEC can be massive.[34]

§ 11.04 SEC Administrative Enforcement Remedies

The SEC has a number of administrative enforcement remedies it may invoke when asserted violations of the federal securities laws have been perpetrated by persons and entities subject to the Commission's administra-

---

[30] *SEC v. Dresser Industries, Inc.*, 628 F.2d 1368, 1375-76 (D.C. Cir. 1980) (*en banc*).

[31] *Id.* at 1376, 1391.

[32] See, *e.g.*, *Permian Corp. v. United States*, 665 F.2d 1214 (D.C. Cir. 1981).

[33] 5 U.S.C. § 552.

[34] For more extensive treatment of parallel proceedings see Pickholz, *The Expanding World of Parallel Proceedings*, 53 Temple L.Q. 1100 (1982); Steinberg & Brennan, *Parallel Proceedings*, 8 Corp. L. Rev. 335 (1985); Note, *Using Equitable Powers to Coordinate Parallel Civil and Criminal Actions*, 98 Harv. L. Rev. 1023 (1985).

tive jurisdiction. The following discussion highlights key SEC administrative enforcement remedies.

[A] Refusal and Stop Orders

Section 8 of the Securities Act generally governs the time in which SEC filed registration statements of securities offerings and amendments thereto become effective. Section 8(b) and Section 8(d) respectively authorize the Commission to issue refusal orders and stop orders in connection with materially incomplete, inaccurate, or false and misleading registration statements. Furthermore, Section 8(e) empowers the SEC to make an examination in any case in order to determine whether a stop order should be issued under Section 8(d).[35]

[B] Summarily Suspending Trading in a Security

Summary suspensions of over-the-counter or exchange trading of a security are imposed by the SEC under Section 12(k) of the Exchange Act. This sanction is not to exceed ten days. The Supreme Court in *SEC v. Sloan*[36] held that the Commission was not authorized to summarily suspend trading in a security for successive ten-day periods, unless such successive suspension was based on new circumstances. The Court thus required the SEC to provide notice and right to a hearing with regard to suspensions for extended periods of time.

[C] Broker-Dealer Disciplinary Sanctions

Broker-dealer (and associated persons) disciplinary sanctions may be imposed pursuant to Section 15(b)(4), Section 15(b)(6), as well as Sections 15(a) and 19(h) of the Exchange Act. Persons or entities registered as broker-dealers, as well as any person "associated" with a broker-dealer, are vulnerable to SEC discipline under these provisions. After providing notice and opportunity for a hearing, broker-dealer sanctions may include outright revocation of registration (or denial of registration), suspension of registration, censure, or barring an associated person from associating with a broker-dealer. Moreover, pursuant to Section 15(a), a broker-dealer or associated person, *inter alia*, can be barred from becoming a member (or becoming associated with a member) of a registered securities association (*i.e.*, the NASD). Also, pursuant to Section 19(h) of the Exchange Act, the SEC can suspend or revoke the registration or take other disciplinary action against a registered securities association as well as suspend or expel a member or person associated with a member of such association.[37]

---

[35] See McLucas, *Stop Order Proceedings Under the Securities Act of 1933: A Current Assessment*, 40 Bus. Law. 515 (1985).

[36] 436 U.S. 103 (1978).

[37] See Mathews, *Litigation and Settlement of SEC Administrative Enforcement Proceedings*, 29 Cath. U.L. Rev. 215, 222-23 (1980). For SEC disciplinary proceedings against investment advisers, see §§ 203(e), (f) of the Investment Advisers Act, 15 U.S.C. §§ 80b-3(e), (f).

[D] Section 15(c)(4) Disciplinary Proceedings

Administrative proceedings involving certain defective Exchange Act reports filed with the SEC may be adjudicated pursuant to Section 15(c)(4) of the 1934 Act. Section 15(c)(4) authorizes the Commission to order compliance with the provisions of Section 12, 13, 14 or 15(d) of the Exchange Act and the rules or regulations thereunder. For example, if a Section 12 or 15(d) registrant fails to comply with, in any material way, the continuous reporting requirements of Section 13, such as the timely and accurate filing of annual and other periodic reports, the Commission may, after notice and opportunity for hearing, publish its findings and issue an order requiring compliance. The order may be directed not only to the registrant but also to any person who "caused" such registrant's failure to comply.[38]

In 1984 Congress enacted the Insider Trading Sanctions Act (ITSA). The ITSA, *inter alia*, expands Section 15(c)(4) so as to enable the SEC to bring administrative actions to remedy violations of the proxy and tender offer provisions contained in Section 14 of the Exchange Act. The Act also clarifies that the Commission may proceed administratively against persons (such as officers, directors, and perhaps attorneys) who are a "cause" of a failure to comply with Sections 12, 13, 14 or 15(d).[39]

[E] Section 21(a) Reports of Investigation

Section 21(a) of the Exchange Act allows the Commission, in its discretion, to "make such investigations as it deems necessary to determine whether any person has violated, is violating, or is about to violate any provision of this title," and "to publish information concerning any such violations." Moreover, pursuant to Section 21(a), the SEC "may require or permit any person to file with it a statement in writing . . . as to all the facts and circumstances concerning the matter . . . investigated."[40] Although a Section 21(a) report is not actually an adjudicatory type of proceeding, it is used by the SEC as a substitute for administrative disciplinary or civil injunctive suits in marginal, nonegregious cases, at times having the effect of inducing subject parties to settle.

These settlements frequently enable the Commission to present its position regarding the conduct in question, thereby providing notice of the SEC's future enforcement posture on the issue. Moreover, through the Section 21(a) report procedure, the Commission can avoid the usual requirement of having to find an actual violation while persuading subject parties to modify their conduct or take, what the SEC views as, corrective steps. Hence, in these Section 21(a) reports, the Commission criticizes policies and decisions made

---

[38] See McLucas & Romanowich, *SEC Enforcement Proceedings Under Section 15(c)(4) of the Securities Exchange Act of 1934*, 41 Bus. Law. 145 (1985).

[39] *Id.* See *In re Kern*, [1988 Transfer Binder] Fed. Sec. L. Rep. (CCH) ¶ 84,342 (ALJ 1988).

[40] 15 U.S.C. § 78u(a).

by subject parties, thus directing to all concerned the areas in which the Commission desires reform.[41]

§ 11.05 SEC Injunctions

[A] Standards for Injunctive Relief

As in any other type of case where permanent injunctive relief is sought, a defendant's violation of the federal securities laws is not by itself sufficient for the SEC to obtain an injunction. Rather, the test applied in practically all federal courts is whether there is a reasonable likelihood that the defendant, if not enjoined, will again engage in the violative conduct.[42] In identifying the relevant factors that demonstrate a reasonable likelihood of future violations, the Second Circuit has pointed to

> the degree of scienter involved, the sincerity of defendant's assurances against future violations, the isolated or recurrent nature of the infraction, defendant's recognition of the wrongful nature of his conduct, and the likelihood, because of defendant's professional occupation, that future violations might occur.[43]

Other courts have also deemed relevant the gravity of the offense committed,[44] the time elapsed between the violation and the court's decision,[45] whether the defendant, in good faith, relied on advice of counsel,[46] and the adverse effect an injunction would have on the defendant.[47]

The Supreme Court's decision in *Aaron v. SEC*[48] casts light on this issue. There, the Court held that the SEC must prove scienter in civil enforcement actions to enjoin violations of Section 10(b) of the Exchange Act, Rule 10b-5 promulgated thereunder, and Section 17(a)(1) of the Securities Act,[49] but need not prove scienter under Section 17(a)(2) or 17(a)(3).[50] The Court noted that under Sections 17(a)(2) and 17(a)(3), "the degree of intentional wrongdoing evident in a defendant's past conduct" is an important factor in determining

---

[41] For further discussion see M. Steinberg & R. Ferrara, *supra* note 2, at § 4:01, *et seq.*

[42] See, *e.g.*, *SEC v. Advance Growth Capital Corp.*, 470 F.2d 40, 53 (7th Cir. 1972).

[43] See, *e.g.*, *SEC v. Universal Major Indus. Corp.*, 546 F.2d 1044, 1048 (2d Cir. 1976).

[44] See, *e.g.*, *SEC v. Manor Nursing Centers, Inc.*, 458 F.2d 1082, 1102 (2d Cir. 1972).

[45] See, *e.g.*, *SEC v. Monarch Fund*, 608 F.2d 938, 943 (2d Cir. 1979).

[46] See, *e.g.*, *SEC v. Lum's, Inc.*, 365 F. Supp. 1046, 1066 (S.D.N.Y. 1973).

[47] See, *e.g.*, *SEC v. Manor Nursing Centers, Inc.*, 458 F.2d 1082, 1102 (2d Cir. 1972).

[48] 446 U.S. 680 (1980).

[49] *Id.* at 687-96.

[50] *Id.* at 696-700.

whether the Commission has "established[ed] a sufficient evidentiary predicate to show that such future violation may occur."[51] The presence or lack of scienter is "one of the aggravating or mitigating factors to be taken into account" in a court's exercise of its equitable jurisdiction.[52] In a concurring opinion, former Chief Justice Burger asserted that the SEC "will almost always" be required to show that the defendant's past conduct was more culpable than negligence. The Chief Justice concluded that "[a]n injunction is a drastic remedy, not a mild prophylactic, and should not be obtained against one acting in good faith."[53]

It has been contended that the *Aaron* Court's language, even apart from the former Chief Justice's concurring opinion, could require the SEC to prove scienter in order to make a "proper showing" for procuring injunctive relief under *any* section of the securities acts.[54] This may overstate *Aaron's* implications. It appears that the majority merely stated that the presence of scienter is an important factor for a court to weigh in determining whether to grant the Commission's request for injunctive relief. The absence of scienter may not preclude the granting of such relief where the applicable statutory provision requires only negligent culpability. Indeed, where a defendant has committed prior violations, where his or her carelessness has been egregious, where public investors have been severely injured, or where the defendant's occupation increases the probability of future violations, a court considering the totality of the circumstances may order injunctive relief.[55]

[B] Collateral Consequences

Although the above factors are important in determining whether an injunction should issue, the primary purpose of injunctive relief under the federal securities laws is to deter future violative conduct, not to punish the violator.[56] As Judge Friendly noted, however, an injunction can have severe collateral consequences.[57] For example, an injunction not only harms one's reputation but it also serves as the basis for contempt sanctions if the injunctive order subsequently is violated.[58] Issuance of an SEC injunction can

---

[51] *Id.* at 701.

[52] *Id.*

[53] *Id.* at 703 (Burger, C.J., concurring).

[54] See Huffman, *Aaron Restricts SEC Enforcement*, Legal Times, June 9, 1980, at 2.

[55] See *SEC v. Washington County Utility District*, 676 F.2d 218 (6th Cir. 1982); *SEC v. Murphy*, 626 F.2d 633 (9th Cir. 1980). For further discussion on *Aaron*, see §§ 7.03[B] and 8.04[B], *supra*.

[56] See *Aaron v. SEC*, 446 U.S. 680 (1980); *Hecht Co. v. Bowles*, 321 U.S. 321 (1944).

[57] See *SEC v. Commonwealth Chemical Securities, Inc.*, 574 F.2d 90, 99 (2d Cir. 1978).

[58] See, *e.g.*, *United States v. Custer Channel Wing Corp.*, 327 F.2d 675 (4th Cir. 1967).

cause the suspension or revocation of a broker-dealer's registration, or constitute grounds for prohibiting any person from associating with a broker-dealer.[59] Similarly, an injunction disqualifies the subject party from serving as a director, officer, or employee of a registered investment company.[60] It can constitute a basis for barring an attorney, accountant, or other professional from practicing before the SEC.[61] Additionally, a Regulation A exemption from Securities Act registration may be unavailable to an enjoined issuer of securities.[62] As a final example, the Commission frequently requires that an injunction be disclosed in certain filings, reports, statements, or other information sent to shareholders and investors.[63]

Largely because of these consequences, the courts have required the SEC "to go beyond the mere facts of past violations and demonstrate a realistic likelihood of recurrence."[64] Employing this standard, courts have concluded in a number of cases that the SEC has not made a sufficient showing and have denied the Commission's request for injunctive relief.[65]

[C] Ancillary or Other Equitable Relief

Over the years, the SEC has sought, and successfully obtained, ancillary or other equitable relief against an enjoined party. Examples of such relief include disgorgement, appointment of a receiver, appointment of independent members to the board of directors, and appointment of a special counsel.[66] Proponents assert that the authority for ordering such relief derives from the general equitable powers of the federal courts.[67] Indeed, even if a

---

[59] See § 15(b)(4)(C) of the Exchange Act, 15 U.S.C. § 78o(b)(4)(C); *SEC v. Geon Indus., Inc.*, 531 F.2d 39, 55 (2d Cir. 1976).

[60] See § 9(a)(2) of the Investment Company Act (ICA), 15 U.S.C. § 80a-9(a)(2). The SEC can lift or waive this disqualification pursuant to § 9(c) of the ICA.

[61] See SEC Rule 2(e)(3)(i), 17 C.F.R. § 201.2(e)(3)(i). Rule 2(e) is discussed in § 11.06[A], *infra*.

[62] See Rule 252(c)(4) of Regulation A, 17 C.F.R. § 230.252(c)(4).

[63] See Item 401(f) of Regulation S-K, 17 C.F.R. § 229.401(f). See generally Andre, *The Collateral Consequences of SEC Injunctive Relief: Mild Prophylactic or Perpetual Hazard?*, 1981 U. Ill. L. Rev. 625.

[64] *SEC v. Commonwealth Chemical Securities, Inc.*, 574 F.2d 90, 100 (2d Cir. 1978).

[65] See, *e.g.*, *SEC v. Caterinicchia*, 613 F.2d 102 (5th Cir. 1980).

[66] See, *e.g.*, *SEC v. Manor Nursing Centers, Inc.*, 458 F.2d 1082 (2d Cir. 1972) (disgorgement); *SEC v. Fifth Ave. Coach Lines, Inc.*, 289 F. Supp. 3 (S.D.N.Y. 1968), *aff'd*, 435 F.2d 510 (2d Cir. 1971) (receiver); *SEC v. Coastal States Gas Corp.*, SEC Lit. Rel. No. 6054 (S.D. Tex. Sept. 12, 1973) (independent members of board of directors). See generally Farrand, *Ancillary Remedies in SEC Civil Enforcement Suits*, 89 Harv. L. Rev. 1779 (1976).

[67] See *SEC v. Wencke*, 622 F.2d 1363, 1369 (9th Cir. 1980). See generally Hazen, *Administrative Enforcement: An Evaluation of the Securities and Exchange Commission's Use of Injunctions and Other Enforcement Methods*, 31 Hastings L.J. 444 (1979).

court refuses to grant the SEC's request for an injunction, it may nevertheless grant other equitable relief.[68] Some authorities assert, however, that a number of the more far-reaching forms of equitable relief, such as appointment of directors, may exceed the scope of a court's equitable powers.[69]

[D] Modification or Dissolution of SEC Injunctions

In view of the collateral consequences imposed by SEC injunctions, subject parties may seek to have the particular injunction modified or dissolved. The apparent majority view, derived from the Supreme Court's decision in *United States v. Swift & Co.*,[70] places a heavy burden upon the party seeking modification or dissolution. Writing at the time he was a federal appellate judge, Justice Blackmun construed *Swift* as follows:

> (1) [T]hat, where modification and amendment of an existing decree is under consideration, there are "limits of inquiry" for the decree court and for the reviewing court; (2) that the inquiry is "whether the changes are so important that dangers, once substantial have become attenuated to a shadow;" (3) that the movants must be "suffering hardship so extreme and unexpected" as to be regarded as "victims of oppression;" and (4) that there must be "[n]othing less than a clear showing of grievous wrong evoked by new and unforeseen conditions." Phrased in other words, this means for us that modification is only cautiously to be granted; that some change is not enough; that the dangers which the decree was meant to foreclose must almost have disappeared; that hardship and oppression, extreme and unexpected, are significant; and that the movants' task is to provide close to an unanswerable case. To repeat: caution, substantial change, unforeseeenness, oppressive hardship, and a clear showing are the requirements.[71]

Swift's stringent guidelines thus have been applied by numerous courts in a variety of contexts, including where modification or dissolution of an SEC injunction is sought.[72] A number of courts, however, have declined to follow *Swift's* rigorous requirements. These courts reason that subsequent Supreme Court decisions have departed from *Swift's* restrictive standards.[73] Hence, the Second Circuit, while noting that changes in fact or law provide the strongest reasons for modifying an injunction, held that modification or dissolution also is appropriate "where a better appreciation of the facts in light of

---

[68] See, *e.g., SEC v. Commonwealth Chemical Securities, Inc.*, 574 F.2d 90, 102-03 (2d Cir. 1978).

[69] See Dent, *Ancillary Relief in Federal Securities Law: A Study in Federal Remedies*, 67 Minn. L. Rev. 865 (1983).

[70] 286 U.S. 106 (1932).

[71] *Humble Oil & Refining Co. v. American Oil Co.*, 405 F.2d 803, 813 (8th Cir. 1969).

[72] See, *e.g., SEC v. Advance Growth Capital Corp.*, 539 F.2d 649 (7th Cir. 1976).

[73] See *United States v. United Shoe Machinery Corp.*, 391 U.S. 244 (1968); *System Federation v. Wright*, 364 U.S. 642 (1961).

experience indicates that the decree is not properly adapted to accomplishing its purposes."[74]

A significant decision departing from the *Swift* standards in the securities law area is *SEC v. Warren*.[75] Distinguishing *Swift*, the district court in *Warren* exercised its

> inherent equitable power to weigh the severity of the alleged danger which the injunction was designed to eliminate against the continuing necessity for the injunction and the hardship brought by its prospective application.[76]

Weighing these factors, the court granted the motion to dissolve the injunction.[77] On appeal, the Third Circuit affirmed on substantially the same reasoning.[78]

Another development in this area has been that, even where the SEC makes the necessary showing, some courts have hesitated to order an unconditional permanent injunction. The conditions that courts have attached to the imposition of an injunction include automatic dissolution after a fixed number of years, suspension after the defendant fulfills certain requirements, and permitting a petition for dissolution after a fixed period of time on a lesser showing than that required by *Swift*.[79] Although the SEC, at times, has agreed to certain of these limitations pursuant to the consent process, the Commission's position appears to be that upon making a proper showing, it is entitled as a matter of statutory right to the ordering of a permanent injunction.[80]

Hence, the continued viability of the stringent *Swift* standard is open to debate. Perhaps a better approach would be for courts faced with a motion to modify or dissolve an injunction to apply an ad hoc balancing test. This standard would consider such factors as (1) subsequent change of fact or law, (2) the extent of adverse, unforeseen collateral consequences, (3) whether the injunction has fulfilled its objectives, (4) whether the individual deterrent effect of the injunction has ceased, (5) the decree's effect on societal deterrence, (6) whether a government entity is a party to the litigation and the adverse effect that granting of the motion would have on the entity's resources, and (7) the extent and nature of the public or other countervailing interest involved.

---

[74] *King-Seeley Thermos Co. v. Aladdin Industries, Inc.*, 418 F.2d 31, 35 (2d Cir. 1979).

[75] 76 F.R.D. 405 (W.D. Pa. 1977), *aff'd*, 583 F.2d 115 (3d Cir. 1978).

[76] 76 F.R.D. at 408.

[77] *Id.* at 407-08.

[78] 583 F.2d at 120-22.

[79] See, *e.g.*, the district court's ruling in *SEC v. Blazon Corp.*, 609 F.2d 960 (9th Cir. 1979), the validity of which the Ninth Circuit did not resolve.

[80] See *Brief of the SEC* at 10, *SEC v. Associated Minerals, Inc.*, Nos. 79-1449, 79-1450 (6th Cir. 1980).

This list of considerations is not exhaustive, but should serve as a fairly comprehensive benchmark for assessing motions for modification or dissolution. Although the formulation may resemble a balancing test, such a characterization may be misleading. The importance of each factor may change from case to case, depending on the totality of the circumstances. Further, if the factors are to be weighed, they should not be weighed equally. For example, when a party seeks modification or dissolution of an injunction that was obtained by a government entity, such as the SEC, the public interest criteria should be of paramount importance. In such a case, dissolution or modification may still be granted — but only if the public interest is relatively minute or, in the alternative, if the other variables clearly are predominant.[81]

§ 11.06 Professional Responsibility

This section will address select issues with respect to a securities lawyer's professional responsibilities. In addition to discussing Rule 2(e), the section will focus on counsel's obligations where his or her client engages in violations of law.

[A] Rule 2(e)

SEC Rule of Practice 2(e) provides that the Commission may suspend, limit, or bar "any person" from practicing before it "in any way." Despite the broad language of Rule 2(e), its application to date has been limited to disciplining attorneys, accountants, engineers, and other similar professionals. Although the securities laws do not give the SEC explicit authority to discipline such professionals, the Commission and the courts have held that the Rule is a necessary adjunct "to the Commission's power to protect the integrity of its administrative procedures and the general public."[82]

It has been argued without success that the SEC is exceeding or abusing whatever Rule 2(e) authority it may have by administratively litigating matters involving conduct which arguably does not come within the ambit of "practicing before the Commission."[83] This assertion stems from the fact that the SEC defines "practicing before the Commission" in a broad manner. Thus, the disciplinary authority of Rule 2(e) may come into play in connection with the numerous registration provisions, as well as the periodic

---

[81] For further discussion see Steinberg, *SEC and Other Permanent Injunctions — Standards for Their Imposition, Modification, and Dissolution*, 66 Cornell L. Rev. 27, 71-73 (1980).

[82] *Touche Ross & Co. v. SEC*, 609 F.2d 570, 582 (2d Cir. 1979). See *In re Carter & Johnson*, [1981 Transfer Binder] Fed. Sec. L. Rep. (CCH) ¶ 82,847 (SEC 1981).

[83] See *In re Keating, Muething & Klekamp*, [1979 Transfer Binder] Fed. Sec. L. Rep. (CCH) ¶ 82,124 (SEC 1979) (Karmel, Comm'r, dissenting); Kelleher, *Scourging the Moneylenders from the Temple: The SEC, Rule 2(e), and the Lawyers*, 17 San Diego L. Rev. 501 (1980).

and other reporting requirements, to the extent that any or all of these filings and registration applications can be denominated as "practicing" before the SEC. For example, attorneys who, under Rule 2(e), engage in improper counseling of their clients with respect to required reports filed with the SEC, can be suspended from practicing before the Commission.[84]

[B] Legal and Ethical Standards

Under the American Bar Association's *Model Rules of Professional Conduct*, a lawyer, with certain exceptions, is obligated to preserve his or her client's confidences and secrets.[85] This duty is more protective of client confidentiality than the attorney-client privilege, applying "not merely to matters communicated in confidence by the client but also to all information relating to the representation, whatever its source."[86] In this regard, however, counsel should be wary when the client is engaging in violations of law. Under such circumstances, counsel's rendering of substantial assistance with knowledge of the fraud (such as the drafting by counsel of an SEC disclosure document which the lawyer knows presents a materially false impression of the issuer's financial condition) may result in his or her being held liable as an aider and abettor under the *Model Rules*, the federal securities laws, and state law.[87]

The *Model Rules* make clear that a lawyer has discretion to reveal to third parties information relating to the representation of a client only to the extent counsel reasonably believes such disclosure is necessary to prevent the client from engaging in a criminal act that "is likely to result in imminent death or substantial bodily harm."[88] Hence, counsel under the *Model Rules* may not disclose information in order to prevent the client from perpetrating a crime or fraudulent act which counsel believes is likely to result in serious economic harm. Under such circumstances, counsel if he or she stays in the representation, must be careful not to become an aider or abettor. An alternative is for counsel to withdraw from the representation.[89] In this regard, however, a number of states have adopted a modified version of the *Model Rules* which permit counsel to disclose to third parties otherwise confidential information relating to a crime in order to prevent the client from unlawfully causing serious financial injury.[90]

---

[84] See, *e.g., In re Fields*, [1972-1973 Transfer Binder] Fed. Sec. L. Rep. (CCH) ¶ 79,407 (SEC 1973), *aff'd without opinion*, 495 F.2d 1075 (D.C. Cir. 1974).

[85] See Rule 1.6 of the *Model Rules of Professional Conduct* (1983).

[86] *Id.* (comment to Rule 1.6). See *Upjohn v. United States*, 449 U.S. 383 (1981).

[87] See, *e.g.*, Rule 1.2(d) of the *Model Rules*; *SEC v. Spectrum, Ltd.*, 489 F.2d 535 (2d Cir. 1973); *SEC v. National Student Marketing Corp.*, 457 F. Supp. 682 (D.D.C. 1978).

[88] *Model Rule* 1.6(b).

[89] *Id.* Rule 1.16. See *In re Carter & Johnson*, [1981 Transfer Binder] Fed. Sec. L. Rep. (CCH) ¶ 82,847 (SEC 1981).

[90] See Hall, *States Modifying ABA's Ethics Rules*, Legal Times, Aug. 12, 1985, at 1. See also Hacker & Rotunda, *Representing the Corporate Client and the Proposed Rules of Professional Conduct*, 4 Corp. L. Rev. 269 (1981).

The disclosure obligations in the securities law area are magnified by the concept that commission of a past unlawful act may materially impact on the present financial condition of the issuer. Accordingly, nondisclosure of the unlawful act(s) (and their financial consequences) may violate the federal securities laws and thereby constitute an ongoing fraud. Hence, the securities lawyer's dilemma when counseling a client in this setting can be unsettling.[91]

In the securities law context, counsel may be retained by the corporate entity. Generally, directors, officers, shareholders, employees, and affected communities may be considered constituents of the corporation.[92] In determining to whom to look as embodying the various interest groups of the corporation, the incumbent board of directors (who are elected by the shareholders) and members of executive management (who in turn are appointed by the board) may be deemed as the appropriate decisionmakers of corporate policy.[93]

In this regard, decisions made by an executive officer, properly designated to make such determinations, generally should be accepted by the lawyer as one made by the corporation. However, when such determinations involve violations of law, different considerations apply. In such situations, counsel should take appropriate measures which may include (depending on the seriousness of the situation and the corrective steps, if any, taken): (1) asking the officer or other decisionmaker to reconsider the matter; (2) if the situation is not corrected, referring the matter to higher authority in the corporation, such as the chief executive officer or the board of directors; (3) advising that a separate legal opinion on the matter's legality be procured; (4) fully informing the independent directors of the matter and its consequences; (5) if all else fails and the client seeks to engage in the illegal action without taking corrective action, resigning from the representation; and (6) in some states, having discretion to inform shareholders, affected third parties, and government agencies of the fraud.[94]

The SEC in the *Carter and Johnson*[95] administrative Rule 2(e) proceeding focused on this subject. Although the Commission held that the respondents did not violate Rule 2(e), it set forth standards that apply today:

---

[91] See generally Gruenbaum, *Clients' Frauds and Their Lawyer's Obligations*, 68 Geo. L.J. 191 (1979); Kramer, *Clients' Frauds and Their Lawyer's Obligations: A Study in Professional Irresponsibility*, 67 Geo. L.J. 991 (1978); Lorne, *The Corporate and Securities Adviser, the Public Interest, and Professional Ethics*, 76 Mich. L. Rev. 425 (1978); Sonde, *The Responsibility of Professionals Under the Federal Securities Laws — Some Observations*, 68 Nw. U.L. Rev. 1 (1973).

[92] See *Model Rule* 1.13 (comment).

[93] *Id.* See Steinberg, *Corporate/Securities Counsel — Conflicts of Interest*, 8 J. Corp. L. 577 (1983); *Developments in the Law — Conflicts of Interest in the Legal Profession*, 94 Harv. L. Rev. 1244 (1981).

[94] See *Model Rules* 1.13(b), (c) (and comment thereto). See *supra* note 90 and accompanying text.

[95] *In re Carter and Johnson*, [1981 Transfer Binder] Fed. Sec. L. Rep. (CCH) ¶ 82,847 (SEC 1981).

The Commission is of the view that a lawyer engages in "unethical or improper professional conduct" under the following circumstances: When a lawyer with significant responsibilities in the effectuation of a company's compliance with the disclosure requirements of the federal securities laws becomes aware that his client is engaged in a substantial and continuing failure to satisfy those disclosure requirements, his continued participation violates professional standards unless he takes prompt steps to end the client's non-compliance. . . .

We do not imply that a lawyer is obliged, at the risk of being held to have violated Rule 2(e), to seek to correct every isolated disclosure action or inaction which he believes to be at variance with applicable disclosure standards, although there may be isolated disclosure failures that are so serious that their correction becomes a matter of primary professional concern. It is also clear, however, that a lawyer is not privileged to unthinkingly permit himself to be co-opted into an ongoing fraud and cast as a dupe or a shield for a wrongdoing client.

Initially, counselling accurate disclosure is sufficient, even if his advice is not accepted. But there comes a point at which a reasonable lawyer must conclude that his advice is not being followed, or even sought in good faith, and that his client is involved in a continuing course of violating the securities laws. At this critical juncture, the lawyer must take further, more affirmative steps in order to avoid the inference that he has been co-opted willingly or unwillingly, into the scheme of non-disclosure.

The lawyer is in the best position to choose his next step. Resignation is one option, although we recognize that other considerations, including the protection of the client against foreseeable prejudice, must be taken into account in the case of withdrawal. A direct approach to the board of directors or one or more individual directors or officers may be appropriate; or he may choose to try to enlist the aid of other members of the firm's management. What is required, in short, is some prompt action that leads to the conclusion that the lawyer is engaged in efforts to correct the underlying problem, rather than having capitulated to the desires of a strong-willed, but misguided client.

Some have argued that resignation is the only permissible course when a client chooses not to comply with disclosure advice. We do not agree. Premature resignation serves neither the end of an effective lawyer-client relationship nor, in most cases, the effective administration of the securities laws. The lawyer's continued interaction with his client will ordinarily hold the greatest promise of corrective action. So long as a lawyer is acting in good faith and exerting reasonable efforts to prevent violations of the law by his client, his professional obligations have been met. In general, the best result is that which promotes the continued, strong-minded and independent participation by the lawyer.

> We recognize, however, that the "best result" is not always obtainable, and that there may occur situations where the lawyer must conclude that the misconduct is so extreme or irretrievable, or the involvement of his client's management and board of directors in the misconduct is so thorough-going and pervasive that any action short of resignation would be futile. We would anticipate that cases where a lawyer has no choice but to resign would be rare and of an egregious nature.[96]

It should be emphasized that the Commission in the *Carter and Johnson* proceeding focused on counsel's obligations to seek the undertaking of corrective action *within* the corporate structure where fraud is afoot. The SEC did not address counsel's duty to disclose to the public or to affected third parties.[97]

---

[96] *Id.* at 84,172-84,173.

[97] *Id.* at 84,173 n.78. See authorities cited note 91, *supra*.

GLOSSARY

GLOSSARY

This Glossary is designed to familiarize the reader with key securities law terms, statutes, rules, and other regulations. Although not intended to be comprehensive or exhaustive, the Glossary should prove useful.

General Terms

Acceleration

Process by which the SEC can expedite a registration statement's effective date, thereby avoiding § 8(a)'s twenty day waiting requirement. *See Section 8(a) of the Securities Act; Rule 460.*

Accredited Investor

Class of investor defined in § 2(15) of the Securities Act and Rule 501(a), for purposes of the exempt offering provisions of Regulation D and § 4(6) of the Securities Act, to include certain institutional investors as well as financially sophisticated and/or wealthy investors.

Affiliate

Generally, an affiliate of an issuer is one who controls, is controlled by, or is under common control with, either directly or indirectly through one or more intermediaries, such issuer. *See Controlling Person; Rule 405.*

"All-or-None" Offering

Type of offering whereby all the securities offered must be sold at a specified price within a specified time with the amount due to the seller at a specified date and where the purchase price will be refunded in whole or in part if the offering is not fully subscribed. Pursuant to Rule 10b-9, such offerings are prohibited unless such conditions are met.

American Stock Exchange (AMEX)

Exchange where the securities of smaller and perhaps newer companies are traded, as opposed to the New York Stock Exchange with its larger companies and more stringent listing requirements. *See Securities Exchanges.*

Annual Report to Security Holders

Pursuant to Rule 14a-3 and Rule 14c-3, an annual report is to be furnished to an issuer's security holders. The annual report is not deemed a filed document for § 18(a) liability purposes. *See § 14(a) of the Exchange Act; Rule 14a-9.*

"Bad Boy" Disqualifications

Refers to provisions contained in certain SEC rules (such as Rule 252(c) and (d)) disqualifying an issuer from using certain exemptions from registration if the issuer or its affiliated persons, executive officers, directors, or other like persons have been subject to disciplinary action during the previous five years (or ten years for Rule 252(d)(1)), including a criminal conviction relating to the sale of securities and the imposition of an SEC injunction.

"Best Efforts" Underwriting

Type of underwriting arrangement where the underwriters agree to act as agent for the issuer and use their "best efforts" in finding purchasers for the securities being offered. To the extent that the underwriters are unsuccessful in finding purchasers, the securities are not sold. *See Underwriting; "Firm Commitment" Underwriting.*

"Blue Sky" Laws

Term used to refer to the body of state securities statutes. Some states have statutes that only require disclosure of material information, while other states have merit regulation which requires, in addition to full disclosure, that the securities offered meet a test of substantive fairness. *See Merit Regulation; Regulation by Qualification.*

Bond

Type of security which is an evidence or certificate of a debt on which the issuing governmental body or corporation promises to pay the holder of the bond a specified amount of interest for a predetermined length of time, with repayment of the principal amount at a specified expiration date. A bond (as distinguished from a debenture or other debt security) is secured by the corporation's assets. *See Debentures; Debt Securities.*

"Change in Circumstances" Doctrine

Doctrine which holds that the concept of underwriter status can be avoided if a party can establish that he or she purchased the subject securities with investment intent but that subsequent unforeseen changes compelled the earlier than planned sale of the securities. Although the SEC has evidently rejected this defense to underwriter status, courts nonetheless may accept its validity.

Churning

Refers to the practice of a broker-dealer engaging in excessive trading in a customer account over which it has control for the purpose of generating commissions.

Comfort Opinion

A statement furnished by an attorney, acting either as counsel for the issuer or for the underwriter, providing that, based on counsel's participation in the preparation of the registration statement and conferences with representatives of the issuer, underwriters and public accountants, he/she has no reason to believe that the registration statement violates § 11. In order to avoid § 11 liability, counsel should ensure that neither the opinion nor its contents appear in the registration statement.

"Commercial/Investment" Test

Test adopted by several lower federal courts, used to ascertain whether a note is a security for purposes of § 2(1) of the Securities Act and § 3(a)(10) of the Exchange Act. Under this test, the focus is on the underlying commercial or investment character of the transaction. Applying the "unless the context otherwise requires" language of §§ 2(1) and 3(a)(10), courts adhering to this view hold that a note is not a security where it arises from a transaction that is essentially commercial in nature even when its terms are literally within the Acts' coverage. *See "Plain Language" Test; Risk Capital Test.*

Conditioning the Market

See "Gun-jumping."

Controlling Person

Pursuant to Rule 405, a controlling person is any person who directly or indirectly possesses the power to direct the management or policies of an entity. *See Rule 405.*

Crown Jewel

Antitakeover device whereby the target company sells (or grants an option to purchase) its most valuable asset — its "crown jewel" — to a third party in order to make the company less attractive to an unfriendly bidder.

Debentures

Type of debt security that is not secured by a mortgage on the issuing corporation's assets, but is only backed by the company's general credit. Issuances of debentures are subject to the Trust Indenture Act of 1939 as well as the Securities Act of 1933. The antifraud provisions of § 10(b) of the Exchange Act also apply. *See Bonds; Debt Securities.*

Debt Securities

Refers to bonds, notes, debentures, and other evidences of indebtedness in which investors furnish capital to a corporation in return for a promise by the corporation to repay the principal in full at a future specified date and to pay the investor a fixed rate of interest thereon for the term of the loan. The issuance of debt securities is subject to the Trust Indenture Act of 1939 and to the Securities Act. The antifraud provisions of § 10(b) of the Exchange Act apply as well. *See Bonds; Debentures.*

Deficiency Letter

Letter sent by the SEC's Division of Corporation Finance to an issuer notifying it of deficiencies in its registration statement. Amendments to the registration statement are subsequently filed in response thereto. This letter also is known as a "letter of comments."

"Disclose or Abstain" Rule

Doctrine promulgated by the courts in the insider trading context which provides that under certain circumstances (see *Chiarella*, 445 U.S. 222 (1980), and *Dirks*, 463 U.S. 646 (1983)) one with material nonpublic information concerning a company's securities, the affairs of a company, or the market for the company's stock must either refrain from trading (or tipping) based on such information or must disclose such information to the investing public before trading (or tipping) on it.

Due Diligence

In the securities offering context, refers to the functions performed by various parties, including underwriters, to help ensure that the prospectus contains no material misstatement or omission. The standard of conduct required of parties to successfully invoke the due diligence defense varies depending on the statute implicated (*e.g.*, § 11 of the Securities Act as compared to § 10(b) of the Exchange Act), the party's relationship with the issuer, whether the defendant is an expert or non-expert, and whether the portion of the offering document in question is an expertised or non-expertised portion.

"Economic Reality"

Looking at the prefatory language, "unless the context otherwise requires," contained in § 2 of the Securities Act and § 3(a) of the Exchange Act, courts, in ascertaining whether a security exists, decipher the economic reality of a transaction rather than applying a literal construction.

"Economic Risk" Test

Under Rule 146 (which has been superseded by Rule 506), test used to determine whether offerees or purchasers of securities are able to bear the economic risks of the investment and, hence, help qualify the offering for exemption from registration pursuant to § 4(2). Rule 506 has eliminated this test. The test, however, still may be applicable under certain states' Blue Sky laws.

"Firm Commitment" Underwriting

Type of underwriting arrangement whereby the underwriters agree to purchase from the issuer the securities being offered for the purpose of reselling them to participating dealers and the public. To the extent that the underwriters are not successful in finding purchasers, they must pay for and hold the securities for their own account. *See Underwriting; "Best Efforts" Underwriting.*

Foreign Corrupt Practices Act (FCPA)

A 1977 amendment to the Exchange Act, this legislation requires a reporting company to maintain reasonably accurate and detailed books and records (in addition to its normal Exchange Act reporting requirements) and to devise and maintain an internal accounting system that will reasonably insure proper accountability of assets and internal control of accounting practices and procedures. *See §§ 13(b)(2) and 30A of the Exchange Act.*

"Fraud on the Market" Theory

Theory used by courts (and acquiesced in by the Supreme Court) to apply the presumption of reliance in securities litigation (*e.g.*, § 10(b) litigation). This theory posits that the market price of an issuer's stock reflects all available public information regarding the issuer and does not include deceptive or manipulative conduct.

"Free Writing"

Term used to refer to written sales literature (unless otherwise exempted, such as a § 10 prospectus, tombstone ad, or identifying statement) that is prohibited during the pre-filing and waiting periods and only permitted in the post-effective period. However, if there is such "free writing" in the post-effective period, a statutory § 10(a) prospectus must precede or accompany it or such "free writing" will be deemed a separate prospectus under § 2(10), thereby resulting in a violation of § 5(b)(1).

Glass-Steagall Act

Popular name for the Banking Act of 1933. In essence, this legislation requires that investment banking be separated from commercial banking. *See Investment Banking.*

Going-Private

Refers to a transaction or series of transactions in a publicly-held company whereby the controlling (or other) group substantially reduces or eliminates entirely the number of shares held by the public by inducing shareholders to exchange their stock for cash, thereby causing the company to attain private status. Such transactions are regulated by Rules 13e-3 and 13e-4 and, of course, state law. *See Leverage Buyout (LBO); § 13(e) of the Exchange Act; Rules 13e-3, 13e-4; Schedule 13E-3.*

Going-Public

Process whereby an issuer embarks upon a plan of financing in which securities are sold to the investing public. The issuer thereby becomes subject to the reporting requirements of the Exchange Act. *See Initial Public Offering (IPO).*

Golden Parachute

A generous severance package that compensates certain key executives if control of a target company changes in the event of a corporate takeover.

"Greenmail"

The purchase of a substantial block of the subject company's securities by a (potentially) unfriendly suitor with the primary purpose of inducing the subject company to repurchase the block at a premium over the amount paid by the potential suitor.

"Gun-Jumping"

The publication of information of an offering or other conduct in the pre-filing period resulting in a conditioning of the public market or a stimulation of interest in the securities to be registered, thereby resulting in a violation of the § 5(c) proscriptions against offers to sell in the pre-filing period.

Horizontal Commonality

One of the two types of "common enterprise" for purposes of the *Howey* investment contract test. Generally, horizontal commonality looks to the relationships which exist between an individual investor and the pool of other investors. A pooling of the interests of the investors is essential to finding the presence of horizontal commonality; all courts have held that horizontal commonality is sufficient to meet the common enterprise requirement of the *Howey* test. *See Vertical Commonality; Howey Test.*

"Hot Issue"

Occurs where the price of an offering of securities quickly rises to a substantial premium above the initial offering price. The demand for the securities offered may be accompanied by an investor stampede to purchase the coveted "hot" stock.

Howey Test

Test promulgated by the Supreme Court in the *Howey* case, 328 U.S. 293 (1946), to determine when an investment contract exists for purposes of § 2(1) of the Securities Act and § 3(a)(10) of the Exchange Act. "The test is whether the scheme involves an investment of money in a common enterprise with profits to come solely from the efforts of others." The test subsequently has been elaborated upon by the lower courts. *See Investment Contract.*

Identifying Statement

Pursuant to Rule 134, a communication concerning an offering, not deemed to be a prospectus under § 2(10), which may be published or transmitted during the waiting period (and post-effective period). Used to ascertain what parties are interested in the securities and the extent of such interest. Mention of price of the securities is permitted. *See Rule 134.*

In Registration

Refers to the entire registration process, generally from the pre-filing period until the prospectus delivery requirements have been satisfied.

Initial Public Offering (IPO)

The first public offering of securities that an issuer makes. By so doing, the issuer "goes public" and becomes subject to the Exchange Act's reporting obligations. *See "Going-Public".*

Insider Trading Sanctions Act (ITSA)

Enacted in 1984, and amended in 1988, this legislation authorizes the SEC, *inter alia*, to seek the imposition of a civil monetary penalty amounting to three times the profit received or loss avoided against any person unlawfully purchasing or selling securities while in possession of material nonpublic information, unlawfully tipping material nonpublic information, or substantially contributing to the violation's occurrence by a brokerage firm's (or investment adviser's) failure to maintain and enforce an adequate law compliance monitoring system.

Integrated Disclosure

Refers to the Commission's integrated disclosure framework which simplifies registrant reporting by (1) making uniform the disclosure requirements under the Securities Act and the Exchange Act, (2) allowing periodic reporting under the Exchange Act to satisfy much of the Securities Act registration statement disclosure requirements, and (3) encouraging (but not requiring) the use of informal shareholder communications to satisfy certain of the Act's formal disclosure requirements.

Integration of Offerings

Doctrine by which seemingly separate offerings are construed as one integrated offering, thereby vitiating otherwise exempt offerings and usually resulting in a violation of the Securities Act's registration requirements. The SEC has set forth criteria to determine when integration should apply as well as safe harbor rules. *See Rules 147(b)(2) and 502(a).*

Investment Advisors Act of 1940

Requires registration of all non-exempt investment advisors and obligates such advisers to conform their conduct to statutory norms. The Act, *inter alia*, addresses fee arrangements between advisors and clients, prohibits fraudulent practices, precludes assignment of an investment advisory contract without the client's consent, requires advisors to maintain books and records consistent with rules that may be promulgated by the SEC, and authorizes the SEC to inspect such books and records.

Investment Company Act of 1940

Requires companies engaged primarily in the business of investing, reinvesting, and trading in securities and whose securities are offered to and held by the investing public to register with the SEC and to disclose their financial condition and investment policies. The Act contains antifraud provisions and private remedies. Investment companies also may be subject to the provisions of the 1933 and 1934 Acts.

"Investment Contract"

Term used in § 2(1) of the Securities Act and § 3(a)(10) of the Exchange Act as a type of instrument that constitutes a security. *See Howey Test.*

"Letter of Comments"

See "Deficiency Letter."

"Letter of Intent"

Signed letter between an issuer and its managing underwriter outlining the proposed terms of the offering as well as the underwriting compensation, but not binding either party, with the possible exception of a provision concerning payment of expenses upon abandonment by one of the parties.

Leveraged Buyout (LBO)

Corporate control transaction frequently characterized by public shareholders of a corporation being cashed-out, with corporate insiders obtaining a substantial equity interest in the ongoing enterprise. The funds borrowed to finance the acquisition are collaterized by the corporation's assets, with repayment of the loans to be made out of the company's future revenue stream and by the sale of certain divisions or subsidiaries. *See Going-Private.*

Lock-Up

An arrangement, made in connection with the contemplated acquisition of a publicly-held entity, that gives the prospective acquiror an advantage in acquiring the subject company over other potential acquirors.

Market Information

Information about the market for a particular entity's securities as contrasted with information about the corporation or its business.

Market Maker

Refers to a broker-dealer in the over-the-counter market who buys and sells securities as a principal for its own account on a regular or continual basis. The market maker conducts "two-way" bids; *i.e.*, it stands willing to both buy and sell the securities for which it is making a market. Market makers are subject to regulation by the National Association of Securities Dealers (NASD) and the SEC.

Merit Regulation

Refers to state Blue Sky statutes that, in addition to requiring full and adequate disclosure, require that securities offerings be substantively fair, just, and equitable. *See "Blue Sky" Laws; Registration by Qualification.*

NASD (National Association of Securities Dealers, Inc.)

Self-regulatory organization (SRO) of broker-dealers organized and governed under the supervision of the SEC pursuant to § 15 of the Exchange Act.

NASDAQ (National Association of Securities Dealers Automated Quotation System)

Electronic means of publicizing buy and sell quotes to be used in the over-the-counter market. *See Market Maker; Over-The-Counter Market.*

New-Issue Markets

That part of the securities market which consists of initially issued securities, often from companies. These securities are issued to the investing public through a network of underwriters and dealers. *See Trading Markets.*

New York Stock Exchange (NYSE)

The dominant stock exchange in the United States. Most of this country's largest commercial and industrial companies have their securities listed and traded on the NYSE. *See Securities Exchanges.*

"No-Action" Letter

Letter issued by the SEC's staff, sought by a party prior to engaging in the contemplated conduct, in order to help ensure that such conduct will not raise the Commission's ire. After a no-action letter has been issued, the SEC is not precluded from subsequently bringing an enforcement action; however, as a practical matter, the chances of such an action being initiated are slim. Prospective plaintiffs are not affected by the issuance of an SEC no-action letter.

Over-The-Counter Market (OTC Market)

Generally, securities transactions in the secondary trading markets which do not take place on exchanges are said to be conducted over-the-counter. The NASDAQ and the Pink Sheets are the vital components of the OTC market. *See Market Maker; NASDAQ; Pink Sheets.*

Pac-Man Defense

A tender offer by the subject company for the securities of the bidder.

"Piggy-Back" Registration

Term used to refer to a manner in which a control person can register his/her stock in a public offering. If a control person has covenanted with the issuer for the right of "piggy-back" registration, he/she is authorized to "piggy-back" his/her stock or a portion thereof at the time that the issuer elects to file a registration statement.

Pink Sheets

System used in the over-the-counter market to record quotes and reports of transactions of securities not traded on the NASDAQ System. *See Over-The-Counter Market.*

"Plain Language" Test

Test adopted by the Second Circuit which is used to ascertain whether a note is a security. Under this test, much deference is given to the statute (§ 2(1) of the Securities Act or § 3(a)(10) of the Exchange Act) and the burden of proof is upon the party seeking to avoid the plain language of the statute to show that the "context otherwise requires." *See "Commercial/Investment" Test; Risk Capital Test.*

Poison Pill

Generally, an antitakeover provision whereby certain securities (such as rights or warrants) of the target company are triggered upon consummation of any enumerated transaction or event into the common stock or other security of the target or of the acquiror or cash.

Post-Effective Period

Time period after the registration statement filed with the SEC becomes effective. Sales can be made only by means of a statutory § 10(a) prospectus; § 10 summary prospectus permitted for certain issuers (reporting companies) for solicitation purposes only; preliminary § 10 prospectus not permitted in post-effective period; "free-writing" permitted if accompanied or preceded by a statutory § 10(a) prospectus; certain broker-dealer published information is permitted pursuant to Rules 137-139; the "tombstone ad" and "identifying statement" may be used; prospectus delivery requirement for dealers generally applies; unsolicited brokers' transactions without prospectus delivery requirements generally permitted if, *inter alia*, transactions executed on an exchange or in the over-the-counter market; and the interstate commerce requirement applies.

Pre-Filing Period

Time period before a registration statement has been filed with the SEC. Subject to certain exceptions, offers to sell as well as offers to buy are prohibited; sales are prohibited; negotiations and agreements with underwriters who are or will be in privity with the issuer are permitted; Rule 135 announcements are permitted; certain broker-dealer published information is permitted pursuant to Rules 137-139; and the interstate commerce requirement must be met in order for § 5 to apply.

Preliminary Prospectus

Prospectus used pursuant to Rule 430 in the waiting period as a written offer in satisfaction of § 10's prospectus delivery requirement. The preliminary prospectus contains substantially the same information as the § 10(a) statutory prospectus. A legend in red ink must be included, stating among other things, that the registration statement has yet to become effective. This document also is called a "red herring" prospectus. *See Rule 430.*

Presumptive Underwriter Doctrine

Under this doctrine, one who purchases more than ten percent of the securities offered in a registered offering may be deemed an underwriter unless such person establishes sufficient investment intent. The SEC staff apparently has abandoned the presumptive underwriter doctrine.

Private Offering Exemption

Transactions by an issuer which are exempt from the registration requirements of § 5 of the Securities Act because they do not involve any public offering, and hence, fall within the § 4(2) exemption of the Securities Act. *See § 4(2) of the Securities Act; Rule 506.*

Prospectus

Generally, with certain exceptions, any written communication (or by radio or television) which offers any security for sale or confirms the sale of any security, including confirmations, letters, brochures, circulars, notices, and advertisements. Solely oral communications (if not by radio or television) do not constitute a prospectus. *See §§ 2(10) and 10 of the Securities Act.*

Public Utility Holding Company Act of 1935

Statute regulating interstate holding companies which are engaged through their subsidiaries in the retail distribution of manufactured or natural gas or in the electric utility business. This Act requires such holding companies, unless exempted by the Act, to register with the SEC and to file initial and periodic reports detailing the financial structure, organization, and operations of such companies and their subsidiaries.

Racketeer Influenced and Corrupt Organizations Act (RICO)

RICO establishes criminal offenses and penalties as well as a civil private right of action for treble damages and attorneys' fees. Although enacted largely due to the concern of the extent to which organized crime had penetrated the national economy, controversy has arisen regarding the use of the private monetary right of action against accepted, legitimate businesses.

"Red Herring"

See Preliminary Prospectus; Rule 430.

Refusal Order

Proceeding initiated by the SEC pursuant to § 8(b) of the Securities Act empowering the Commission, after providing an opportunity for a hearing, to declare a registration statement deficient on its face, and thereby issue a refusal order. To issue a refusal order, the SEC must act within ten days after the filing of such registration statement. The effect of the Commission's order is to prevent the registration statement from becoming effective until amended in accordance with such order. *See § 8(b) of the Securities Act.*

Regional Exchanges

The Boston (BSE), Philadelphia (Phlx), Midwest (MSE), and Pacific (PSE) stock exchanges are examples of exchanges known as regional exchanges. The volume of trading conducted on such exchanges accounts for only a small percentage of all the trading done in the securities markets. *See Securities Exchanges; New York Stock Exchange; American Stock Exchange.*

Registration by Coordination

Type of state Blue Sky registration available to an issuer when a registered offering is being made under the Securities Act. This type of state registration requires only the filing of three copies of the 1933 Act registration statement as well as any additional information required by the state securities administrator.

Registration by Notification

Type of state Blue Sky registration requiring the filing of a short-form registration statement. Such form of registration generally is available only when an issuer and its predecessors have had a seasoned business for at least five years (*e.g.*, no default and average net earnings).

Registration by Qualification

Type of state Blue Sky registration requiring, in addition to full and adequate disclosure, that the offering meet the strictures of merit regulation; *i.e.*, that the offering be substantively fair, just, and equitable. *See Merit Regulation.*

Registration Statement

The basic disclosure document which must be filed with the SEC pursuant to the 1933 Act's registration requirements for public offerings. The registration statement consists of the § 10(a) statutory prospectus, which must be delivered to prospective purchasers before or at the time that sales are consummated, and supplemental information which is placed on file and available for public inspection at the SEC's office.

Reporting Company

Generally refers to issuers subject to the periodic reporting requirements of the Exchange Act. With certain exceptions, these registrants include: (1) those which have had a public offering under the Securities Act (*see § 15(d) of the Exchange Act*), (2) those which have securities traded on a national stock exchange (*see § 12(b) of the Exchange Act*), and (3) those which have more than $5 million in assets and a class of equity securities owned by at least 500 persons (*see § 12(g) of the Exchange Act*).

Repurchase Agreement

Financing arrangement whereby a person owning securities agrees to transfer the securities to another party for cash at a certain price. The original owner also simultaneously agrees to "repurchase" these securities at a fixed, higher price from the other, "lending" party, on a fixed date, the price differential being the return to the lender on the investment. Whether a "repo" is construed as a purchase and sale of a security or as a loan will determine how it will be scrutinized under the securities laws.

Restricted Security

Generally, securities acquired directly or indirectly from an issuer or its affiliate in a nonpublic offering, or securities subject to the Regulation D resale limitations. *See Rule 144.*

"Risk Capital" Test

Under this test, an investment contract generally may be found if an investor invests money, property, or services in an enterprise or venture with the expectation of some pecuniary or non-pecuniary benefits to the investor to be derived essentially from the efforts of others; horizontal or vertical commonality need not be required. This important alternative to the *Howey* Test has been embraced by a number of states, although generally not by the federal courts. *See Howey Test.*

Sale of Business Doctrine

This doctrine, rejected by the Supreme Court in the *Landreth Timber Co.*, 105 S.Ct. 2297 (1985), and *Gould*, 105 S.Ct. 2308 (1985), companion cases, provides that the transfer of stock incidental to the sale of a business does not constitute a security.

Scorched Earth Defense

Antitakeover device whereby the directors of the subject company take actions to sell off the subject company's assets, or failing this, to destroy the character of the company in an effort to defeat the bidder's tender offer.

Section "4(1-1/2)" Exemption

A hybrid exemption from registration, not enumerated in the Securities Act, yet ostensibly within its intent. This exemption, based largely on SEC no-action letters and other SEC pronouncements, seeks to fill the gap in the statutory exemptive scheme concerning sales of securities by affiliates, and sales of restricted securities by non-affiliates, who desire to sell such securities in a routine private transaction. Certain "established criteria" of the § 4(1) and § 4(2) exemptions must be met in order for a party to successfully invoke this exemption.

Securities Act of 1933

The first federal securities statute enacted, this "Truth in Securities" Act focuses on the initial offering context. It requires all securities offered for sale, unless otherwise exempted, to be registered with the SEC. The Act sets forth the requirements for registration of securities that are offered for sale to the public. The Act also contains exemptions from registration, private remedies, and antifraud provisions. Full disclosure, and not merit regulation, is the guiding principle.

Securities Exchange Act of 1934

Federal statute establishing the Securities and Exchange Commission and setting forth provisions governing the public trading of securities. The Act, for example, contains antifraud provisions, extensive reporting as well as other requirements for certain issuers of securities, oversight of broker-dealers and national securities exchanges, requirements focusing on proxy solicitation, and provisions covering tender offers and going-private transactions.

Securities Exchanges

Forum with established rules and procedures where securities are traded by exchange members. The securities must be admitted to trading by the exchange and the members thereof trade for either their own accounts or for customers. By the provisions of the Exchange Act, the exchanges are subject to SEC oversight. *See American Stock Exchange; New York Stock Exchange; Regional Exchanges; § 6 of the Exchange Act.*

"Shark Repellents"

Amendments to a potential target company's certificate of incorporation or by-laws that have been devised to discourage unsolicited approaches from unwanted bidders.

"Shelf" Registration

Refers to Rule 415 which concerns Securities Act registration of securities to be offered or sold on a delayed or continuous basis in the future. Rule 415 allows, *inter alia,* Form S-3 (or F-3) issuers to file primary-at-the-market offerings of equity securities which they plan to offer within two years of the effective date of the registration statement. *See Rule 415.*

Shingle Theory

Posits that broker-dealers are to be held to a fairly strict standard of conduct because by hanging out its "shingle," a broker-dealer impliedly represents that its conduct and the behavior of its employees will be fair and will comport with professional norms.

Short Sale

Practice where an investor places an order to sell at the current market price a security which he/she does not then own. By so doing, he/she incurs an obligation to sell which is to be fulfilled by purchasing the securities at a later date, hopefully for a lower price, and thereafter delivering such securities to the purchaser. Rules promulgated by the SEC pursuant to its § 10(b) authority regulate short sales. Moreover, § 16(c) of the 1934 Act prohibits short sales by insiders.

Short-Swing Profits

For purposes of § 16(b) of the 1934 Act, short-swing profits are profits realized by insiders (directors, officers, 10% shareholders) from the purchase and sale (or sale and purchase) of stock within a six-month period. Pursuant to § 16(b), such profits are subject to disgorgement to the corporation. Strict liability attaches in order to effectuate the remedial purpose of the statute.

"Soft" Information

Refers to appraised asset valuations, projections, future earnings, and other less than "hard" information about an issuer which traditionally have not been required to be disclosed to investors and shareholders, but which are increasingly becoming subject to disclosure concerns. *See Rule 175.*

Specialist

A trader on a securities exchange who, pursuant to SEC and self-regulatory organization (SRO) regulations and for the purpose of maintaining "a fair and orderly market," purchases securities for his/her own account or executes orders for other broker-dealers, while specializing in the securities of particular issues or companies.

Statutory Prospectus

The § 10(a) (of the 1933 Act) prospectus, which is used only after the registration statement becomes effective and which must be sent or given to the investor before or at the time that a sale is effectuated. The statutory prospectus constitutes the first portion of the registration statement and must conform with the requirements set forth in Schedule A of the 1933 Act. *See § 10(a) of the Securities Act.*

"Stickering"

Refers to the practice of using a prospectus supplement, a "sticker," to update a registration statement to reflect "material" changes. Such "stickering" may be used in a "shelf" registration. *See "Shelf" Registration.*

Stock

Type of corporate security, the purchase of which by an investor generally gives him/her the potential to share in the corporation's profits in the firm by way of dividends as well as (in regard to common stock) the right to elect the directors of the corporation and to vote on matters that will fundamentally change the structure or nature of the corporation. Stockholders, as equity owners of the corporation, can be said to own the corporation.

Stock Exchanges

See Securities Exchanges.

"Stop Order"

Proceeding initiated by the SEC pursuant to § 8(d) of the Securities Act in response to materially false, incomplete, inaccurate, or misleading information in a registration statement. Once such a proceeding is initiated, and violations are found, the effectiveness of the registration statement becomes suspended until amended in accordance with the stop order. The Commission must provide notice and an opportunity for a hearing. *See §§ 8(d), (e) of the Securities Act.*

Summary Prospectus

Prospectus that may be used by reporting companies pursuant to Rule 431 and § 10(b) of the 1933 Act as a written offer in the waiting period and for solicitation purposes only in the post-effective period. *See Rule 431.*

Target Company

Refers to a company that is the subject (target) of a takeover bid.

Tender Offer

A means frequently used to acquire control of a corporation characterized by active solicitation to purchase a substantial percentage of the issuer's stock at a premium over the market price, offered for a limited period of time and often contingent upon the tender of a specific number of shares. Tender offers are governed by the Williams Act which was enacted by Congress as an amendment to the Exchange Act. *See Williams Act; §§ 13(d), (e), 14(d), (e), and (f) of the 1934 Act.*

"Tombstone Ad"

Advertisement of an offering, not deemed to be a prospectus under § 2(10) of the 1933 Act, which may be published during the waiting period (and post-effective period). It provides basic information about the offering and identifies the members of the underwriting syndicate. Such an ad is used to ascertain what parties are interested in the securities and the extent of such interest. Mention of price of the securities is permitted.

Trading Markets

Generally, that part of the securities market which consists of securities that have previously been issued. These securities are bought and sold on stock exchanges and in the over-the-counter market.

Transactional Exemptions

Refers to transactions which are exempt from the registration requirements of § 5 of the Securities Act due to a perfection of one of the Securities Act's statutory exemptions (or pursuant to an exemption prescribed by the SEC under its rulemaking authority).

Trust Indenture Act of 1939

Federal legislation regulating the issuance of debentures, notes, bonds, and similar debt securities offered to the public pursuant to trust indentures under which more than $1 million of securities at any one time may be outstanding. Often these securities must also be registered under the 1933 Act. The Trust Indenture Act regulates the conduct of the indenture trustee and the issuer and provides rights for security holders.

Two-Tier Offer

A two-step acquisition technique in which the first-step (front-end) is a cash tender offer and the second-step (back-end) often is a merger in which remaining shareholders of the subject company may receive securities of the bidder valued below the cash consideration offered in the first-step tender offer.

Underwriter

Any person who has purchased securities from an issuer (or from a controlling person) with a view to their distribution, offers or sells for an issuer (or for a controlling person) in connection with the distribution of securities, or directly or indirectly participates in any such undertaking, or the direct or indirect underwriting thereof. *See § 2(11) of the 1933 Act; "Best Efforts" Underwriting; "Firm Commitment" Underwriting.*

Uniform Limited Offering Exemption (ULOE)

Provides issuers with a uniform exemption from state registration and is intended to coordinate with SEC Regulation D. A majority of the states have adopted some form of ULOE and it is the goal (albeit unlikely to eventuate) of the SEC and the North American Securities Administrators Association (NASAA) to achieve general uniformity in all the states.

Vertical Commonality

One of the two types of "common enterprise" for purposes of the *Howey* test. Vertical commonality generally requires only that the investor(s) and promoter (or third party) be involved in some common venture. The lower federal courts widely disagree on whether vertical commonality satisfies the *Howey* common enterprise element. *See Horizontal Commonality; Howey Test.*

Waiting Period

Time period after a registration statement has been filed with the SEC but before it becomes effective. Oral offers and written offers by means of a § 10 prospectus are permitted; however, only in the post-effective period, may securities be sold and offers to buy be accepted; certain broker-dealer published information is permitted pursuant to Rules 137-139; the § 2(10) "tombstone ad" and Rule 134 "identifying statement" may be used; and the interstate commerce requirement must be met in order for § 5 to apply.

White Knight

The name given to a party sought out by a subject company in an attempt to fend off an unwanted bidder. Action taken by a white knight may include purchasing a large block of the target company's stock or making a competing tender offer.

Williams Act

Act adopted in 1968 as an amendment to the Exchange Act dealing generally with tender offers. Provisions of the Williams Act include §§ 13(d), (e), 14(d), (e), and (f) of the Exchange Act. *See Tender Offer.*

SECURITIES ACT OF 1933

Section 2

Provides the definitions of terms used throughout the Securities Act.

Section 3(a)

Specifies and enumerates specific securities or categories of securities that are exempt from Securities Act (§ 5) registration, largely due to the intrinsic character or nature of the issuer itself. These exempt securities include, for example, certain short-term promissory notes or bills of exchange, securities issued or guaranteed by municipalities, state or federal governments, and securities issued by nonprofit, religious, educational or charitable organizations. Certain of the exempt securities, although not subject to 1933 Act registration, are regulated by other agencies (*e.g.*, securities issued by national banks are subject to regulation by the Comptroller of the Currency). Section 3(a)(2) through 3(a)(8) provides a listing of the exempt securities. Even an exempt security, however, is subject to the securities acts' antifraud provisions.

Section 3(a)(9)

Provides that securities exchanged by an issuer exclusively with its existing security holders, except those exchanged in a Title 11 bankruptcy proceeding, are exempt from Securities Act registration, provided that no commission or other remuneration is paid for soliciting such an exchange.

Section 3(a)(10)

Generally exempts from Securities Act registration securities which are issued in exchange for bona fide legal claims, securities, or property interests when a court or other specified tribunal, after conducting an adversary proceeding on the transaction's fairness, grants such approval.

Section 3(a)(11)

The "intrastate" exemption provides an exemption from Securities Act registration for securities offered and sold only to persons resident within the same state as the issuer is resident and doing business (or incorporated and doing business). *See Rule 147.*

Section 3(b)

Empowers the SEC, through the promulgation of rules and regulations, to define additional exemptions from registration where, in the Commission's view, the public interest and the protection of investors does not require such securities to be registered either because of the limited character of the offering or the small amount involved. However, no offering of over

$5,000,000 may be exempted under this subsection. *See Rules 504, 505, 701; Regulation A.*

Section 4(1)

Exempts from the registration requirements of § 5 "transactions by any person other than an issuer, underwriter, or dealer." Hence, this provision generally permits individual investors who are not affiliates to resell their securities without registration, provided such resales are viewed as "transactions" rather than part of a "distribution." *See Rule 144.*

Section 4(2)

The private offering exemption provides that "transactions by an issuer not involving any public offering" are exempt from the registration requirements of § 5 of the Securities Act. The requirements for perfecting the § 4(2) exemption are detailed. There is no monetary limit to the amount of funds that can be raised under this exemption. *See Private Offering Exemption; Rule 506.*

Section 4(3)

This exemption concerns the prospectus delivery requirements of dealers. The prospectus delivery time periods have been shortened by the SEC pursuant to Rule 174. Nonetheless, a participating dealer selling part of its allotment is subject to the prospectus delivery requirements, irrespective of the time period elapsed. *See Rule 174.*

Section 4(4)

Exempts from the registration requirements of § 5 "brokers' transactions executed upon customers' orders on any exchange or in the over-the-counter market but not the solicitation of such orders." *See Rule 144.*

Section 4(6)

Provides an exemption for offerings not exceeding $5,000,000 in any twelve-month period. Available to an unlimited number of accredited investors only. No general solicitation or advertising is permitted, there are no issuer qualifications, restrictions on resale apply, and no specific information need be furnished to investors.

Section 5(a)

Prohibits the use of the mails or any instrument or means of interstate commerce to sell or to deliver a security for purposes of sale before the effective date of the registration statement. *See Pre-Filing Period; Waiting Period.*

Section 5(b)

Prohibits the use of the mails or any means of interstate commerce to transmit any prospectus, unless such prospectus meets the requirements of

§ 10. Also, the provision prohibits securities to be carried through the mails or in interstate commerce for purposes of sale or for delivery after sale unless accompanied or preceded by a § 10(a) prospectus. *See Post-Effective Period; Rules 430 and 431.*

Section 5(c)

Prohibits, subject to certain exceptions, the use of the mails or any means of interstate commerce to offer to sell or offer to buy the securities offered in the time period before a registration statement has been filed with the Commission or while the registration statement is the subject of a stop order, refusal order, or any public proceeding or examination under § 8. *See Pre-Filing Period.*

Section 6

Sets forth the filing requirements for registration statements including who must sign the statement, the effect of a signature affixed thereto, and the fee to be paid upon filing. This section also states that a registration statement is deemed effective only as to the securities offered therein, that the registration statement or amendments thereto are considered to be filed as of the receipt thereof by the SEC (provided the proper fee accompanies the statement), and that the information contained in or filed with a registration statement shall be available for public inspection and copying.

Section 7

Generally provides that a registration statement shall contain the information and be accompanied by the documents specified in Schedule A. *See § 10(a) of the Securities Act; Schedule A.*

Section 8(a)

Provides that the effective date of a registration statement is the twentieth day after it is filed or such earlier date as the SEC may determine (based upon factors stated therein). The statute also provides that the effective date of a registration statement begins to run anew if amendments are filed thereto (unless filed with the SEC's consent or pursuant to an SEC order). *See Rule 460.*

Section 8(b)

Provides that if the Commission determines that a registration statement is deficient on its face, upon affording an opportunity to a hearing, it can issue a refusal order, so long as it acts within ten days after the filing thereof, preventing the registration from becoming effective until amended in accordance thereto. *See "Refusal Order".*

Section 8(d)

Provides that the SEC may initiate a stop order in response to materially false, incomplete, inaccurate, or misleading information in a registration statement, suspending the effectiveness of the registration statement until amended in accordance with the stop order. Notice and an opportunity for a hearing must be provided. *See Stop Order.*

Section 8(e)

Empowers the SEC to make an investigation into whether a stop order under § 8(d) should issue. *See Stop Order.*

Section 10(a)

Provides that a statutory prospectus must contain the information contained in the registration statement (see § 7) except the documents referred to in paragraphs (28) through (32) of Schedule A (or paragraphs (13) and (14) of Schedule B for foreign governmental issuers); however, the SEC may by rules or regulations omit this required information from any prospectus if it determines that such information is not necessary or appropriate for the protection of investors and the public interest. Also provides under certain circumstances for the updating of information in a prospectus that is used more than nine months after the effective date of the registration statement. *See Statutory Prospectus; Schedule A.*

Section 10(b)

Empowers the SEC to promulgate rules and regulations permitting the use of prospectus that will satisfy § 5(b)(1). *See Preliminary Prospectus; Summary Prospectus; Rules 430 and 431.*

Section 11(a)

Establishes a private right of action for damages on behalf of purchasers against an enumerated list of persons and entities who may be subject to civil liability for material misstatements or omissions contained in the registration statement (including the prospectus which is part of the registration statement). The action may be brought by "any person acquiring such security" unless it can be shown that, at the time of purchase, the purchaser knew of the misstatement or omission.

Section 11(b)

Provides defenses for subject parties other than the issuer for claims arising under § 11(a) of the Securities Act, the most important of which is the "due diligence" defense of § 11(b)(3). *See Rule 176.*

Section 11(c)

States that the appropriate standard of reasonableness in determining what constitutes reasonable investigation and reasonable grounds for belief for purposes of the § 11(b)(3) "due diligence" defense is "that required of a prudent man in the management of his own property." *See Rule 176.*

Section 11(e)

Provides for the measure of damages in suits brought under § 11(a) of the 1933 Act, as well as the payment of costs and attorney's fees. The provision also permits a defendant in a § 11(a) action to prove that the plaintiff's loss was due to factors other than the material misrepresentation(s) or nondisclosure(s) contained in the registration statement. The statute limits the damages of an underwriter to the dollar amount of the securities offered to the public by such underwriter.

Section 11(f)

Provides for joint and several liability for the subject parties specified in § 11(a). The statute also allows for contribution unless the parties who are liable were guilty of fraudulent misrepresentation and the others were not.

Section 11(g)

Prohibits recovery under § 11 of an amount exceeding the public offering price of the security.

Section 12(1)

Provides the purchaser of securities with an express private right of action for rescission (or if he/she no longer owns the securities, for damages) against his/her seller if such seller offers or sells a security in violation of § 5. Generally, if a violation of § 5 has been committed by the seller, strict liability is imposed.

Section 12(2)

Affords an express private right of action to a purchaser against his/her seller for rescission (or damages if the securities have been disposed of) where the purchaser acquired the securities by means of a prospectus or oral communication which contained a material misstatement or omission. The seller under § 12(2) has a "reasonable care" defense.

Section 13

Provides the statute of limitations for actions brought under §§ 11, 12(1), and 12(2) of the 1933 Act.

Section 14

Provides that any provision, condition, or stipulation that binds any person acquiring a security to waive compliance with any provision of the 1933 Act or the SEC's rules and regulations thereunder shall be void.

Section 15

Provides that a person who controls a person held liable under § 11 or 12 of the 1933 Act shall be jointly and severally liable with such controlled person, unless such controlling person did not have knowledge of the facts or reasonable grounds to believe in the existence of such facts upon which the controlled person's liability is predicated.

Section 16

Provides that the rights and remedies provided by the 1933 Act shall be in addition to whatever rights or remedies exist at law or in equity.

Section 17(a)

Makes it unlawful to engage in fraudulent or deceptive practices in the offer or sale of securities.

Section 17(c)

Provides that the exemptions from registration contained in § 3 of the 1933 Act shall not apply to the provisions of § 17.

Section 19(a)

Empowers the SEC to promulgate rules and regulations deemed necessary to carry out the provisions of the 1933 Act. Also states that good faith reliance on SEC rules or regulations will preclude 1933 Act liability.

Section 19(b)

Empowers the SEC to subpoena witnesses, administer oaths and affirmations, take evidence, and request the production of documents for the purpose of enforcing the Securities Act.

Section 19(c)

Authorizes the SEC to cooperate with state securities regulators in order to achieve greater uniformity and effectiveness of federal and state regulations and minimum interference with capital formation, particularly for small businesses.

Section 20(b)

Empowers the SEC, when it appears that a person is engaged in or is about to engage in a practice or act violative of the 1933 Act or the rules or regulations promulgated thereunder, to bring an action in United States District Court to enjoin such practice or act, and upon a proper showing, an injunction or restraining order shall be granted without bond. The statute also authorizes the SEC to transmit evidence concerning such practices or acts to the Attorney General who may bring the appropriate criminal proceedings under the 1933 Act.

Section 22(a)

Provides that the United States District Courts shall have jurisdiction over offenses and violations under the 1933 Act and the rules and regulations promulgated thereunder, and concurrent jurisdiction with the states for suits at law or in equity brought to enforce any duty or liability created by the 1933 Act. The statute also provides for venue of suits, service of process, and judicial review. It prohibits the removal of properly instituted 1933 Act cases from state court to federal court.

Section 22(b)

Provides that, if a person refuses to obey a subpoena, a federal district court, upon application by the SEC, may issue an order to such person requiring him/her to appear before the SEC and produce evidence; failure to obey such order is punishable by contempt of court.

Section 23

States that just because a registration statement has been filed or is in effect or no stop order has been issued in no way implies that the SEC represents that the registration statement is true and accurate and devoid of material misrepresentations or omissions or that the SEC has passed upon the merits of the security, and any representation to the contrary to any prospective purchaser shall be unlawful.

Section 24

States that any person who willfully violates any provision of the 1933 Act or any rule or regulation promulgated thereunder, or who willfully makes a material misrepresentation or omission in a registration statement, shall upon conviction be subject to fines and/or imprisonment.

SECURITIES EXCHANGE ACT OF 1934

Section 2

States the necessity for the Securities Exchange Act of 1934, and enumerates reasons in support thereof.

Section 3(a)

Provides the definition of terms used throughout the Exchange Act.

Section 4(a)

Establishes the SEC and sets forth the criteria and rules governing the appointment of its five commissioners and the terms of their office.

Section 6(a)

Permits an exchange to be registered as a national securities exchange pursuant to the terms and conditions of § 6 of the 1934 Act and the provisions of § 19(a) of the Act upon filing a registration application with the SEC in such form as the SEC may, by rule, prescribe containing the rules of such exchange and any other information or document as the SEC, by rule, may prescribe as germane for the public interest or the protection of investors.

Section 6(b)

Sets forth basic conditions that must, in the Commission's view, be satisfied in order for an exchange to be registered as a national securities exchange.

Section 7(a)

Provides that the Federal Reserve Board shall prescribe rules and regulations regarding the amount of credit which may be initially extended and subsequently maintained on a non-exempt security, and sets forth a standard upon which such rules and regulations shall be based for the initial extension of credit.

Section 7(b)

States that notwithstanding the provisions of § 7(a), the Federal Reserve Board may from time to time raise or lower margin requirements for the initial extension of credit or the maintenance thereof.

Section 9

Provides an express private remedy for purchasers and sellers injured by manipulation of securities which are traded on a national securities exchange.

Section 10(b)

The basic antifraud provision of the securities laws makes it unlawful to employ deceptive or manipulative devices in connection with the purchase or sale of securities. *See Rule 10b-5.*

Section 12(a)

Makes it unlawful for any broker or dealer to conduct transactions in securities on a national securities exchange (other than for an exempted security) that has not been registered pursuant to the 1934 Act.

Section 12(b)

Provides for 1934 Act registration of a security which is listed on a national securities exchange by filing an application with the exchange as well as with the SEC containing specified information.

Section 12(g)

Requires registration of a security for 1934 Act purposes by the issuer filing specified information with the SEC. Pursuant to Rule 12g-1, this requirement occurs when the issuer has assets of greater than $5 million and has a class of equity security held of record by at least 500 persons.

Section 12(i)

Vests the administration and enforcement of §§ 12, 13, 14(a), 14(c), 14(d), 14(f), and 16 with respect to federally insured banks and savings and loan institutions in their respective governing bodies, which are empowered to promulgate rules and regulations necessary to execute their functions under this subsection, provided such rules and regulations are substantially similar to the SEC's rules and regulations promulgated under the above sections (unless not necessary or appropriate in the governing agency's view).

Section 13(a)

Requires issuers of a security registered pursuant to § 12 of the Exchange Act to file annual and other periodic reports as the Commission shall prescribe containing specified information. This periodic reporting obligation also is incurred by publicly-held issuers under § 15(d). *See § 15(d); Forms 8-K, 10-K, 10-Q.*

Section 13(b)(2)

Generally requires publicly-held issuers to maintain reasonably accurate books and records and internal accounting controls. This statute was passed as part of the Foreign Corrupt Practices Act. *See Foreign Corrupt Practices Act (FCPA).*

Section 13(d)

Requires any person (or group) who acquires, either directly or indirectly, a greater than five percent beneficial ownership interest in any equity security of a class subject to the 1934 Act's reporting requirements to file a Schedule 13D statement of ownership with the SEC within ten business days after attaining such percentage of ownership. *See Schedule 13D.*

Section 13(e)

Makes it unlawful for any 1934 Act § 12 reporting company to purchase its own shares in contravention of SEC rules. *See Going-Private; Rules 13e-3, 13e-4; Schedule 13E-3.*

Section 14(a)

Gives the SEC broad authority to regulate the solicitation of proxies with respect to securities registered under § 12 of the Exchange Act. The statute makes it unlawful for any person to violate SEC rules and regulations prescribed pursuant to § 14(a). *See Annual Reports to Security Holders; Rule 14a-9.*

Section 14(d)

Requires any person making a tender offer for equity securities subject to the Exchange Act's reporting requirements and registered pursuant to § 12 of the Exchange Act to file with the SEC certain materials. Also, the statute sets forth procedural mandates, such as the offering period, pro rata rights, and the time within which tendered shares may be withdrawn. *See Tender Offer; Regulation 14D; Schedules 14D-1, 14D-9.*

Section 14(e)

Prohibits deceptive, manipulative, and fraudulent practices in connection with any tender offer, invitations or requests for tenders, or any solicitation of security holders for or against any such offer, invitation, or request. *See Tender Offer.*

Section 14(f)

Requires a tender offeror to file with the Commission disclosures of the names and descriptions of individuals who are to be elected directors and other agreements affecting directors that will occur in connection with a change of management control pursuant to a tender offer for Exchange Act reporting equity securities.

Section 15(c)(1)

Prohibits fraudulent, deceptive, or manipulative conduct by broker-dealers in the over-the-counter market (or on exchanges of which they are not members) in connection with the purchase or sale of securities.

Section 15(c)(4)

Authorizes the Commission in an administrative proceeding, after providing notice and an opportunity for hearing, to order compliance by subject parties with the provisions of §§ 12, 13, 14, and 15(d) of the Exchange Act and SEC rules and regulations promulgated thereunder. The SEC also may proceed administratively against persons who are deemed to be a "cause" of a failure to comply with § 12, 13, 14, or 15(d).

Section 15(d)

Generally obligates issuers of public offerings of securities made pursuant to the Securities Act to file annual, periodic, and other specified reports with the SEC. *See Forms 8-K, 10-K, 10-Q.*

Section 16(a)

Requires beneficial owners of over ten percent of any non-exempt security registered pursuant to § 12 of the 1934 Act and directors and officers of the issuer of such stock to file with the SEC (and with any national securities exchange that such stock is listed on) a statement specifying how much of the issuer's stock is owned by such person and monthly changes in such ownership interest.

Section 16(b)

Provides that profits realized by insiders (as defined in § 16(a)) from the purchase and sale (or sale and purchase) of stock within a six-month period are subject to disgorgement to the corporation; strict liability attaches. If the corporation does not institute the action, a shareholder may bring the suit on behalf of the corporation. *See Short-Swing Profits.*

Section 16(c)

Generally prohibits short sales and sales against the box by insiders (as defined in § 16(a)). *See Short-Sale.*

Section 18(a)

Provides an express right of action for damages when an investor purchases or sells a security in reliance upon a materially false or misleading statement that is contained in a document filed with the SEC pursuant to the Exchange Act. Because of § 18(a)'s strict reliance and causation requirements ("eyeball" reliance is required), suits based solely on § 18(a) thus far have had little chance of success.

Section 20(a)

Imposes joint and several liability on persons directly or indirectly controlling one held liable under the Exchange Act (or rules or regulations promulgated thereunder), unless such controlling person acted in good faith and neither directly nor indirectly induced the violation.

Section 20A

Enacted as part of the Insider Trading and Securities Fraud Enforcement Act of 1988, this statute provides an express private right of action for those who traded securities contemporaneously with, and on the opposite side of, a transaction from the insider trader.

Section 21

Gives the SEC broad authority to investigate possible violations, subpoena witnesses, require the production of memoranda and other records, initiate contempt proceedings, transmit evidence to the Attorney General (who may institute criminal proceedings), and bring actions for injunctive relief. Also, the statute permits the Commission to seek a treble monetary penalty against those engaged in insider trading.

Section 21A

Enacted as part of the Insider Trading and Securities Fraud Enforcement Act of 1988, this statute imposes an affirmative duty upon broker-dealers and investment advisers to maintain and enforce reasonable supervisory mechanisms to prevent insider trading violations and imposes treble monetary penalties under specified conditions. The statute also addresses the amount of penalty that can be assessed against a controlling person, contains procedures for collection, and gives the SEC authority to award bounties to informants.

Section 28(a)

Provides that the rights and remedies contained in the Exchange Act shall be in addition to any other rights and remedies that may exist at law or in equity. The statute limits recovery in 1934 Act private damages actions to actual damages. It also states that nothing in the Exchange Act shall affect the jurisdiction of state securities commissions to the extent that the latter do not conflict with the Act or the rules and regulations promulgated thereunder.

Section 29(a)

Provides that any condition, stipulation or provision binding a person to waive compliance with any provision of the 1934 Act or any SEC rule or regulation thereunder (or any stock exchange rule) shall be void.

Section 29(b)

Provides that every contract formed or performed in contravention of the 1934 Act or any rule or regulation prescribed thereunder "shall be void" as regards the rights of the violating party or his/her successor who takes with knowledge.

Section 30A

Enacted as part of the Foreign Corrupt Practices Act, the provision makes it unlawful for any publicly-held registrant or any person acting on behalf of such issuer to engage in bribery of any foreign official, foreign political party, or candidate for foreign political office. *See Foreign Corrupt Practices Act (FCPA).*

Section 32(a)

Generally provides for fines and/or imprisonment for willful violation of any provision of the Exchange Act or any pertinent SEC rule or regulation thereunder. The provision states, however, that no person shall be subject to imprisonment for the violation of any rule or regulation if he/she proves that he/she had no knowledge of such rule or regulation.

SEC RULES

Securities Act Rules

Rule 134

Rule specifying what may be included in an "identifying statement." An identifying statement meeting the terms of Rule 134 is a communication not deemed to be a § 2(10) prospectus and may be published or transmitted during the waiting period (and post-effective period). It is used to ascertain what parties are interested in the securities and the extent of such interest. *See "Identifying Statement".*

Rule 135

Permits a pre-filing announcement by an issuer of a proposed registered offering that will not be deemed a violation of § 5. This rule provides that certain enumerated information may be publicly disseminated by the issuer as long as the notice contains only specified information and states that the offering will only be made by means of a prospectus. Mention of the underwriter and the offering price generally are not permitted.

Rule 137

Permits a dealer not participating in a distribution to publish and distribute in its regular course of business information, recommendations, and opinions regarding securities of a reporting company that has filed or proposes to file a registration statement, provided that the dealer receives no remuneration from the issuer for such activities or from the ensuing distribution. The rule applies to the pre-filing, waiting, and post-effective periods.

Rule 138

Permits dealers participating in an offering of non-convertible senior securities which are registered on Form S-2 or S-3 (as well as Form F-2 or F-3) to publish recommendations and opinions concerning the issuer's common stock, and vice-versa. The rule applies to the pre-filing, waiting, and post-effective periods.

Rule 139

Generally permits participating dealers to publish recommendations or opinions concerning offerings of S-2 (or F-2) issuers as long as said publication is (1) disseminated at regular intervals, (2) includes similar information regarding a substantial number of companies in the registrant's industry or is part of a comprehensive list of securities currently recommended by such dealer, (3) does not give special prominence to the issuer, and (4) does not give a more favorable opinion or recommendation with respect to the issuer than the last previous opinion issued before the dealer became a participant. With respect to S-3 (or F-3) issuers, a participating dealer is given greater latitude under Rule 139. The rule mandates only that, with respect to such issuers, the recommendation must be contained in a publication which is distributed with reasonable regularity in the normal course of the dealer's business. Nonetheless, Rule 10b-6 concerns may be present. *See Rule 10b-6.*

Rule 144

Provides a safe harbor under the § 4(1) exemption for all shareholders who are selling their restricted securities and for affiliates who are selling their unrestricted securities without registration, and a safe harbor for brokers under the § 4(4) exemption who execute such transactions. If shareholders or brokers make a sale in compliance with the full set of objective conditions of Rule 144, they will not be deemed to be underwriters or involved in a distribution. *See § 4(1) and 4(4) of the Securities Act.*

Rule 145

Unless an exemption from registration is available, Rule 145 requires that securities issued in connection with mergers, consolidations and certain other recapitalizations must be registered under the Securities Act. The rule also addresses issuer communications in the pre-filing period and applicable restrictions on resales by persons other than the issuer. *See Form S-4.*

Rule 146

Former SEC safe harbor rule to the § 4(2) exemption from Securities Act registration. Rule 146 is no longer in effect and has been superseded by Rule 506 of Regulation D. *See § 4(2) of the Securities Act; Rule 506.*

Rule 147

Safe harbor to the § 3(a)(11) intrastate exemption. Generally, the rule includes an 80% "in state" business requirement upon the issuer, a nine-month out-of-state resale prohibition, a principal residence test for purchasers and offerees, and precautions against interstate offers and sales. The doctrine of integration applies. Unlike the § 3(a)(11) exemption, the rule is only available for offerings by issuers. *See § 3(a)(11) of the Securities Act.*

Rule 174

Provision, promulgated by the SEC pursuant to § 4(3) of the Securities Act, nullifying to a large degree, the prospectus delivery requirements of said statute. The rule generally provides that a dealer is not subject to the prospectus delivery requirements if the issuer is a reporting company under the Exchange Act. Moreover, the time period in which a prospectus must be delivered under § 4(3) for first-time issuers has been significantly shortened pursuant to Rule 174. Participating dealers selling part of their allotment, however, must comply with the prospectus delivery requirements irrespective of the time period elapsed. *See § 4(3) of the Securities Act.*

Rule 175

Provides a safe harbor for forward-looking statements made by an issuer in a 1933 Act registration statement and in an SEC filed document pursuant to the Exchange Act by a reporting company if made with a reasonable basis and in good faith. The 1934 Act's counterpart to Rule 175 is Rule 3b-6. *See "Soft" Information.*

Rule 176

Lists a number of factors for an adjudicator to take into account as "circumstances affecting the determination of what constitutes reasonable investigation" for purposes of the due diligence defense of § 11(b)(3). *See § 11(b) of the Securities Act.*

Rule 405

Sets forth the definition of terms used throughout Regulation C. *See Regulation C.*

Rule 415

Concerns the Securities Act registration of securities to be offered or sold on a delayed or continuous basis in the future. Allows, inter alia, Form S-3 (or F-3) issuers to file primary-at-the-market offerings of equity securities which they plan to offer within two years of the effective date of the registration statement. *See "Shelf" Registration.*

Rule 430

Authorizes the use of a preliminary prospectus or so-called "red herring" to be used in the waiting period as a written offer in satisfaction of the prospectus delivery requirements. *See Preliminary Prospectus; § 10(b) of the Securities Act.*

Rule 430A

Under this rule, issuers engaging in offerings of securities for cash are not required to file a pre-effective "pricing" amendment (*i.e.*, information relating to price and the underwriting syndicate). The information omitted in reliance on Rule 430A must be contained either in the final prospectus which will be deemed a part of the registration statement if filed within five business days after the registration statement's effective date or in a post-effective amendment to the registration statement.

Rule 431

Provides for the use of a summary prospectus by reporting companies under § 10(b) of the 1933 Act for purposes of § 5(b)(1) of the Act. *See Summary Prospectus; § 10(b) of the Securities Act.*

Rule 460

Declares the SEC's policy of not accelerating a registration statement's effective date unless the preliminary prospectus has been distributed to underwriters and participating dealers of the offering.

Rule 501

Sets forth the definitions of terms used throughout Regulation D.

Rule 502

Sets out four general conditions that are applicable to Regulation D offerings. The conditions concern the integration of offerings, with a safe harbor provided therefor; the information that must be disclosed by an issuer to purchasers under a Regulation D offering (except for offerings made pursuant to Rule 504 or solely to accredited investors); the prohibitions against advertising and general solicitation (with the exception of Rule 504(b)(1)); and the limitations on resale (except as provided in Rule 504(b)(1)).

Rule 503

Sets forth the requirements for filing a Form D with the SEC pursuant to a Regulation D offering.

Rule 504

Provides an exemption from Securities Act registration under § 3(b) for offerings not exceeding $500,000 in any twelve-month period (or $1 million if $500,000 of such offerings are state registered). The number of investors is unlimited, there are no investor qualifications, and reporting companies and investment companies do not qualify for use of the exemption. The prohibitions on general solicitation and advertising and the restrictions on resale apply, unless the offering is registered in states that require registration and delivery of a disclosure document. Pursuant to federal law, no information need be specifically disclosed.

Rule 505

Provides an exemption under § 3(b) for offerings not exceeding $5 million in any twelve-month period. The exemption is limited to 35 purchasers plus an unlimited number of accredited investors. Specified information must be delivered to all non-accredited purchasers. The prohibitions on general solicitation and advertising apply, as well as the restrictions on resale. Investment companies and issuers disqualified under Regulation A do not qualify for use of the exemption.

Rule 506

Safe harbor to the § 4(2) exemption. The exemption permits sales to 35 purchasers plus an unlimited number of accredited investors. Information supplying requirements (unless all purchasers are accredited), investor sophistication requirements (unless the purchaser is accredited), resale limitations, and prohibitions on advertising and general solicitation apply. No dollar limitation applies to Rule 506 offerings. *See § 4(2) of the Securities Act.*

Rule 701

Adopted pursuant to § 3(b) of the Securities Act as part of Regulation D. The rule generally provides an exemption from registration up to $5 million based on a formula during any twelve-month period for offers and sales of securities for certain compensation benefit plans adopted for the participation of employees, officers, directors, consultants, and advisers of an eligible company. The exemption can only be used for compensatory purposes (rather than for capital raising purposes) and can be used only by nonreporting companies. Restrictions on resale apply to securities sold in Rule 701 offerings.

SEC RULES

Exchange Act Rules

Rule 10b-5

Promulgated pursuant to § 10(b) of the 1934 Act, this rule makes it unlawful to employ any deceptive or manipulative device in connection with the purchase or sale of a security. *See § 10(b).*

Rule 10b-6

Subject to certain exceptions, the rule generally prohibits persons who are engaged in a distribution of securities from bidding for or purchasing such securities (or inducing others to do so) until after they have completed their participation in the distribution.

Rule 13e-3

Generally, the rule prohibits fraudulent, deceptive, and manipulative acts or practices in connection with going-private transactions and prescribes filing, disclosure, and dissemination requirements as a means reasonably designed to prevent such acts or practices. *See Going-Private; § 13(e) of the Exchange Act.*

Rule 13e-4

Governs issuer tender offers for a company's own securities. The rule prohibits fraudulent, deceptive, and manipulative acts and practices and establishes filing, disclosure, and dissemination requirements. An issuer tender offer regulated by Rule 13e-4, that also constitutes a going-private transaction under Rule 13e-3, must comply with both rules. *See Tender Offer; Going Private; § 13(e) of the Exchange Act; Rule 13e-3; Schedule 13E-3.*

Rule 14a-9

Prohibits the solicitation of proxies which contain any materially false or misleading statement. *See Annual Report to Security Holders; § 14(a) of the Exchange Act.*

Rule 14d-1

Sets forth the scope of Regulations 14D and 14E and the definitions applicable thereto.

Rule 14d-8

Extends the right of shareholders to receive proration of their shares in a tender offer that is oversubscribed from the previous ten-calendar-day period (as provided in § 14(d)(6)) to the entire period that the offer remains open.

Rule 14d-9

Requires the subject (target) company of a tender offer to file with the Commission a Schedule 14D-9, which calls for the disclosure of specified information. *See Schedule 14D-9.*

Rule 14d-10

Requires that a tender offer be open to all shareholders and that the best price paid to any security holder be paid to any other tendering security holder.

Rule 14e-3

Prohibits insider and tippee trading in the tender offer context by applying the disclose-or-abstain provision where an individual is in possession of material information relating to a tender offer where he/she knows or has reason to know that such information is nonpublic and was obtained directly or indirectly from the offeror, the subject corporation, any of their affiliated persons, or any person acting on behalf of either company.

SEC REGULATIONS

Regulation A

Provides an exemption from Securities Act registration for offerings of securities not exceeding $1.5 million in any twelve-month period. Pursuant to this exemption, a Regulation A offering is available to an unlimited number of investors with no investor qualification requirements. No investment companies are permitted to use the exemption and issuers and underwriters subject to "bad boy" prohibitions are disqualified. The issuer is subject to certain disclosure and notification requirements that resemble a "mini registration." Generally, no restrictions on resale apply.

Regulation C

Sets forth the procedural rules (Rules 400 through 494) governing the registration of securities under the 1933 Act. *See Rule 405.*

Regulation S-K

Sets forth the substantive disclosure requirements for filing forms under the 1933 and 1934 Acts.

Regulation S-X

Delineates the accounting rules and procedures to be followed in the preparation of the audited financial statements and SEC filings required by the 1933 and 1934 Acts.

Regulation 14D

Prescribes the filing and disclosure requirements promulgated by the SEC under § 14(d) of the Exchange Act. *See § 14(d) of the Exchange Act; Schedules 14D-1, 14D-9.*

SEC FORMS

Form S-1

Used primarily by first-time issuers, this is the basic, long-form registration statement and requires full registrant and transaction-related information to be contained in the prospectus. No incorporation by reference is permitted.

Form S-2

Generally available to companies which have reported for three or more years, this registration form allows incorporation by reference from the Form 10-K and other SEC periodic reports into the prospectus. Issuers using this Form also must deliver a copy of the annual security holder report along with the prospectus describing the offering or present registrant-oriented information in the prospectus comparable to that contained in the annual security holder report along with a description of the offering.

Form S-3

Available to companies meeting the three-year requirement of Form S-2 as well as a "market following" test requiring the issuer to have either $150 million of voting stock held by non-affiliates or $100 million voting stock held by non-affiliates and a minimum three million share annual trading volume. Companies meeting these requirements are allowed the fullest incorporation by reference of 1934 Act documents into the registration statement. They need only include the transaction-specific description of the offering in the prospectus, as well as events that occurred after the filing of the most recent 1934 Act report incorporated by reference.

Form S-4

Form which may be used for the registration of securities issued in combinations, mergers, consolidations, recapitalizations, acquisitions of assets, and other transactions that require registration under Rule 145. *See Rule 145.*

Form S-8

Available to reporting companies offering securities to their employees or their subsidiaries' employees pursuant to a stock benefit plan.

Form S-18

As compared to the Form S-1, a somewhat less demanding form of registration statement available for non-reporting issuers where the aggregate offering price for the securities is no greater than $7.5 million. No incorporation by reference is permitted.

Form 8-K

Form that requires disclosure of specified events that may arise in the period between 1934 Act periodic filings. Disclosure of events other than those called for by the form are permissive rather than mandatory. *See §§ 13(a), 15(d) of the Exchange Act.*

Form 10-K

The form used by issuers which are Exchange Act reporting companies for filing their annual reports pursuant to § 13 or 15(d) of the Exchange Act. Information required to be included in the Form 10-K includes, for example, audited financial statements, a meaningful description of the issuer's business and financial condition, and financial data summaries appropriate for trend analysis. *See §§ 13(a), 15(d) of the Exchange Act.*

Form 10-Q

The form used by issuers which are Exchange Act reporting companies for the filing of quarterly reports pursuant to § 13 or 15(d) of the 1934 Act. *See §§ 13(a), 15(d) of the Exchange Act.*

SEC SCHEDULES

Schedule A

Sets forth the information required to be contained in a statutory § 10(a) prospectus, which is filed as part of the registration statement. *See §§ 7 and 10(a) of the 1933 Act.*

Schedule 13D

Statement of ownership disclosure form which must be filed pursuant to § 13(d) of the 1934 Act when a person (or group) acquires over five percent beneficial ownership of a reporting class of equity security. The purpose is to alert investors, the marketplace, and the target company's management of a potential change in corporate control. *See § 13(d) of the Exchange Act.*

Schedule 13E-3

A comprehensive disclosure document which must be filed by an issuer (and its affiliates) pursuant to Rule 13e-3 in the event of a going private transaction. *See Going-Private; § 13(e) of the Exchange Act; Rules 13e-3 and 13e-4.*

Schedule 14D-1

Must be filed with the Commission by a tender offeror, pursuant to § 14(d)(1) of the Exchange Act. The Schedule must contain information regarding the tender offeror, including its identity and background, as well as its purpose for the tender offer and its proposals or plans. *See § 14(d) of the 1934 Act; Regulation 14D.*

Schedule 14D-9

Statement which must be filed with the SEC by a subject (target) company of a tender offer, pursuant to Rule 14d-9, and containing information including, if material, a description of any arrangement or other understanding and conflicts of interest between, among others, the offeror, the subject corporation, and their affiliates. Certain negotiations and transactions undertaken by the target company in response to the tender offer and its position in regard to the tender offer (and the reasons therefor) must be disclosed. *See Tender Offer; § 14(d) of the Exchange Act; Rule 14d-9.*

INDEX

[References are to pages.]

A

[References are to pages.]

B

C

[References are to pages.]

[References are to pages.]

[References are to pages.]

[References are to pages.]

E

[References are to pages.]

[References are to pages.]

[References are to pages.]

[References are to pages.]

[References are to pages.]

[References are to pages.]

[References are to pages.]

N

O

[References are to pages.]

[References are to pages.]

[References are to pages.]

R

[References are to pages.]

[References are to pages.]

[References are to pages.]

[References are to pages.]

[References are to pages.]

[References are to pages.]

[References are to pages.]

TABLE OF CASES

[References are to pages.]

[References are to pages.]

D

E

[References are to pages.]

[References are to pages.]

[References are to pages.]

[References are to pages.]

T

U

V

W

[References are to pages.]

Y

Z

TABLE OF STATUTES, RULES & REGULATIONS

[References are to pages.]

FEDERAL STATUTES

FEDERAL STATUTES—Cont.

[References are to pages.]

FEDERAL STATUTES—Cont.
INVESTMENT COMPANY ACT OF 1940 (ICA)—Cont.

MAIL FRAUD STATUTE

PUBLIC UTILITY HOLDING COMPANY ACT OF 1935

RACKETEER INFLUENCED & CORRUPT ORGANIZATIONS ACT (RICO)

SECURITIES ACT OF 1933

Statutes

FEDERAL STATUTES—Cont.
SECURITIES ACT OF 1933—Cont.
Statutes—Cont.

[References are to pages.]

FEDERAL STATUTES—Cont.
SECURITIES ACT OF 1933—Cont.
Statutes—Cont.

S.E.C. Securities Act Rules

FEDERAL STATUTES—Cont.
S.E.C. Securities Act Rules—Cont.

[References are to pages.]

FEDERAL STATUTES—Cont.
S.E.C Securities Act Rules—Cont.

SECURITIES EXCHANGE ACT OF 1934

Statutes

FEDERAL STATUTES—Cont.
SECURITIES EXCHANGE ACT OF 1934—Cont.
Statutes—Cont.

[References are to pages.]

FEDERAL STATUTES—Cont.
SECURITIES EXCHANGE ACT OF 1934—Cont.
Statutes—Cont.

S.E.C. Securities Exchange Rules

FEDERAL STATUTES—Cont.
S.E.C. Securities Exchange Rules—Cont.

SECURITIES EXCHANGE COMMISSION REGULATIONS

SECURITIES INVESTOR PROTECTION ACT OF 1970

TENDER OFFER REFORM ACT OF 1987

TRUST INDENTURE ACT OF 1939

UNIFORM COMMERCIAL CODE (UCC)

[References are to pages.]

FEDERAL STATUTES—Cont.

UNITED STATES CODE

Title 5

Title 9

Title 15

Title 18

Title 29

UNITED STATES CONSTITUTION

Amendments

FEDERAL STATUTES—Cont.

WILLIAMS ACT OF 1968

STATE STATUTES

DELAWARE CODE ANNOTATED

Title 8

GEORGIA CODE ANNOTATED

INDIANA BUSINESS CORPORATION ACT

INDIANA CODE

MINNESOTA STATUTES ANNOTATED

NEW YORK BUSINESS CORPORATION LAW

OKLAHOMA STATUTES

Title 71

PENNSYLVANIA STATUTES ANNOTATED

TABLE OF RELEASES

[References are to pages.]

SECURITIES ACT RELEASES

SECURITIES ACT RELEASES—Cont.

SECURITIES EXCHANGE ACT RELEASES